CHRISTIANIZING PEOPLES
AND CONVERTING INDIVIDUALS

INTERNATIONAL MEDIEVAL RESEARCH

Volume 7

CHRISTIANIZING PEOPLES AND CONVERTING INDIVIDUALS

Edited by

Guyda Armstrong
&
Ian N. Wood

BREPOLS

British Library Cataloguing in Publication Data

Christianizing peoples and converting individuals. –
(International medieval research ; 7)
1. Conversion – Christianity – History – To 1500 2. Evangelistic work – History – To
1500 3. Church history – Middle Ages, 600-1500 4. Europe – Church history – 600-
1500
I. Armstrong, Guyda II. Wood, Ian, 1950-
270.3

© 2000, Brepols Publishers n.v., Turnhout, Belgium

D/2000/0095/88
ISBN 2-503-51087-6

Transferred to Digital Printing in 2009.

Contents

The Early Medieval East

The Early Medieval West

The Conversion of Scandinavia

The Conversion of
Central and Eastern Europe

The Conversion of the Jews

Crusade and Conversion
in the Mediterranean Region

Competing Faiths in Asia:
Muslims, Christians,
Zoroastrians, and Mongols

The Theology of Conversion

Conversion in Art

Introduction

IAN N. WOOD

T he anniversary of Augustine's arrival in Kent in 597, and the subsequent christianization of England, made conversion an obvious theme for the 1997 International Medieval Congress. It was also a theme which attracted massive interest, and not just from early medievalists interested in the christianization of England and its near-contemporary parallels. Indeed, if anything Augustine's mission was underrepresented in the considerable number of papers dealing with conversion and christianization.

If the Anglo-Saxons, and indeed the West Germanic peoples, were underrepresented, the Early Middle Ages were present in a number of papers concerned with Central and Eastern Europe—and as far east as Georgia. In addition, interest in the Baltic region took this aspect of the christianization of Europe well into the fourteenth century. Papers on these regions constitute a good proportion of the present volume, and they provide a very useful point of entry into work currently being done on christianization in areas which are less well known to most historians than is Western Europe—not least because of the range of languages involved.

At the same time, interest in christianization and conversion in later periods of the Middle Ages was fully apparent in numerous papers. Two issues predominated: one was the interface between Christians and Muslims—in Spain and in the Holy Land—and also between Christians and Jews—once again in Spain, but also in England, and more generally in Western Europe. The other was the rather more theological question of the nature of conversion, as discussed by Aquinas, and in Franciscan writings.

In deciding to devote a volume of the IMR series to the topic of conversion, we also decided to make that volume as wide-ranging as possible. Limitations of space meant that certain topics had to be excluded—and there was a decision to concentrate on historical approaches to the topic, which meant leaving aside, with regret, a number of essentially literary studies. Within those limitations, however, we have been able to gather together a considerable range of papers. Chronologically they begin in the early fourth century with the christianization of Georgia, and they stretch to missions to Asia almost exactly a millennium later. Quite apart from the chronological range, the different types of questions posed and materials used are a fascinating indication of the different interpretations of the topic to be found among specialists in different fields. Christianization, as a process affecting complete peoples, or at least large groups, attracts attention, as does conversion of the individual. By putting these varying approaches together, we hope we have given some indication of the range of current work on christianization and conversion history—and that the range itself, quite apart from the individual studies, will prove to be an eye-opener.

The Early Medieval East

The Life of St Nino:
Georgia's Conversion
to its Female Apostle

EVA M. SYNEK

Traditions of Georgia's Conversion

T here is a tradition that attributes the first missionary enterprise in Georgia to the Apostle Andrew. But it became *en vogue* only in the second millennium. Then it served to stress the apostolic origins of Georgian Christianity and to justify Georgian autocephaly vis-à-vis the patriarch of Antioch.[1] One variant of the Andrew legend says that in principle the *Theotokos* herself was appointed to bring the Gospel to Georgia. But feeling that she would die soon, she made Andrew, the first-called disciple of the Lord, and Simon of Kana her delegates. In a further version, the *Theotokos* did not send Andrew, but wanted to have her country converted by a woman. Therefore her choice was St Nino, who enlightened Iberia in the time of Constantine the Great.[2]

> She took with her Jacob the priest, who had come from Greece, and an *erist'hav* [a kind of duke], and went away to Tsoben, and called the Mt'heulians, Dchart'halians, P'hkhovians, and Tsilcanians [i.e. the mountain clansmen], and preached the faith of

This is a slightly revised version of a paper first published in *Ostkirchliche Studien*, 47 (1998), 139–48. Thanks are due to the editorial staff for permission to reprint.

[1] See Julius Aßfalg, 'Georgien', in *Theologische Realenzyklopädie*, ed. by Gerhard Krause and Gerhard Müller (Berlin, 1984), XII, 390.

[2] See Eva Maria Synek, *Heilige Frauen der frühen Christenheit. Zu den Frauenbildern in hagiographischen Texten des christlichen Ostens,* Das östliche Christentum, n.f., 43 (Würzburg, 1994), p. 93.

Christ; but they would not receive it. The *erist'hav* raised the sword a little, and with fear they gave up their idols to be broken. They passed to Ertsu, and baptized the Ertsu-T'hianians. And the Quarians heard this, and fled to T'hoshet'hi, but were at last subdued, King T'hrdat baptizing them. And she became frail, and set out for Mtzkhet'ha. And when she arrived in Ctoet'ha, in the village which is called Bodini, she could go no farther. And there came forth from the city of Uzharma, Rev, the king's son, and Salome, his wife, and his daughter, to watch over her. The king and his wife, Nana, sent Iovane [John], the archbishop, to see her and bring her back. But she did not wish to go, and entreated that after him Jacob the priest should be appointed. And she gave to him the letter written by Queen Helena, who wrote to Nino as queen, apostle, and evangelist. She gave the wood of life [i.e. a cross-relic] to Queen Nana. And Iovane [John] gave Nino of the body and blood of Christ, and she took the provision for her soul's journey, and committed her spirit into the hands of God, in the fifteenth year from her arrival in Kart'hli, from the ascension of Christ three hundred and thirty-eight years, from the beginning five thousand eight hundred and thirty-eight.[3]

There are two main medieval sources for Georgia's conversion by St Nino. The quotation is from the so-called *Conversion of Kartli (Mokcevaj Kartlisaj)*, a compilation that has been handed down in two versions.[4] The final version of the so-called *Šatberdi-text* is from the tenth century (the so-called 'text A'). There is a selected English translation of this text in the appendix of Marjory and J. O. Wardrop's translation of the slightly differing Life of St Nino as provided by the *Sakart'hvelos Samot'hkhe*, the standard collection of Georgian saints. A fully annotated German translation, based upon the new critical edition of Ilia V. Abuladze, was provided by Gertrud Pätsch in the 1970s. A second version of the *Conversion* (the so-called text B) is provided by the *Čeliši-manuscript* (presumably from the fourteenth century). For a long time, this text was held to be much younger than the *Šatberdi-text*. But recently found text-fragments from St Catherine's Monastery of Mount Sinai seem to challenge the traditional ranking. As argued by Fairy von Lilienfeld there is now good reason to believe that the main substance of the text transmitted in the *Čeliši-manuscript* is at least as old as the *Šatberdi-text*.[5] The second main source is the Georgian chronicle, the *Life of Kartli*. Its narratives concerning St Nino are attributed to Leonti Mroweli, a Georgian bishop from

---

[3] *Life of Kartli*, ch. 1; translation from Marjory Wardrop and J. O. Wardrop, 'Life of St Nino', *Studia Biblica et Ecclesiastica*, 5 (1900), 63–64; cf. Gertrud Pätsch, 'Die Bekehrung Georgiens. Mokcevay Kartlisay', *Bedi Kartlisa. Revue de Kartvelologie*, 33 (1975), 296.

[4] Compare Pätsch, 'Die Bekehrung Georgiens', p. 288.

[5] Fairy von Lilienfeld, 'Amt und geistliche Vollmacht der heiligen Nino, "Apostel und Evangelist" von Ostgeorgien, nach den ältesten georgischen Quellen', in *Horizonte der Christenheit. Festschrift für Friedrich Heyer zu seinem 85. Geburtstag*, Oikonomia, 34, ed. by Michael Kohlbacher and Markus Lesinski (Erlangen, 1994), pp. 227–28.

the eleventh century.[6] His work obviously depends on the same source material as the 'Conversion'.[7] 'It will be found that the different versions, through about a thousand years, show no essential disagreement':[8] the Wardrops' affirmation remained true also after the discovery of several new manuscripts during the twentieth century.[9]

Nino's Displacement and her Rehabilitation in the Georgian Sources

The striking point is that we do not hear anything of Nino in layers prior to the seventh century, though she became very prominent from this time on. One might suspect that the whole Nino-story is just a pious invention if there were only the medieval Georgian sources about this woman. But there is a report of the conversion of Iberia already in the church history of Rufinus (i.e. in his additions to the church history of Eusebius), which influenced various other church historians (Sokrates, Sozomenos, Theodoret, Gelasios of Kyzikos, and Theophanes). Rufinus attributes the conversion of the Iberian royal family to a woman, a Christian *captiva*.[10] The story was composed on the basis of the oral account of a Georgian prince named Bacurius, whom Rufinus had met in Jerusalem towards the end of the fourth century. St Nino of the Georgian hagiography is unquestionably the same person as Rufinus's anonymous *christiana*. Certainly, the Georgian cycles of Nino stories are much more elaborate. But the heart is the same: a foreign Christian woman wins influence over the royal family by curing the Iberian Queen Nana.[11] Due to her miraculous recovery the queen becomes the first convert of the royal family. Her husband, King Mirian, is converted after a striking personal religious experience.[12] In a threatening situation he remembers the stranger's God and makes a vow to worship him in the case of being rescued. The royal

---

[6] Gertrud Pätsch, *Das Leben Kartlis. Eine Chronik aus Georgien 300–1200*, Sammlung Dietrich, 330 (Leipzig, 1985), pp. 12–13.

[7] See Pätsch, *Das Leben Kartlis*, p. 17.

[8] Wardrop and Wardrop, 'Life of St Nino', p. 4.

[9] Compare Pätsch, *'Die Bekehrung Georgiens'*, p. 288; Pätsch, *Das Leben Kartlis*, pp. 10–11.

[10] Rufinus, *Historia ecclesiastica*, I, 10–11; for an English translation see, for example, David Braund, *Georgia in Antiquity. A History of Colchis and Transcaucasian Iberia, 550 BC–AD 562* (Oxford, 1994), pp. 248 ff.

[11] See *Life of Kartli*, part 2 (Pätsch, *Das Leben Kartlis*, pp. 158–59); *Conversion of Kartli*, ch. 1, 4 (Pätsch, 'Die Bekehrung Georgiens', p. 294); ch. 8 (Pätsch, 'Die Bekehrung Georgiens', p. 318).

[12] See *Life of Kartli*, part 2 (Pätsch, *Das Leben Kartlis*, pp. 163–65); *Conversion of Kartli*, ch. 1, 4 (Pätsch, 'Die Bekehrung Georgiens', p. 294); not very elaborated in the *Šatberdi-text*, but see *Čeliši-manuscript*, ch. 6 (Pätsch, 'Die Bekehrung Georgiens', pp. 320–21).

couple is instructed in the new faith by the Christian woman, though only baptized together with its people after the arrival of clerics called from Constantinople.[13]

Today there is a broad scholarly consensus that the Iberian royal family adopted Christianity about AD 330,[14] which brought about the principal christianization of East Georgia. There is some archaeological evidence for earlier Christian traces from the end of the second century,[15] not only in the Roman dominated western parts of the Georgian region, antique Colchis and Lazica respectively, but also in Iberia. Armenian influence might have contributed to the settlement of Christianity at least in the frontier area of Iberia.[16] But the tradition that makes Grigor, the enlightener of Armenia, also the apostle of Iberia, certainly lacks serious historical evidence.[17] Though 'the beginnings of Christianity are obscure',[18] Aßfalg seems to be quite right to stress that 'the conversion of East Georgia by St Nino has to be retained'.[19] Peeters's theory that Georgia only adopted the Nino story from outside, precisely from the Armenian church historian Moses of Chorene,[20] has been ruled out:[21] there are too many details in the Georgian narrative that seem to be very old local tradition, such as the tradition of Nino's burial in Bodbe. It is remarkable that on the way from Mcxeta and Bodbe a church connected with the memorial of St Nino goes back already to the end of the sixth century. Recently it was argued by Lilienfeld that also Nino's connections with the Georgian Jewish diaspora, her ascetic image and those elements of the story which link the Georgian church with Jerusalem might point to very old layers.[22] One interesting point is that contrary to Rufinus's idealistic report as well as to the narrative of Moses of Chorene, the Georgian legend does not fail to mention the fact that the christianization process was complicated. As Lang put it: 'Whereas the Iberian kings, possibly for reasons of state, adopted Christianity quite readily, paganism did not give up its hold on the

---

[13] Compare *Life of Kartli*, part 2 (Pätsch, *Das Leben Kartlis*, pp. 165–66, 171–73); *Conversion of Kartli*, ch. 1, 4–5 (Pätsch, 'Die Bekehrung Georgiens', p. 294); chs 9, 11, 12 (Pätsch, 'Die Bekehrung Georgiens', pp. 321, 325, 327).

[14] See, for example, David Marshall Lang, *A Modern History of Georgia* (London, 1962), p. 11; idem, 'The Georgians', in *Ancient Peoples and Places* (London, 1966), LI, 94; Aßfalg, 'Georgien', p. 390; Braund, *Georgia*, p. 239; and Heinz Fähnrich, *Geschichte Georgiens von den Anfängen bis zur Mongolenherrschaft* (Aachen, 1993), p. 77, propose 337.

[15] See Braund, *Georgia*, p. 239

[16] See, for example, Michael Tarchnišvili, 'Die Legende der heiligen Nino und die Geschichte des georgischen Nationalbewußtseins', *Byzantinische Zeitschrift*, 40 (1940), 72–73.

[17] See Aßfalg, 'Georgien', p. 390.

[18] Ibid.

[19] Ibid.

[20] See Paul Peeters, 'Les débuts du christianisme en Georgie d'après les sources hagiographiques', *Analecta Bollandiana*, 50 (1932), 5–58.

[21] See Tarchnišvili, 'Die Legende der heiligen Nino', pp. 52–57.

[22] See Lilienfeld, 'Amt und geistliche Vollmacht der heiligen Nino', pp. 235–36.

populace without a struggle'.[23] The *Conversion* and the *Life of Kartli* make quite clear that Christianity was not only advanced by preaching but also by force and some kind of sword mission. One might speculate whether the tensions between the royal family and Nino indicated in the *Conversion of Kartli* and even more in the narrative of Leonti might have a historic nucleus connected with the question of missionary strategies.[24] In the context of medieval historiography the respective passages mark an obvious inter-dependence with the politics of royal centralisation.[25]

However, insistence upon an old indigenous tradition of Georgia's female apostle does not answer the question at all why written Georgian sources kept silent about Nino for centuries. On the contrary, it seems to complicate matters even more. Nevertheless, we do not have to become completely fatalistic about this obscure lacuna in history. The medieval sources themselves seem to reveal a lot about the mystery of Nino's apparent fading from Georgian historical consciousness and her abrupt return during the seventh century. Tarchnišvili thought Nino's social position to be the key to her irritating treatment in early medieval tradition:[26] Nino was a woman, who came to Iberia as a captive according to Rufinus, a fact the Georgian sources more or less try to cover by silence. On the other hand, they reveal that the Georgian people were irritated by the fact that their faith depended on a woman, even worse, a slave woman. The narrative of Nino's death in Bodbe frankly says that one felt injured by the low status of the enlightener. The dying Nino is addressed: 'Why do you speak of captivity, freer of captives?' The Georgian royal women and other nobles remind her that Nino herself taught them concerning the prophets, the twelve and the further seventy-two apostles: 'And God has sent none to us save thee'.[27]

It seems that in the sixth-century Grigor of Armenia served as an honourable substitute for the slave woman:[28] as long as the Armenian and Georgian Church had a good relationship it was logical to celebrate Grigor, the bishop of noble origin, as a common apostle. Things changed significantly in the seventh century. While in Armenia Zenon's *Henotikon* was retained as common christological doctrine, the Georgian church adopted the decision of the Chalcedonian synod. Strengthened by the national renaissance under Arabic domination, the schism between the Armenian and the Georgian Church fostered the re-activation of the indigenous Nino-tradition. The stressing of Nino's apostolic significance accompanied the progress of Georgia's political unification and the winning of full ecclesiastical independence. In the ninth

---

[23] Lang, 'The Georgians', p. 97; See also Fähnrich, *Geschichte Georgiens*, p. 80.

[24] See *Life of Kartli*, part 2 (Pätsch, *Das Leben Kartlis*, pp. 181–82).

[25] See Pätsch, *Das Leben Kartlis*, pp. 33–34.

[26] See Tarchnišvili, 'Die Legende der heiligen Nino', pp. 57–58.

[27] See *Conversion of Kartli* (Pätsch, 'Die Bekehrung Georgiens', p. 303); *Life of Kartli*, part 2 (Pätsch, *Das Leben Kartlis*, p. 183).

[28] For the following paragraph, see Synek, *Heilige Frauen der frühen Christentheit*, pp. 107–8.

century the cult of St Nino was widely established in Georgia. At the same time the Grigor tradition was nearly completely ruled out. Some traces of the former intimate relationship of the Georgian Church and of the Armenian Church survived, but were transformed in a way that served the new politics.[29] For instance, the tradition of St Hripsime, whose martyrdom was traditionally connected with Grigor's missionary success, was not completely dropped. But now, it was stressed that Georgia had its own enlightener, St Nino, who had brought the Gospel directly from Jerusalem. St Hripsime was deprived of her role as Grigor's co-apostle to Georgia and changed into a disciple and godchild of St Nino.[30] Moreover, it was remembered that the first clergy came from Constantinople, not from Armenia.[31] As pointed out by *Gavachišvili* and *Tarchnišvili*: it is the very aim of the *Conversion of Kartli* to show that Georgia's Christianity does not depend on the Armenian Grigor but on Nino.[32]

Solutions for the Status Problem by Narrative Theology

Good reasons for Nino's displacement and her rehabilitation since the seventh century are one point. Another point is how the remaining status problem was handled by the hagiographers. I will continue with some examples, stressing the hagiographers dealing with the enlightener being a woman. It has to be added that the narratives are also concerned with the fact that Nino was a foreigner and a slave. Certainly both handicaps—as the Georgians saw it—cannot be neatly separated.

As already mentioned the legends try everything to conceal the fact that Nino has come to Georgia as a captive. Instead, one is told that the young woman, encouraged by her teacher and a dream-vision, decided to become a missioner. The patriarch of Jerusalem who is said to be her uncle on the maternal side gives the 'official' ecclesiastical confirmation to Nino's ambitious plan.[33] He blesses her at the steps of the altar and prays over her: 'O Lord God of the Fathers and centuries [. . .] I send her to preach Thy divinity and to spread the good tidings of Thy resurrection, wherever it pleases Thee'.[34]

---

[29] See Pätsch, *Das Leben Kartlis*, p. 28.

[30] See *Life of Kartli*, part 2 (Pätsch, *Das Leben Kartlis*, p. 128); *Conversion of Kartli*, ch. 4 (Pätsch, 'Die Bekehrung Georgiens', p. 308).

[31] See *Life of Kartli*, part 2 (Pätsch, *Das Leben Kartlis*, pp. 166, 171–73); *Conversion of Kartli*, ch. 1, 4 (Pätsch, 'Die Bekehrung Georgiens', p. 294); chs 9, 11, 12 (Pätsch, 'Die Bekehrung Georgiens', pp. 321, 325).

[32] See Tarchnišvili, 'Die Legende der heiligen Nino', p. 71.

[33] For the chronological tensions see Lilienfeld, 'Amt und geistliche Vollmacht der heiligen Nino', p. 238.

[34] See *Conversion of Kartli*, ch. 4 (Pätsch, 'Die Bekehrung Georgiens', p. 308); *Life of Kartli*, part 2 (Pätsch, *Das Leben Kartlis*, pp. 137–38).

When relating the story of Nino's arrival in Georgia and her confrontation with the pagan cults, it is said that she remembers another word of the patriarch: 'I send you like a real man'.[35] This ambiguous wish reminds one of a formula for the ordination of deaconesses. Also the rite of Nino's appointment by the patriarch as described by the hagiographer is very reminiscent of an ordination ceremony.[36]

A further passage that obviously deals with the gender problem introduces the beginning of Nino's mission with a dream-vision.[37] One hears that she has come near the royal city of Mcxeta and is quite desperate. While she is asleep on a stone a man passes a book to her, saying: 'Bear this swiftly to Mcxeta to the king of the pagans'. But Nino weeps and stumbles: 'O Lord, I am a strange and unskilled woman, when I go there, I do not even know, in what tongue I should speak with the strange tribes'. Then she is ordered to read the book, that comprises sentences such as: 'Wheresoever this gospel shall be preached, there shall also this, that this woman has done, be told for a memorial of her'; 'there is neither male nor female: for ye are all one'. Or: 'Jesus said to Mary Magdalene: go, o woman, and preach the gospel to my brethren'. And in this context maybe even more striking: 'he that receiveth you receiveth me; and he that receiveth me receiveth him that sent me'. As Nino in the fictional dream scene, the reader or listener of the legend is confronted with a kind of topical version of the Ten Commandments made up of quotations from the gospel (Matthew 26. 13, Galatians 3. 28, Matthew 28. 19, Luke 2. 32, Matthew 26. 13, Mark 14. 9, Matthew 10. 40, Luke 10. 38–42 (heavily shortened), Matthew 10. 28, Mark 16. 9, John 20. 17), ending with an invocation of the Holy Trinity. This composition is compared to the tablets of stone, delivered to Moses, by the hagiographer himself. Its genre is that of a prophetical convocational vision as very common already in the Old Testament.[38] The intention is clearly the scriptural sanction for female apostleship. Though missing in the *Šadberti-text*, the composition is a common tradition of the Nino story as told by Leonti and the *Čeliši-manuscript* of the *Conversion of Kartli*.

Other passages are more subtle. One way to deal with the scandal of the female apostle is to turn it to the opposite: the hagiographers composed a setting where Nino is just one of many formidable women in striking positions. One hears of Georgian Jewish women who believed in Jesus as the Saviour, of noble female converts of the saint, and also of a personal relationship to the Roman Empress Helena. One hears of Nino's mother who serves in an ecclesiastical office in Jerusalem, and most strikingly,

---

[35] See *Conversion of Kartli*, ch. 6 (Pätsch, 'Die Bekehrung Georgiens', p. 312); *Life of Kartli*, part 2 (Pätsch, *Das Leben Kartlis*, p. 147).

[36] See Synek, *Heilige Frauen der frühen Christenheit*, pp. 116–17.

[37] See *Conversion of Kartli*, *Čeliši-manuscript*, ch. 4 (Pätsch, 'Die Bekehrung Georgiens', p. 310); *Life of Kartli*, part 2 (Pätsch, *Das Leben Kartlis*, pp. 143–44); according to Lilienfeld, 'Amt und geistliche Vollmacht der heiligen Nino', p. 243 (referring to information from Z. Aleksidze) this passage is also part of one of the Sinai fragments.

[38] See, for example, Jeremiah 1. 4–10.

of her teacher in Jerusalem. This woman is said to be no less than the best contemporary theologian! In a prophetic word she compares her pupil with the lioness and the female eagle, praising the first for roaring louder than all other four-footed animals and the latter for its force and its ability to fly even higher than male eagles.[39]

One further striking point is that most narratives are ascribed to the testimony of women, who are also said to be the scribes and portrayed as excellent theologians: the Georgian queens Salome of Užarma and Perozavri of Sivneti and a woman with a Jewish background, Sidonia, one of Nino's first Georgian converts. It is a pity that we have very little chance to verify the historical nucleus of this information.[40] Did female circles play a special role in keeping alive the Nino tradition? Were there actually female hagiographers? Were there memories of Salome, Perozavri, and Sidonia playing a special role in the christianization process? Or are they mainly part of the setting that should release Nino from the reproach that being an apostle is not a fitting role for a woman?

Interdependence of Nino's Promotion and the Social Status of Women

However, Nino's victory was great but not perfect. Even at the top of her career, in the eleventh and twelfth century, the wish continued to have a more respectable enlightener. So the *Vita of Josef of Alvaverdi* says that he was the pupil of a Syrian monk named John: 'This John and his twelve disciples were called by God to go to Georgia, because there had been no apostle and the land had only been converted by St Nino'.[41] In the beginning I mentioned briefly the Andrew legend. The version of the legend, which describes Nino as the personal choice of the *Theotokos* seems to be an attempt to justify the enlightener's gender. Presumably, it is older than the Andrew version.[42]

It is obvious that the social status of women in Georgia rendered the reception of St Nino difficult for several centuries. In the introduction to her translation of the Georgian chronicle, Pätsch pointed out that in Georgia Christianity was understood as constructing social norms ('als Setzung gesellschaftlicher Normen').[43] A dream-vision related in the *Conversion of Kartli* as well as in the *Life of Kartli* is interpreted by Sidonia in the way that Nino has come to change Georgian law completely: of course,

---

[39] See *Conversion of Kartli*, ch. 3 (Pätsch, 'Die Bekehrung Georgiens', p. 307); *Life of Kartli* (Pätsch, *Das Leben Kartlis*, p. 135).

[40] See Ruth Albrecht, *Das Leben der heiligen Makrina auf dem Hintergrund der Thekla-Traditionen. Studien zu den Ursprüngen des weiblichen Mönchtums im 4. Jahrhundert in Kleinasien,* Forschungen zur Kirchen- und Dogmengeschichte, 38 (Göttingen, 1986), pp. 235–36.

[41] See Tarchnišvili, 'Die Legende der heiligen Nino', p. 63.

[42] See Synek, *Heilige Frauen der frühen Christenheit*, pp. 110–11.

[43] See Pätsch, *Das Leben Kartlis*, p. 33.

first, one thinks of religious order. But second, one should not forget the interdependence of religious and social order.

The question whether Christianity was better or worse for women has already been raised very often. At the conference 'Women in the Christian Tradition' which was held under the patronage of the European Science Foundation (1995), Jenny Jochens made it the leading-question for her investigation of the conversion of the Norse people. But maybe one should not only be a bit sceptical towards the controversial answers to this question but also towards the question itself. First of all, one would have to define what one considers 'better or worse' in individual aspects, though today there is often no general western and, even less, an intercultural consensus in this crucial preliminary question. Moreover, one has to be aware that the question somehow implies believing in an abstract 'essence of Christianity' (*Wesen des Christentums*). But from a historical point of view, Christianity is everything but an abstract idea: the writings that became the Christian 'Holy Scripture' mirror plurality and heterogeneity respectively, of the interpretation of the Jesus event already in the first Christian generations. There is no 'pure' Christianity but always enculturated Christianity from the very beginning, which continued to develop in an enormous variety in different historical contexts. Christianity has been formed in an extremely pluralistic manner by its social, economic, political, religious, and mental surroundings as could be demonstrated, for example, for the development of ecclesiastical institutions as well as doctrines, spiritual forms as well as liturgical expressions. Of course, theological doctrine on women and role-models for women provided for in such normative Christian texts as canon law, liturgical rubrics, and hagiography make no exception to this general observation. Also Nino's displacement and her rehabilitation may serve as a nice example for the impact of various factors in Christian development in general and in the gender question in particular. At the same time Nino's 'career' indicates a reciprocal process. Scholars in Georgian history widely agree upon the interdependence of Nino's promotion and significant changes in Georgia's social structure. Tarchnišvili and Hauptmann, in particular, argued that Georgia's conversion to its female apostle was accompanied by a general improvement of the social status of women.[44]

The regency of Tamar (1184–1213) was Georgia's 'golden age', the zenith of Georgia's power. The Georgian chronicle characterizes it as a time of social peace and general wealth.[45] Is it completely accidental that the glorious rule of Georgia by a woman fell together with Nino's 'victory'? In Georgia's national epic poem, Rustaveli's *Vepkhistqaosani*,[46] we read: 'The lion's whelps are equal (alike lions), be they male or

---

[44] See Tarchnišvili, 'Die Legende der heiligen Nino', p. 62; Peter Hauptmann, 'Unter dem Weinrebenkreuz der heiligen Nino. Kirchengeschichte Georgiens im Überblick', *Kirche im Osten*, 17 (1974), 9–41.

[45] See *Life of Kartli* (Pätsch, *Das Leben Kartlis*, p. 452). See Fähnrich, *Geschichte Georgiens*, pp. 142–66.

[46] See, for example, Lang, 'The Georgians', pp. 172–78 (with further literature).

female'.[47] An homage to the queen, certainly; no description of social reality but a programmatic verse, of course. Nevertheless: things have changed in medieval Georgia. When Tarchnišvili and Hauptmann maintain a connection with the Nino cult it seems hard to argue against it.

In general, promoting somebody as a saint implied that one looked at him or her as an embodiment of what one imagined to be an important Christian virtue at the respective time. Therefore the shaping of saints in hagiographical literature and iconography as well as the rising or fading of their cult is sometimes a very good indicator for the interdependence of the general culture and the specific shape of Christianity. One only has to think of the western medieval aristocratic saints: their promotion generally served such worldly reasons as the political strengthening of a dynasty or the empowering of a territory. In the second Middle Ages quite often the aim of promoting a new cult seems to have been even more materialistic: the 'discovery' of relics followed by the establishing of a great pilgrimage was a quite practicable way to make money, obviously followed in some great monasteries; thus, the implementation of the cult of St Mary Magdalene and the 'discovery' of her relics in the monastery of Vézelay led to an unquestionable economic success.[48] On the other hand, aristocratic saints also served to provide role models for contemporary bishops, abbots, kings, but also for queens and other female rulers.

So it seems that Nino was also first rehabilitated for political reasons but at the same time provided the background for an increasing estimation of women in general and also for their practical possibilities in the Georgian cultural context. As demonstrated by the convocational vision, the biblical saint, Mary Magdalene,[49] the 'apostle of the apostles', and other biblical heritage helped to understand Nino's apostleship as well as to legitimize it. The medieval Georgian hagiographers who were interested in promoting St Nino completely dropped the reinforcement of the traditional 'house-order' which is to be found in the Bible as well. From a twentieth-century theological point of view one could argue that the selective exegesis is adequate within a canonical approach to the Bible and even call it a great theological achievement within our own, western, cultural framework. One could also point out analogies in several hagiographical traditions. We already mentioned that the cult of Mary Magdalene served as a source of income in medieval France. In the circulating legends she was celebrated as the apostle of the French territory. This might have provoked con-temporary women to long for more active roles, for example, to preach the gospel as

---

[47] Shot'ha Rustaveli, *Vepkhistqaosani*, n. 39; trans. by Marjory S. Wardrop, *The Man in the Panther's Skin. A Romantic Epic by Shot'ha Rust'haveli* (London, 1912; repr. Tbilisi, 1966), p. 29.

[48] See, for example, Susan Haskins, *Die Jüngerin. Maria Magdalena und die Unterdrückung der Frau in der Kirche* (Bergisch Gladbach, 1994), pp. 124–59.

[49] For the appeal to Mary Magdalene see also other passages in the medieval Georgian hagiography: e.g. *Conversion of Georgia*, ch. 3 (Pätsch, 'Die Bekehrung Georgiens', p. 306).

Mary was said to have done. Whether intended by the hagiographers or not, the celebration of a female apostle offered a role-model for women. Not only the Georgian hagiographers, but also early forerunners of the nineteenth- and twentieth-century women's movement such as Christine de Pizan referred to Mary Magdalene: the female apostle could be called to witness in order to improve women's freedom of action as well as their general reputation and their specific theological ranking.

Such observations might lead us to overlook for a moment that other biblical layers, especially the so-called pastoral epistles, are not only quite hostile to women's religious teaching, they also reinforce the ideology of women's general inferiority to men, which was, as we know, a commonplace in pagan Antiquity and continued to be so in Christian Middle Ages in Western as well as in Eastern contexts. The memory of Mary Magdalene and other female disciples of the Lord, the ancient baptismal formula in Galatians 3. 28, and some other biblical and later traditional elements supplied further generations with legitimate potential for singular unconventional women as Georgia's female enlightener or in later centuries, for its female ruler, Queen Tamar. They could even provoke or at least strengthen efforts at emancipation. But on the other hand, the affirmation of female inferiority within the same Holy Scripture, which reminds us of Mary's Easter experience and her announcement of the good tidings, could work and actually has worked until today in the opposite way.

I am not sure whether the scholarly debate on whether Christianity was better or worse for women should be continued at all. But if one wants to go on with it, one should at least be very precise: after having defined what one considers 'better or worse' in singular aspects one could try to show what elements of Christian tradition worked in one or the other way in a specific missionary context.

Why Orthodoxy Did Not Spread among the Bulgars of the Crimea during the Early Medieval Era: An Early Byzantine Conversion Model

THOMAS S. NOONAN

T his study began as an attempt to explain why the Bulgar inhabitants of the Crimea were not converted to either Orthodoxy or Judaism during the Early Middle Ages. As the research progressed, two salient points emerged. First, there is no evidence that the Jewish population of Khazaria ever had any desire to evangelize the pagan Bulgars. Consequently, there was no reason to explore why the Bulgars did not become Jews. Second, to understand why a successful proselytizing religion like Orthodoxy made no concerted effort to convert the Crimean Bulgars, it became necessary to examine why Orthodoxy succeeded in evangelizing both the Rus' and the Danubian Bulgars during the same time period. This analysis led to the formulation of what I have termed an early Byzantine conversion model. This model attempts to explain why Byzantium actively sought to convert some of its neighbours in the Early Middle Ages and made little effort to evangelize others.

The Bulgars of the Crimea

By the sixth century various groups that can be identified as Turkic-speaking Bulgar nomads had appeared in the north Pontic steppes. During the first-half of the seventh century, a confederation of Bulgar groups formed in the area of the Azov-Don steppes. This Bulgar state, often referred to as Magna Bulgaria, was initially headed by Kubrat who had apparently led the Bulgar revolt against Avar domination of this region. Kubrat maintained good relations with Byzantium and even converted to Orthodoxy.[1]

---

[1] There is a good, brief account of these events in Peter B. Golden, 'The Peoples of the South

However, around the mid-seventh century, the Khazars destroyed Magna Bulgaria and established their rule over the Don-Azov steppes. Prior to the Khazar conquest, many nomadic Bulgars seeking green pastures had grazed their flocks in the Crimea during the spring. Now, however, these Bulgars were marooned in the Crimea and could not continue with their annual circuit which brought them back to the Don-Azov region during the winter. Since the Crimean steppes could not support all these Bulgars with their flocks on a full-time basis, many of the Crimean Bulgars were forced to adopt a sedentary way of life in order to survive.[2] During the period c. 650–c. 965, the society of the new Bulgar agriculturalists of the Crimea was shaped by two powerful forces. The Saltovo-Maiatskaia culture, with its well-developed traditions of agriculture and craft production, appeared in the Khazar khaganate during the first-half of the eighth century and soon spread to the Crimean Bulgars. This development was aided by the fact that Khazar rule came to encompass most of the Crimea during this period. In addition, the sedentary Crimean Bulgars were greatly influenced by the society of their provincial, Byzantinized neighbours. Over the course of time, the Bulgars came to live in homes built like these neighbours', they had extensive trade ties with them, and a few even began to convert to Orthodoxy.[3] At some point which is the still the subject of great controversy (probably between c. 750 and c. 865), the Khazar elite converted to Judaism. Consequently, the sedentarized Crimean Bulgars were ruled by Jewish overlords while at the same time they came into close contact with an Orthodox Christian population.

The political tensions between Byzantium and Khazaria which periodically erupted in the Crimea quite naturally had a religious dimension. For example, an eighth-century *notitia episcopatuum,* listing the names of bishoprics subject to the Patriarch of Constantinople, enumerated seven bishoprics subject to the eparchy of Gothia in the Crimea. These seven bishoprics were all within the Khazar khaganate and some have interpreted their existence as evidence of an evangelization policy by Byzantium designed to erode Khazar political control and further Byzantine secular interests.[4] While this interpretation has been disputed, other Byzantine *notitiae* from the ninth and tenth century included bishoprics located in the Khazar regions of the Crimea.[5] In addition, there is no doubt that Jews lived in the Crimea during the Early Middle Ages. The famous Byzantine missionary, St Constantine, 'learned the Hebrew language and

---

Russian Steppes', in *The Cambridge History of Early Inner Asia*, ed. by Denis Sinor (Cambridge, 1990), pp. 261–63.

[2] I. A. Baranov, *Tavrika v epokhu rannego srednevekov'ia (saltovo-maiatskaia kul'tura)* (Kiev, 1990), pp. 14–18.

[3] Baranov, *Tavrika*, examines these developments in great detail.

[4] C. de Boor, 'Nachträge zu den Notitia episcopatuum', *Zeitschrift für Kirchengeschichte,* 12 (1891), 519–34, and 14 (1894), 573–99.

[5] Alexander A. Vasiliev, *The Goths in the Crimea* (Cambridge, MA, 1936), p. 135.

scriptures' while in the Crimea c. 861.[6] In short, Byzantium and Khazaria both had co-religionists in the Crimea who could serve as the vehicle for an active evangelization campaign.

Despite these seemingly propitious circumstances, there is no evidence that either Byzantium or Khazaria ever initiated a concerted effort to convert the Bulgars of the Crimea. Judaism has seldom been a proselytizing religion.[7] Furthermore, the Khazar elite was well aware that any concerted attempt to convert their subjects to Judaism would create serious problems among the religiously diverse peoples of the khaganate. Individual Orthodox missionaries sporadically tried to convert the pagans of the Crimea. Constantine, for instance, burned the sacred oak tree of the people of Phullae near Kherson and reportedly converted all the natives.[8] This episode is revealing since it demonstrates that two-hundred years after the Bulgars began to settle in the Crimea, pagan natives in the vicinity of the Byzantine city of Kherson had still not been converted. The remarkable passivity of Orthodox missionary interest in the Crimea was reaffirmed by the events of c. 920. In that year a group of Christians from 'Khazaria' travelled to Constantinople to complain to the patriarch, Nicholas I Mysticus, that they lacked a bishop to ordain priests and teach the faith. Nicholas ordered the new archbishop of Kherson to remedy these problems and he later complimented the archbishop on having saved the Khazars who were in danger of abandoning Orthodoxy.[9] These letters show a Byzantine clergy in the Crimea that ignored its flock and failed to provide even the minimum of religious support for them. In sum, neither the Jews who constituted the Khazar elite nor the Byzantine Church and state saw any need to mount a major drive to convert the pagan Bulgars of the Crimea. Those Bulgars who did convert to Orthodoxy were soon forgotten by the Byzantine hierarchy.

The Motivations behind Conversion: Religious Competition

If the Jewish ruling elite of Khazaria had little interest in proselytizing, such was not the case with Byzantium. Thus, it is important to consider the motivations behind the successful Byzantine efforts to convert the Rus' of Kiev and the Danubian Bulgars. Why was Byzantium so intent on converting these peoples while it literally ignored the Crimean Bulgars? The conversion of the Rus' and the Danubian Bulgars is sometimes explained by a combination of propinquity and the strategic military and political

---

[6] *The Vita of Constantine and the Vita of Methodius,* trans. and comm. by Marvin Kantor and Richard S. White, Michigan Slavic Materials, 13 (Ann Arbor, 1976), pp. 20–21.

[7] P. B. Golden ('Khazaria and Judaism', *Archivum Eurasiae Medii Aevi,* 3 (1983), 132) notes that 'Mass conversion to Judaism or the Judaization of the ruling strata of a state [. . .] was an uncommon, but not unknown phenomenon'.

[8] *The Vita of Constantine,* pp. 42–43.

[9] Nicholas I Patriarch of Constantinople, *Letters,* ed. and trans. by R. J. H. Jenkins and L. G. Westerlink (Washington, 1973), letters 68 and 106, pp. 314–15, 554–55, 388–91, 569.

interests of Byzantium. The Danubian Bulgars were the immediate neighbours of Byzantium in the Balkans, and their rulers had presented a serious military threat to Constantinople. Similarly, the Rus' threatened Byzantine cities in the Black Sea including Constantinople and their Grand Prince Sviatoslav had even attempted to take over Bulgaria. This argument seems plausible until we remember that the Crimean Bulgars lived in close proximity to key Byzantine centres in the Crimea such as Kherson and that Kherson was the linchpin of the entire Byzantine strategic position in the northern Black Sea.[10] Propinquity and strategic considerations by themselves were not sufficient to inspire a concerted Byzantine policy to convert the pagans. In order to explore why Byzantium sought to convert some peoples on its borders but was content to let the Crimean Bulgars remain pagans, it is necessary to consider the situation in both Rus' and Danubian Bulgaria prior to their acceptance of Orthodoxy.

A comparison of the Rus' and Danubian Bulgar situation with that of the Crimean Bulgars reveals two significant differences. First, in both Rus' and Danubian Bulgaria there was an element of real competition between Byzantine Orthodoxy and Latin Catholicism. In the Crimea, by way of contrast, there was no real competition among religions of the book to convert the Bulgars. Second, both Rus' and Danubian Bulgaria were independent states ruled at the time of conversion by strong leaders who concluded that there was a compelling state interest in converting to Christianity. The Crimean Bulgars were dominated by the Khazars whose ruling elite clearly saw no compelling state interest in their conversion to either Judaism or Orthodoxy. Let us examine each of these two factors in more detail.

The eventual conversion of the Rus' to Orthodoxy sometimes leads us to forget that there was a real possibility that Rus' might have turned to Latin Catholicism. In the mid-950s, the regent, Princess Olga, had been baptized an Orthodox Christian with the emperor serving as her godfather. Nevertheless, serious disagreements apparently existed between Olga and Byzantium regarding the status of a Rus' Church. Fearing that conversion might bring both religious and political subordination to Constantinople, Olga probably demanded an autonomous Rus' Church structured along national lines.[11] In any event, in 959 Olga sent an embassy to the German Emperor Otto I asking for a bishop and priests to convert the Rus'. In 960, Otto had the monk Adalbert of Trier ordained bishop of the Rus' and sent to Olga. Adalbert's mission was unsuccessful and he soon returned home.[12] While Adalbert unquestionably encountered pagan opposition to Christianity, his embassy also failed because Otto presumably did not grant Olga's wish for an autonomous Church and the princess had no desire for a Rus' Church

---

[10] Constantine Porphyrogenitus, *De Administrando Imperio*, ed. by G. Moravcsik, trans. by R. J. H. Jenkins (Budapest, 1949), chs 5–8, pp. 52–57; Dmitri Obolensky, *The Byzantine Commonwealth: Eastern Europe 500–1453* (London, 1971), pp. 42–51, 235–37.

[11] George Vernadsky, *Kievan Russia* (New Haven, 1948), pp. 40–41.

[12] Vernadsky, *Kievan Russia*, p. 41; A. P. Vlasto, *The Entry of the Slavs into Christendom: An Introduction to the Medieval History of the Slavs* (Cambridge, 1970), p. 251.

controlled by German clergy who had close ties to the German emperor.[13] Grand Prince Sviatoslav (962–972) was a strong pagan but under his successor, Iaropolk (972–980), ties with the Latin Church resumed. In 973, Iaropolk sent an embassy to Otto I which may have had the same purpose as that sent by Olga earlier. This embassy did not produce any results.[14] Nevertheless, contacts with the Latins continued and in 979 a papal envoy from Rome visited Iaropolk.[15]

Under Vladimir, ties with the Latin Church intensified. In 986, Germans claiming to be emissaries of the pope visited the grand prince in Kiev.[16] A few years later, after Vladimir seized Kherson and agreed to accept Orthodoxy and marry the emperor's sister, a papal ambassador came to him bringing holy relics.[17] Another papal envoy visited Vladimir in 992 bringing assurances of friendship and respect.[18] Vladimir was not unresponsive to these embassies from the papacy. In 994, the envoys he had dispatched to the pope in Rome returned to Kiev.[19] In 1000, papal envoys again visited Kiev along with representatives from the Kings of Bohemia and Hungary.[20] Finally, Vladimir sent commercial envoys to Rome and the Near East the very next year. It is not known whether they visited the pope or carried any message to him from Vladimir.[21] The second-half of the tenth century was thus characterized by intensive contacts linking Kiev with the German Church and the papacy.

It is very clear that both the Holy Roman Emperor and the German Church as well as the papacy entertained serious hopes of winning the Rus' over to Latin Christianity. Furthermore, Rus' rulers from Olga to Vladimir were willing to listen to these entreaties and, in the case of Olga, actively sought western bishops and priests. It can, of course, be argued that the Rus' rulers only 'played their Latin card' as a ploy to pressure Byzantium to concede to their demands for an autonomous Church. However, it is equally arguable that once the Rus' rulers had decided on conversion to Christianity,

---

[13] Vernadsky, *Kievan Russia*, p. 41.

[14] Vlasto, *The Entry of the Slavs*, p. 253.

[15] *The Nikon Chronicle, I: From the Beginning to 1132,* ed. by Serge A. Zenkovsky, trans. by Serge A. and Betty Jean Zenkovsky (Princeton, 1984), p. 73, s.a. 979. While some scholars are reluctant to credit information in the sixteenth-century *Nikon Chronicle* that is not found in earlier chronicles, S. H. Cross (*The Russian Primary Chronicle: Laurentian Text,* trans. and ed. by S. H. Cross and O. P. Sherbowitz-Wetzor (Cambridge, MA, 1953), p. 245 n. 92) makes a good argument that these *Nikon Chronicle* entries relating to early Rus' ties with the Latin Church are much more likely to have been omitted from earlier chronicles than invented by sixteenth-century scribes.

[16] *The Russian Primary Chronicle*, p. 97, s.a. 986

[17] *The Nikon Chronicle*, p. 107, s.a. 987.

[18] *The Nikon Chronicle*, p. 111, s.a. 992.

[19] *The Nikon Chronicle*, p. 113, s.a. 994.

[20] *The Nikon Chronicle*, p. 118, s.a. 1000.

[21] *The Nikon Chronicle*, p. 118, s.a. 1001.

they were somewhat indifferent to the specific version. While Rus' had strong economic and political ties with Orthodox Byzantium, it also had very active ties with Scandinavia, Poland, and Hungary where Latin Christianity was spreading rapidly. For Byzantium, however, the constant embassies going between Kiev, the German emperor, and the papacy represented a major threat. Given the Byzantine position on the northern Black Sea and the dependence on Rus' for mercenaries, among other things, it was imperative to win the Rus' over to Orthodoxy. Consequently, it was Latin competition that led to a determined Byzantine interest in converting the Rus'.

The competitive conversion environment that developed in Rus' was not unique. A very similar situation had arisen a century earlier in Danubian Bulgaria under Khan Boris.[22] Around 863, Boris decided to convert to Christianity and turned to the Franks who were his political allies. Boris sought an autonomous Christian Church and, from this perspective, the distant Franks were more promising than the neighbouring Byzantines who might well use the Church to further their political objectives. After all, it was a basic tenet of Byzantine political philosophy that a nation which accepted the Byzantine faith became subject to the Byzantine empire.[23] Byzantium, fearing Frankish political penetration into Bulgaria, immediately attacked and defeated the Bulgars. Boris was forced to sever his ties with the Franks, accept Orthodoxy for himself and his country, and allow Greek priests to begin the formal conversion of his people. Boris soon realized that Byzantium would not accept an autonomous Bulgarian Church and instead sought to control this Church while subordinating Boris as well. Consequently, Boris formally requested Patriarch Photius to permit Bulgaria to have its own patriarch, a position which would permit much greater autonomy for the new Bulgarian Church. When Photius did not respond to this request, Boris turned to Pope Nicholas in 866. The Bulgarian embassy was warmly greeted and within a few months a papal embassy had reached Bulgaria to take over the conversion while the Byzantine clergy were expelled. Boris had also approached the Franks since a Frankish embassy with a number of missionaries reached Bulgaria during 867. Boris thus made it very clear that he had no compunctions about accepting Latin Christianity if that was what it took to obtain an autonomous Bulgarian Church.

Boris soon found, however, that the papacy was very jealous of its power. Pope Nicholas told Boris that newly converted Bulgaria could not have its own patriarch, although, it would have its own bishops. Furthermore, Bishop Formosus, the head of the papal delegation, soon became the favourite of Boris. When Boris asked the pope

---

[22] The account of the conversion of Bulgaria under Khan Boris given here is based upon the following works: Vlasto, *The Entry of the Slavs*, pp. 158–62; Obolensky, *Byzantine Commonwealth*, pp. 116–29; Robert Browning, *Byzantium and Bulgaria: A Comparative Study across the Early Medieval Frontier* (Berkeley, 1975), pp. 144–53; and John V. A. Fine, Jr., *The Early Medieval Balkans: A Critical Survey from the Sixth to the Late Twelfth Century* (Ann Arbor, 1983), pp. 117–26.

[23] Obolensky, *Byzantine Commonwealth*, pp. 117–18.

to appoint Formosus the archbishop of Bulgaria, Nicholas refused. Instead of leaping at this opportunity to have one of his own men installed as the head of the Bulgarian Church, Nicholas apparently reacted negatively to the idea of Boris selecting the head of the Bulgarian Church. In early 868, the new pope, Hadrian, turned down Boris's second nominee for the position of archbishop of Bulgaria. The papacy had thus succeeded in alienating Boris.

Rebuffed by the papacy, Boris was now receptive to suggestions coming from Constantinople that it was ready to compromise with him about the Bulgarian Church. By early 870, a Bulgarian embassy was in Constantinople negotiating for a conversion agreement acceptable to both sides. A Church council meeting in Constantinople at the time declared that Bulgaria came under the jurisdiction of Byzantium. The patriarch quickly appointed an archbishop for Bulgaria and pledged that the new head of the Bulgarian Church would have substantial autonomy. Boris was quite satisfied with this arrangement since, once appointed, the new archbishop apparently possessed great freedom of action. Boris had thus obtained the type of Church he wanted. As in the case of Vladimir, it can be argued that Boris blackmailed Byzantium by 'playing the Latin card'. However, it can be argued with equal force that Rome might well have brought Bulgaria into the Latin sphere had the popes not misplayed their hands.

The struggle between Rome and Constantinople over the right to evangelize Bulgaria continued for several more years. A Byzantine Church council even agreed around 880 that Bulgaria should come under Rome, a decision made to appease the pope. But Patriarch Photius knew that Boris was quite happy with his quasi-autonomous archbishop and would ignore all of the pope's letters. Nevertheless, as late as the pontificate of Stephen V (885–891), Rome was still ordering Boris to respect its jurisdiction over Bulgaria.

There can be no doubt that real competition existed between Rome and Constantinople regarding the evangelization of Bulgaria. This serious rivalry forced Byzantium to take vigorous and decisive action in order to ensure that Boris was brought into the Orthodox fold. In sum, both in Rus' and in Bulgaria Byzantium only became very serious about conversion when faced with the threat of another religion evangelizing a country in which it had important secular interests.

The Motivations behind Conversion: State Interests

Competition between Constantinople and Rome was only one of the major forces behind conversion. Both in Rus' and Bulgaria important internal developments prompted strong and determined leaders to decide that conversion to Christianity was advantageous. In Rus', Vladimir became grand prince after a long and bloody civil war. For eight years members of the Rurikid dynasty had fought each other for the throne of Kiev. Vladimir realized that the Rurikid dynasty constituted the only cement uniting diverse peoples who inhabited a huge area and had little in common. These peoples had never formed part of a single state before. In fact, terms like East Slav and Finn, which are frequently used to label the majority of the population in Vladimir's state, are very misleading since both East Slavs and Finns were divided into a number of different and often hostile tribes which lacked any sense of a common identity. In short, Vladimir had inherited a motley assemblage of very heterogeneous peoples who had no common history and whose only real unifying force, the Rurikid dynasty, had just torn itself apart for almost a decade. There was a desperate need to create stronger bonds linking these diverse peoples together. Furthermore, it was essential to strengthen the power of the grand prince and legitimize his right to rule over the Rus' lands. Such enhanced power was crucial if Vladimir were to consolidate his realm and centralize his power.

Vladimir wisely saw that religion was the new force besides the Rurikid dynasty that would help to bind the diverse peoples conquered by his ancestors into a more unified state.[24] During the first years of his reign, Vladimir tried to create a syncretic paganism that would appeal to the various peoples in his realm. However, he soon discovered that paganism did not provide the cohesiveness he sought. After all, there were East Slavic pagans, Finnic pagans, Scandinavian pagans, and Baltic pagans each of whom was perfectly satisfied with their brand of paganism. Furthermore, a syncretic paganism, no matter how carefully constructed, risked favouring one group of pagans and alienating the others. Consequently, Vladimir abandoned his quest for a syncretic paganism that would help unify his peoples and apparently began to consider the various religions of the book.

The stories of Vladimir's conversion are incomplete and contradictory. Nevertheless, it is clear that he considered, if only briefly, Judaism, Islam, Orthodoxy, and Latin Catholicism. The first two were not serious competitors. The real choice was between Constantinople and Rome/Germany. Either religion would have served Vladimir's purpose, and there were some Christians of both kinds in Rus' at the time. The turning point came when Vladimir captured Kherson and forced the Byzantine emperor, Basil II, to send his sister Anna to him as his bride provided that he converted personally and undertook the evangelization of his peoples. Vladimir's new commitment to Orthodoxy was symbolized by his having the pagan idols of Kiev dumped unceremoniously into the Dnepr river. Orthodoxy, in turn, provided Vladimir with a valuable new force for unity. The inhabitants of his realm now became Rus', meaning Orthodox people ruled by the Rurikids, and they slowly lost their tribal affiliations. In addition, grand prince Vladimir now had a Church organization that would buttress his secular power, and he had a high place in the hierarchy of rulers who governed this world. For all practical purposes, Vladimir and his successors were chosen by God to rule over the Rus' lands; they were no longer opportunists who ruthlessly destroyed local chieftains, brutally extracted tribute from their peoples, and forcibly welded them into a new state to serve their personal interests. In sum, conversion served Vladimir's needs, and Orthodoxy, in particular, was chosen because the Rus' elite were familiar

---

[24] Janet Martin, *Medieval Russia, 980–1584* (Cambridge, 1995), pp. 5, 10, puts it very succinctly: Vladimir sought a common religion to integrate the diverse tribes into a single society and to introduce an ideology that would legitimize his rule.

with Byzantium and because the metropolitans sent to govern the new Rus' Church soon realized that they kept their positions at the sufferance of the grand prince and had to accommodate his desires.

In Bulgaria, Boris had also decided that conversion would well serve his secular needs. Khan Boris very much wanted to elevate his position above that of the pagan boyars. The power of the boyars rested in large part upon the support that paganism provided for a traditional order in which boyars were the heads of sacred clans and the khans were only the first among equal clan leaders.[25] As Fine has put it so succinctly: 'Christianity was a means to crush the religious and ideological basis of boyar privileges, and advance Boris's position as an autocrat. The new religion allowed him to stand high above the boyars and, in imitation of the Christian emperor, be prince "by the Grace of God" and God's representative on earth'.[26] In addition, Boris ruled a realm traditionally composed of two different peoples, Turkic Bulgars and South Slavs. A common Christian religion, distinct from the traditional paganisms of each, would greatly facilitate their assimilation into a single people, a process that was already underway.[27] Either Orthodoxy or Catholicism might have met the political needs of Boris, but Byzantium won out because it was eventually willing to satisfy Boris's demands regarding the semi-independent status of the new Bulgarian Church.

The above analysis is not meant to belittle the purely religious motivations that may have prompted rulers like Vladimir and Boris to seek conversion. The point is that conversion everywhere in Eastern Europe met strong resistance from the pagan population. A ruler needed very good reasons to seek evangelization and face the wrath of his pagan peoples. In his very illuminating recent study of Grand Prince Gediminas of Lithuania (1315–41), Rowell offers some important observations regarding the predicament of a pagan ruler who might consider conversion. First, Gediminas's Orthodox and pagan subjects had gone so far as to threaten him with death if he converted to Catholicism.[28] But Gediminas was willing to face their wrath if Latin Catholicism could satisfy one crucial secular need: the abolition of the Teutonic knights who threatened the very existence of Lithuania.[29] Since neither the pope nor the German emperor would or could meet Lithuania's price, conversion was simply not worth it. But Gediminas welcomed Christians, and especially merchants and artisans, into his realm and provided them with churches and freedom of worship as long as they did not attempt to proselytize the pagan population.[30] The relatively well-documented situation of Gediminas provides some insight into the considerations that no doubt entered the

---

[25] Fine, *Early Medieval Balkans*, p. 119.

[26] Fine, *Early Medieval Balkans*, p. 118.

[27] Fine, *Early Medieval Balkans*, p. 118; Browning, *Byzantium and Bulgaria*, p. 144.

[28] S. C. Rowell, *Lithuania Ascending: A Pagan Empire Within East-Central Europe, 1295–1345* (Cambridge, 1994), pp. 61, 139, 214, 222–23, 226.

[29] Rowell, *Lithuania Ascending*, pp. 199, 225.

[30] Rowell, *Lithuania Ascending*, pp. 72, 134, 148, 204–5.

minds of Vladimir, Boris, and their predecessors when they thought about conversion and its implications.

The Evangelization of the Alans

The Crimean Bulgars were not the only neighbour of Byzantium whose conversion to Orthodoxy was neglected. Since the sixth century, the Alans of the central-north Caucasus had been close allies of Byzantium. Their ruler even held the high imperial title of *exousiastes*. Nevertheless, the earliest evidence of Christianity in Alania dates from the ninth century and the Alan king was only converted in the early tenth century at which time the first archbishop was sent there.[31] However, Byzantine interest in the conversion of the Alans was motivated primarily by immediate political considerations. The Khazars also sought an alliance with the Alans, and during the reign of King Benjamin (c. 880–900), the Alans came to the aid of the Khazars when the latter were attacked. Under Aaron, Benjamin's successor (c. 900–920), Byzantium bribed the Alans to attack the Khazars and simultaneously sought to convert the Alans. The Alans, however, were defeated by the Khazars and reconciled with them. Soon after (perhaps in 932), it was reported that the Alans had abandoned Christianity and had expelled the priests and bishops sent by Byzantium.[32] Byzantium made no special efforts to convert the Alans until it needed their services against the Khazars. The Alans, like the Crimean Bulgars, were not the object of conversion competition. Islam apparently made little progress in the Alania while only a few Alans had converted to Judaism. Consequently, for many centuries there was no need to convert them. Serious but short-lived efforts at evangelization among the Alans only developed in the early tenth century when Byzantium tried to turn the Alans against the Khazars.

Conclusions

Conversion was a very difficult and complex societal change. It did not take place spontaneously or with the preaching of a few missionaries. Successful Byzantine evangelization in southeastern Europe during the Early Middle Ages required the coincidence of two factors which constituted what can be called the early Byzantine conversion model. First, Byzantium had to believe that its political interests were threatened by the spread of Catholicism into areas considered part of the Byzantine sphere of influence. Second, the ruler/ruling elite of the pagan country had to believe that Christianity offered such significant practical advantages that it was worth risking the wrath of devout pagans. Only when these two conditions were operative did Orthodoxy spread from Byzantium to one of its neighbours.

---

[31] Obolensky, *Byzantine Commonwealth*, p. 235.

[32] Norman Golb and Omeljan Pritsak, *Khazarian Hebrew Documents of the Tenth Century* (Ithaca, 1982), pp. 104, 112–15, 135–36.

The Early Medieval West

Some Historical Re-identifications
and the Christianization of Kent

IAN N. WOOD

My purpose in this paper is to raise certain questions about religion in Kent and in the rest of England in the years on either side of Augustine's arrival in 597. For Kent itself several questions seem to me to follow logically from Rob Meens's 1994 article 'A Background to Augustine's Mission to Anglo-Saxon England':[1] an article of crucial importance, which provides the chief 're-identification' of my title, but which, I think, has not yet been fully brought into discussion of religion in England at the end of the sixth century. More generally, several years of grappling with continental paganism has led me to the conclusion that far too much has been assumed about our knowledge of its counterpart in England.[2] It is with one aspect of this problem that I shall start, before coming back to Rob Meens's argument.[3]

In a famous letter written to Mellitus in 601, Gregory explained that the *fana idolorum* of the English should not be destroyed, but that the idols in them should be,

---

[1] R. Meens, 'A Background to Augustine's Mission to Anglo-Saxon England', *Anglo-Saxon England,* 22 (1994), 5–17.

[2] For my views on Germanic paganism, see I. N. Wood, 'Pagan Religion and Superstitions East of the Rhine from the Fifth to the Ninth Century', in *After Empire: Towards an Ethnology of Europe's Barbarians*, ed. by G. Ausenda (Woodbridge, 1995), pp. 253–79.

[3] Meens's response to the current paper is already available in R. Meens, 'Questioning Ritual Purity: The Influence of Gregory the Great's Answers to Augustine's Queries about Childbirth, Menstruation and Sexuality', in *Saint Augustine and the Conversion of England*, ed. by R. Gameson (Stroud, 1999), pp. 176–77.

and that altars with relics should be placed in the purified buildings. Similarly, the sacrifices of cattle which used to be offered on pagan festivals should instead be made on Christian holy days, when the people would set up wattle huts round the churches (*ecclesias*) constructed out of idolatrous *fana*.[4]

In this letter Gregory was responding to an eye-witness account of Kentish paganism, and its information must, therefore, be taken seriously as evidence for religion in Kent between 597 and 601. It reveals that the pagans had *fana* and made sacrifices, which appear to have involved the setting-up of booths. This much must be accepted. But Gregory also pushes us to a particular understanding of the word *fana*, which I have carefully not translated. These *fana* are clearly of some size, at least in Gregory's imagination: they can serve as churches, and they have altars in them. They could be similar to the *fanum* of King Rædwald, who, according to Bede, had an altar for Christian sacrifice and an altar for sacrifices to demons in the same building.[5] Although one might question whether Rædwald's religious position became quite as straightforwardly pagan as the *Ecclesiastical History* implies, the type of syncretism envisaged, with old gods being thought still to have some power, is not uncommon among first-generation Christians elsewhere in the Early Middle Ages.[6] And there is also the *fanum* at Goodmanham destroyed by the priest Coifi: though it should be noted that Bede makes Coifi speak not of *fana*, but of *templa* in his rejection of Christianity.[7]

Colgrave clearly saw no problem in swithering between translating *fanum* as 'temple' or as 'shrine'. In doing so he may be accurately reflecting a vagueness in Gregory and Bede: yet to the modern ear at least there may be a difficulty. The word 'temple' tends to carry with it a greater impression of size than does the word 'shrine'. Did the Anglo-Saxons have sizeable temples? John Blair thinks they did, and he may have identified some.[8] Brian Hope-Taylor thinks there is one at Yeavering—though I personally have my doubts about his interpretation of many of the individual buildings

---

[4] Gregory I, *Register*, XI, 56, ed. by P. Ewald and L. Hartmann, *Monumenta Germaniae Historica, Epistolae*, 1 and 2 (Berlin, 1887–99); Bede, *Historia Ecclesiastica*, I, 30, ed. and trans. by B. Colgrave and R. A. B. Mynors, *Bede's Ecclesiastical History of the English People* (Oxford, 1969). See especially R. A. Markus, 'Gregory the Great and a Papal Missionary Strategy', *The Mission of the Church and the Propagation of the Faith*, ed. by G. J. Cuming, Studies in Church History, 6 (Cambridge, 1970), pp. 29–38 (reprinted in Markus, *From Augustine to Gregory the Great* (London, 1983)).

[5] Bede, *Historia Ecclesiastica*, II, 15.

[6] For the Hungarian ruler Géza, see Thietmar of Merseburg, *Chronicon*, VIII, 4, ed. by W. Trillmich (Darmstadt, 1957). For Helgi the Lean, see P. Meulengracht Sørensen, 'Religions Old and New', in *The Oxford Illustrated History of the Vikings*, ed. by P. Sawyer (Oxford, 1997), p. 223.

[7] Bede, *Historia Ecclesiastica*, II, 13.

[8] J. Blair, 'Anglo-Saxon Pagan Shrines and their Prototypes', *Anglo-Saxon Studies in Archaeology and History*, 8 (1995), 1–28.

on the site.[9] Nevertheless, Gregory the Great and Bede thought that there were *fana* in England in the sixth century, and that a *fanum* could be big enough to house at least two altars. On the whole, I suspect that we are not just dealing with Gregory's imagination: there are enough indications in Gregory and Bede to show that there were *fana* big enough to hold one or more altars in England, though there may have been very few of them outside Kent, and there they may not have been found because we may not know what to look for.

In thinking about the whole issue of temples in England, we should remember that Germanic temples have not been found on the continent, and here, for once, arch-aeological evidence is in tune with what Tacitus tells us about the *Germani*.[10] Of course, there may have been considerable differences between the religions of Tacitus's *Germani* and those of the Germanic peoples of the sixth century: indeed there is some reason to believe that this was the case. One need only look at the linguistic evidence for the spread in popularity of certain Germanic gods in the course of Roman and post-Roman periods.[11] Nevertheless, there is an absence of references to temples not only in Tacitus's *Germania*, but also in most texts referring to the Germanic peoples of the *Völkerwanderungzeit*: and this taken together with the absence of temples in the archaeological record should be significant. Further, the negative point seems all the stronger in that Slav temples are very much in evidence in both literature and arch-aeology.[12]

The one area on the continent where sources make regular reference to *fana* is Frisia. They are referred to, for instance, in accounts of the desecration, first by Willibrord and then by Liudger, of the cult site of Fosite, probably on Helgoland.[13] Although Altfrid in his *Vita Liudgeri* borrowed from Alcuin's *Life of Willibrord*, it should be remembered that he was the nephew of Liudger, and may have heard an eye-witness account of the *fana* with their holy spring. Thus, while Alcuin's references to shrines in the *Vita Willibrordi* might be attributed to literary licence, it is possible that he and Altfrid were presenting a recognisable image of the realities of Frisian religion. The one other temple which is frequently cited by modern historians is that at the

---

[9] P. Hope-Taylor, *Yeavering* (London, 1977), pp. 97–102.

[10] Tacitus, *Germania*, 9, ed. by A. A. Lund (Heidelberg, 1988); Wood, 'Pagan Religion and Superstitions East of the Rhine from the Fifth to the Ninth Century', pp. 255–56.

[11] K. Helm, *Altgermanische Religionsgeschichte*, II, *Die nachrömische Zeit, 2, Die West-germanen* (Heidelberg, 1953), provides a careful survey of the development of each major cult.

[12] L. P. Slupecki, *Slavonic Pagan Sanctuaries* (Warsaw, 1994); M. Müller-Wille, *Opferkult der Germanen und Slawen* (Stuttgart, 1999), pp. 81–88.

[13] Alcuin, *Vita Willibrordi*, 10, ed. by H.-J. Reischmann, *Willibrord, Apostel der Friesen* (Darmstadt, 1989); Altfrid, *Vita Liudgeri*, I, 22, ed. by W. Diekamp, *Die Vitae sancti Liudgeri* (Münster, 1881). Compare *Vita Willehadi*, 4, ed. by A. Poncelet, *Acta Sanctorum*, November 8th, III (Brussels, 1910).

Irminsul in Saxony, but only the *Annales Regni Francorum* mention such a building: other sources are silent.[14] A temple at the Irminsul may well be the fantasy of one Carolingian—and most modern historians.

It seems, therefore, that *fana* had some significance for pagan religion among the Frisians and Anglo-Saxons, but rather less elsewhere in the Germanic world, and that one has to move east to the Slav lands to find unquestionably temple-based religions. One possible explanation for the significance of temples in England and Frisia is that both areas had either been under direct Roman rule, or, in the case of parts of Frisia, were Roman frontier territory. If this explanation is right, while temples are unlikely to have been traditional aspects of Germanic paganism, they could well have been borrowings from the Roman world.

That pagan cult sites in England and Frisia had a Roman past might have an echo in Alcuin's account of Willibrord's actions at a shrine in the *villa* at Walcheren, which may well have been associated with the trading site of Domburg.[15] One might guess further and postulate that this Frisian *villa*, which was run by a *custos*, was in some way connected to the Roman temple of the goddess Nehalennia. Roman temples, dilapidated though they might have been, might well have provided the pagan *Germani* with a model for their own shrines on the lower Rhine and in England. On the other hand, if pagan Germanic *fana* in England and in Frisia did take over previously existing sacred places, one should consider the possibility that the sites taken over were actually Christian: put simply, Christian churches of the Late Roman period could have provided the model for Germanic temples within what had been the Roman Empire, and on occasion may even have constituted the physical building itself.

In other words, since Frisians and Anglo-Saxons seem to have been unusual among the Germanic peoples in the religious significance that they accorded to buildings, it may well be that this stemmed from the fact that they settled in areas where the religion of the indigenous population was associated with buildings (which must usually have been churches, although some pagan survival is not impossible, since sites associated with pagan cult continued to be religious centres).[16] In short, I would like to suggest that Anglo-Saxon paganism was already modelled in part on Christianity, even before Augustine arrived. Further, if there are Germanic shrines or temples to be found, some are likely to be reused Roman temples or churches.

It may not only have been holy buildings, or at least the notion of sacredness being found in buildings, which the Anglo-Saxons borrowed from the Romano-British: there is an absence of a priestly caste in our sources for traditional Germanic religion of the

---

[14] *Annales Regni Francorum*, s.a. 772, ed. by F. Kurze, *Monumenta Germaniae Historica, Scriptores Rerum Germanicarum in usum scholarum* (Hannover, 1895). See Wood, 'Pagan Religion and Superstitions East of the Rhine from the Fifth to the Ninth Century', p. 255.

[15] I owe this observation to Stephane Lebecq.

[16] M. Henig, *Religion in Roman Britain* (London, 1984), pp. 224–27.

Migration period and the centuries on either side.[17] There is the *custos* at Walcheren,[18] if he may be called a priest, and, more obviously, Coifi in Northumbria:[19] otherwise, kings fulfill a priestly function, at least in officiating over such rites as the casting of lots.[20] It is not impossible that Coifi's role—assuming that he existed—was itself a borrowing from Christianity.

Anglo-Saxon paganism, then, was made in England, however much certain gods, rituals, and aspects of cosmology may have been traditional to the Germanic peoples. It was, thus, syncretist, before Augustine's arrival, because it had already borrowed from Christianity. This, of course, instantly raises the problem of British survival, but in a rather different way from, say, the question of Eccles place-names. It is not my intention to enmesh myself in this question here. Instead, I wish to turn to the second aspect of my enquiry, which is to ask whether there are any traces of British Christian practices in what can be deduced about Anglo-Saxon religion prior to Augustine's arrival. Once again it is necessary to turn to Gregory the Great, this time to the *Responsiones*: for the most part I follow Meens's reading of them, although I wish to reconsider the transmission of ideas of ritual purity, which, Meens argued, resulted from British influence on the *Angli*.

What Meens's article of 1994 did, beyond any doubt, was to show that the questions relating to ritual purity, that is sections 8 and 9 of Gregory's *Libellus Responsionum* to Augustine, could well have been written by the pope, and that they relate not to questions which originated with pagans, but rather to questions raised by Christians influenced by Irish and British ideas of purity of the type expressed in the penitentials, even if Augustine heard them from Anglo-Saxons.[21] Further, Meens dealt with the relationship of the *Libellus* to Augustine's meetings with the British bishops. According to Bede, there was a showdown in those encounters, over the dating of Easter and also over Augustine's authority.[22] Meens argued that, since Bede places these

---

[17] Wood, 'Pagan Religion and Superstitions East of the Rhine from the Fifth to the Ninth Century', pp. 257–59.

[18] Alcuin, *Vita Willibrordi*, 14.

[19] Bede, *Historia Ecclesiastica*, II, 13.

[20] For example, Alcuin, *Vita Willibrordi*, 11; *Vita Vulframni*, 6–8, ed. by W. Levison, *Monumenta Germaniae Historica, Scriptores Rerum Merovingicarum*, 5 (Hannover, 1910).

[21] Meens, 'A Background to Augustine's Mission to Anglo-Saxon England'; on the authenticity of the *Liber Responsionum*, see also P. Meyvaert, 'Le *Libellus Responsionum* à Augustin de Cantobéry: Une oeuvre authentique de Grégoire le Grand', in *Grégoire le Grand, Colloques internationaux du C.N.R.S. Chantilly, Centre culturel Les Fontaines, 15–19 septembre 1982*, ed. by J. Fontaine (Paris, 1986), pp. 543–49; and H. Chadwick, 'Gregory the Great and the Mission to the Anglo-Saxons', in *Gregorio Magno e il suo tempo*, Studia Ephemeridis, Augustinianum, 33–34 (Rome, 1991), pp. 207–11.

[22] Bede, *Historia Ecclesiastica*, II, 2. On this episode, see I. N. Wood, 'Augustine and

meetings after the *Libellus Responsionum*, which itself is dated to 601 in Gregory's *Register*,[23] the questions of ritual purity must have come up separately, asked by *Angli*, who had already experienced British missionary activity.

Before accepting the whole of Meens's argument, it is necessary just to remember the problems of the *Libellus Responsionum*. It exists in more than one version, and it has yet to be properly edited, though Meens himself is currently doing that. That edition will no doubt solve many of the problems associated with the work. What can be said is that, despite a considerable amount of argument to the contrary, the majority of the answers are now known to be Gregorian.[24] Further, since the text of the *Libellus* in Gregory's *Register* has a date of 601, it is reasonable to infer that Gregory answered questions put to him in that year over and above the famous question concerning *fana* and sacrifice. Certainly, the seventh question on relations between Augustine and the bishops of Gaul and Britain seems particularly appropriate for the year 601, since it can be juxtaposed with points made in the letters of commendation which Gregory sent to the Frankish bishops on behalf of Mellitus and Laurentius in that year.[25]

Whether all the *Responsiones* came from the same original document of 601 is, however, not quite so clear—and what that original document looked like is distinctly problematic. Most obviously, Augustine cannot have asked one of the questions ascribed to him at any moment after he arrived in Gaul in 596. In Colgrave's translation of Bede's *Historia Ecclesiatica,* Augustine is made to ask, 'Even though the faith is one are there varying customs in the churches? and is there one form of mass in the Holy Roman Church and another in the Gaulish churches?' As Gregory points out, Augustine has already found (*invenisti*) that there are varying customs, so the first part of the question is otiose, and must be an editorial invention. Since there are three known versions of the *Libellus Responsionum*, and only one of them has the form of a set of questions and answers, there is no difficulty in seeing 'Augustine's questions' as having been added to the Gregorian statements.[26]

Working from the standpoint that the *Responsiones* are Gregorian, even though they have been subject to early medieval editorial intervention, it is worth returning to

---

Aidan: Bureaucrat and Charismatic?', in *L'Église et la mission au VIe siècle*, ed. by C. de Dreuille (Paris, 2000), pp. 160–62, 172–74.

[23] Gregory I, *Register*, XI, 56.

[24] Meyvaert, 'Le *Libellus Responsionum* à Augustin de Cantobéry: Une oeuvre authentique de Grégoire le Grand'; and Chadwick, 'Gregory the Great and the Mission to the Anglo-Saxons'.

[25] Gregory, *Register*, XI, 45; I. N. Wood, 'Augustine's Journey', *Canterbury Cathedral Chronicle* (1998), p. 38.

[26] For the variations in the texts, see P. Meyvaert, 'Bede's Text of the *Libellus Responsionum* of Gregory the Great to Augustine of Canterbury', in *England before the Conquest*, ed. by P. Clemoes and K. Hughes (Cambridge, 1971), pp. 15–33 (reprinted in Meyvaert, *Benedict, Gregory, Bede and Others* (London, 1977)). See also, Meens, 'A Background to Augustine's Mission to Anglo-Saxon England', p. 7.

Meens's argument, in particular, to his view that the *Responsiones* predate the meeting with the British bishops, and that they are evidence of the attitudes of *Angli* who had already been converted to Christianity by British clergy before Augustine's arrival.[27] Quite apart from the date of the *Responsiones* in Gregory's *Register*, the reference to the British bishops in the context of the seventh question, about Augustine's relations with the bishops of Gaul and Britain, does give us a date of 601, by which time Augustine was clearly thinking about the British Church. It may well suggest that Augustine was already looking forward to the meeting at Augustine's Oak, which Meens would place sometime in the future. Yet although Bede places the meeting later than the *Responsiones*, he gives it no date, and there is no reason to think that he had any knowledge of the chronology of Augustine's dealings with the British Church —indeed there are signs that his account of the mission is schematically arranged:[28] the episode may have been misplaced. In other words, Augustine might have asked Gregory questions about ritual purity before his meeting with the British bishops, but he might also have asked it after meeting them for the first time.

This, however, need not invalidate Meens's point that it was the English who had raised the question of ritual purity with Augustine, whose question in Bede's version concludes with the statement: 'All these things the ignorant English need to know'. The problem here is that Gregory makes no reference to the English in his answer: and given the fact that the question concerning variety of ecclesiastical ritual cannot have been posed by Augustine in the way presented in Bede's text of the *Responsiones*, we cannot rely on the questions on ritual purity as preserved in the *Historia Ecclesiastica* as the sole proof that it was the English rather than the British who raised the issue in Augustine's mind, even if the issue originated with the latter.

Here it is worth considering the extent to which Gregory's *Responsiones*—as opposed to 'Augustine's questions'—concern the English, as opposed to other groups. Although the first of 'Augustine's questions' is set out as a general enquiry about the life of bishops, Gregory's response is explicitly couched in terms of the nascent English Church, the *Ecclesia Anglorum*, as is the sixth response, dealing with episcopal consecration. So too the second question which concerns variety of custom is answered specifically with regard to the *Ecclesia Anglorum*. The response to the fifth question on incest deals directly with the *gens Anglorum*. Gregory must, therefore, have been answering questions about practices among the *Angli*. Less directly concerned with the English Church is the seventh response, which explicitly deals with Augustine's relations with Gallic and British bishops. The other answers are unspecific in their regional application, although number four, on incest, may be treated as a subsection of five, and thus can be seen as being relevant to the English. The third response deals with the very general issue of theft from churches. This leaves the eighth and ninth

---

[27] Meens, 'A Background to Augustine's Mission to Anglo-Saxon England', pp. 16–17.

[28] On the extent to which Bede's account of Augustine's mission is a literary construct, see Wood, 'Augustine and Aidan: Bureaucrat and Charismatic?'.

responses on ritual purity, where the answers once again lack any geographical specificity, although, as Meens has shown, they relate to British practices.

Given the uncertain authenticity of 'Augustine's questions', as opposed to Gregory's answers, we do not have to conclude that *Responsiones* eight and nine concern the English rather than the British—though it is possible that a full survey of the manuscripts of all three versions of the *Responsiones*, which after all survive outside Bede's *Ecclesiastical History*, will clarify the status of those questions. What we can say is that Augustine was having to deal with traditions of the British Church over a much wider range of issues than is suggested by Bede's account of the meeting at Augustine's Oak: a point which itself suggests close association with that Church, something which in turn can be inferred from Gregory's seventh response.

That Augustine's dealings with the British Church were much more complex than Bede implied is shown above all by an additional response of Gregory, the so-called *Obsecratio Augustini*, not contained in Bede's selection, which deals with the problem raised by the cult of a martyr called Sixtus, whom Augustine could not identify. Gregory simply tells him to equate the cult with that of the martyred pope of the same name.[29] The cult may have been based at Chich in Essex, and in any case shows Augustine having to deal with British Christians on his own doorstep. It is not impossible that Bede himself was responsible for excluding it from his version of the *Libellus*.

If we do accept that the responses on purity relate to problems raised by the English, as opposed to the British—and this is called into question, but is not ruled out, by my caveats—then like Meens we have to accept that British clergy had started to evangelize the English before Augustine's arrival. We might, moreover, think that questions of ritual purity had arisen through direct contact between the *Angli* and surviving pockets of British Christians in eastern England. On the other hand, whereas the English might have taken their notions of temples from the conquered British, notions of purity are perhaps more likely to have been transmitted from the free British Churches of the West, since the surviving evidence tends to suggest that the religious traditions to which the notions of purity belonged were developed by the British and Irish Churches after the beginning of the English settlement in the East.[30]

There is one further point which, I think, ought to be fitted into this model. Before news reached Gregory that the English wished to be converted, they had turned to *sacerdotes e vicino*,[31] who had refused to provide them with missionary help. Most

---

[29] M. Deanesly and P. Grosjean, 'The Canterbury Edition of the Answers of Pope Gregory I to Augustine', *Journal of Ecclesiastical History,* 10 (1959), 28–29. See the discussion in N. Brooks, *The Early History of the Church of Canterbury* (Leicester, 1984), p. 20.

[30] Our earliest dateable evidence for such notions comes from Gildas's Penitential: R. Sharpe, 'Gildas as a Father of the Church', in *Gildas: New Approaches,* ed. by M. Lapidge and D. N. Dumville (Woodbridge, 1984), pp. 193–205.

[31] Gregory, *Register,* VI, 49, 57.

historians have assumed that the reference is to British clergy. It is, however, clear from Gregory's recurrent use of the phrase that the *sacerdotes e vicino* were Frankish, not British.[32] In other words, Gregory's letters do not prove that the British remained aloof from evangelizing the Anglo-Saxons. Despite the fact that some British did not wish to work among the English, as can be seen in the canons of the Synod of the Grove of Victory,[33] there is no reason to think that all British clergy had refused to do so in the years before 596. That the people of Kent turned first to the Franks and then to Rome for missionary help, and not to the Britons, might be explained by the fact that the Britons could be seen as a conquered people, and that victors rarely take a new God from their victims: though it is interesting to note that in this case they did take the God of their victims, even if they preferred to do so from a third party.

What all this suggests is that early Anglo-Saxon religion was a much less fixed entity than is often supposed. However much Germanic tradition they brought with them, the Anglo-Saxons seem to have borrowed from religious practices within Britain in developing their own religion. Even as they did so, it seems possible that the British Church of the West, with its developing ideas, made some attempt to keep an eye on Christians who remained in the conquered territory, but perhaps also to spread Christianity to the invaders. The latter, however, turned not to the British, but to the Franks and ultimately to Rome for the last stage in their conversion, and this in time prompted Gregory the Great's policy of assimilation of tradition, rather than a hard-line break, in order to facilitate the process of mission. Instead of a static model of pagan versus Christian, in early Anglo-Saxon England we seem to be faced with non-stop religious development and fluctuation in which paganism and Christianity were never hermetically separate.

---

[32] I. N. Wood, 'The Mission of Augustine of Canterbury to the English', *Speculum*, 69 (1994), 8.

[33] *The Irish Penitentials*, ed. by L. Bieler (Dublin, 1975), pp. 68–69.

Converting Monks: Missionary Activity in Early Medieval Frisia and Saxony

WOLFERT VAN EGMOND

At the latest, from the early seventh century onwards, the Franks attempted to christianize the Frisians and Saxons living to the north and east of their kingdom. We have only scant information about these attempts. They appear to have been undertaken by bishops and monks from the northern dioceses of the Frankish realm, such as Cologne, and by monks who came from further away, such as Wulfram (d. 711), who came from the abbey of Fontenelle in Neustria. Later in the seventh century, monks from the British Isles joined these Frankish missionaries. It appears as if the arrival of these newcomers marks the intensification of the attempts to make Frisia and Saxony part of Christendom. The insular missionaries certainly received better press than their Frankish colleagues. However, we should not forget that they were not the first, and that their arrival did not end the activities of Frankish missionaries.

The ideas in this paper have been influenced by the two other speakers in the session 'Monasticism and Conversion II' at the International Medieval Congress, July, 1997: Anne-Marie Helvétius, who spoke on 'Christian Behaviour in Neustrian Hagiography', and Marco Mostert, who spoke on 'Christian Behaviour in Utrecht Hagiography' (later published as 'New Perspectives for the Study of East Central European Christianization? Christian Behaviour in Utrecht Hagiography', in *Early Christianity in Central and East Europe*, ed. by P. Urbańczyk, Christianity in East Central Europe and its Relations with the West and the East, 1, Wydawnictwo Naukowe Semper (Warsaw, 1997), pp. 175–86.

Our sources, primarily hagiographical texts, give lively accounts of the activities of all these missionaries. We are told that they converted multitudes of people to the Christian faith. When they were working in areas where other missionaries had been active before them, they would have corrected the people that had lapsed into old pagan beliefs and practices. The sources recount that the missionaries built churches and founded monasteries in newly converted areas.

Here we shall have a closer look at this latter aspect. The foundation of new monasteries may have been the most important feature of all missionary activity in these areas, and not just because several monastic foundations later became the seats of new dioceses. Even the briefest of glances at the background of the missionaries makes clear that monks played a major role in the christianization of early medieval Frisia and Saxony. However, the influence of monasticism is not just apparent in the spiritual origins of the first missionaries. The term 'monks' is here taken in the sense of 'clerics living together in a community', be they male Benedictines, nuns, or male or female canons. The term 'monastery' in this context refers to a 'community of clerics', whether its members lived up to the ideals of the synods of Aachen of 816–817 or not.[1]

One short remark on the geographical limits of our enquiry should be made. The title mentions Frisia and Saxony, but the sources adduced are mainly written in Utrecht, at that time the seat of the Frisian diocese.[2]

Christianization

What does christianization imply? Ludo Milis has developed a model of the process meant to be applicable to all times and places where Christianity takes hold.[3] According

---

[1] Compare J. Semmler, 'Die Beschlüsse des Aachener Konzils im Jahre 816', *Zeitschrift für Kirchengeschichte*, 74 (1963), 15–82; idem, 'Mönche und Kanoniker im Frankenreiche Pippins III und Karls des Grossen', in *Untersuchungen zu Kloster und Stift* (Göttingen, 1980), pp. 78–111.

[2] Still indispensable for the study of medieval narrative texts from the area of the present-day Netherlands is M. Carasso-Kok, *Repertorium van verhalende historische bronnen uit de middeleeuwen. Heiligenlevens, annalen, kronieken en andere in Nederland geschreven verhalende bronnen*, Bibliografische reeks van het Nederlands Historisch Genootschap, 2 ('s-Gravenhage, 1981). The most recent survey of hagiographical texts written in the diocese of Utrecht before 1200 AD is M. Carasso-Kok, 'Le diocèse d'Utrecht, 900–1200', in *Corpus Christianorum. Hagiographies* II, ed. by G. Philippart (Turnhout, 1996), pp. 373–411. A similar survey for the Germanic-speaking areas east of the Rhine until 950 AD is given by T. Klüppel, 'Die Germania (750–950)', in *Corpus Christianorum. Hagiographies* II, pp. 161–209.

[3] L. Milis, 'La conversion en profondeur: Un processus sans fin', *Revue du Nord*, 68 (1986), 487–98; idem, 'Monks, Mission, Culture and Society in Willibrord's Time', in *Willibrord, zijn wereld en zijn werk*, ed. by P. Bange and A. G. Weiler (Nijmegen, 1990), pp. 82–92; M. de Reu, 'De missionering: het eerste contact van heidendom en christendom', in *De Heidense Mid-*

to this model the christianization of a given area develops in three, partly overlapping phases. In the first phase, new forms of collective public behaviour are enforced. This means, for example, that people are baptized and that old cults are suppressed. In the second phase, the people are confronted with a new moral code, reflecting Christian values. Being required to live according to that code, people change their public behaviour. In the last phase, inner individual behaviour is changed through the interiorization of the Christian moral code. Thus, christianization is not the result of many sudden conversions, but rather a long-term process, especially when large groups of people are concerned. Any social group (and any person) may undergo this process at a different speed.

This model certainly helps to put some order into our thoughts on christianization. There are, however, problems when it is applied to particular situations, as Bert Demyttenaere recently pointed out.[4] For example, there is a danger in the distinction between 'public' and 'inner' behaviour. Although the influence of the new Christian doctrines varied, we should be wary of exaggerating this distinction. It might lead to an image of the newly baptized Frisians and Saxons as being Christians only in their outward behaviour, while in their hearts and thoughts they were still praying to the old gods. It is undoubtedly true that public behaviour influences thoughts and feelings, but these in their turn influence public behaviour.

Another, related problem is the question of the group whose public behaviour is supposedly changed in the first phase of christianization. How large was this group? If it was large, how could its behaviour be modified? It seems impossible that a handful of missionaries completely changed the behaviour of all people in such large areas as Frisia and Saxony. Such a change must have been brought about gradually; it cannot have been accomplished in all persons simultaneously.

It was impossible for the missionaries to reach all people at once, and to convince them of the need to change their behaviour at the same moment. Hence they had first to devote their attention to small groups. There was also another reason to concentrate on small groups. If the people at large were to be convinced of something new, there had to be some who had been convinced already. Since christianization was a long process, again and again there had to be new people who were completely convinced: new missionaries had to be trained.

The awareness that a small group could spread Christianity is evident in the writings of Bishop Radbod of Utrecht (899/900–917). In a miracle story about St Martin, the *Libellus de miraculo sancti Martini*, he writes:

---

deleeuwen, ed. by L. Milis (Brussels and Rome, 1991), pp. 19–46. See also the chapters written by Milis himself in this last volume.

[4] A. Demyttenaere, *The Claustralization of the World* (Utrecht, 1997) (also published in *Klasztor w społeczeństwie średniowiecznym i nowożytnym*, Congress of the LARHCOR, Opole, 9–11 May 1996, ed. by M. Derwich and A. Pobóg-Lenartowicz (Wrocław, 1997), pp. 23–41).

In a certain sense the glory of the things invisible grows through the tongues of men, until what is incessantly praised by the celestial beings also resounds among mortals through preaching mouths, and stretches out everywhere, having been brought to the farthest reaches of the world by a few and having been dispersed and disseminated by many. Thus did the Christian religion grow, which, at first solely confined to the lands of the Jews, posed as a poor religion because of its small number of believers. But afterwards, when it was spread throughout the world thanks to the preaching of the Apostles, it was no longer worthy to be called poor, but rather imperial and dominant. That is to say: it had gained many kingdoms and had triumphed over the mightiest kings and had crushed through its own power the necks of the proud and the sublime.[5]

Radbod presents the growth of Christianity as having occurred in concentric circles. First it was brought to a region by a few missionaries. Afterwards it was dispersed widely within that region.

Missionaries had to be trained in small groups which were partially secluded from the rest of society. This partial seclusion was necessary to provide for an environment in which Christian ideas and values were far more present than in the rest of society. In this way the members of these small groups could absorb these ideas and values. Future missionaries preferably entered these groups at a young age, so that they could more easily be imbued with a Christian world view.

It is not surprising that in the eighth and ninth centuries monasteries were the obvious institutions to form such small groups. Most monks began their monastic career as oblates. From an early age they were formed within the cloister. They lived in a community that was thoroughly permeated with Christian values. Because of their tender age, it was possible to shape their behaviour and to encourage them to adopt Christian values. As a consequence of their monastic upbringing, as adults they were able to act as missionaries and preachers in the world outside the monasteries.[6]

---

[5] *Libellus de miraculo sancti Martini auctore Radbodo episcopo Traiectensi*, ed. by O. Holder-Egger, *Monumenta Germaniae Historica, Scriptores* (henceforth *MGH, SS*), 15, 2 (1888), p. 1240, prologue: Crescit enim quodam modo per hominum linguas invisibilium excellentia rerum, dum, quod apud superos sine cessatione laudatur, apud mortales quoque per ora sermocinantia volvitur, et usque ad extremum terrae a singulis progressa et per plures sparsa ac disseminata, per omnia dilatatur. Hoc denique modo christiana crevit religio, quae primum in solis Iudeorum terminis angustata, paupertatem fidei ob raritatem credentium praetendebat; postmodum vero in universum mundum apostolorum praedicatione diffusa, iam non dignata est vocari paupercula, sed potius imperatrix et domina, sane quia multa sibi regna adquisierat regesque potentissimos vicerat, superborum et sublimium colla propria virtute calcaret. *Bibliotheca Hagiographica Latina*, Subsidia hagiographica 6 and 70 (Brussels, 1898–99 and 1986) (henceforth *BHL*), 5656.

[6] Compare Mayke de Jong, *In Samuel's Image: Child Oblation in Early Medieval West* (Leiden, 1996).

Hagiography and its Audience

The importance of the monasteries for the christianization of Frisia and Saxony is reflected in the hagiographical texts written in these regions during the eighth and ninth centuries. These texts were first of all intended for a monastic audience. In their prefaces we find only some rather uncertain indications that, even if only in translation and pronounced orally, they might be aimed at a lay public as well. In the prologue of the *Libellus de miraculo sancti Martini* the author writes:

> We think that this extraordinary fact is worthy of committing to writing and to memory, so that, in the course of times to come, Christ will everywhere be proclaimed, Christ will everywhere be praised, that Christ will be on the tongue, Christ will be in the mouth, Christ will be in the hearts of everybody.[7]

'Everybody' has to know the miracle. But is the author really concerned with everybody? The introductions of many texts explicitly address monks. We also encounter implicit indications. The *Homilia de Lebuino* suggests an appropriate time to read the text, namely during the meal. In this way not just the physical hunger but also—and much more importantly—spiritual hunger may be satisfied.[8] This passage suggests a monastic community in which texts are read aloud during meals. The appearance in our texts of saints in 'choirs' of patriarchs, prophets, apostles, martyrs, confessors, and virgins also suggests an ideal of communal worship.[9] The earthly community of clerics is here represented as a reflection of the perfect, heavenly order. Finally, should we assume that names like those of the Venerable Bede, Pythagoras, Plato, or Tullius, which are explicitly mentioned in our texts,[10] meant anything to an uneducated lay audience? There is consensus among scholars that the Carolingian *vitae* were in the first place intended for a clerical public.[11]

---

[7] *Libellus de miraculo sancti Martini*, prologue, p. 1240: Dignum etiam ducimus tam insigne factum stilo et memoriae commendare, ut per successiones temporum Christus ubique adnuntietur, Christus ubique laudetur, Christus in lingua, Christus in ore, Christus omnium versetur in corde.

[8] *Homilia sancti Radbodi de sancto Lebuino*, *Patrologia Latina* (henceforth *PL*), 132 (Paris, 1853), col. 553; *BHL*, 4814.

[9] *Sermo Radbodi de vita sanctae virginis Christi Amelbergae*, *PL*, 132 (Paris, 1853), col. 554, ch. 8. *BHL*, 322; *Vita altera Bonifatii*, ed. by W. Levison, *Vitae sancti Bonifatii archiepiscopo Moguntini*, *MGH*, *Scriptores in usum scholarum* (Hannover and Leipzig, 1905), p. 63, ch. 2; *BHL*, 1401; *Libellus de miraculo sancti Martini*, p. 1241, ch. 1.

[10] *Sermo sancti Radbodi de sancto Switberto*, *PL*, 132, cols. 547–49, chs 1–3; *BHL*, 7939. *Vita altera Bonifatii*, p. 77, ch. 21; *Libellus de miraculo sancti Martini*, prologue, p. 1240.

[11] K. Heene, 'Merovingian and Carolingian Hagiography: Continuity or Change in Public and Aims?', *Analecta Bollandiana*, 107 (1989), 421–24.

Hagiographical texts were an aid in instructing monks in correct behaviour. As the *Vita Sturmi* relates, Sturm returned to Fulda after a year spent in Italy 'inquiring into the customs, observances and traditions' of the monks there:

> Then there was a great desire in the community to adapt their mode of life to the observances either described or shown to them or exemplified in the lives of the saints. They carried out in every detail the Rule of Saint Benedict which they had vowed to follow.[12]

Not just *vitae*, but all Latin hagiographical texts from this period and region were primarily destined for clerics and monks. If the first intended audience of these texts was clerical or monastic, then their message was also first meant for a clerical or monastic public. Since in Frisia and Saxony virtually all clerics were monks, the constant appeal to imitate the saints in the hagiographical texts produced there is aimed at monks. They were to be the exemplary Christians who had to follow the example of the saints. They had to strive constantly to improve their behaviour to become perfect Christians.

And yet might sermons, miracle collections, and accounts of translations not also have been used in attempts to reach laymen? This is a very appealing suggestion. If the answer to this question is positive, then it offers us possibilities to say something of the religiosity of large groups in early medieval society. As we have seen, there are some vague indications in the hagiographical texts themselves that their authors also thought of laymen.[13] However, most Frisians and Saxons did not understand Latin in the least. This means that they needed interpreters before they could have access to the contents of these hagiographical texts. The texts may have been prepared with the intention that their contents be used in preaching to laymen. The texts should, however, be considered as sources for preaching, rather than as the very texts used in preaching. The only substantial group to have had direct access to these texts remained that of the clerics, particularly monks, the clerics living in communities.[14]

---

[12] *Vita Sturmi*, ed. by G. H. Pertz, *MGH, SS,* 2 (1829), p. 372, ch. 14: Desiderium tunc ingens inerat fratribus ad omnia quae eis dicta vel ostensa fuerant, sanctorum exemplis semetipsos toto adnisu aptare, et regulam sancti Benedicti, quam se implesse promiserant, ad omnia observabant; *BHL*, 7924. Translation by C. H. Talbot in *Soldiers of Christ: Saints and Saints' Lives from Late Antiquity and the Early Middle Ages*, ed. by T. F. X. Noble and T. Head (London, 1995), p. 177.

[13] H. Röckelein, 'Zur Pragmatik hagiographischer Schriften im Frühmittelalter', in *Bene vivere in communitate: Beiträge zum italienischen und deutschen Mittelalter Hagen Keller zum 60. Geburtstag überreicht von seinen Schülerinnen und Schülern*, ed. by T. Scharff and T. Behrmann (Münster, 1997), pp. 233–35.

[14] For a consideration of how laymen could be reached by the contents of hagiographical texts, see W. S. van Egmond, 'The Audience of Early Medieval Hagiographical Texts: Some

Let us consider as an example the *Translatio sancti Viti*. It is an account of the translation of the relics of St Vitus from St Denis to Corvey in 836. The text was written in Corvey in the ninth century.[15] It consists of four parts. It begins with an introduction (part I), followed by a short account of the foundation of Corvey (part II). Then comes the account of the translation proper, including the miracles that took place on the way (part III). The text concludes with a report of the miracles happening in the first year after the arrival of the relics (part IV). It is possible that the story of the translation itself, as well as the miracle stories in the third and fourth parts, were used in preaching to laymen. However, it seems unlikely that people from outside Corvey abbey cared for part II, the account of the foundation of the abbey. The beginning of the story of the translation proper seems to confirm that it was used independently from the first two parts. Its first sentences date the event with precision, and enumerate the most important people involved in the translation.[16] All this information can also be found in the preceding paragraphs of part II, and some of it is mentioned merely a few lines before. It must have been possible to simply ignore the first two parts and read the proper translation account as if it were an autonomous text.

Missionaries

The hagiographical texts written in the ninth and tenth century in the diocese of Utrecht repeatedly pay attention to the missionaries who worked in the region. The first of these were Willibrord (d. 739) and Boniface (d. 754). They should be admired and their example followed because of their way of living, rather than for the number of people they converted. In his writings, Bishop Radbod shows concern for the preservation of the clerical institutions of his diocese. They had seriously suffered from the incursions of Vikings and the confusion following the disintegration of the Carolingian empire. He wrote for the clerics of his diocese. He encouraged them to improve themselves so that they might not only gain eternal salvation for their own souls, but might also show others the way.[17]

In the epilogue of the *Vita altera Bonifatii* the author, possibly the same Bishop Radbod, reports how he read out his recently finished text to his brethren. They were unsatisfied with his work because he ought to have included some miracles accomplished by Boniface. This infuriated the author. Using words from the gospels, he berated them for their inability to have faith without visible signs. He then continued with a lengthy explanation. Although Boniface doubtlessly did miracles, he should be

---

Questions Revisited', in *New Approaches to Medieval Communication*, ed. by M. Mostert, Utrecht Studies in Medieval Literacy, 1 (Turnhout, 1999), pp. 41–67.

[15] *Translatio sancti Viti martyris—Übertragung des hl. Märtyrers Vitus*, ed. and trans. by I. Schmale-Ott (Münster, 1979); *BHL*, 8718–19a.

[16] *Translatio sancti Viti*, pp. 46–48, ch. 5.

[17] *Sermo de sancto Switberto*, col. 547b–c, ch. 1.

venerated and imitated above all for his inner virtues and correct behaviour. For those virtues made it possible for him to do his great deeds.[18]

The hagiographical texts written in Frisia and Saxony before the end of the first millennium were primarily meant to educate monks. It was they who needed to be converted and become exemplary Christians. This could not be accomplished in the twinkling of an eye. It was brought about through protracted teaching in the monasteries. From the monasteries Christianity would slowly spread out in the world, a process that was to take even longer. Spreading Christianity could only come about through the accumulation of monasteries. That is why the foundation of new monasteries in Frisia and Saxony was the most important step in christianizing these areas. People who had grown up in old monasteries founded new ones.

The history of the dioceses of Utrecht and Münster provides a good example.[19] At the end of the seventh century, Willibrord founded a small monastery in the old Roman fortress of Utrecht (Traiectum). This served as a base for his activities among the Frisians. It was in this monastery that Liudger, who later also studied with Alcuin in York (probably during the years 767–772), was raised. Subsequently, Liudger worked as a missionary among the Frisians and Saxons, cooperating with the Utrecht monastery. Still later he moved further eastwards and founded the monasteries of Münster (793) and Werden-Ruhr (799). In 777 Alberic, the head of the monastery in Utrecht, had been ordained the first bishop of Utrecht. In 804 Liudger in his turn became the first bishop of Münster (804–809). The case of Utrecht and Münster shows how a pupil from one monastery in Frisia founded several monasteries in Saxony.

Other examples could be given. The first two bishops of Paderborn, Hathumar (806/7–815) and Badurad (815–852), were probably educated in the cathedral chapter of Würzburg. Three of the first bishops of Verden (Spatto (785–788), Thanco (788–808), and Harud (808–830)) were simultaneously abbots of the monasteries of Amorbach and Neustadt am Main, both in the diocese of Würzburg.[20] Willehad, the first bishop of Bremen (787–789), was a monk who had started his missionary career in the region of Dokkum, in Frisia. And monks from Corbie founded the monastery of Corvey.

---

[18] *Vita altera Bonifatii*, pp. 74–78, chs 18–23.

[19] For a recent summary in English of the early history of the diocese of Utrecht, see J. M. van Winter, 'The First Centuries of the Episcopal See at Utrecht', in *Utrecht, Britain and the Continent. Archaeology, Art and Architecture*, ed. by E. de Bièvre, British Archaeological Association Conference Transactions (London, 1996), pp. 22–29. For Münster, see Arnold Angenendt, *Mission bis Millennium, 313–1000*, Geschichte des Bistums Münster, 1 (Münster, 1998).

[20] A. Wendehorst, *Das Bistum Würzburg, I: Die Bischofsreihe bis 1254*, Germania Sacra Neue Folge, 1.1 (Berlin, 1962), pp. 35–36; idem, 'Das Bistum Würzburg: Ein Überblick von den Anfängen bis zur Säkularisation', in *Freiburger Diözesan-Archiv*, 86 (= 3. Folge 18. Bd.) (1966), pp. 13–15; H. Schoppmeyer, 'Paderborn', in *Lexikon des Mittelalters*, 10 vols (Munich, 1977–), VII, 1613.

The general picture is clear. In about two centuries a network of monasteries was laid over Frisia and Saxony. In the present-day region of Westphalia twenty monastic foundations predate the year thousand.[21] In Saxony as a whole almost fifty monasteries for women were established in the two centuries between c. 820 and c. 1040.[22] It was in these monasteries that small groups could be thoroughly imbued with Christian values. Here the real foundations for the comprehensive christianization of the region were laid. The conversion of the monks in Frisia and Saxony was thus the most important step towards the conversion of all Frisians and Saxons.

---

[21] Compare the data in *Westfälisches Klosterbuch: Lexikon der vor 1815 errichteten Stifte und Klöster von ihrer Gründung bis zur Aufhebung*, ed. by K. Hengst, 2 vols (Münster, 1992–94).

[22] M. Parisse, 'Les femmes au monastère dans le Nord de l'Allemagne du IXᵉ au XIᵉ siècle: Conditions sociales et religieuses', in *Frauen in Spätantike und Frühmittelalter. Lebensbedingungen—Lebensnormen—Lebensformen: Beiträge zu einer internationalen Tagung am Fachbereich Geschichtswissenschaften der Freien Universität Berlin, 18. bis 21. Februar 1987*, ed. by W. Affeldt (Sigmaringen, 1990), p. 312.

Deliberate Ambiguity:
The Lombards and Christianity

WALTER POHL

C onversion in Europe had many faces. It might be symbolized by a ruler's grand gesture, like those of Constantine or Clovis, and be the result of great battles and visions of victory. It might be the result of careful planning and missionary activity, as with Anglo-Saxons and Avars. Conversions could be described as achievements of holy men, for instance Ulfila, Augustine, or Cyril and Methodius. They might be endangered by bloodshed, as in the case of the Saxons, or martyrdom, as with Boniface or King Olaf the Saint. Christian rulers broke with the pagan past and had to overcome armed resistance, as in the case of Anglo-Saxons, Bulgarians, or Hungarians. Dramatic conflict and far-reaching decisions not only accompanied the conversion to Christianity, but often also the fight between Catholicism and heresy, especially Arianism; the baptism of Clovis at the beginning and the council of Toledo at the end of the sixth century clearly mark the transition to confessional unity between Germanic warriors and the Roman population. In many of these cases, we may argue that contemporary and modern narratives simplify and condense the complex process of conversion into a single, dramatic act or ascribe it too smoothly to a single actor.[1] But at least these narratives exist and still help us to understand. Syncretism and heterodoxy

---

[1] For some critical remarks, see Patrick J. Geary, 'Die Bedeutung von Religion und Bekehrung im frühen Mittelalter', in *Die Alemannen und Franken bis zur 'Schlacht bei Zülpich' (496/97)*, RGA Erg. Bd. 19, ed. by Dieter Geuenich (Berlin and New York, 1998), pp. 438–50; Alain Dierkens, 'Christianisme et "paganisme" dans la Gaule septentrionale aux Vᶜ et VIᶜ siècles', in ibid., pp. 451–74.

almost certainly played a more important part than our handbook narratives allow for;[2] but still, few would doubt that in the sixth century, the Franks were mostly Catholics, the Goths Arians, and the Saxons pagans.

With the Lombards, we lack such a condensed narrative. No grand gestures, dramatic royal conversions, or decisive missionary interventions are recorded. There was plenty of conflict, to be sure, and there were repeated attempts to give the Lombards a clear confessional profile, for instance by King Authari, who promoted Arianism, or his widow Theodelinda who tried to contain it. But these were exceptions. In the case of the Lombards, we have to deal directly with the ambiguity and the contradictions that in many other conversion narratives are only hidden in the background. Not that modern scholarship has been too disconcerted by this fact; the 'real' religious history of the Lombards has been reconstructed and reconsidered many times. The Italian school inspired by Gianpiero Bognetti underlined the importance of the pagan element that allowed the Lombards in Italy to preserve their separate identity.[3] Others assumed that most of the Lombards were already Arians when they invaded Italy in 568.[4] Whether they only became Arians under Alboin and before that had been Catholics in Pannonia, as Procopius seems to claim, has often been debated.[5] Stephen Fanning discarded Lombard Arianism as rather peripheral.[6] A solution to some of the contradictions, which was proposed by several scholars, was to differentiate between the fundamentally pagan creed of part of the people up to the seventh century and the various political confessions chosen by successive Lombard rulers. The very flexibility of Lombard religious policy also seems to indicate that neither Catholicism nor Arianism was too deeply rooted among their subjects.[7] Chris Wickham has underlined 'the near-total irrelevance of personal religious alignment inside a resolutely secular

---

[2] See Ian N. Wood, 'Pagan Religions and Superstitions East of the Rhine from the Fifth to the Ninth Century', in *After Empire. Towards an Ethnology of Europe's Barbarians*, ed. by Giorgio Ausenda (Rochester, 1995), pp. 253–68.

[3] Gianpiero Bognetti, 'Appunti per una storia dei Longobardi in Italia', in *L'età longobarda*, 4 vols (Milan, 1968), IV, 611–68: In the seventh century, at least in central Italy, 'alla base, non si era superato il paganesimo germanico originario'; idem, 'S. Maria foris Portas di Castelseprio e la storia religiosa dei Longobardi', in *L'età longobarda* (Milan, 1967), II, 37–45. Stefano Gasparri, *La cultura tradizionale dei Longobardi* (Spoleto, 1983), p. 8.

[4] Arnold Angenendt, *Das Frühmittelalter. Die abendländische Christenheit, 400–900* (Stuttgart, 1990), p. 168: 'Die Eindringlinge bekannten sich, wohl im Hinblick auf die noch in Italien lebenden Ostgoten, zum gotisch-arianischen Christentum'.

[5] For a Catholic phase in Pannonia, see Carl Blasel, *Die Wanderzüge der Langobarden* (Breslau, 1909), pp. 582 ff.; Bognetti, 'Appunti', p. 639; against it: Ludwig Schmidt, *Die Ostgermanen* (Munich, 1934), pp. 620 f.

[6] Steven Fanning, 'Lombard Arianism Reconsidered', *Speculum*, 56 (1981), 241–58.

[7] Schmidt, *Die Ostgermanen*, p. 621; Jörg Jarnut, *Geschichte der Langobarden* (Stuttgart, 1982), p. 53.

political system'.[8] Neil Christie has introduced a gendered view, assuming that the Church was quite popular among women, whereas 'its appeal to male minds must have been rather lack-lustre'.[9]

In this paper, I do not intend to offer a new coherent narrative of Lombard conversion or even to present a thorough discussion of the evidence. I will, rather, propose a few methodological reflections that may be of use. My basic approach is not new, but has not been used systematically in a discussion of Lombard conversion so far. I would like to argue that it is necessary to contextualize the passages from the sources, in a way in which, for instance, Ian Wood has dealt with the Merovingian material and is currently dealing with missionary hagiography.[10] Traditional scholarship has analysed the sources as reflections of a coherent reality, asking whether they are accurate or distorted, comparing them with similar passages from other texts. This enabled scholars to decide which category to apply: for instance, a person described as worshipping trees or snakes was a pagan, as was somebody buried with grave goods, unless these contained crosses or other symbols regarded as Christian. Ideally, all forms of expression, whether texts, symbols, or objects, should be the key to either paganism or Christianity, to either Catholicism or Arianism. Paganism in Lombard Italy could only be Germanic paganism. Of course, this view allowed for certain forms of transition or syncretism, but as secondary phenomena that would sometimes blur our vision, but not threaten the basic validity of our clear-cut concepts. I have no doubt that this epistemological optimism has brought admirable results, but I am afraid it has been pushed to the limit. We have to ask whether our sources really describe an underlying, pre-existing reality in which religious practices naturally fell in the set categories of paganism, Arianism, and Catholicism. Could it be that, instead, these very texts and symbols only aim at establishing such clear categories in a world in which religious creeds and practices were much more varied and elusive? Or could it be that the texts sometimes even fail, or do not care, to establish such distinctions? Furthermore, it is often doubtful whether our definition of religion as a social field that incorporates religious practices and beliefs into supernatural phenomena, moral codes, and priestly institutions corresponds to past realities. Doubtless, the Church strove to establish, and control, such a field, but pagan religion was organized, and perceived, in a very different way.[11]

---

[8] Chris Wickham, *Early Medieval Italy. Central Power and Local Society, 400–1000* (Ann Arbor, 1989), p. 36.

[9] Neil Christie, *The Lombards* (Oxford, 1995), p. 185.

[10] Ian N. Wood, *The Merovingian Kingdoms 450–751* (London and New York, 1994); idem, *The Missionary Life* (forthcoming).

[11] Walter Pohl, *Die Germanen* (Munich, 2000), pp. 78–85.

Let us take the example of paganism first.[12] It is clear enough that several Latin texts from the sixth to the ninth centuries describe, or at least allude to, pagan elements. The *Dialogi* of Gregory the Great describe how Roman peasants captured by the Lombards were forced to attend to the sacrifice of a goat's head to the devil, at which these Lombards danced around it and sang a *carmen nefandum*.[13] It is possible to connect the rite, as Grönbech and Gasparri did, with the goats of Thor in the *Prose Edda*.[14] However, Thor is said to have slaughtered two billy-goats, eaten their meat, thrown the bones on the goatskin, and revived the goats by brandishing his hammer, whereas the Lombards adored a *caput caprae* of a female goat, and danced around it, and there is no reference to eating the meat (there is a story about captives forced by the Lombards to eat sacrificial meat elsewhere in the *Dialogi*).[15] Apart from the fact that over six hundred years and almost two thousand miles lie between the stories told by Gregory and by Snorri, it requires some fantasy to see them both as reflections of the same rite: they have nothing in common but the occurrence of goats.[16] Rather than from the Roman peasants who refused to take part in these sacrilegious ceremonies and were therefore all killed, as Gregory says, he knew about such rites from books. He could, for instance, find ample material about sacrificing goats in a book he had most certainly read: the Old Testament. The stories about Moses and Aaron in the *Liber Leviticus* are full of detailed descriptions of sacrifices of female goats, and other animals, and different ways in which the head and other parts of the body should be cut off and arranged on the altar. Gregory himself commented on these passages in the *Moralia in Iob*.[17]

---

[12] For some general remarks on the problem of 'Germanic' religion, see Pohl, *Die Germanen*; *Germanische Religionsgeschichte. Quellen und Quellenprobleme*, ed. by Heinrich Beck, D. Ellmers, and K. Schier (Berlin, 1992).

[13] Gregory the Great, *Dialogi*, 3, 28: 'more suo immolaverunt caput caprae'. Cf. Gasparri, *La cultura tradizionale*, p. 45 f.

[14] Snorri Sturluson, *The Prose Edda*, trans. by Jean I. Young (Berkeley, 1954), pp. 69 f; Vilhelm Grönbech, *Kultur und Religion der Germanen*, 3rd edn (Darmstadt, 1987), II, 235 f.; Gasparri, *La cultura tradizionale*, pp. 47–49; Wilfried Menghin, *Die Langobarden. Archäologie und Geschichte* (Stuttgart, 1985), p. 145; see also W. Schutz, 'Die Langobarden als Wodanverehrer', *Mannus*, 24 (1932), pp. 215–31.

[15] Gregory the Great, *Dialogi*, 3, 27: 'a Langobardis capti carnes immolaticias comedere conpellentur'.

[16] Gasparri, *La cultura tradizionale*, p. 48, acknowledges that his intention is not to 'proporre un'identità più o meno assoluta tra il rito longobardo del caput caprae e la Gylfaginning stessa, ma di intendere semplicemente il primo come una della possibili, lontane radici del secondo'.

[17] Leviticus 1. 8, 3. 12–17, 4. 27–31. Gregory the Great, *Moralia in Iob*, c. 32, 3, 4, in *Patrologia Latina* (henceforth *PL*), 76, col. 635 f. Here, the goat symbolizes the *vita contemplativa*; Christian authors commenting on the Old Testament of course always sought a spiritual interpretation. Augustine, *Ennarationes in psalmos*, in *PL*, 37, col. 1361, took the sacrificial goat divided in three parts as an image for the *ecclesia in gentibus*.

Goats were sometimes taken as symbols of the sinner and connected with the devil.[18] Needless to say, classical religion also knew sacrifices of goats. The passage about being forced to eat sacrificial meat could be found in many martyrs' lives set in the persecutions of the second and third century AD. This does not mean that the Lombards might not have sacrificed goats, or eaten the meat of immolated animals; it simply suggests that accounts like Gregory's about barbarian paganism are not ethnographic descriptions, but take their images of pagan rites from biblical and classical texts. A Christian author had no interest whatsoever in investigating the difference between Germanic and classical paganism, which he took to be the same fundamental error.

Similarly, the material in the ninth-century life of Barbatus about sacred trees and snakes is problematic. The seventh-century saint is depicted opposing a Lombard rite regularly taking place outside Benevento, which involved the veneration of snakes.[19] Again, one is tempted at first glance to interpret this in the context of Germanic paganism. The *Edda* contains many references to sacred snakes, and the ninth-century *Historia Langobardorum codicis Gothani* mentions that the forefathers of the Lombards were believed to be descended from snakes, 'asserunt antiqui parentes Langobardorum [. . .] serpentibus parentes eorum breviati exissent'.[20] Had the Lombards really introduced the snake cult into the Beneventan area? Already, Augustine specifically mentions that the Marsi (who lived in the mountains north of Benevento) venerated snakes, and this seems to have been common knowledge among early Christian authors, for it is also mentioned in a poem by Avitus of Vienne.[21] This was long before the Lombards came to Italy. It is unlikely that this was a coincidence; two interpretations are possible. Either, the author of the *Vita Barbati* again derived his information about pagan practices in the area from books at a time when Lombard paganism had been more or less eradicated, and he knew nothing about it. Or, perhaps, Lombard paganism in seventh-century (or ninth-century) Italy had been deeply influenced by traditional rural cults in the area. The same question arises with the veneration of sacred trees and

---

[18] Augustinus, *Sermo* 261, in *PL*, 39, col. 2227.

[19] *Vita Barbati*, c. 1, ed. by Georg Waitz, *Monumenta Germaniae Historica, rerum Langobardicarum* (henceforth *MGH, rer. Lang.*) (Hannover, 1878), p. 557: 'Langobardi [. . .] priscum gentilitatis ritum tenentes [. . .] bestiae simulacro, quae vulgo vipera nominatur, flectabant colla [. . .] Verum etiam non longe a Beneventi menibus quasi sollempnem diem sacram colebant arborem, in qua suspendentes corium, [. . .]' and then rode past on horseback trying to tear off little bits from this animal skin.

[20] *Historia Langobardorum codicis Gothani*, ed. by Georg Waitz, *MGH, rer. Lang.*, p. 7. For an extensive discussion of the passage in the *Vita Barbati*, see Gasparri, *La cultura tradizionale*, pp. 69 ff.

[21] Augustinus, *De Genesi ad litteram*, 11, ed. by Joseph Zycha, Corpus scriptorum ecclesiasticorum Latinorum, 28, 1, p. 361: 'putantur audire et intellegere serpentes verba Marsorum'. Avitus, *De originali peccato, Poemata*, 2, ed. by R. Peiper, *MGH, Auctores Antiquissimi*, 6, 2 (Berlin, 1883), p. 220. I owe both references to Ian Wood.

sources. King Liutprand's law in the early eighth century explicitly forbade the cult of sacred trees and sources.[22] Sacred trees and sources were as much part of the classical heritage of the *rustici* mentioned in the lawcode as of Germanic tradition.

The argument should be extended to the archaeological evidence.[23] It is quite likely that the Germanic animal style decoration on Lombard brooches and belt-fittings conveyed something more than just aesthetic pleasure. But I suppose most historians would not even be able to explain the symbolic significance of the intricate graffiti that young spray-paint artists nowadays put on the walls and trains of this world, which have a surprising resemblance to Germanic animal style, and certainly are full of hidden significance only insiders understand. One might say that in both cases, a pictorial language was found that could be modulated to express the specific identity of street gangs, or warrior groups, and that served to distinguish the way of life of these groups as a whole from the rest of the population.[24] Whatever distinction animal-style decoration may have expressed, it was not paganism versus Christianity, otherwise animal style decoration could not be found on gold sheet crosses, for instance in some pieces in the museum at Cividale.[25] Neither was such a polarity expressed in inhumation with grave goods or, from the other side, with gold sheet crosses; the phenomena overlap too much, and early medieval Christianity certainly did not exclude the use of grave goods in the inhumation ritual.[26] Of course, taken as a whole, the development of inhumation rituals and of the types of objects found in the graves correspond to a process of acculturation and christianization. But that comes as no surprise. How difficult it may be to describe the details of this process on the basis of burial evidence is exemplified by the controversial debate on the cemetery of Castel Trosino between Bierbrauer, Jørgensen, and Martin.[27] Were these romanized Lombards, or barbarized Romans?

---

[22] *Leges Liutprandi*, ed. by Friedrich Bluhme and Alfred Boretius, *MGH, Leges Langobardorum*, 4 (Hannover, 1868), c. 84, p. 142: 'qui ad arbore, quam rustici sanctivum vocant, atque ad fontanas adoraverit, aut sacrilegium vel incantationis fecerit'.

[23] Compare Christie, *The Lombards*, pp. 188–90.

[24] A similar interpretation is offered by Lotte Hedeager, 'The Creation of Germanic Identity', in *Frontières d'Empire*, ed. by Patrice Brun (Nemours, 1993), pp. 121–31. In general, see Günter Haseloff, *Die germanische Tierornamentik der Völkerwanderungszeit*, 2 vols (Berlin, 1981).

[25] *I Longobardi. Catalogo della Mostra* (Milano, 1990), pp. 223, 227.

[26] Fred Paxton, *Christianizing Death. The Creation of a Ritual Process in Early Medieval Europe* (Ithaca, 1990); Guy Halsall, 'Burial, Ritual and Merovingian Society', in *The Community, the Family and the Saint*, ed. by Joyce Hill and Mary Swan (Turnhout, 1998), pp. 325–38; idem, *Early Medieval Cemetries: An Introduction to Post-Roman Burial Archaeology* (Glasgow, 1996).

[27] Volker Bierbrauer, 'Die Landnahme der Langobarden in Italien aus archäologischer Sicht', in *Ausgewählte Probleme europäischer Landnahmen des Früh- und Hochmittelalters: methodische Grundlagendiskussion im Grenzbereich zwischen Archäologie und Geschichte*, Vorträge und Forschungen, 41.1, ed. by Michael Müller-Wille and Reinhard Schneider (Sigmaringen, 1993), p. 163; L. Jørgensen, 'Castel Trosino and Nocera Umbra', in *Acta Archaeologica*, 62

Thus, it is hard to be precise about conversion and christianization. The extensive appearance of gold sheet crosses in graves demonstrates the spread of a Christian symbolic language, but does not prove, or disprove, that an individual's grave was Christian.

What, then, do the texts tell us about Lombard Christianity? Three observations can easily be made. First, even the earliest contemporary sources that describe the integration of the Lombards in the late Roman world regard them as Christians. Procopius, writing in the middle of the sixth century, remarks that at the end of the fifth, the Heruls subdued the Lombards 'who were Christians'.[28] And Bishop Nicetius of Trier, writing to King Alboin's Frankish wife soon after 560, regards Lombard Arianism, but not paganism, as an issue. Second, in the sixth and seventh centuries, there was not one Christianity the Lombards were faced with in Italy but three: Catholicism, Arianism, and the defenders of the so-called 'Three Chapters'. In Peter Brown's terminology, one could call these rival micro-Christendoms.[29] Third, choices and perceptions in this minefield of religious identities were mainly influenced by political reasoning. Political alliances and loyalties sometimes affirmed and reinforced the religious boundaries, but sometimes they tended to obscure them, to an extent that has not been fully realized yet.

Let us look at a few examples. An alliance that fell reassuringly within the categories of religious factions was that between Byzantines and the Franks, with active support from the Catholic bishops in Italy; the rhetoric was adequate to this type of confrontation. For instance, in 585, King Childebert II wrote to Bishop Laurentius of Milan asking him to broker an alliance with the exarch against the Lombards, 'gentem [. . .] relegioni ac fidei iniquissimae perfidem'.[30] Similar phrases can often be found in the letters of Gregory the Great.[31] When, after 590, Frankish offensives in Italy ceased, and a stable tribute relationship between Lombards and Franks began, the rhetoric changed as well.[32] Gregory of Tours, who wrote a few years after that, was certainly averse to Arianism, and expounds in unpleasant detail how Arius, as a punishment for

---

(1991), 1–58; Max Martin, 'Grabfunde des 6. Jahrhunderts aus der Kirche St. Peter und Paul in Mels SG', in *Archäologie der Schweiz*, 11 (1988), 167–81.

[28] Procopius, *The Wars*, ed. by H. B. Dewing (London, 1914; repr. Cambridge, MA, 1979), VI, 14, 9.

[29] Peter Brown, *The Rise of Western Christendom: Triumph and Diversity A.D. 200–1000* (Oxford, 1996).

[30] *Epistolae Austrasicae* 46, ed. by Wilhelm Gundlach, *MGH, Epistolae Merovingici et Karolini aevi*, 1 (Munich, 1892), p. 151.

[31] See Robert Markus, *Gregory the Great and his World* (Cambridge, 1997).

[32] Walter Pohl, 'The Empire and the Lombards: Treaties and Negotiations in the Sixth Century', in *Kingdoms of the Empire. The Integration of Barbarians in Late Antiquity*, ed. by Walter Pohl (Leiden, New York, Cologne, 1997), pp. 75–134.

heresy, died a terrible death from diarrhea in the toilet. But he does not mention that the Lombards were Arians at all.[33]

For the Lombard rulers, Catholicism or Arianism represented political and economic options. When, in the conflict with the Arian Gepids, King Audoin's ambassadors sought to negotiate Byzantine support, they claimed to be Catholics.[34] The basis of this claim obviously was that in Lombard Pannonia, the remnants of a Catholic Church organization still existed—there is evidence for a bishop of Scarabantia after the middle of the sixth century—but no Arian hierarchy, whereas a Gepid Arian bishop resided in Sirmium.[35] A dozen or so years later, the situation had changed, as Bishop Nicetius's concerns about Alboin's religious policy show. Alboin already prepared, so it seems, his intervention in Italy as the heir of the Gothic kingdom by accommodating Arian missionaries and sending Lombards on pilgrimages to Italy, instead of letting them go to the shrine of St Martin at Tours. There was a large discontented faction of Arian clerics in Italy at the time, being dispossessed of their churches and purged by the Byzantine authorities to the benefit of the Catholic hierarchy, as some of the Ravenna papyri and remarks in Pope Gregory's letters clearly show.[36] We have a fragment from a long list of seized Arian property that the Catholic Church of Ravenna received between 565 and 570.[37] The role of disowned Arian clerics, who were experts both in religious matters and civic administration, in the integration of the Lombards must have been considerable, and may explain the pro-Arian measures taken in the 580s by King Authari.[38] Were they intended to keep the Lombards aloof from the indigenous population? More likely, they were the result of an alliance with the restored Arian

---

[33] Walter Pohl, 'Gregory of Tours and Contemporary Perceptions of Lombard Italy', in *Gregory of Tours*, ed. by Kathleen Mitchell and Ian N. Wood (forthcoming). See also Fanning, 'Lombard Arianism Reconsidered'; and John Moorhead, 'Gregory of Tours on the Arian Kingdoms', in *Studi Medievali*, 36 (1995), 903–15.

[34] Walter Pohl, 'Premesse e conseguenze della formazione del regno longobardo in Italia', in idem, *Le origini etniche dell'Europa* (Rome, forthcoming); idem, 'Die Langobarden in Pannonien und Justinians Gotenkrieg', in *Ethnische und kulturelle Verhältnisse an der mittleren Donau im 6.–11. Jahrhundert,* ed. by Darina Bialeková and Jozef Zabojník (Bratislava, 1996), pp. 27–36.

[35] Heinrich Berg, 'Bischöfe und Bischofssitze im Ostalpen- und Donauraum vom 4. bis zum 8. Jahrhundert', in *Die Bayern und ihre Nachbarn*, ed. by Herwig Wolfram and Andreas Schwarcz (Vienna, 1985), I, 61–110, esp. p. 85.

[36] Gregorius Magnus (Gregory the Great), *Registrum epistolarum*, ed. by Dag Norberg, Corpus Christianorum series Latina, 140–140a (Turhout, 1982), 3, 19.

[37] *Die nichtliterarischen lateinischen Papyri Italiens aus der Zeit 445–700*, 2 vols, ed. by Jan-Olof Tjäder (1955; repr. Lund, 1982), I, no. 3.

[38] Gregory the Great, *Registrum epistolarum* 1, 17; cf. Piergiuseppe Scardigli, *Goti e Longobardi* (Rome, 1987), pp. 193–96.

hierarchy at the expense of the Catholic faction, without, however, launching an anti-Catholic policy in its support similar to the anti-Arian policy of the Byzantines.

Towards the end of the sixth century, the Arian bias shown by Authari gradually gave way to a more balanced policy advocated by Queen Theodelinda. Now, the Lombards profited from a degree of religious tolerance in sharp contrast with the massive attempts by the Byzantine authorities, supported by Pope Gregory, to curb all dissent on the Three Chapters in the exarchate.[39] The letter by a number of north Italian bishops to the Emperor Maurice, in which they threatened to turn to the Lombard side,[40] and later the Aquileian schism in 607, in which one of the contenders returned from Byzantine Grado to Lombard Aquileia, are clear cases in point. Even Pope Gregory had to pour some water into his wine with regard to the Three Chapters, as far as the Lombard kingdom was concerned. A problem arose in 593 when three bishops, with Queen Theodelinda's support, seceded from the new archbishop of Milan, Constantius (who resided in exile in Byzantine Genova), who was considered too eager in the condemnation of the Three Chapters.[41] Gregory sent a letter, via Constantius, to Theodelinda briefly expounding the papal doctrine and enumerating the five oecumenical councils. Constantius, afraid that this would make things even worse, refused to transmit the letter to the queen and asked the pope to send another one, omitting the reference to the fifth oecumenical council, the one in Constantinople in 553 at which the condemnation of the Three Chapters had been decided. Gregory responded saying: 'If you believed she could have been scandalized because the fifth synod was mentioned in it, it has been right that you did not transmit it. [. . .] But we, as you wished, have done it in a way that we did not recall this synod'.[42] The pope's caution was rewarded because he was able to establish a relatively reliable cooperation with Queen Theodelinda, whose son Adaloald later received a Catholic baptism.[43]

But the cautious policy towards the dissenters in the question of the Three Chapters in the Lombard kingdom was also severely criticised in a letter by Saint Columbanus to Pope Boniface, probably in 613, motivated by King Agilulf's discontent with religious factionalism: 'For the division of his people is grief to him, for the sake of the

---

[39] Compare Thomas S. Brown, *Gentlemen and Officers. Imperial Administration and Aristocratic Power in Byzantine Italy, AD 500–800* (Rome, 1984).

[40] *Acta conciliorum oecumenicorum*, 4, 2 (Berlin), pp. 132f.; cf. Berg, 'Bischöfe und Bischofssitze', pp. 82f.

[41] *Acta conciliorum*, 4, 2–4; 4, 33.

[42] Gregory the Great, *Registrum epistolarum* 4, 37: 'Quos autem scripsistis quia epistulam meam reginae Theodelindae transmittere minime voluistis, pro eo quod in ea quinta synodus nominabatur, si eam exinde scandalizari posse credidistis, recta factum est ut minime transmitteretis. [. . .] Nos tamen sicut voluistis ita fecimus, ut eiusdem synodi nullam memoriam faceremus'.

[43] Paul the Deacon, *Historia Langobardorum*, ed. by Ludwig Bethmann and Georg Waitz, *MGH, rer. Lang.*, IV, 27.

queen (Theodelinda), of their son (Adaloald), and perhaps for his own sake also; for he is said to have remarked, that if he knew for certain, he also would believe' (fertur enim dixisse, si certum sciret, et ipse crederet).[44] Columbanus's letter shows Agilulf as a *rex gentilis Longobardus*,[45] a pagan king, pursuing religious matters mainly for the sake of his wife Theodelinda, but thus offering the opportunity to confirm the Catholic faith after a period of Arianism.[46] Lombard religious history is rich in paradox, and this letter is an impressive example. An Irish holy man, only recently arrived in Italy, but worried about the orthodoxy of its church, writes a letter to the pope imploring him to declare himself on the matter and thereby clear himself from the suspicion of heresy, and to take action to promote the Catholic cause. He then states that his main reason to write the letter was that a pagan Lombard king asked him to do so because he was worried about religious unrest in his kingdom. A pagan king as an arbiter between quarrelling bishops, and a pope unable to keep peace in his church even though he carefully avoided touching any controversial issue—this is the view on Italy that Columbanus offers in the same years when Christianity was triumphant in Anglo-Saxon England. Scholars have usually used the letter simply to debate whether Agilulf was really pagan, or rather Arian, or Catholic; compared to the complexity of the situation, this is a reductive argument.

In spite of Columbanus's zealous intervention, the religious situation remained tense and confused, and hardly gave Agilulf the opportunity to 'know for certain and believe'. Too many people around him knew for certain in too many different ways. It took another century until Christian unity was re-established in the Synod of Pavia in 698, where the heresy of the Three Chapters was finally overcome, with the active support of King Cunincpert, 'sublimatus tempore / moderno rector fortis et piissimus / devotus fidem christianam colere / ecclesiarum ditator et opifex'.[47] It may be no coincidence that the poem *De synodo Ticinensi* about the synod is transmitted in two Bobbio manuscripts.[48] One of them is a sixth-century copy of the Acts of the Council of Chalcedon, written in capital letters on blotted-out fragments by the Arian Gothic

---

[44] Columbanus, Ep. 5, in *Opera*, ed. by G. S. M. Walker, Scriptores Latini Hiberniae, 2 (Dublin, 1970), p. 44. For the context, see Donald Bullough, 'The Career of Columbanus', in *Columbanus, Studies on the Latin Writings*, ed. by Michael Lapidge (Woodbridge, 1997), pp. 1–28, esp. pp. 23–28; Carlo Guido Mor, 'San Colombano e la politica ecclesiastica di Agilulfo', in idem, *Scritti di storia giuridica altomedievale* (Pisa, 1977), pp. 605–14.

[45] Columbanus, Ep. 5, p. 52.

[46] Columbanus, Ep. 5, p. 54: 'Reges namque Arrianam hanc labem in hac diu regione, calcando fidem Catholicam, firmarunt; nunc nostram rogant roborari fidem'.

[47] Compare the *Carmen de Synodo Ticinensi*, ed. by Ludwig Bethmann, in *MGH, rer. Lang.*, pp. 189–91.

[48] The MSS are Milan, Ambrosianus, E 147 sup., and C 105 infer.: Ludwig Bethmann, in *MGH, rer. Lang.*, p. 189. Paul the Deacon, *Historia Langobardorum*, VI, 14, mistakenly mentions a synod in Aquileia instead.

Bishop Wulfila, in which a contemporary scribe inserted the poem—a manuscript that is almost emblematic for the complex story of conversion and heresy in Italy.

There is no field in early medieval history in which social boundaries and distinctions were so clearly defined, and continually maintained, as between good and bad Christianity, between Christianity and that troubled universe of traditional beliefs that the Christians called paganism.[49] A few words could decide to which party one belonged, and numerous Christian authors and churchmen devoted a considerable part of their energy to sharpen these criteria even more, and to mark conversions by unmistakable ritual and rhetoric. Therefore, to use these categories—paganism, Catholicism, Arianism, etc.—in our historical narratives makes a lot of sense. But in all their seductive clarity, they should not tempt us to believe that they necessarily corresponded to clear-cut groups of people. The Lombards are a good example of the ambiguity that persisted in spite of all efforts of definition.

In the period around 600, influential Italian clerics even accepted and supported ambiguities that would otherwise have been unacceptable. A pagan king favouring ecclesiastical unity seemed better than a fervent Arian, and tacit acquiescence with supporters of the Three Chapters was better than unity at all costs. In the words of the dissident patriarch John of Aquileia, in a letter to King Agilulf: 'What unity is said to be achieved, where swords, where prison cells, where beating with sticks, and where long exile and judgements with cruel penalties were employed?'.[50] A more or less pagan king was asked by one of the highest clerics in the country to intervene so that 'fides catholica vestris augeatur temporibus', by which he understood the schismatic side of the Three Chapters controversy. In other instances, a Christian Lombard king like Rothari who preserved internal peace and issued a lawcode might seem acceptable to many Catholics even though he was Arian. This is still reflected in Paul the Deacon's *History of the Lombards*; in it, the Catholic monk from Montecassino resolves this tension with a miracle story: when a grave robber disturbs Rothari's grave in the church of St John the Baptist, the Baptist himself appears to declare himself in favour of the Arian king: 'He may not have been of the right creed, but still he commended himself to me'.[51] Such ambiguities were the basis of political and religious compromise that kept the troubled situation in Italy from exploding and made it possible that three different

---

[49] Walter Pohl, 'Einleitung—soziale Grenzen und Spielräume der Macht', in *Grenze und Differenz im frühen Mittelalter*, ed. by Walter Pohl and Helmut Reimitz (Vienna, forthcoming).

[50] *Epistolae Langobardicae*, no. 1, ed. by Wilhelm Gundlach, *MGH, Epistolae Merovingici et Karolini aevi*, 1 (Munich, 1892), p. 693: 'Qualis autem unitas dicitur facta, ubi spata, ubi claustra carcerum, ubi flagella fustium et ubi longa exsilia crudeliumque penarum discrimina parabantur?'.

[51] Paul the Deacon, *Historia Langobardorum*, IV, 47. Cf. Walter Pohl, 'Paulus Diaconus und die "Historia Langobardorum"', in *Historiographie im frühen Mittelalter*, ed. by Anton Scharer and Georg Scheibelreiter (Vienna, 1994), pp. 375–405.

Christian confessions coexisted over one hundred years without excessive unrest or bloodshed, a rare occurrence in the history of the Church. This also accounts for the slow rhythm in Lombard conversion, and its blurred edges. We need not see that as a flaw in our narrative. We can also take it as a trace of the variety and unpredictability of lives past.

The Conversion of Scandinavia

New Perspectives on an Old Problem: Uppsala and the Christianization of Sweden

ANNE-SOFIE GRÄSLUND

M aster Adam, the cleric of Bremen, wrote his church history of the diocese Hamburg-Bremen in the 1070s. Together with Rimbert's *Vita Anskarii,* the *Gesta Hammaburgensis ecclesiae pontificum* is the only detailed historical evidence of the course of events that constituted the conversion of Sweden and is therefore of great importance, although some source criticism is necessary.

A crucial part of Adam's work in his fourth book, devoted to a description of Scandinavia and the circumstances there, is his account of the pagan temple and cult in Uppsala (today Old Uppsala, situated five kilometres to the north of modern Uppsala). In Chapter 26 we read about the famous heathen temple, a building entirely decorated with gold and enclosed with a golden chain. In this temple there were three images: one of Thor, the most powerful of the gods; one of Oden; and one of Frej. The Svear/ Swedes sacrificed to Thor when there was threat of dearth and disease, to Oden when war was at hand, and to Frej at weddings. Frej had a special connection with the Svear/Swedes, as he was believed to be the ancestor of the Ynglinga dynasty of Uppsala. The next chapter tells us about the great ritual festival, held for nine days every ninth (or eighth, see below) year at the vernal equinox. Nine heads of all kinds of male creatures were offered, and the bodies were hung up in the trees of the grove near the temple.

Adam's description of the temple and the cult has had an enormous impact on our conception of the conversion of Sweden, and for centuries it has coloured our picture of pre-Christian cult. From the Middle Ages up to modern times, historians have used his account; above all, questions about the appearance and the location of the temple have been discussed.[1]

Which was the real background for his depiction? We know that Adam stayed with the Danish king, Sven Estridsen, for some time. Here he must have found much information about circumstances in Scandinavia. He has also used Rimbert's *Vita Anskarii* as a source, not only for the presentation of Church matters but also for the setting, concerning the conditions of the Svear/Swedes for example. In that connection it is interesting to note the possibility that Rimbert himself had visited Birka. Adam also relies on information from merchants who had travelled in Scandinavia. However, it is important to note that Adam's description of Uppsala was not based on his own inspection of the place.

Many efforts have been made at reconstructing the temple (Figure 1). It has also been pointed out that the concrete portrayal of the temple seems more likely to be inspired by the description of Solomon's temple in the Old Testament or influenced by west Slavonic temple buildings.[2] Even the Lateran Palace in Rome has been suggested as the model.[3]

The myths about the temple consist of many different elements. In Adam's text the topography is described, the grove, the evergreen tree, the spring, as well as the human sacrifices and the temple. Since Adam describes a Scandinavian temple, it seems more appropriate to search for the model in Old Norse mythology. The evergreen tree, the spring, and the gold-decorated temple, the three foundation stones of Adam's text, are all found in Snorre's *Edda* concerning Valhalla or other cult places. One suggestion is that Adam's informant, when asked to describe the temples of the Svear/Swedes, gave an account of his own mythological cult sites instead.[4] There may have been several informants, and perhaps Adam confused the information, or he may have deliberately mixed fact and fiction in order to make Uppsala a worthy adversary to Hamburg-

---

[1] Kurt Johannesson, 'Adam och hednatemplet i Uppsala', in *Adam av Bremen, Historien om Hamburgstiftet och dess biskopar*, trans. by E. Svenberg, comment. by C. F. Hallencreutz, K. Johannesson, T. Nyberg, and A. Piltz (Stockholm, 1984), pp. 379–407.

[2] Harald Wideen, 'Till diskussionen om Uppsala hednatempel', *Fornvännen*, 46 (1951), 127–31; Olaf Olsen, 'Hørg, hov og kirke. Historiske og arkaeologiske vikingetidsstudier', *Aarbøger for nordisk Oldkyndighed og Historie* (1966), 119; Wilhelm Holmqvist, 'Die Ketten des Tempels in Uppsala', *Offa*, 37 (1980),120ff; Lescek Pawel Slupecki, 'Die slawischen Tempel und die Frage des sakralen Raumes bei den Westslawen in vorchristlichen Zeiten', *Tor*, 25 (1993), 250ff.

[3] Henrik Janson, 'Adam av Bremen, Gregorius VII och Uppsalatemplet', in *Uppsalakulten och Adam av Bremen*, ed. by A. Hultgård (Nora, 1997), pp. 166ff.

[4] Magnus Alkarp, 'Adam av Bremen och Gamla Uppsala' (unpublished master's seminar paper, Uppsala University, 1993); 'Källan, lunden och templet—Adam av Bremens Uppsala-skildring i ny belysning', *Fornvännen*, 92 (1998), 155–61.

Bremen.[5] In this case, the 'real' Uppsala temple should have been modelled on mythological cult sites. Another suggestion has been that Snorre, when describing the mythological cult building, has used an old anecdote, formulated by someone with the Uppsala temple in mind.[6] In the latter case, the mythological cult building should have been modelled on the real Uppsala temple.

Unfortunately, the foundations of the reconstructions of the temple are very weak. The documentation from the archaeological excavations below and outside the present church, undertaken in connection with the restoration of the church in 1926, has only recently been fully analysed (Figure 2).[7] It shows a number of postholes under the church, which previously, with some complementary addition, was interpreted as indicating a square building, that is, Adam's temple (Figure 3). At this level a large amount of clay had once been spread out on the ground in order to make the surface even. However, a critical examination of the evidence has clearly demonstrated that these postholes could not be reconstructed as a square pagan temple but must be the remains of a secular building. There are, in fact, many more postholes than those used for the reconstruction, and, furthermore, some postholes have clearly been imagined in order to fit the reconstruction. In addition, the cultural layer over the clay indicates settlement. Thus the reconstruction of the temple is now outdated.

On top of the layer with the postholes, a new clay layer had been laid, possibly connected to an early wooden church. This conclusion is drawn due to some obvious Christian graves in the layer, in spite of the lack of any visible remains of such a church. The building of the stone church, the cathedral, with its foundation dug through the clay layer, had not started until this, possibly older, wooden church had been demolished.[8] The present church is only a minor part of the very large original cathedral. In a partly dubious source with a thirteenth-century origin, the building of the cathedral is said to have begun in 1138 when King Sverker 'joined it to the ancient pagan building of three gods, purified by fire and sanctified by Yggemundus'.[9] If the source is reliable, is this a reflection of the myths created by Adam? It has been suggested that 'the ancient pagan building' was instead the proposed wooden church.[10]

Sweden's first archdiocese was established in 1164 and located in Old Uppsala. The cathedral was probably completed soon after the middle of the twelfth century, and scarcely a century later a large part of it was demolished by a violent fire just before

---

[5] Alkarp, 'Adam av Bremen och Gamla Uppsala', p. 57.

[6] Sune Lindqvist, 'Valhall—Colosseum eller Uppsalatemplet?', *Tor,* 2 (1952), 91.

[7] Else Nordahl, [. . .] *templum quod Ubsola dicitur* [. . .] *i arkeologisk belysning. Med bidrag av Lars Gezelius och Henrik Klackenberg,* Aun 22 (Uppsala, 1996).

[8] Ann Catherine Bonnier, 'Gamla Uppsala—från hednatempel till sockenkyrka', in *Kyrka och socken i medeltidens Sverige,* ed. by O. Ferm, Studier till det medeltida Sverige, 5 (Stockholm, 1991), pp. 101 ff.

[9] Bonnier, 'Gamla Uppsala', p. 88.

[10] Bonnier, 'Gamla Uppsala', pp. 91 f.

1245. After that, the archdiocese was moved to modern Uppsala and the remains of the cathedral were converted into a parish church.[11] Old Uppsala maintained its importance during the Middle Ages, as shown by the fact that the election of a new Swedish king had to be confirmed at Old Uppsala. It should also be noted that the royal manor in Old Uppsala was by far the largest village in the province of Uppland in the Middle Ages.[12]

Radiocarbon datings from the layers below the church indicate human activity and settlement already from the third century AD. The upper clay layer has been dated to the eighth to ninth centuries. These early datings correspond with evidence from excavations in the close surroundings of the church, where settlement remains, a well and traces of a fence probably enclosing the royal and cultic area, were found.[13] The settlement seems to have been continuously used from the third century up to the Viking Age. The conclusion must be that the whole site was settled and agriculture was carried out there soon after the year AD 200. It was, in fact, argued in the 1930s by archaeologists, studying Old Norse literature, that the royal site in Uppsala could be traced back to the third century.[14] At that time it was not possible to prove such an early dating archaeologically, but obviously it is now.

During the last fifteen years, many small excavations have been carried out in the area.[15] They have made it possible to define several settlement sites, dated by radiocarbon analyses to a major part of the first millennium AD, starting already around the year 0, but with the main point AD 500–1000. These results are of great importance for the understanding of the settlement history of Old Uppsala. Ljungkvist's interpretation so far is that of a non-regulated village with farms spread over a wide area, probably more widely spread in the first half of the millennium and more concentrated in the second half (Figure 5). Some of the farms have yielded remains of craft activities of partly exclusive character: bronze casting, glass bead production, and, possibly, even gold work, as well as metal forging and pottery. Old Uppsala is not unique in its structure, but it is an extremely large settlement area, at least for Swedish circumstances.

---

[11] Bonnier, 'Gamla Uppsala', pp. 86, 93 f.

[12] Sigurd Rahmqvist, 'Gamla Uppsala by—Upplands största', in *Från Östra Aros till Uppsala. En samling uppsatser kring det medeltida Uppsala,* Uppsala stads historia, 7 (Uppsala 1986), pp. 254 ff.

[13] Ulf Alström and Wladyslaw Duczko, 'Norra gärdet Raä 281', in *Arkeologi och miljögeologi. Studier och rapporter,* ed. by Wladyslaw Duczko, Occasional Papers in Archaeology, 7 (Uppsala, 1993), pp. 39 ff; Lars-König Königsson, Jemt Anna Eriksson, and Magnus Hellqvist, 'Människa, ekonomi och miljö i Gamla Uppsala', in *Arkeologi och miljögeologi i Gamla Uppsala* (Uppsala, 1993), pp. 79ff; *Arkeologi och miljögeologi i Gamla Uppsala, II: Studier och rapporter,* ed. by Wladyslaw Duczsko, Occasional Papers in Archaeology, 11 (Uppsala, 1996).

[14] Bo Gräslund, 'Folkvandringstidens Uppsala. Namn, myter, arkeologi och historia', *Kärnhuset i riksäpplet* (Uppland, 1993), p. 191.

[15] John Ljungkvist, 'Den förhistoriska bebyggelsen i Gamla Uppsala. Preliminära tolkningar och omtolkningar av bebyggelseutveckling och organisation', *Fornvännen,* 95 (2000, in press).

Another important fact is that, in the Middle Ages, all this land belonged to the king; the western part as a royal estate, the eastern part as royal land, settled by farmers. This may be traced back to the second half of the first millennium, as all examples of exclusivity in the archaeological material, artefacts, remains of crafts as well as structures, are found in the western part of the area, while the finds from the eastern area rather indicate ordinary (although well-to-do) farms.[16]

On the so-called Royal Manor terrace immediately to the north of the present church and churchyard, excavations in the 1980s have revealed the burnt remains of a large long-house, dated to the sixth to ninth century.[17] Its dimensions imply that it was a royal hall. Through literary evidence, we know that the cult practice in the late Iron Age of sacrificial meals took place in the halls of the kings and chieftains. Therefore, this hall may have been the scene of some of the religious activity in (Old) Uppsala.

However, this exact hall cannot be connected to the time of Adam's informants. On a map from the beginning of the eighteenth century, a number of grave mounds can clearly be seen at this spot.[18] Such mounds are ancient monuments typical of the Viking Age. When the hall was burnt down they obviously used the terrace as burial ground. Without a doubt a new royal hall was built somewhere in the area. Why not on the spot where the church was later built?

In an eighteenth-century drawing there is a rune stone, probably from Adam's time, standing close to Viking Age mounds.[19] Only a few fragments have been preserved, built into the wall of a building in the nearby vicarage, but according to oral tradition the stone earlier stood somewhere among the mounds at the Royal Manor. On stylistic grounds the carving can be dated to the second half of the eleventh century.[20] Although it has no cross decoration, it is in all probability, like most of the Upplandic Viking Age rune stones, a Christian monument. Really, this would be remarkable in the actual setting as given by Adam. He writes that everyone in the country were required to send gifts and attend the pagan festival, but Christians could buy themselves off from this duty. It is worth noting that no indications of religious conflict, neither in text nor in ornamentation, are seen on any of the rune stones in or around the neighbourhood of Old Uppsala, and they can all be dated to the eleventh century. Unlike Adam's text, the rune stones give an impression of a more peaceful conversion.

---

[16] Ljungkvist, 'Den förhistoriska bebyggelsen i Gamla Uppsala'.

[17] Else Nordahl, 'Kungsgårdsplatån', in *Arkeologi och miljögeologi i Gamla Uppsala. Studier och rapporter*, ed. by Duczko, pp. 59ff; Gunnar Hedlund, 'Utgrävningen 1992', in *Arkeologi och miljögeologi i Gamla Uppsala*, pp. 64f; Cf. Ljungkvist, 'Den förhistoriska bebyggelsen i Gamla Uppsala', who argues that the dating rather should be the sixth to the tenth century.

[18] Johan Peringskiöld, *Monumenta Uplandica per Thiundam* (Stockholm, 1710).

[19] Peringskiöld, *Monumenta Uplandica per Thiundam*.

[20] Anne-Sofie Gräslund, 'Runstenar—om ornamentik och datering II', *Tor*, 23 (1992), 177–201, stylistic group Pr 4.

Adam's description of the temple as completely decorated with gold and encircled in a golden chain hanging from the roof has caused much trouble for the text's editors through the centuries.[21] The chain has been especially difficult to explain. In my opinion, one explanation could be that Adam had seen some of the small Celtic reliquary shrines shaped like houses, which appeared even in Scandinavia in the eleventh century, and had that in mind when he wrote about the temple in Old Uppsala (Figure 6). One of these shrines has a preserved chain along the roof ridge, obviously for carrying the shrine. There are also remains of gilding on the shrine; in all probability the whole house-shaped shrine was once covered in gold.[22]

A find from the royal hall in Gudme on Fyn, Denmark, (Roman Iron Age) shows that at least parts of such a hall in fact could be gilt.[23] Melted gold was found in some of the postholes. The posts were probably decorated with gold that melted when the hall burnt down.

Recent astronomic research has pointed out a probable mistake in the translation and interpretation of Adam's text.[24] *Post novem annos* is normally translated 'every ninth year'. However, in the way the Scandinavians counted, it was most probably every eighth year, as they had no zero, but counted the first year from its first day and not, like us, after it was finished. It is difficult to understand how a nine-year cycle could work in connection with cult activities at a special time of the year and in a special moon phase. The nine-year cycle gives a maximal fluctuation of date (plus/minus fourteen days and nights), while an eight-year cycle only gives a displacement of one-and-a-half days and nights.

Based on astronomic calculations and supported among other things by sixteenth-century information about the date for the famous winter market in the area (*distinget*), it has therefore been argued that the Uppsala sacrifice took place every eighth year. The preparations probably started at the first full moon after the winter solstice and the offerings were held at the next full moon.

Old Uppsala is a crucial site for the question of what has been called cult continuity —perhaps cult site continuity is a better term. Place-name studies have shown a frequent connection in Scandinavia between church sites and teophoric place-names, indicating a pagan cult, such as Torsåker, Fröslunda, etc.[25] The archaeological evidence for

---

[21] Adam IV, 26, skolion 139.

[22] Martin Blindheim, 'A House-Shaped Irish-Scottish Reliquary in Bologna and its Place among the Other Reliquaries', *Acta Archaeologica,* 55 (1986), 1–53.

[23] Peter Vang Petersen, 'Excavations At Sites of Treasure Trove Finds at Gudme', in *The Archaeology of Gudme and Lundebog. Papers Presented at a Conference at Svendborg, October 1991*, ed. by P. O. Nielsen, K. Randsborg, and H. Thrane (København, 1991), p. 36.

[24] Göran Henriksson, *Arkeoastronomi i Sverige* (Uppsala, 1994), pp. 3 ff.

[25] Lars Hellberg, 'Hedendomens spår i uppländska ortnamn', *Ortnamnssällskapets i Uppsala årsskrift* (1986), 40–71; Stefan Brink, 'Kultkontinuitet från bosättningshistorisk utgångspunkt',

continuity, however, has been rather sparse. Ever since the days of Master Adam, Old Uppsala has been regarded as the best example of such cult site continuity. Even the strongest opponent to the idea of cult site continuity, Olaf Olsen, has admitted that.[26] Recently, another good example has appeared: in Frösö, Jämtland, a cult site with animal bones (at least six bears and many other species) has been found precisely below the choir of the medieval church.[27]

But if there was no heathen temple beneath the church in Old Uppsala, what about the continuity? First, cult site continuity does not necessarily mean the exact spot, the pagan cult could well have been carried out in the close vicinity of the church place. That Uppsala really was an important cult site is demonstrated by its illustrious fame, the most well-known Scandinavian place from the middle of the first millennium AD through the Middle Ages. There is a possibility of a spot continuity similar to that in Mære in Trøndelag, Norway, where the remains of a large long-house were found under the medieval church, a Viking Age hall where small gold foil pictures of an embracing couple were found; the artefacts probably played a role in the fertility cult.[28] In the same manner, there could have been a royal hall beneath the Old Uppsala church. Perhaps Adam was right when he described the temple as a *triclinium*,[29] a banquet hall with three benches, which has actually been found in a very large hall in northern Norway,[30] and when he uses the word *libatur* for the offering, which means a sacrifice of drink—that is exactly what can be expected to have happened in the hall.

---

in *Kontinuitet i kult och tro från vikingatid till medeltid,* ed. by B. Nilsson, Projektet Sveriges kristnande, Publikationer, 1 (Uppsala, 1992), pp. 105–27.

[26] Olsen, 'Hørg, hov og kirke', p. 237.

[27] Margareta Hildebrandt, 'En kyrka byggd på hednisk grund?', *Populär arkeologi,* 3.4 (1985), 9–13; Elisabet Iregren, 'Under Frösö kyrka—ben från en vikingatida offerlund', *Arkeologi och religion. Rapport från arkeologidagarna 16–18 Januari 1989,* ed. by L. Larsson and B. Wyszomirska, University of Lund, Institute of Archaeology, Report Series, 34 (1989), pp. 119–33.

[28] Hans-Emil Lidén, 'From Pagan Sanctuary to Christian Church. The Excavation of Mære Church in Trøndelag', *Norwegian Archaeological Review,* 2 (1969), 3–32.

[29] Francois-Xavier Dillmann, 'Kring de rituella gästabuden i fornskandinavisk religion', in *Uppsalakulten och Adam av Bremen,* ed. by A. Hultgård (Nora, 1997), pp. 65 ff.

[30] Frands Herschend and Dorthe Mikkelsen, 'The Main House at Borg', in *Borg, en høvdingegård i Lofoten,* ed. by G. Stamsø Munch (forthcoming).

Figure 1. The pagan temple in Uppsala as the sixteenth-century historian Olaus
Magnus imagined it. From Magnus, *Historia om de nordiska folken* [Historia de
Gentibus Septentrionalibus], 1555, ed. by Michaelisgillet (Uppsala, 1909).

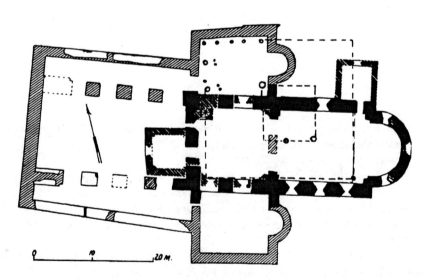

Figure 2. Plan of the cathedral and (in black) the present parish church.
The broken line (---) indicates the pagan temple suggested by Sune Lindqvist.
From Lindqvist, 'Uppsala hednatempel. Gamla och nya spekulationer',
Ord och bild, 36 (1927), 641–54.

Figure 3. Sune Lindqvist's reconstruction of the pagan temple. Model made
by Hilmer Gelin in the 1930s for the Museum of Scandinavian Antiquities
at Uppsala University. Note the hall buildings.

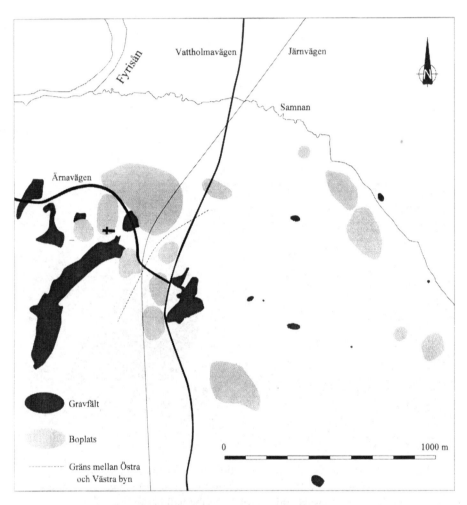

Figure 4. Map of the Old Uppsala area with burial grounds marked in black and defined settlement sites marked in grey. The broken line (---) marks the borderline between the east and west part of the medieval village. From John Ljungkvist (2000). Reprinted by permission.

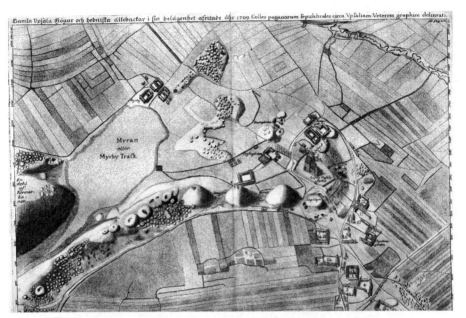

Figure 5. Johan Peringskiöld's map of Old Uppsala, drawn in 1709. From Peringskiöld, *Monumenta Uplandica per Thiundam* (Stockholm, 1710).

Figure 6. A Celtic house-shaped shrine with a chain attached
to the roof, now in the Museum of Bologna. From Blindheim,
'A House-Shaped Irish-Scottish Reliquary in Bologna and its Place
among the Other Reliquaries', *Acta Archaeologica*, 55 (1986), 1–53.

Early Christian
Burials in Sweden

BERTIL NILSSON

W hen dealing with the process of conversion to Christianity in Sweden, it is appropriate to ask some questions about the burial customs. They concerned everybody. What new did the Church bring to Sweden regarding burial customs? Where do we find the first Christian burials? How do we know that they are Christian?

Attempts to describe 'The ideal burial custom during the Viking Age', or 'The medieval burial', or 'The Christian burial custom', have been made during the last decades in many handbooks. Perhaps they come quite close to the truth, but they still give the impression that there was an homogeneity that in reality did not exist at all. For present research it is therefore important to let the details just be details and nothing more and not to let them explain more than what is possible. It is thus necessary to present examples from different types of source material, different periods, and geographical regions.

Examples from Pre-Christian Grave Fields

In 1980 Anne-Sofie Gräslund published an analysis of about 1100 graves from Björkö in Lake Mälaren, the island where the famous trading centre Birka was situated.[1]

---

[1] There is a comprehensive analysis of the grave finds made in Birka in Anne-Sofie Gräslund, 'Resultate der Birka-Forschung in den Jahren 1980 bis 1988. Versuch einer Auswertung', in *Birka II, 3. Systematische Analysen der Gräberfunde* (Stockholm, 1989), pp. 151–74; see p. 153 about the grave fields, pp. 156–57 about the different grave types, p. 160 about the Christian influence. A comprehensive bibliography is given, pp. 167–74.

How many grave fields there were once upon a time on the island we do not know for sure; the area was subsequently cultivated intensively and is, therefore, from archaeological point of view partially destroyed. Six zones have been analysed, which date back to the time of the existence of the commercial town Birka,[2] that is mainly the ninth century.

The material has been analysed from several different aspects. The relative allocation of cremation graves and inhumations is numerically even, that is 566 cremations and 544 inhumations.[3] The local distribution over the area, on the other hand, differs. The cremations are mainly found in specific zones.[4]

The inhumations have been studied among others with regard to how the deceased has been placed in the grave, but also with regard to the grave in relation to the four cardinal points, what usually is called the grave's orientation. When the deceased has been placed in an east-west direction with the head to the west, it is usually taken as a Christian custom. This position is determined by the belief that Christ is going to come back from east on the very last day, like the rising sun. If the grave is placed north-south, on the other hand, it has been regarded as a sign of a non-Christian burial custom. On Björkö the vast majority of the inhumations, about 85 per cent, are placed with the skull within the sector southwest-northwest, to a great extent exactly due west. Only a small number of skeletons have been found where the skulls are placed in the sector southeast-northeast. However, the number indicates that this is not just happenstance; there must be a reason for this praxis; though, it is for the time being not possible to determine why. One can point to the possibility that topographical circumstances have played a part.[5]

At different times, parts of northern Uppland have been investigated. About 6600 graves from a little more than 270 grave fields have been registered. The main part of the investigated grave fields belong to the Viking Age. The graves vary considerably in size,[6] and there are several different types: mounds, ship tumuli, barrows, and round or four-sided stone circles.[7]

The round stone circles, which is the most common type, are found in more than 80 per cent of the material in some parishes. They contain both cremations and

---

[2] See map over the extension of the grave fields in Anne-Sofie Gräslund, *Birka IV. The Burial Customs. A Study of the Graves on Björkö* (Stockholm, 1980), p. 4, and about their origin in Gräslund, *Systematische Analysen der Gräberfunde*, p. 160.

[3] Additionally, there are obviously a number of uncertain respectively indeterminable graves; see Gräslund, *Systematische Analysen der Gräberfunde*, p. 87, where all the graves are classified.

[4] Gräslund, *The Burial Customs*, p. 50.

[5] Gräslund, *The Burial Customs*, pp. 26–27.

[6] See table in Anders Broberg, *Bönder och samhälle i statsbildningstid. En bebyggelse-arkeologisk studie av agrarsamhället i Norra Roden 700–1350*, Upplands fornminnesförenings tidskrift, 52 (Uppsala, 1990), p. 40.

[7] Broberg, *Bönder och samhälle i statsbildningstid*, p. 31.

inhumations of men and women of different age. Also the finds of artefacts vary.[8] The mounds are almost as common; in some grave fields they make up 70 per cent. Also the mounds contain persons of both sexes, as well as burned and unburned remains of bone.[9] Both round stone circles and mounds had been used up to the middle of the eleventh century.

The four-sided stone circles, though, are partly different. First of all, there is a concentration of them in six out of thirteen parishes investigated. These graves contain almost only inhumations; just occasionally cremated persons are found. Together with other graves from the Mälar region, they can be dated to the very last period of the Viking Age. It is also notable that they sometimes occur in only one of the total number of grave fields which belonged to one village.[10] The four-sided stone circles are thus regarded as constituting an important link in the conversion from pre-Christian burial to Christian. At the same time as the number of mounds decreases, or even do not appear at all, the number of four-sided stone circles increases.[11] Despite this, the question must be asked how widespread the use of this type of stone circle actually was. For example, in Finnveden, in the southern part of Sweden, this type of construction seems not to have been used at all, but instead grave mounds alone have been built till the end of the Viking Age.[12] The regional and local variation could thus be considerable in this case. But we should also ask whether the grave fields in other regions, where there are no four-sided stone circles with inhumations, were not used during the last part of the Viking Age.[13]

Christian Burial Custom Gains Influence: How Do We Know?

The examples from Birka and the province of Uppland lead us back to the questions which I asked at the beginning: how and when did Christian influence have effect on the burial customs in Sweden? These questions immediately lead us to the

---

[8] Broberg, *Bönder och samhälle i statsbildningstid*, pp. 32–33.

[9] Broberg, *Bönder och samhälle i statsbildningstid*, pp. 33–34.

[10] Broberg, *Bönder och samhälle i statsbildningstid*, p. 34; see also Anne-Sofie Gräslund, 'Kultkontinuitet—myt eller verklighet? Om arkeologins möjligheter att belysa problemet', in *Kontinuitet i kult och tro från vikingatid till medeltid*, Projektet Sveriges kristnande, Publikationer, 1, ed. by Bertil Nilsson (Uppsala, 1992), pp. 129–50, here esp. p. 143.

[11] Anne-Sofie Gräslund, 'Arkeologin och kristnandet', in *Kristnandet i Sverige. Gamla källor och nya perspektiv*, ed. by Bertil Nilsson (Uppsala, 1996), pp. 19–44, here esp. pp. 29–30.

[12] Ulf Bodin, *Ett vikingatida skelettgravfält i Finnveden. Gravar och boplatsrester från arkeologiska undersökningar 1990 och 1936–1937 inom ett gravfältskomplex i Nästa, Kärda socken, Värnamo kommun, Småland* (Jönköping, 1994), pp. 29–30, 50–51.

[13] See also Anders Broberg, 'Religionsskifte och sockenbildning i Norduppland', in *Kyrka och socken i medeltidens Sverige*, ed. by Olle Ferm, Studier till det medeltida Sverige, 5 (Stockholm, 1991), pp. 49–79, here esp. pp. 49–52, 66–67.

problem of criteria. How can we determine if a single grave or graves together, which do not obviously belong to a Christian cemetery/churchyard, are 'Christian' or show 'Christian influence'? The discussion among scholars about the criteria for determining Christian burial customs in relation to other cultures' way of taking care of the dead are found in many different international writings.[14] During the last decade in Sweden, it is mainly Gräslund who has devoted her interest to questions of this kind, because of her close investigations in the trading town of Birka. We know for sure that there were Christian persons of different categories in the town. Her investigations show, however, that it is difficult to identify Christian graves with certainty, but she suggests that a little part of one of the grave fields may have been used for Christians only.[15] Hypothetically, this is absolutely the oldest example from Sweden where you find quite a number of Christian graves together in a delimited area.

It is certain that during the period which is of interest, only inhumation was officially accepted by the Church. That had always been the case. Thus cremations can be excluded from Christian burial customs. The difficulties, though, have to do with the fact that inhumation is not exclusively a Christian feature. The pre-Christian burial customs have included cremation as well as inhumation until the middle of the eleventh century, as my examples show.

The orientation of the graves has been regarded as Christian if the dead person has been buried in east-west direction with the head in the west, allowing, of course, a reasonable limit of variation. It appears, however, that even this criterion is not sufficient on its own; the east-west orientation was also used for pre-Christian burials in Europe.

With regard to the contents in the graves, it is obvious that the Church was against the use of grave gifts. Thus Christian graves should be empty, apart from clothing of the deceased or things which obviously have a symbolic Christian value.

---

[14] See for example Dorothy Watts, *Christians and Pagans in Roman Britain* (London, 1991), pp. 38–78, where mainly English research is treated. A sort of summary has recently been published: Christopher Daniell, *Death and Burial in Medieval England. 1066–1550* (London and New York, 1997).

In Oslo an unpublished thesis for the degree of Master of Arts (mag. art.) was discussed in spring 1994 and written by Sjur Harby, who rather thoroughly treats 'Christian burial custom' and 'variation'. His thesis is challenging, though some objections must be raised against it. It should therefore be the object for further discussions. This cannot be done in this article, but it should be noticed that Harby, though not the first, in a meritorious way has pointed to the importance of studying the grave as a whole and not just looking for separate details, which are supposed to confirm either the pre-Christian or the Christian burial custom. How to do that is, unfortunately, not very well described by Harby. See his 'Variasjon og folkelig religiøsitet i tidligmiddelaldersk gravskikk' (unpublished master's thesis, Oslo University, 1994), pp. 25–40.

[15] Gräslund, *The Burial Customs*, pp. 73–74.

In connection with this, another feature concerning the graves in Birka can be taken into account, namely their frequency. During pre-Christian times, the graves were laid side by side, and thus the grave field grew with every new corpse which was buried. The Christian custom was to use a clearly defined area, marked off from its surroundings and possibly blessed by the bishop. Therefore, Christian graves came to lie over each other, thereby destroying older graves when new burials took place.[16] Excavated examples of such areas are found also in regions in Sweden other than Birka and from later times.[17]

Recently, another criterion has also been used within archaeological research, that is the distribution of sexes on the grave fields or cemeteries. It is most likely that it was with the arrival of the Christian Church that the custom of segregating men and women in the cemetery was introduced in the Scandinavian countries: the women were buried to the north of the church, men to the south. Where the segregation is provable, even in a mainly pre-Christian grave field without traces of a church building, it thus indicates that there has been a church. You may indeed ask if this custom has been put into practice also in grave fields without a church building. The criterion of segregation of sexes is, however, not very easily used when we study grave fields which are only partly preserved. On the other hand, this criterion might help us to determine if the grave field is a Christian one or not when a church building made of wood has totally disappeared.[18] One problem, though, is that, for uncertain reasons, the segregation of sexes has not been practised altogether consistently over the centuries.[19]

From the later part of the Viking Age there is a touching example where segregation has not been used. In a cemetery in the province of Östergötland a family grave has been excavated, which turned out to contain the remains of several persons buried under

---

[16] The best survey in Swedish regarding criteria for pre-Christian, as well as Christian, Scandinavian burial customs is found in Anne-Sofie Gräslund, 'Var Mammen-mannen kristen?', in *Mammen. Grav, kunst og samfund i vikingetid*, Jysk arkæologisk selskabs skrifter, 28, ed. by M. Iversen (Højbjerg, 1991), pp. 205–10, here esp. pp. 205–7; see also Anne-Sofie Gräslund, 'Den tidiga missionen i arkeologisk belysning—problem och synpunkter', *Tor. Tidskrift för nordisk fornkunskap*, 20 (1985), pp. 291–313, here esp. pp. 296–301; on the orientation as a criterion see Gräslund, *The Burial Customs*, pp. 46–47, with examples from Birka; see also Gräslund, 'Arkeologin och kristnandet', pp. 24–25.

[17] Gräslund, 'Den tidiga missionen i arkeologisk belysning', pp. 296–301; Anne-Sofie Gräslund, 'Arkeologi som källa för religionsvetenskap. Några reflektioner om hur gravmaterialet från vikingatiden kan användas', in *Nordisk hedendom. Et symposium*, ed. Gro Steinsland et al. (Odense, 1991), pp. 141–47, here esp. pp. 144–46.

[18] See Bertil Nilsson, *Kvinnor, män och barn på medeltida begravningsplatser*, Projektet Sveriges kristnande, Publikationer, 3 (Uppsala, 1994), pp. 12–13.

[19] For this see Bertil Nilsson, *De sepulturis. Gravrätten i Corpus Iuris Canonici och i medeltida nordisk lagstiftning*, Bibliotheca theologiae practicae, 44. Kyrkovetenskapliga studier (Stockholm, 1989), pp. 142–43.

stone slabs with runic inscriptions. The latest buried persons are a man and his wife together in the same grave holding hands.[20]

Concerning the criteria (there are several others than the ones I have just mentioned, but they are of a more peripheral and uncertain character),[21] it should be underlined that the general character of a grave from the early period of conversion does not bring any actual knowledge either about the deceased person's Christian commitment or about those who have been in charge for the burial rituals and the interment. It is no longer possible to establish who the persons were, who actually decided in each different case how to take care of the dead, whether in the heathen way or in the Christian.[22]

There are several instances of graves from Swedish grave fields of the Viking Age, which have been regarded as Christian, or at least influenced by Christian burial customs, when using the criteria which I have just presented. As mentioned, from that point of view it is in Birka that we find the oldest Christian graves in a delimited area in a larger grave field. In other cases the number of the graves are fewer, or in some cases just a single grave is found.[23] In these cases, it is not possible to decide whether they have been influenced by Christian burial custom as a result of actual conversion among some individuals or as a result of a gradually ongoing change of the burial customs, which in an early phase had nothing to do with how influential the Church was in a local area. In a certain period it might instead be a question of fashion or, on the other hand, local variation or changes due to the very comprehensive pre-Christian burial customs, changes which occurred independently of influence from the Church. It should also be underlined that it is difficult to use the criteria for Christian burial custom when it comes, among other things, to the distinction between a necessary condition and a sufficient one respectively, since there is not a sufficient one. Therefore, it is of great importance every time when judging that the grave is studied as a whole and that also the close environment is taken into consideration.

Despite all the difficulties, the conclusion is that some graves which are connected with or found in mainly pre-Christian grave fields from the Viking Age are to be regarded as the oldest evidence for Christian influence on the burial customs in Sweden. Nothing, though, is preserved from these graves which can be regarded as grave stones or other memorials apart from a very small number of rune stones.

---

[20] Berit Wallenberg, *Grav under runhällar i Skänninge* (Stockholm, 1984), passim.

[21] See Dorothy Watts, *Christians and Pagans in Roman Britain*, pp. 51–78, including a table with evaluation of the different criteria, p. 79.

[22] See also Gräslund, 'Den tidiga missionen i arkeologisk belysning', pp. 292–94.

[23] See, e.g., Broberg, *Bönder och samhälle i statsbildningstid*, pp. 35, 76; Lena Thunmark-Nylén, 'Samfund och tro på religionsskiftets Gotland', in *Medeltidens födelse,* Symposier på Krapperups borg, 1, ed. by Anders Andrén (Lund, 1989), pp. 213–32, here esp. pp. 213–15.

The Burial Places of the Established Church

Has there always been a church building in connection with a large number of Christian burials? Beyond doubt, the ecclesiastical ideal which had developed during the early Church and the early Middle Ages, in light of theological reflection on the destiny of man beyond death as waiting for the Last Judgement, was that burial places and church buildings belonged together.[24] In Sweden no traces of church buildings have been found on such pre-Christian grave fields which mainly contain non-Christian burials in addition to some Christian ones. On the other hand, it is obvious that a number of medieval parish churches, for instance in the province of Uppland, have been erected close to or even on a grave field from the Viking Age.[25] Therefore we should also ask if a Christian churchyard successively took over the pre-Christian grave field, so that there are no signs of burials other than Christian ones today, at least not on the surface. It is possible, though, that future archaeological excavations may also reveal pre-Christian burials in areas which became churchyards during the Middle Ages.

The other oldest Christian burials are thus those which are found in the oldest churchyards, and that is, of course, normal. The earliest Christian burials are immediately related to the erection of the first church buildings. In the light of recent research concerning regional and local conditions, it is not unlikely that churches in Sweden as well as in Denmark and Norway have been built on private initiatives by petty kings or great men on their estates. Five such churches have been pointed out in the province of Uppland, and a number of others presumably belong to the same category.[26] However, it is not likely that the pattern has been the same all over the country.

Investigations made by Stefan Brink have shown that the circumstances as regards the erection of a parish church were different in the northern part of Sweden (Norrland) than in the other provinces. The province of Hälsingland may serve as an example, where there is no reason to believe that great men or landowners on their own stood behind the building of churches.[27] In the province of Jämtland it is likely that the earliest

---

[24] Nilsson, *De sepulturis*, pp. 37–40.

[25] Gräslund, 'Kultkontinuitet', pp. 142–43.

[26] Olle Ferm and Sigurd Rahmqvist, 'Stormannakyrkor i Uppland under äldre medeltid', in *Studier i äldre historia tillägnade Herman Schück, 5/4 1985*, ed. by Robert Sandberg (Stockholm, 1985), pp. 67–83, here esp. p. 82, where more than twenty churches are listed, which are regarded as of interest concerning on whose initiative they were built.

[27] Stefan Brink, *Sockenbildning och sockennamn. Studier i äldre territoriell indelning i Norden*, Acta academiae regiae Gustavi Adolphi, 57. Studier till en svensk ortnamnsatlas, 14 (Uppsala, 1990), pp. 151–61; see also Stefan Brink, 'Tidig kyrklig organisation i Norden—aktörerna i sockenbildningen', in *Kristnandet i Sverige. Gamla källor och nya perspektiv*, Projektet Sveriges kristnande. Publikationer, 5, ed. by Bertil Nilsson (Uppsala, 1996), pp. 269–90, here esp. pp. 281–82.

church buildings were erected on the pre-Christian so-called *Hov*-estates or very close to them. The initiative in those cases to build a church may have come from a combination of a decision made collectively by the peasants and a great man's economic willingness. Later on, stone parish churches were built in these places.[28] So, the oldest churchyards are likely to be found at this type of manor-houses, the *Hov*-estates, which had a special connection with the pre-Christian cult.

In connection with this, it should be asked if there was a time when there were grave fields sharply marked off from the surroundings and intended only for Christian burials but without any connection either to a pre-Christian grave field or to a church building, free-standing cemeteries, so to speak.[29] Has there ever been a stronger mark of conversion than the repudiation of the pre-Christian burial custom? There is no certain evidence for totally separate Christian grave fields in Sweden. The reason for this might be that they have subsequently been connected to a church building, but that is not very likely. On the contrary, chronologically, church buildings and cemeteries were founded at the same time. As already mentioned, Christian burial fields without connection to a church building were something which was not approved of from the Church's normative point of view.[30] However, it has been suggested that some areas in the pre-Christian grave fields have been used for Christian burials only[31] and that these areas have in some way been blessed or consecrated and possibly marked out by a rune-

---

[28] See Bertil Nilsson, 'Det tidigaste kyrkobyggandet i Jämtland', in *Jämtlands kristnande, Projektet Sveriges kristnande. Publikationer, 4*, ed. by Stefan Brink (Uppsala, 1996), pp. 117–53, here esp. pp. 130–33.

[29] See Gustaf Trotzig, 'Gegensätze zwischen Heidentum und Christentum im archäologischen Material des 11. Jahrhunderts auf Gotland', in *Kirche und Gesellschaft im Ostseeraum und im Norden vor der Mitte des 13. Jahrhunderts*, Acta Visbyensia, 3 (Visby, 1969), pp. 21–30, here esp. p. 24 concerning the island of Gotland; about the ecclesiastical ideal, see Nilsson, *De sepulturis*, p. 50, esp. n. 28.

[30] Nilsson, *De sepulturis*, p. 50, esp. n. 28.

[31] About Norway see Inger Helene Vibe Müller, 'Fra ættefellesskap til sognefelleskap. Om overgangen fra hedensk til kristen gravskikk', in *Nordisk hedendom*, ed. by Steinsland, pp. 359–67, where she has pointed to possible Christian grave areas without church buildings dating from an early phase of the christianization; concerning Denmark, see Leif Nielsen 'Hedenskab og kristendom. Religionsskiftet afspejlet i vikingetidens grave', in *Fra stamme til stat i Danmark. 2. Høvdingesamfund og kongemagt*, ed. by Peder Mortensen and Birgit M. Rasmussen (Aarhus, 1991), pp. 245–67, here esp. p. 253, whose material seems to indicate the opposite result.

On account of Vibe Müller's hypothesis, the question should be asked what kind of society it was where there was a need for separate burial places for Christians but a lack of possibilities for the practice of the cult. Heikki Valk has also given interesting contributions on this problem when comparing Estonia and Finland; see Heikki Valk, 'Neighbouring but Distant: Rural Burial Traditions of Estonia and Finland during the Christian Period', *Fennoscandia archaeologica*, 11 (1994), pp. 61–76, here esp. pp. 62, 64, 67, 72–74.

stone with a cross on it.[32] It is also likely that in an early phase of christianization there were small private churches or chapels in connection with pre-Christian grave fields.[33] These churches lost their function when a parish church was built somewhere in a central place or maybe as soon as such a church was founded, the reason being that the cemetery could have been in use long before the parish church was actually consecrated. Therefore, in at least some parts of Sweden there could have existed a number of small wooden churches, of which no traces are likely ever to be found, since they have been situated in places other than the medieval parish churches. On the other hand, the sensational finds which were made in the parish of Karleby in the province of Västergötland in 1986, when the remains of two small wooden churches were found, one upon the other, with a cemetery around them should be mentioned. One of the interesting things is that these chapels in one sense were actually known to the local inhabitants, but only in an indirect way. The oral tradition had preserved the name *kapellgärdet*, or 'the chapel field', for the area where the churches were found.[34] Before 1986 no one actually believed that this name had anything to do with a chapel dating back to the early Middle Ages. How many more such chapels are still hidden underneath Swedish meadows?

In connection with this lovely little story about archaeological prosperity it should be stressed that from the ecclesiastical point of view it was really important that churches or chapels—the terminology is somewhat complicated—were built as early as possible,[35] which was, of course, regarded as a fundamental result of mission. For the Church in the abstract sense of the word, the church in the concrete sense was of great significance. It was generally part of missionary strategy that churches should be built, because it was there, in principal, that the cult was going to be practised. It was prescribed, at least from the later part of the eighth century, that the celebration of the Mass was allowed to take place only at a consecrated altar, preferably at an *altare fixum*. When circumstances so demanded, portable altars were also allowed to be used, for

---

[32] Gräslund, 'Kultkontinuitet', pp. 144–46. In this respect it is not without interest if a rune-stone, for instance like the one in Järvsta, Valbo parish, Gästrikland (*Gästriklands runinskrifter*, Gs no. 11), is located on or by the pre-Christian grave field; see also Bertil Nillson, 'Från gravfält till kyrkogård. Förändringar och variation i gravskicket', in *Kristnandet i Sverige*, ed. by Nilsson, pp. 349–85, here esp. pp. 357–58.

[33] Gräslund, 'Kultkontinuitet', p. 143; about Norway see Vibe Müller, 'Fra ættefellesskap til sognefelleskap', pp. 367–69.

[34] Maria Vretemark, 'Torkan gav traditionen liv', *Populär arkeologi*, 7.1 (1989), 12–15.

[35] With regard to the development of christianization in Norway, Dagfinn Skre has presented an opposite opinion in this case, which according to my interpretation, however, is not definitely supported by the material; see Dagfinn Skre, *Gård og kirke, bygd og sogn. Organiseringsmodeller og enheter i middelalderens kirkebyggning i Sør-Gudbrandsdalen* (Oslo, 1984), pp. 143–44.

instance on missionary journeys.[36] We can note that when Rimbert talks about Ansgar's first visit to Birka, he stresses the fact that the result was that a chapel was now erected, originally on the property which belonged to the king's captain (*hövitsman*) Hergeir. With regard to the second visit, it is said that the king gave Ansgar 'a piece of land where he could build a chapel. [. . .]'[37] The existence of these chapels, mentioned in Rimbert's text, has not been archaeologically confirmed. But in this case it does not matter if these chapels never existed and if the stories about them were related just to emphasize the fortunate result of the mission, because the stories themselves tell us how important church foundation was thought to be. As the cult was at the centre of the Christian religion, church building was something you could not be without.

And with church buildings, burial customs were connected to the development of the Christian memorial tradition since the time of the early Church. Of especial importance were the relics in the altar. According to canon law, it was only parish churches which had burial rights (*ius funerandi*),[38] but this was the ideal when the organization of parishes had taken place. Before that the immediate surroundings of a private chapel on local property could be used as a burial ground for the first generation of Christians, especially if the missionaries had been able to convey some of the official ecclesiastical beliefs, such as the importance of the grave being placed close to an altar, as well as the role played by the prayers for the dead.

---

[36] Joseph Braun, *Der christliche Altar in seiner geschichtlichen Entwicklung, 1* (München, 1924), pp. 71–73.

[37] Rimbert, *Vita Anskarii auctore Rimberto*, 11, 28. *Scriptores rerum Germanicarum in usum scholarum ex Monumentis Germaniae Historicis recusi,* ed. by G. Waitz (Hannover, 1884).

[38] About this see Nilsson, *De sepulturis*, pp. 42–58.

Adam of Bremen and the Conversion of Scandinavia

HENRIK JANSON

I n the process of christianization of Scandinavia a decisive role has been attributed to the conversion of one particular locality, in which the old pagan beliefs are held to have defended their positions until the second half of the eleventh century. The destruction of the golden temple of Old Uppsala has long been reckoned the final step by which the Old Norse religion eventually lost its status as the ideological basis of society in the Scandinavian kingdoms.[1] In the 1920s the famous Swedish archaeologist Sune Lindqvist excavated inside the twelfth-century cathedral church. Amongst a few other things, he found some postholes, and in the following decades scholars produced a great number of reconstructions built on a combination of these postholes and the description of the temple in Adam of Bremen's history of the archbishops of Hamburg-Bremen.

---

[1] See for example Helge Ljungberg, *Den nordiska religionen och kristendomen. Studier över det nordiska religionsskiftet under vikingatiden* (Stockholm, 1938), pp. 74, 273; Birger Nerman, *När Sverige kristnades* (Stockholm, 1945), p. 162; Sven Ulric Palme, *Kristendomens genombrott i Sverige* (Stockholm, 1959), p. 155; Thomas Lindkvist and Kurt Ågren, *Sveriges Medeltid* (Stockholm, 1985), pp. 60–64, 94–95; Bibi and Peter Sawyer, *Medieval Scandinavia* (Minneapolis, 1993), p. 101; Lesley Abrams, 'Kings and Bishops and the Conversion of the Anglo-Saxon and Scandinavian Kingdoms', in *Church and People in Britain and Scandinavia,* ed. by Ingemar Brohed, Bibliotheca historico-ecclesiastica Lundensis, 36 (Lund, 1996), p. 15 with n. 2. Abrams is a victim of the late seventeenth-century forgery *Annotationes ex scriptis Karoli episcopi Arosiensis excerptæ*; see also five of the six articles in *Uppsalakulten och Adam av Bremen,* ed. by Anders Hultgård (Nora, 1997).

These speculations came to a sudden end in 1965 when Olaf Olsen published his doctoral thesis 'Hørg, Hov og Kirke'.[2] Here he could show that there was not a shred of evidence for temple buildings in Viking-Age Scandinavia. The postholes under the cathedral of Old Uppsala were no exception. Already in 1951 it had been pointed out by Harald Wideen that these postholes could amongst other things just as well be remains of an older church building.[3] That such a building must have existed on the site was proved by the fact that the stone church was built on older Christian graves. Moreover, it was stressed by both Wideen and Olsen that there was no compelling reason to combine the postholes with the description of the temple by Adam of Bremen. This description, they briefly remarked, seemed to be adorned with literal and theological symbols.

In Olsen's view, Old Uppsala was in any case a unique place. In the whole of Scandinavia it was only here, he thought, that cult continuity could be asserted with at least some probability. Hence, even if the idea of Scandinavian pagan temples was demolished by Olsen's work, the cult place Uppsala was left untouched as the last stronghold for pagan Scandinavian religion and cult until the end of the eleventh century.

When I, some ten years ago for my doctoral thesis, began to approach the question of the formation of the medieval Scandinavian kingdoms, I also of necessity came across the problem of the cult at Old Uppsala. Adam of Bremen described the temple and the cult containing human sacrifices by kings and peoples as something that was still going on when he was writing in the middle of the 1070s. It soon became clear to me that there was something definitely strange with this cult place. A vast amount of material from the eleventh century consisting of skaldic poetry and amusing stories in connection with the great issues of the time was transmitted into the earliest Old Norse literature, and especially into the extensive king's saga compilations from the first half of the thirteenth century. Nowhere in this material is there any trace of the central pagan cult place Uppsala. Nor is there any trace of how this cult was stopped. Furthermore, there are no reliable indications of Swedish paganism in conflict with the key Christian figures of this time, in spite of the fundamental prejudice of the sagas regarding Swedish backwardness.[4] Apart from Adam there is indeed no source whatsoever that

---

[2] Olaf Olsen, 'Hørg, Hov og Kirke. Historiske og arkæologiske vikingetidsstudier', in *Aarbøger for Nordisk Oldkyndighed og Historie* (1966), pp. 1–307.

[3] Harald Wideen, 'Till diskussionen om Uppsala hednatempel', *Fornvännen*, 46 (1951), 127–31.

[4] Cf. Peter Foote, 'Icelandic Historians and the Swedish Image. Comments on Snorri and his Precursors', in *Snorre Sturlasson och de isländska källorna till Sveriges historia. Fyra föreläsningar från ett symposium i Stockholm hösten 1988*, ed. by G. Dahlbäck, Sällskapet Runica et Midiævalia, Opuscula 1 (Stockholm, 1993), pp. 9–42. The Blot-Sven episode and the story of 'Kalmar-ledungen' is of no value in this connection. The first is obviously related to the Swedish legend of St Eskil and does not, by the way, say anything about Uppsala. This is also true of the

mentions the eleventh-century royal cult at Uppsala or how it came to an end. This is somewhat strange, since Adam says that if only this head of the barbarian *superstitio* was destroyed, all the people who offered human sacrifices would be converted. The importance attributed to this cult place by Adam and the silence in all other sources are not compatible.

But Adam's picture becomes even more suspicious when we look at the milieu in which his famous temple cult is said to have taken place. In the province of Uppland where Uppsala is situated, over 1100 rune stones were raised during the eleventh century. The great majority of these stones are explicitly Christian. None, however, is explicitly pagan, and most scholars agree today that the raising of rune stones was by this time an exclusively Christian habit, in particular in the Upplandic region.

It is also clear that the people raising these stones must have had a prominent position in society, and we must consequently come to the conclusion that the Upplandic aristocracy, at the time Adam described the golden temple *Ubsola*, consisted of thousands of individuals who reckoned themselves within the Christian Church. It is of course tempting to suggest, as some scholars have done, that the many rune stones in Uppland were a result of a particularly severe conflict between pagans and Christians in this region.

Yet again, apart from Adam, there is no clear evidence, neither written nor archaeological, for the presence of paganism, and Adam of Bremen himself often talks about the *sueones* or *suedi* as almost pious. He blames the misfortune of what he calls 'our religion' on the fact that the Swedes had been guided by bad teachers, such as the *episcopus girovagus* Osmund, who at the royal court of the *pessimus,* but nevertheless Christian, King Emund rejected the claims of the archbishop of Bremen. But Adam also says that they would be converted if only the temple Uppsala was demolished. There seems to be some kind of contradiction in these statements. If the problem was simply bad teachers why was it of such a crucial importance to destroy a pagan temple? It is rather curious that some sources connect this *pessimus* King Emund with Uppsala.

These and other circumstances have forced me to go one step further than Wideen and Olsen, and to call into question not only the temple but the pagan cult place as well. This step is however far more complicated because it has wide reaching implications for our picture of northern Europe during the so-called 'Dark Ages'. We have, for example, to confront the question of where, when, and how we can identify a society based on a religion that was not Christian on source critical grounds.[5]

---

latter, and the *ledung* concerned was in 1123 directed against a region with at least one stone church and presumably a rather advanced Christian society; see, for example, the papers collected in *Möres kristnande,* ed. by H. Williams, Projektet Sveriges kristnande, publikationer, 2 (Uppsala, 1993).

[5] A related problem is to be found in the Christianity of Beowulf; for a discussion, see Mary A. Parker, *Beowulf and Christianity* (New York, 1987). Consider also in this connection Eric Gerald Stanley, *The Search for Anglo-Saxon Paganism* (Cambridge, 1975).

It is an understatement to say that the picture of the persistence of paganism in Scandinavia until the end of eleventh century is well established. But the significance of the concept of conversion depends on how we reconstruct the religion on the other side of the borderline. The pagan cult place Uppsala makes it possible to fill the space on the other side with the 'Germanic' religion reconstructed mostly from the Old Norse literature from the thirteenth century. The suppression of the pagan cult at Uppsala still marks the passage of this religion from the position of ideology of a society outside the Church, to the world of demons inside the Church under constant oppression from the Catholic Church and kingdom.

This all depends, however, on the assumption that Adam is credible at least when he describes Uppsala as a pagan cult place. But why did he put in a temple of gold into this cult place where there was no temple? Why did he indeed describe Uppsala as he did? Confronted by all these problems, we are forced to answer a question, that should have been answered long ago: Why did Adam write the *Gesta* of the archbishops of Hamburg-Bremen? The answer to this question might shed new light on the pagan temple at Uppsala and on the religious life in Viking Age Scandinavia. I have devoted a large part of my doctoral thesis to this question.[6]

In this paper, however, I can only very briefly sketch out the main points of my conclusions. First, Adam was occupied by hastily writing the major parts of the *Gesta* during 1075 and during the winter 1075 and 1076. This was the winter when Europe witnessed the open split between the two power systems that we could characterize as the imperial around Henry IV and the papal around Gregory VII. Adam dedicated his work to his archbishop, Liemar, and this prelate seems to be one of the more underestimated figures in the building up of this conflict. Already in April 1074, Liemar as leader of the imperial episcopate confronted and rejected the demands of Gregory's legates, and in connection with this he seems to have made clear that the imperialists were prepared to take the position which was indeed later taken at Worms in January 1076, when the king and the imperial episcopate declared Gregory as *invasor* and Antichrist in the apostolic see. These actions by Liemar in the spring 1074 led Pope Gregory to take the extreme step of suspending Liemar from his episcopacy at the end of the year, and some months later he excommunicated him for his arrogant disobedience from 'the body and blood of the Lord'. At Canossa in 1077 Liemar stood by the side of his lord the king, and throughout his life he persisted as one of the most devoted followers of Henry IV.[7] This consistency of his standpoint gained him respect even from the king's enemies. Nevertheless, Pope Urban II is said to have characterized

---

[6] *Templum nobilissimum. Adam av Bremen, Uppsalatmplet och konfliktlinjerna i Europa kring år 1075,* Avhandlingar från Historiska institutionen i Göteborg, 21 (Göteborg, 1998). This paper, however, was written in 1997, before the publication of the thesis.

[7] I show in my thesis that Liemar did not go to Rome in 1075, as has been maintained since Bernhard Schmeidler, 'Ein Brief Bischof Immads von Paderborn an Papst Gregor VII', in *Neues Archiv der Gesellschaft für ältere deutsche Geschichtskunde,* 37 (1912), 804–9.

Liemar as *scismaticorum princeps*. At the time Liemar was excommunicated, Gregory himself declared that disobedience to him was idolatry.

To this man, Adam dedicated his *Gesta*, and it can be shown that he wrote with his eyes fixed on this conflict and that he stood firmly on the side of Liemar and the king. His description of the bad side of Archbishop Adalbert is, for example, an obvious parallel to the picture of the Antichrist Gregory presented by the king and his bishops in 1076. From an analysis of the documentary material, Wolfgang Seegrün has to some extent reached the same conclusion regarding the position of Adam's work by showing that the *Gesta* is to be seen in connection with Liemar's defence against Gregory.[8]

Putting together then the lack of evidence for paganism in Uppland at this time with the political and theological position of Liemar and Adam, it becomes quite probable that there is some kind of connection between Uppsala and the fundamental religious question of the time. Who was to be followed, the pope or *caesar*? A closer comparison between on the one hand the position of the imperialists in 1076, and Adam's Uppsala on the other, reveals striking correspondences. In a *triclinium* of a temple totally made of gold, the *sueones* worshipped the statues of three deadly sins: *superbia* with a sceptre, *furor* with arms, and *luxuria* with a huge *priapus*. According to Henry IV and his bishops, the false monk Hildebrand bought the *favor* that got him the arms that elevated him to the see of peace, from which he destroyed peace. From the papal throne in the *Triclinium majus* of the Lateran palace he acted in *superbia* as if *regnum* and *imperium* had been not in God's but in his own hands, robbed Henry of the kingdom of Italy, reigned with a new senate of women, and filled the Church with the stench of the gravest scandal by living together more familiarly than necessary with one of these. He furthermore cloaked violence with religion and endowed the *furor* of the mob with the administration of the Church.

I would like to stress that the correspondences between the imperialist's view on Gregory and Adam's description of Uppsala can not be accidental. It is, however, difficult to decide how the parallels are to be explained from a literal point of view. They do not seem to work as a complete allegory. A clue is given, though, in Adam's description of the Slavic temple of Rethra. Here Adam ends by pointing out that the picture given signified the lost souls of the worshippers. In his interpretation, the cult depicted was a mirror of the desires of the worshipping people. The cult was a mirror of their souls.

By suspending and excommunicating Liemar, Gregory brought northern Europe directly under his own papal jurisdiction, and he immediately sent letters to King Sven of Denmark, trying to persuade him to become a vassal of St Peter. In Sven, however, the empire and the archbishop of Bremen seem to have had a firm ally, and through him the Norwegian kingdom was also attached to the empire. But the leading bishop in the kingdom of the Danes was a fugitive clerk from the Church of Paderborn, who had

---

[8] Wolfgang Seegrün, *Das Erzbistum Hamburg in seinen älteren Papsturkunden*, Studien und Vorarbeiten zur Germania Pontificia, 5 (Köln and Wien, 1976), pp. 91, 94–100.

good reasons to support the new offensive strategy of Gregory in the north, and he may even have initiated it. The kings of Denmark and Norway were probably obstacles here. In Sweden, however, the political situation in these years is very unclear, but it is indeed clear that the archbishop of Bremen had no ecclesiastical control in this kingdom, where the old mythical seat of the king was in old Uppsala. If the king, who at this time had his seat in Uppsala, supported the policy of the bishop of Lund in following the papal line, it is no wonder that in the eyes of Adam the religion of the Swedes is very similar to that of the Gregorians. The object for their veneration was the same and, as far as Adam was concerned, so were their desires.

The cult in Uppsala, which must have been intimately connected with the Swedish king, could be described as a mirror of the Gregorian religion. It was from this religion that the Swedes were to be converted in the 1070s. The *templum* and *domus* of Uppsala was not a pagan temple in our sense, but a church resisting the sacred Roman Empire for reasons not very different from those of the Gregorians and other enemies of Henry IV gathering around Gregory VII.

Approaches to the Conversion of the Finns: Ideologies, Symbols, and Archaeological Features

DEREK FEWSTER

A mong modern Finnish archaeologists and historians there is a nearly unanimous interpretation of how and when the conversion of the Finns took place. The Christianization of the Finns began during the later half of the twelfth century, after the Swedish crusade of the 1150s. Despite disagreements regarding the details of the events, the common view shows a general acceptance of a rather late date of the transition from pagan to Christian beliefs.

In order to throw some new light on this well-trodden subject, I aim to turn the question around, beginning with the researchers and their intentions, only later returning to the factual history, whatever may remain of it. The issue might as well be to discover the ideological tendencies of past and present historians and archaeologists, as to figure out when and how Christian belief and Church organization arrived in the 'Easterland' of the emerging kingdom of Sweden.[1]

The conversion of *one* diocese in Europe is of course of peripheral interest, but as the subject is not easily accessed by foreigners, it could prove fruitful to glance at an example of national history, regardless of the actual events leading to the conversion. I will however try to shed some light on this issue too.

---

[1] For a thought-provoking introduction to the subject of archaeological usefulness, see Carl-Axel Moberg, 'Den nyttiga fornforskningen: En skiss till en åskådnings historia och karakteristik', *Lychnos: Annual of the Swedish History of Sciences Society* (1984), 133–57.

Medieval Finland

Since the region is not too well known outside its present borders, medieval Finland needs a brief presentation to begin with. By modern agreement Prehistory, that is, the 'Viking Age', ends by 1025 or 1050 in Finland, when the 'Crusading Period' begins. The Proper Middle Ages begin in 1200 in the south-west, and around 1300 in the east.

The late prehistoric inhabitants of present day Finland seem to have been divided in several *gentes*: The Finns (*Suomalaiset*) of the south-west coastal region, the Tavastians (*Hämäläiset*) of the interior, and the Karelians (*Karjalaiset*) of the eastern areas around Lake Ladoga. No original name is found for what has become modern Finland. The only ancient idea somehow covering this area was the *Österland* of the Swedes.

'Finland' was a small region in the south-west, where the town of Åbo (*Turku*) later would be founded. As the area was incorporated in the evolving state of Sweden, the word Finland came to be used, by the late fourteenth century, as a technical term for the entire eastern part of medieval Sweden. Only one permanent Catholic diocese was formed in this area. The see was moved twice in the thirteenth century, settling by 1300, at the latest, on its best known site in Åbo.

Three so-called crusades are known to have been undertaken by Swedish forces to Finland. The first one belongs to the mid or late 1150s. Little is known about this venture, no more than that King Erik soon returned to Sweden and that Bishop Henry was murdered by a local farmer, Lalli. Thus St Henry became the patron saint of the diocese. The second crusade was the 'reconquest' of the Tavastian region, dated to around 1238–49. The political aspect is well documented in the sole source for the event, *Erik's Chronicle*. The third crusade was an unambiguous political manoeuvre against Novgorod in 1293, securing some parts of the Karelian region. As a result, the castle of Viborg was founded, being mentioned in 1295. The border against Novgorod was fixed in 1323. The possible Danish crusades of 1191, 1202, and 1210 are difficult to substantiate and might well be misconceptions of medieval copyists. Anyway, visible results of these undertakings are not to be found.

As to historical sources, the bishop's archive was burned in 1318 by the Slavs of Novgorod. The subsequent fires of Stockholm castle in 1697 and of the town of Åbo in 1827 were almost as disastrous. The lack of preserved documentation leaves researchers in an awkward position; the silence of the sources facilitates all kinds of speculation, as we shall see.

Scandinavian Approaches

The publications covering the subject of the conversion are numerous and cannot be surveyed within the scope of this essay. As only a few outlines have been published in languages other than Swedish or Finnish, such publications provide a good point of departure for historiographical scrutiny of the conversion of the Finns. The standard view of the conversion is presented in several modern surveys of the process of christianization in the north.

In *Viking og Hvidekrist,* Olaf Olsen mentions briefly the lack of any Christianity in Finland until well into the thirteenth century. He does not consider the eleventh-century burial customs really Christian, nor does he ascribe much historical value to the first crusade. Olsen represents a traditional and formal Scandinavian view, showing little interest in the subject. Yet he does not use the opportunity provided to emphasise any violent nature of the conversion. His conversion is one of the word, *Wortmission.*[2]

Eric Christiansen gives the question more space in *The Northern Crusades,* but does not present any convincing arguments, as personal speculations and misinterpretations are often presented as facts. However, from a historiographical point of view his text is quite interesting. He considers Sweden a unified and fully developed state, even before Finland is conquered, which is done essentially by force. He basically believes in a late *Schwertmission,* begun by the kings of Sweden. Christiansen's most recent and only truly Finnish reference is a patriotic survey from 1962. After presenting the dismal state of civilization in Finland, he concludes: 'Not an impressive total [. . .] but the starting point was a wholly unchristian, illiterate and ungoverned world, which in two centuries became a fairly harmonious Catholic society'. His non-archaeological synthesis is a good example of latter day Scandinavism.[3]

In a more recent work, *Medieval Scandinavia,* by Birgit and Peter Sawyer, Finland nearly sinks into oblivion. A Swedish conquest is mentioned, as is the border of 1323. Regarding conversion in general, the Sawyers believe in a period of transition, which would rank them among the subscribers to a *Kulturmission.*[4]

There is one common, quite misleading line of thought in all of the works mentioned, which brings us closer to the actual issue. All the authors view medieval history through a certain political theory of the early nineteenth century, Scandinavism, making the history, and conversion, of Finland a separate and special case. It is the fallacy of considering present borders as natural, eternal, and final.

The whole concept of Scandinavia is neither prehistorical nor medieval. The earliest known uses of the word in Sweden are from the years 1810–16. The word only emerges in the Swedish language after the eastern part of Sweden, that is the Grand-Duchy of Finland, was lost to the Russian emperor in 1808–9. This Swedish political catastrophe created a sudden ideological need to see the political realities of the day as a natural and noncontroversial matter of course. Hence nineteenth-century scholars and artists created a sense of Scandinavian unity within the framework of Scandinavism, emphasising a pure Germanic national heritage, while excluding the Finns from the

---

[2] Olaf Olsen, 'Kristendommen og kirkerne', in *Viking og Hvidekrist: Norden og Europa 800–1200,* ed. by Else Roesdahl (Copenhagen, 1992), p. 155: 'Det var næppe megen kristendom i Finland før langt ind i 1200-årene'.

[3] Eric Christiansen, *The Northern Crusades: The Baltic and the Catholic Frontier 1100–1525* (London, 1980), p. 210.

[4] Birgit and Peter Sawyer, *Medieval Scandinavia: From Conversion to Reformation, circa 800–1500,* 2nd edn, The Nordic Series, 17 (Minneapolis, 1996), pp. 100–28.

history of Sweden.[5] In due time the emerging nationalism of the Finns would serve the same purpose: to make Finnish history unique and glorious.

If we attempt to form a picture of the conversion of the Finns, based on Scandinavian research, we would most likely encounter a tendency to disregard 'Finland', as it was only a 'temporary province' of 'Sweden'. This trait, I would argue, is still rather a rule than an exception among modern Scandinavian scholars. A most recent exception must however be mentioned: Anne-Sofie Gräslund's survey of the changing faith in the north in *Kyrka-Samhälle-Stat*. Her approach is to a certain degree both un-Scandinavian, and as we shall see, un-Finnish, in her acceptance of an early and peaceful conversion, beginning in the eleventh century.[6]

The National Approaches

As the Scandinavians neglected the east, the Finnish historians and archaeologists of the nineteenth century were busy creating an equivalent view of Finland as a natural and ancient state. Any historical features of the 'Germanic West' present in the Grand-Duchy, or later in the independent state, became unwanted, unpatriotic, and un-Finnish. An image of a medieval and tribal Finland was emerging. It became a truth that the Swedish crown brought oppression to the native people. Catholic Christianity was soon considered a bad influence also because of the subsequent annihilation of a national and pure heathendom. Medieval Finland became an issue of introvert nationalism.

Any foreigner transgressing on the subject of the medieval history of the Åbo diocese, would either have to learn Finnish, an arduous task, or have to trust the translations of possibly nationalist Finnish scholars. Clearly this seems to be another main problem that the Sawyers, Eric Christiansen, and Olaf Olsen have encountered. These, like other authors, are at the mercy of possibly tendentious and outdated works, even if the Sawyers seem to be aware of how Finnish nationalism has used the period before the 'Swedish conquest' for the creation of a national identity.[7] Yet the Sawyers dare state that 'talk of national symbols and periods of national greatness may be considered anachronistic with no significance for modern historical scholarship'.[8] Now this is an optimistic view, if ever.

---

[5] An excellent presentation of Swedish nationalism in relation to the question of medieval Finland is provided by Per Olof Sjöstrand, *Hur Finland vanns för Sverige: En historia för nationalstater*, Opuscula Historica Upsaliensis, 16 (Uppsala, 1996). For the earliest uses of the word Scandinavia, see 'Skandinav' in *Svenska Akademiens Ordbok* (1973), XXVI, cols 3489–92.

[6] Anne-Sofie Gräslund, 'Religionsskiftet i Norden', in *Kyrka-Samhälle-Stat: Från kristnande till etablerad kyrka*, Historiallinen arkisto, 110.3, ed. by Göran Dahlbäck (Helsingfors, 1997), pp. 11–36.

[7] See, for instance, Claus Ahrens, *Frühe Holzkirchen in nördlichen Europa*, Veröffentlichung der Helms-Museums, 39 (Hamburg, 1981). The text in the chapter 'Christianisierung in Finnland und Lappland', esp. pp. 49–51, provides the traditional Finnish nationalist view.

[8] Sawyer and Sawyer, *Medieval Scandinavia*, pp. 237–38.

In Finland nationalism led to a general lack of source criticism: the surviving brief notices of the baptisms, conversions, and crusades have in general been taken as genuine accounts and acknowledgements of the stated feats. Rarely have the documents been considered overstatements or glorifications of what actually took place, a not unheard of feature of the medieval state and Church. This lack of critique emanates from an inherent wish to believe in the sources: the tremendous struggle of the Church militant battling the heathens, the Swedish kings fighting the proud and strong Finns, the hard-bought victory over the infidels, the glory of the tragic loss of independence, and, implicitly, the late dates provided for these events. The view of the medieval Church suited the modern nationalists.

Finnish nationalism threw a long shadow on the picture of medieval Finland. In almost any historical or archaeological work we would find the term *Ruotsin vallan aika* (the time of Swedish power/sovereignty), suggesting a hierarchy, as Finland of course was *subjected* to Swedish rule. The name of the Swedish kingdom is often given as *Ruotsi-Suomi* (Sweden-Finland), a totally modern invention emphasising Finland as a separate entity. The realm was never so called before 1808, as it never was a double monarchy.

Nationalism did not stop here. There was a need for a truly Finnish prehistory and 'pre-conquest' independence. If Finland was supposed to be a national entity, it could not have been created in recent times, but rather it had to emanate from time immemorial, from the archaeological and heathen past.

Strong emphasis was given to some central concepts marking what was truly Finnish in pre-conquest times. Some of these features are quite close to the early antiquarian views of the Germanic tribes, here adapted for the Finnish tribes. It should be noted that Finnish archaeology was created in the late nineteenth century as a counterreaction to the supposed cultural superiority of the Germanic peoples, a thought popular in Europe around the turn of the century. Within the concept of an independent Finnish heritage the following features would be of central importance:

(1) The Finn was a free warrior of a proud, strong, and just tribe (*heimo*).

(2) The forest was the cultural landscape of Finland, and any agrarian activities would only be subsidiary. The manly Finn was a hunter, having sold furs to the vain south for thousands of years.

(3) The hill-fort was the symbol of a high level of political organization and an early proof of tribal unity. This was the final defence against both Vikings and Slavs.

(4) Any foreign presence in Finland was an act of trespassing, a threat to the indigenous Finns. The would-be conquerors arrived in great numbers, in general to enslave or tax the natives (Figure 1).

(5) Paganism was the national religion, a symbol of ideology. The national 'epos' of *Kalevala* ended with the coming of Christ, and the old mage Väinämöinen leaving his people. Paganism was seen as a part of the national heritage, as it was neither Swedish nor Russian. Regardless of his probable Christian background, the slayer of bishop Henry, Lalli, was considered a pagan and became a symbol of Finnish independence in the early twentieth century. The first Finn known by name was quickly transformed into a political assassin and hero.

(6) Finally, Christianity was forced on the Finns, who after a fierce struggle converted *en masse* during the Swedish crusades. The new religion wiped out the local *Volksgeist*. As the conversion was to Catholicism, the Finns never really felt Christian. Only the Reformation brought true conversion to the north, in the acceptable form of Lutheranism.

These six mentioned values and concepts would probably dominate any archaeological treatise or history book written before 1945, openly or subconsciously.[9] Their shadows reach into the twenty-first century, I would argue.

The Lutheran Approach to Catholic Christianity

There was both a national political reason to emphasise the tragic struggle of the Finns and their ultimate defeat as there was a religious reason to see medieval Christianity as non-Finnish and imposed. As children of a Lutheran upbringing, the Finns of recent centuries would have had very little first-hand knowledge of anything Catholic. Any interest taken in Catholic traditions would embrace the subject with suspicion and only limited understanding. The Lutheran tradition being the point of reference, the scholars would often tend to look at medieval Christianity as a fully developed and final ideology, even from its first inclusion in Finland, as the Catholic Church in Finland was seen as a monolithic, static, and somehow timeless, organization.

To justify the unquestionable state of Catholicism in the Late Middle Ages, a nationalist could write in 1930 that 'the Finnish Catholic church was spared almost completely from the bad conditions creating objections in many other countries. The spirit remained pure thanks to competent bishops', that 'the spirit of the church was national', and that 'it always worked for the best of the Finnish people'.[10]

Not withstanding the general Lutheran continuity in Finland, the reformation also had a profound meaning for the concept of Finnish nationality and language. The first book written in Finnish was a translation of the New Testament, accomplished by Michael Agricola in 1548. Anything medieval would therefore tend to be less civilized, as it would have been written in Latin or Swedish.

Nationalism—Modern Trends

Do these features live on today, as I have implied? Any general degree of nationalism can not, of course, be measured, as all tendencies are personal, variable, and depend on the social and academic background of the researcher. Most scholars are probably indifferent today to questions of national and ethnic identity in their research.

---

[9] For a tremendous illustrated vision of Finnish history see Aarno Karimo, *Kumpujen yöstä: Suomalaisia vaiheita, tekoja ja oloja kivikaudesta nykyaikaan*, 4 vols (Porvoo, 1929–32). The four volumes codified the nationalist interpretation of history for generations of Finns to digest it as the ethnic truth of manifest destiny.

[10] Karimo, *Kumpujen yöstä*, II (1930), 351.

Yet, I would argue that a few crucial topics of the political archaeology and history of the pre-war period do remain in modern scholarship. The point of conversion is one of them.

I would like to give a few examples. In 1987 the leading Finnish Viking Age specialist wrote that 'the conversion signified the destruction of the original Finnish traditions', and that 'the Christian church crushed the self-esteem of the Finns, [. . .] the shock was so great that the Finns have not yet fully recovered, even today'.[11] These are emotional statements of modern national values, heavily dependent on twentieth-century nationalism. Blaming the conversion process for modern drinking behaviour seems a bit out of proportion, but the statement fits well within the nationalist tradition of Finland.

Most popular, assimilated history also tends to follow the traditional view. The listed features mentioned above can all be found in late twentieth-century schoolbooks, comic strips, plays, booklets for tourists, novels, etc. The comic strip *Toinen ristiretki* (The Second Crusade) was drawn by two students of history, both with a master's degree (Figure 2). In this dramatized reconstruction of the events of c. 1238–49 the Finns are highly suspicious of anything Swedish or Christian, and with good reason, too. The work includes nearly all the national symbols of prehistoric Finland.[12]

The greatest archaeological movement of the 1980s was an appeal to preserve and investigate a huge hill-fort, Rapola in Sääksmäki, of quite dubious character. Its fame rests on a long, undated stone foundation winding round the crest, on a seventeenth-century surveyor believing it ancient, and on the name of a fourteenth-century excommunicated farmer, *Cuningas de Rapalum* ('King of Rapola'). The symbolic value of the presumed hill-fort, however, overshadows all possible doubt. It is still considered the administrative centre of a Tavastian 'pre-conquest' kingdom.[13] Three years of recent excavations revealed nothing but traces of ancient fields.

The supposed importance of the hill-forts, these bastions of pagan defence, is further emphasised by several attempts at experimental archaeology in the twentieth century. A researcher, with a PhD in archaeology, attempted in the 1980s to prove the veracity of a pagan chain of beacons in the south-west. By burning polystyrene, car tires, and petroleum he proved the visibility excellent and the defence system ancient. This quite serious experiment echoes a similar one in the 1930s, with professional scholars involved, but which was not as successful as only organic material was used.[14]

---

[11] Pirkko-Liisa Lehtosalo-Hilander, 'The Conversion of the Finns in Western Finland', in *The Christianization of Scandinavia*, ed. by Birgit Sawyer, Peter Sawyer, and Ian Wood (Alingsås, 1987), pp. 34–35.

[12] Pekka A. Manninen and Ilpo Lagerstedt, *Toinen ristiretki*, Suomalaisia sarjakuvia, 1 (Seinäjoki, 1986).

[13] See the exhibition catalogue *Terra Tavestorum: Hämäläisten maa*, ed. by Ritva Wäre (Helsinki, 1994), p. 41. The booklet was published only in Finnish by the National Board of Antiquities, in connection with a new display of the glorious and independent prehistory of one of the supposed early medieval tribes, the *Hämäläiset*.

[14] Jukka Luoto and Pertti Huttunen, 'Tulitedotus tutkimuksen kohteena', *Kotiseutu*, 4 (1987), 194–98.

There are still scholars who attempt to describe Finland as a pre-conquest, independent tribal state with both indigenous currency and taxation.[15] These features of overt nationalism are however limited, and are seldom consciously acknowledged by most archaeologists. But nationalism can also flourish in the subconscious as a self-explanatory scientific basis for the pursuit of historical knowledge. Finnish historiography has only recently begun to acknowledge the fundamental continuity of nationalism in the humanities.

As most archaeologists in post-war Finland believe in a neutral, scientific archaeology, their historiographical insight into the possible uses of the past in the service of the nation would be limited. The archaeologist of today is well aware of the national tendencies until 1917, the year of Finland's declaration of independence, but he sadly neglects the possible nationalist undertones of the later twentieth century.[16]

Nationalism and Archaeology

In archaeology nationalism led to a presumption of paganism in all prehistorical contexts, despite any empirical principles being voiced, or any possible Christian features being visible. Visualizing any combination of Christianity and paganism has not really been a serious option for Finnish scholars. The latent wish to view the conversion of the Finns as a late, abrupt, and preferably violent event has led to a series of national features in the archaeological interpretation of the finds. Slightly exaggerating, the following could be stated:

(1) In Finnish archaeology, it is an absolute requirement that a Christian grave is empty of all grave goods. Little consideration is given to the persistent medieval habit of fitting graves with markers of social status, a feature well documented in all of northern Europe.[17]

---

[15] A good example of this is the symposium report *Muinaisrunot ja todellisuus* [Ancient Folk Poetry and Reality], ed. by Martti Linna, Historian Aitta, 20 (Lohja, 1987). The recently published Jari Hyvärinen, *Hirsilinnojen aika* [The Time of the Log Castles] (Helsinki, 1998) reconstructs dozens of unexcavated hill-forts in beautifully detailed line drawings.

[16] See Ari Siiriäinen, 'Recent Trends in the Finnish Archaeology', in *Congressus Octavus Internationalis Fenno-Ugristarum Jyväskylä 10–15.8.1995. I: Orationes plenarie et conspectus quinquennales*, ed. by Heikki Leskinen (Jyväskylä, 1995), pp. 183–89; Ole Klindt-Jensen, *A History of Scandinavian Archaeology* (London, 1975); and Bruce G. Trigger, *A History of Archaeological Thought* (Cambridge, 1989). None of these authors consider nationalism to be worth more than superficial consideration, at the most. For an opposite view in general see *Cultural Identity and Archaeology: The Construction of European Communities*, ed. by Paul Graves-Brown, Siân Jones, and Clive Gamble (London, 1996); and Don D. Fowler, 'The Uses of the Past: Archaeology in the Service of the State', *American Antiquity,* 52 (1987), 229–48.

[17] Compare Pekka Sarvas, 'Ristiretkiajan ajoituskysymyksiä', *Suomen Museo,* 78 (1971), 51–61, with Jakob Kieffer-Olsen, 'Middelalderens gravskik i Danmark: En arkæologisk forskningsstatus', *Hikuin,* 17 (1990), 105.

(2) An inhumation is never really considered as influenced by Christianity, even if this tradition of burial expands dramatically in the eleventh century in Finland. But then again, if the cemetery also shows contemporary or slightly younger cremations, these are quickly considered examples of a general relapse to an ancient and well-tried paganism. The few known cases of this have become proof of a popular reaction against Christianity over the whole county.[18] The possibility of a complex set of burial customs within the hamlet or tribal unity is not possible within the concept of Finnish national archaeology.

(3) The grave should also definitely be orientated from west to east. Some researchers do not even wish to see this as a sign of any Christian influence, even if this habit also suddenly appears in south-west Finland in the eleventh century.[19]

(4) An archaeologically shown presence of a belltower by the cemetery is not quite sufficient to make an inhumation cemetery Christian, as can be seen in the cases of Nousiainen Moisio or Lieto Ristipelto. Other features must also be provided.[20]

(5) Only cross pendants, crucifixes, book mounts, and other religious artefacts are allowed to imply any form of Christianity, and only then of *primum signum*. These objects are the main focus of Finnish conversion archaeology; the 'to be or not to be' of the cross pendants, that has been the question.[21]

All in all, the graves have to be inhumations without any grave goods, they have to be in the direction of west-east and they have to be by a church to be truly Christian. QED, there is no conversion in Finland before the late twelfth century.[22]

---

[18] Wäre, *Terra Tavestorum*, p. 46; see also Matti Huurre, *9000 vuotta Suomen esihistoriaa* (Helsinki, 1979), pp. 222–26.

[19] Sarvas, 'Ristiretkiajan ajoituskysymyksiä', p. 52. All the author's national opinions of Christianity have been left out of the German summary.

[20] Torsten Edgren, 'Den förhistoriska tiden', in *Finlands historia*, ed. by Märtha Norrback (Esbo, 1992), I, especially the hesitant statement on p. 250: 'Dessa gravfält kan m.a.o. betecknas som kristna'.

[21] Nils Cleve, 'Spår av tidig kristendom i västra Finland', *Finskt Museum*, 54–55 (1947–48), 67–85; Ella Kivikoski, 'Christliche Einflüsse in dem archäologischen Material der Wikingerzeit und der Kreuszugszeit Finnlands', in *Kirche und Gesellschaft im Ostseeraum und im Norden vor der Mitte des 13. Jahrhunderts*, Acta Visbyensia, 3 (Visby, 1969), 31–41; Paula Purhonen, 'Cross Pendants from Iron-Age Finland', in *Byzantium and the North: Acta Byzantina Fennica*, 3 (1987), 31–57; Jukka Luoto, 'Suomen varhaiskristillisyydestä', *Suomen Museo*, 96 (1989), 133–52; Jussi-Pekka Taavitsainen, 'Finnish Limousines: Fundamental Questions about the Organizing Process of the Early Church in Finland', in *Quotidianum Fennicum: Daily Life in Medieval Finland*, Medium Aevum Quotidianum, 19 (Krems, 1989), pp. 75–88.

[22] Compare this with the liberal view presented in Alain Dierkens, 'Het getuigenis van de archeologie', in *De Heidense Middeleeuwen*, ed. by Ludo Milis et al. (Turnhout, 1992), pp. 47–68. Cf. also N. A. Makarov, 'On the Christianization of the Rural Areas of Russia in the 11th–13th Centuries. Burials with Crosses and Small Icons in Beloserie Cemeteries', *Suomen Museo*, 96 (1989), 49–59, esp. p. 58: 'While providing no quantative indicators, the burials with

(6) Finally, little or no difference has generally been made between Western and Eastern Christianity. The issue of Greek Orthodoxy among the Finns involves some historiographical complexity, as might be expected. After the independence achieved in 1917, anything Russian, like Eastern Christianity, was considered to be of little importance for the history of the newborn state. Novgorod was still seen as the ancestor of the Enemy, of the Soviet Union (Figure 3).

Only during the last decade have several scholars turned some attention to the degree of early medieval Slavic influence among the Finns. There is even a tendency to dispute the initial Western Christian influence, as many researchers consider the eastern trading influence paramount in bringing formal Christianity to the Finns.[23]

The shifting political winds of the last decade have made this standpoint possible: nowadays, being in favour of an early eastern influence longer implies a dubious adoration of Finnish-Soviet Union relations. However peaceful the eastern trading option may be, the main issue remains. Archaeologists still contemplate the origins and meanings of the Finnish national identity, be it in comparison to Western Europe, Catholicism, Scandinavia, Sweden, Russia, the Soviet Union, Greek Orthodoxy, or the European Union. Archaeological preferences and questions, such as the first conversion of the Finns, still reflect the political statements and events of the twentieth century.

The Research and the Features of Conversion

Bearing all these features of modern nationalism in mind, what does the archaeological record contain? What about the actual conversion of the Finns? First we have to summarize the main traditions of research in an ideological and roughly chronological order:

The nineteenth- and early twentieth-century patriots, consisting mostly of historians, were the first to tackle the question. These researchers were preoccupied with the events of the surviving written sources: the 'Crusades' and the founding of the diocese in the western region. To them, the conversion was late, apparently also forced and undertaken by a centralized Catholic Church and the young Swedish state. All the same, in this construction the formal Christian culture brought western civilization to

---

crosses and icons are evidence of fundamental shifts in the confessional situation of the 11th and 12th centuries: nominal Christianization of part of the population on the fringes of the Russian lands'.

[23] Taavitsainen, 'Finnish Limousines', does not consider the question at all. For the Slavic and Greek Orthodox presence in Finland and Karelia, see for instance Unto Salo, 'The Early Stage of Finland's Conversion to Christianity', in *Byzantium and the North: Acta Byzantina Fennica*, 4 (1988–89), 95–117; and Makarov, 'On the Christianization of the Rural Areas'. Many general surveys now mention the influence as a fact, as do Liisi Eränkö, 'Henkinen elämä', in *Rautakausi Suomessa*, ed. by Kati Tyystjärvi (Helsinki, 1990), pp. 39–40; and Jaakko Masonen, 'Finnland im Mittelalter. Zur Einführung', in *Quotidianum Fennicum*, pp. 5–12.

the north by means of a *Wortmission*. Russian Christianity could not even be considered a vague influence.

World War I changed the setup and the ideological needs. The twentieth-century nationalists of independent Finland, including the growing host of archaeologists, militarized the past. The pace of the conversion became the main point of interest, as the survival of indigenous pagan elements during the twelfth and thirteenth centuries was of national importance. To the adherents of this tradition the conversion was late, forced, nearly instantaneous, and meant a violent subjugation of the Finns. In essence, the rich pagan culture was destroyed by a Catholic and Swedish *Schwertmission*. This line of research did, as we have seen, survive the turmoils of World War II, and does still influence the general concept of the conversion.

More recently archaeologists and historians, tentatively defined as 'transition scholars' or 'diffusionists', have also been looking in a new direction, east, without much consideration of the internal religious changes in the region. To these researchers the conversion was a successive and nearly secular diffusion of ideas from the eleventh century onwards. The emerging local Christianity is to some degree presented as a social and economic structure, without religious features or internalized beliefs.[24] The Finns somehow remained in charge of their destiny as they slowly adopted 'Christian' customs. Thus, trade was the primary motor as Christian culture became a habit by a *Kulturmission*. This view is in fact a demilitarized version of the previous archaeological nationalism, a construction still filled with Finnish *Volksgeist*.

So where does all of this leave us? As to the actual archaeological and historical record, some matters appear to be hard to dispute. A transition from cremation to inhumation burial is clearly visible before the 'Crusades', beginning among the western Finns in the eleventh century. The graves show that the Finns, among other beliefs, also seem to have been convinced of the resurrection of the body, a Christian-influenced eschatological feature. The surviving family members continued in providing the deceased with grave offerings throughout the final period of the local cemeteries, before the first parish churches were built in Finland. The tradition of hamlet or family cemeteries vanishes completely, apparently in favour of church burials, by the early thirteenth century.

The conflicts and crusades mentioned in the historical sources seem to indicate a possible struggle against increasing state control, not a fight against the new religion. There are no sources or archaeological finds relating to prolonged or hostile wars

---

[24] Paula Purhonen does in fact attempt to re-examine the question from an anthropological and religious standpoint in the most recent study of the Finnish conversion: *Kristinuskon saapumisesta Suomeen: Uskontoarkeologinen tutkimus* [On the Arrival of Christianity in Finland: A Study in the Archaeology of Religion], Suomen muinaismuistoyhdistyksen aikakauskirja, 106 (doctoral thesis, University of Helsinki, 1999). The thesis does however lack a necessary critical historiographical survey of the subject and sees the question as a purely scientific problem, as a question devoid of political tendencies, wishful thinking, and previous Lutheran bias.

against the new power in Finland, comparable with Henry of Livonia's description of the developments in the southern Baltic.

It could be argued that the conversion of the Finns follows closely the process in the Mälaren valley in Sweden: a series of successive transitions, basically peaceful and more or less contemporary with those in Uppland, the main differences being the later date of the organization of the Finnish diocese, and the stronger initial influence of Greek Orthodox Christianity in Finland.

Figure 1. Horned Vikings, sailing under a Christian banner depicting the Blessed
Virgin, fight the Finns. Illustration of 'Länttä vastaan' [Against the West],
from Aarno Karimo, *Kumpujen yöstä*, I (Helsinki, 1929), p. 275.

Figure 2. The Cross is raised on the flaming ruins of a conquered hill-fort. Drawing from comic-strip by Pekka A. Manninen and Ilpo Lagerstedt, *Toinen ristiretki* [The Second Crusade], Suomalaisia sarjakuvia, 1 (Seinäjoki, 1986), p. 29.

Figure 3. A picture depicting coercive conversion of orthodox Carelians, instigated by an ominous Catholic monk. Illustration from 'Karjalaisten toinen kaste' [The Second Baptism of the Karelians], from Aarno Karimo, *Kumpujen yöstä*, II (Helsinki, 1930), p. 191.

The Conversion of
Central and Eastern Europe

Signs of Conversion
in Early Medieval Charters

ZSOLT HUNYADI

A s in the case of other types of sources, such as laws and chronicles, in dealing with charters one should determine and enumerate a group of signs and symbols, which might be taken into account as being indicative of conversion to Christianity. Early medieval charters (in our case from the ninth to the eleventh century) provide evidence of direct, palpable signs of missionary activity and pastoral care, including such indispensable tools as ecclesiastical vestments, liturgical vessels and utensils, and, particularly, books. Nevertheless, neither the nature nor the quantity of the surviving material allows scholars to obtain unquestionable information on the conversion of either the Hungarians or the Slavs of the region. As a result, it is necessary to add many indirect proofs and indications provided by the toponyms (including *patrocinia*), personal names, special institutions (*ecclesia propria*), the practice of Christian burial, particular social groups (e.g. *exsequiales*), and the development of the ecclesiastical hierarchy (the density of parochial and/or country churches, the formation of bishoprics, and the foundation of clan monasteries and their donations). These components may act as indicators of the process of christianization or of the results of conversion. Unfortunately, even these signs are not adequate for tracing the course of conversion step by step in the Carpathian basin, and later in the medieval Kingdom of Hungary. Although several of the features mentioned might be

---

The following article was delivered as part of a panel entitled 'Signs and Symbols of Conversion' in the written sources of medieval Central Europe.

evaluated or judged in terms of Western European analogies, quantitative calculations and the reconstruction of the exact situation are almost impossible and merely illusory.

However, by using some medieval charters as a lens one can find interesting points which shed some light on the visible features of conversion. Accordingly, I would like to start at the very beginning of the tenth century. In autumn of 903, at the time of the Bavarian-Hungarian war, a council was convoked in Passau by the local bishop where Madalwin, the Pannonian *chorepiscopus*, also appeared. He handed over his landed properties and ecclesiastical accessories (vestments and books) to the advocates of the bishop (Ratolf and Alperic)[1] in return for two of his benefices which he received for life.[2] It is known that Madalwin, a former imperial scribe, was active among the Caranthans (Slavs) as a missionary/suffragan bishop (*chorepiscopus*) in Lower Austria. According to some scholars, the well-informed Madalwin escaped from the Magyars, and that is why he swapped his landed properties for Western ones and deposited his missionary accessories in Passau.[3] Burchard, the bishop of Passau issued a charter about this transaction in which he listed *totum apparatum suum*, that is, all the things Madalwin handed over to him.[4]

The list of Madalwin's books unquestionably indicates a certain set of books indispensable or at least necessary for his goals. I share the idea of Franz Zagiba, who assumes that besides the Latin texts there might have been Old High German and Slavic texts in his book collection.[5] The 'stock' can be divided into four groups: (1) liturgical and homiletic, (2) legal, (3) hagiographical, and (4) works concerned with the seven liberal arts. Accordingly, one can find on the list (1) *plenarium*,[6] *epistolare, I Librum Sacramentorum*,[7] *graduale et nocturnale, predicationes per anni circulum, Collectarium*,[8] *tractatum Albini super IIII euangelia, explanatio in regum, liber penitentialis, epistolas Pauli, VII epistolas canonicas*; (2) *canones de diversis conciliis et de capitularibus*

---

[1] *Codex Diplomaticus Hungariae Ecclesiasticus ac Civilis*, ed. by Georgius Fejér (Buda, 1829–44), VII (1831), 1, pp. 84–86. Recent extract: Hans Wagner, *Urkundenbuch des Burgenlandes und der angrenzenden Gebiete der Komitate Wieselburg, Ödenburg und Eisenburg*, 4 vols (Graz, 1955–85), I (1955), 12. For drawing my attention to this document, thanks should be expressed to Dr László Veszprémy.

[2] György Györffy, 'A kalandozások kora', in *Magyarország története* [A History of Hungary], ed. by György Székely (Budapest, 1987), I, 2, p. 1641.

[3] Péter Váczy, 'Magyarország kereszténysége a honfoglalás korában' [Christianity in Pannónia at the Age of the Conquest], in *Emlékkönyv Szent István király halálának kilencszázadik évfordulójára*, ed. by Jusztinián Serédi (Budapest, 1938), I, 222–23.

[4] Fejér, *Codex Diplomaticus*, VII, 1, pp. 84–85.

[5] Franz Zagiba, *Das Geistesleben der Slaven im frühen Mittelalter* (Wien, 1971), p. 85.

[6] Fejér, *Codex Diplomaticus*, VII, 1, p. 85: IIII evangeliorum.

[7] Ibid.: '[. . .] in quo continentur benedictiones ecclesie et benedictiones sacrorum ordinum et cetera omnia que ad ipsum ministerium episcopi pertinent [. . .]'.

[8] Ibid.: 'ab initio XL-e usque in Pascha super omnia cottidiana euangelia'.

Karoli ceterorumque regum, lex Bawariorum et francorum et alemannorum;[9] (3) *II passionales,*[10] *vitam sancti Martini, Dyalogos Severi,*[11] *vitam Sancti Severini Confessoris;* and (4) *computus cum cyclo pleno,* for example. Apart from the books, the charter enumerates precious ecclesiastical vestments that Madalwin, presumably, used during his missionary activity: *pluviale,*[12] *casula,*[13] and *stolas.*[14] The list of things deposited does not mention any liturgical vessels or utensils.

Since Franz Zagiba analysed and determined the importance of the composition, here I would only like to draw a parallel with stated ideals and norms.[15] A prescriptive model can be found in the case of the early ninth-century bishops Gerbald of Liège and Haito of Basel who described the qualities of an ideal country priest in their episcopal statutes. Their purposes were, of course, partly different from those of a missionary bishop, but 'the sorts of episcopal statutes or capitularies which Gerbald's and Haito's works represent, seem to have been widely distributed throughout the Empire'.[16] It is clear from Madalwin's list that he was familiar with the dispositions of the *capitularia* and various councils, thus it is likely that he was well stocked with those liturgical materials (vestments and books) which were also necessary for country/parochial priests who were supposed to guard the faith subsequent to the conversion. Gerbald's statutes prescribed the required apparatus, which included: a 'paten and chalice, chasuble and alb, missal or sacramentary, lectionary, martyrology, penitential, psalter, cross and pyx (or, perhaps, reliquary)'.[17] Furthermore, Bishop Haito wanted his clergy to be familiar with 'sacramentary, lectionary, antiphonary, baptistery, *computus*, penitential, psalter and homiliary'.[18] Certainly, both authors formulated expectations concerning the lowest level of pastoral care and activity. However, the correspondence between the normative source and Madalwin's list can help us to estimate the activity of the *chorepiscopus*.

Following this line of enquiry, one should look at the work of Carl Hammer who investigated eleven inventories of church and clerical goods from Carolingian Bavaria in the period of 788/89 to 899.[19] Instead of repeating Hammer's results, I would like to

---

[9] Fejér, *Codex Diplomaticus*, VII, 1, p. 85: 'in uno corpore'.

[10] Ibid.: 'de Natale domini usque ad missam sancti Johannis; aliud passionale de missa Sancti Michaelis usque in Pascha'.

[11] Ibid.: 'de miraculis que fecit'.

[12] Ibid.: 'purpureum auro paratum'.

[13] Ibid.: 'purpurea sirica, de sirico pretioso'.

[14] Ibid.: 'II cum anfanone auro et gemnis paratum'.

[15] Zagiba, *Das Geistesleben der Slaven*, pp. 84–89.

[16] Carl Hammer, 'Country Churches, Clerical Inventories and the Carolingian Renaissance in Bavaria', *Church History,* 49 (1980), 6; *Monumenta Germaniae Historica, Capitularia regum Francorum* (henceforth *MGH, Cap.*) (Hannover, 1883), I, 237, 242–44, 362–67.

[17] Hammer, 'Country Churches', p. 7.; *MGH, Cap.* I, 243.

[18] Hammer, 'Country Churches', p. 7.; *MGH, Cap.* I, 363.

[19] Hammer, 'Country Churches', pp. 8–17.

highlight one of his, rather general, statements. He remarked that inventories may not list components with no significant importance, only those made of precious metals or cloths. Completely different was the case of books that 'were considered precious items per se, and there is little chance of their omission for reasons of insufficient value'.[20] On the other hand, the nature of book collections analysed by Hammer is slightly more practical and pastoral than that of Madalwin's list. Nevertheless, the repeated occurrences of the *sacramentarium, collectarium, graduale, liber poenitentialis, psalterium,* and other liturgical works in ninth-century charters indicate some similarities within the different 'spiritual weaponry'.

In connection with the process of conversion/christianization, the cited requirements of Bishops Gerbald and Haito were partially responsible for leading László Mezey to suppose that the eleventh-century Hungarian parochial priest was supplied with the same apparatus.[21] Although St Stephen (1000/1–1038) decreed that the king should supply the churches with vestments and altar cloths while the bishop supplied priests and books,[22] it would be an exaggeration to suppose that the lowest level of pastoral care was at the same level in the realm. However, one can only refer to analogies since there is no contemporary Hungarian example, especially prior to the large-scale conversion of the Hungarians, during the eleventh century.

What we can take into account in the Kingdom of Hungary is, at first sight, the foundation charter of the Pécsvárad Benedictine monastery dated to 1015, but the document was actually interpolated in the thirteenth century.[23] The next (in fact, the first) port of call might be those books listed on the reverse side of the foundation charter of the Tihany Benedictine monastery dated to 1055:[24] *duo missales, unum nocturnale, duo gradalia.*[25] Although this list was apparently written by a later hand as an addition in the eleventh century, it should not be regarded as the complete inventory of the monastery. Thus, the first—and for long time the last—reasonably complete inventory to have survived comes from around 1093, when Ladislas I (1077–95) compiled a list of the landed properties and moveable goods of the Pannonhalma Benedictine monastery.[26] Besides the ecclesiastical vestments and liturgical vessels, the

---

[20] Hammer, 'Country Churches', p. 10.

[21] László Mezey, 'A latin írás magyarországi történetéből' [From the History of Latin Writing in Hungary], *Magyar Könyvszemle*, 82 (1966), 1.

[22] *The Laws of King Stephen*, I, 2, p. 1. Cf. *The Laws of the Medieval Kingdom of Hungary. Decreta regni medievalis Hungariae*, 2 vols, ed. by J. M. Bak, G. Bónis, J. R. Sweeney, and L. S. Domonkos (Bakersfield, 1989), I, 9. It reads: 'Vestimenta vero et coopertoria rex prevideat, presbiterum et libros episcopi'.

[23] *Diplomata Hungariae Antiquissima ab anno 1000 usque ad annum 1131*, ed. by Georgius Györffy (Budapest, 1992), I, 62–80.

[24] *Diplomata Hungariae Antiquissima*, I, 145–56.

[25] *Diplomata Hungariae Antiquissima*, I, 152.

[26] *Diplomata Hungariae Antiquissima*, I, 295–301.

collection contains eighty volumes, which meant circa two hundred works. Apart from texts associated with the particular readings and studies of the Benedictine monks, there are more than forty liturgical books for the Mass or chants: *VI textus evangeliorum, VI missales, I bibliotheca, IIII nocturnales, IIII antiphonaria, IIII gradualia, II sequentiales cum trophis, IIII baptisteria, III collectarii, IIII (h)ymnarii, II leccionarii, I breviarius.* Among the books ordered for reading one can find: *III (h)omeliae, II libri sermonum, I collationes, II passionales.*[27]

I am fully aware of those questions and difficulties that are automatically raised in the case of sources of such nature. First of all, the first-mentioned inventories were those of ninth-century country churches, while afterwards I referred to those of mid- and late eleventh-century Benedictine monasteries. Of course, these materials are different and should be treated differently. Nevertheless, one should bear in mind at least two important factors. On the one hand, in the Kingdom of Hungary, the Benedictines themselves played an important role in conversion and/or missionary activity. On the other hand, it is assumed (albeit, with no explicit proof) that the *scriptoria* of the Benedictine monasteries, especially that of Pannonhalma, took a reasonable part in copying books indispensable for spreading or at least retaining the 'new' faith.

Summing up the first part of my argument, I must admit that the charter of 903 containing the list of Madalwin's books provides more immediate information for judging his missionary activity among the Slavs as *chorepiscopus* than similar cases in the Kingdom of Hungary two centuries later. Thus, needless to say, the afore-mentioned Benedictine inventories are simply not suitable for establishing an unquestionable impression not only about the conversion in general, but also about the influence of these book collections on the wider world in particular.

As formulated in the introduction, here, in the second part of my argument I will try to highlight some other fields from which one can gather indirect signs or indications (in the charters) of the process of conversion and the spread of the Catholic faith in the medieval Kingdom of Hungary.

(1) One of the most interesting questions is the vernacular ecclesiastical terminology in the Hungarian language, which is closely connected to the activity of Madalwin, for instance, and other Pannonian *chorepiscopi* as convertors among the Slavs. It is widely accepted—though from time to time challenged—that a reasonable part of the Hungarian ecclesiastical vocabulary derives from the Slovenian language;[28]

---

[27] *Diplomata Hungariae Antiquissima,* I, 300; cf. Mezey, 'A latin írás', pp. 15–16. See also Géza Érszegi, 'A pannonhalmi bencés apátság javainak összeírása, 1093' [Conscription of the Goods of the Benedictine Abbey of Pannonhalma], in *Kódexek a középkori Magyarországon,* ed. by Vizkelety András (Budapest, 1985), p. 84, Előd Nemerkényi, 'Latin klasszikusok Pannonhalmán a 11. században' [Latin Classics in Pannonhalma in the Eleventh Century], *Ókortudományi Értesítő,* 4 (1999), 25–31.

[28] István Kniezsa, *A magyar nyelv jövevényszavai* [Slavonic Loan Words in the Hungarian

that is, the Magyars used basic expressions as loan words (and calques) even before the beginning of Church organization by the first king, St Stephen (e.g. *barát* (brother), *szent* (saint), *malaszt* (grace), *bérmál* (confirm), *apát* (abbot), *apáca* (nun), *pilis* (tonsure), *zsolozsma* (evensong), *péntek* (Friday), *vecsernye* (vespers), *zarándok* (pilgrim)).[29] Certainly, the mentioned missionary activities (or pastoral care) had a great impact on the religious terminology of the Pannonian Slavonic population and, mostly through them, on that of the Magyars as well. If our terminology had developed parallel to Church organization, the loan words would have been taken rather from the German and Moravian (Slavonic) languages.

Nevertheless, there are two layers of ecclesiastical loan words taken from foreign languages prior to the period when the Hungarians met the Southern Slavs. The oldest elements of the Christian terminology (from the eighth and ninth centuries) are of Turkic origin: *gyász* (mourning), *örök* (eternal), *bűn* (sin), *érdem* (merit), *búcsú* (indulgence), *gyón* (confess), *egyház* (church), *ünnep* (holiday), *bocsájt* (forgive).[30] The next layer of the loan words, those of Bulgar-Slavonic origin, are indicative of missionary activity of the Byzantine Church in the region: *kereszt* (cross), *pap* (priest), *szombat* (Saturday), *panasz* (lament), *vádol* (accuse), *diák* (literate), *karácsony* (Christmas).[31]

(2) Toponyms belong to the next group of signs appearing in charters, being created from the *patrocinia* of local churches in the early medieval Kingdom of Hungary.[32] For instance, if one investigated the villages named after St Gall, mostly to be found around the early tribal settlements of the Árpáds in the tenth century (Szentgál),[33] one would

---

Language] (Budapest, 1955), I, 1, pp. 1–2; László Mezey, *Deákság és Európa* [Latinity and Europe] (Budapest, 1979), p. 91; Imre H. Tóth, 'Magyarok és szlávok a 9–11. században', [Hungarians and Slavs in the 9–11th Centuries], in *Árpád előtt és után*, ed. by Gyula Kristó and Ferenc Makk (Szeged, 1996), p. 83.

[29] György Györffy, *István király és műve* [King Stephen and his work] (Budapest, 1977), p. 72. See also János Melich, 'A magyar nyelv keresztény terminológiája' [The Christian Terminology of the Hungarian Language], in *Segédkönyv a szlavisztikai szemináriumi gyakorlatokhoz. Melich János válogatott írásaiból*, ed. by Lajos Kiss and István Nyomárkay (Budapest, 1995), pp. 45–55; Imre H. Tóth, 'The Significance of the Freising Manuscript [FM] for Slavic Studies in Hungary', *Zbornik Brižinski spomeniki*, 45 (1996), 443–50. For examples, see *Magyar oklevélszótár* [Hungarian Charter Vocabulary], ed. by István Szamota and Gyula Zolnai (Budapest, 1902), passim.

[30] On this topic, see András Róna-Tas, 'The Christianity of the Hungarians before the Conquest', in *La civiltà ungherese e il cristianesimo*, ed. by István Monok and Péter Sárközy, 3 vols (Budapest, 1998), I, 29–34.

[31] Imre H. Tóth, 'Magyarok és szlávok', pp. 79–80, 82.

[32] On this topic, see András Mező, *A templomcím a magyar helységnevekben. (11–15. század)* [Patrocinia in the Hungarian toponyms. 11–15th centuries] (Budapest, 1996), pp. 36–44.

[33] These are Kalocsa, Szekszárd, Veszprém, Koppány (Baranya Co.), Orci (Somogy Co.), Veselény (Nógrád Co.); Péter Váczy, 'Sankt Gallen és a magyarok' [Sanktgallen and the Hun-

realize that the *patrocinia* of those local churches (earlier chapels) were closely connected to the missionary activity of a monk from Sankt Gallen. This monk, Bruno, possibly implanted the cult of the patron saint of his monastery as a result of the saint's presence (after 972). These settlements, of course, are not to be confused with those toponyms and *patrocinia* appearing later in other parts of the realm. The origin of a particular *patronicium* or the cult of a given saint must be clarified before using it as a proof—at most a secondary or indirect one—in such a survey.

(3) The question of naming is even more complicated; in particular there are problems in using personal names in the charters in order to estimate how deeply the Christian 'way of life' was rooted in the Hungarian society. Unfortunately, both the eleventh and twelfth centuries lack those sources that would inform us about contemporary naming customs. The only certainty is that in the end of the twelfth century a reasonable proportion of the personal names was still of Hungarian or Turkic origin, that is, they were gentile (non-Christian). Without precise research, one can assume that it was only the thirteenth century that saw the Hungarian situation coming close to conforming to Christian custom or, at least, the Western European model. This process was parallel to the profound social changes of the period.

(4) According to some scholars,[34] in analysing missionary activity through charters certain particular institutions are to be taken into account. One of them is the *ecclesia propria* (*Eigenkirche*, proprietary church), in-as-much as one accepts that, following the Western European or, rather, German pattern, private foundations could also act as starting points or centres for the convertors' activity. It is undeniable that the institution of patronage, in general, had local characteristics in certain cases, such as rituals. In its entirety, it is not easy to make out the nature of *patronatus* exclusively from charters. Foundation charters, donations, inventories can indicate the presence of the Christian faith or can also mark the possible areas of its spread but, in fact, they in themselves are unable to prove anything.

(5) The manner of burial may also act as an indicator of how far the Christian faith was rooted in the life of the once pagan Magyars. Twelfth- and thirteenth-century charters reporting the inspection of the boundaries of landed properties (*reambulatio*) mention isolated burial places.[35] These Hungarians converted superficially to Christianity

---

garians], in *A magyar történelem korai századaiból*, ed. by Ferenc Glatz (Budapest, 1994), pp. 52–56; Györffy, *István király*, pp. 72–73; Mező, *A templomcím*, pp. 75–76.

[34] Compare Hans Erich Feine, *Kirchliche Rechtgeschichte* (Weimar, 1972), pp. 160–72; Mezey, *Deákság és Európa*, pp. 95–96. See also László Koszta's essay in *Korai Magyar Történeti Lexikon, 9–14. század*, [Lexicon of Early Hungarian History: 9th–14th Centuries], ed. by Gyula Kristó, Pál Engel, and Ferenc Makk (Budapest, 1994), p. 422.

[35] Gyula Kristó, 'Sírhelyekre vonatkozó adatok korai okleveleinkben' [Data Concerning Burial Places in Early Charters], *Acta Universitatis Szegediensis. Acta Historica*, 71 (1981), 23, 25; Gyula Kristó, 'Vallási türelem az Árpád-kori Magyarországon' [Religious Tolerance in Hungary in the Árpád Age], in *La civiltà ungherese e il cristianesimo*, ed. by József Jankovics,

but they were still reluctant to be buried in the cemetery next to/around the church of the settlement.

(6) Nonetheless, a remarkable type of donation is to be found in the charters, namely, the *donatio pro remedio animae facta*. The donator gave the Church a gift in return for his (sometimes, for her) spiritual salvation, that is, for the feast of the commemoration of their death. The endeavour of great families as patrons of churches and clan-monasteries yielded a particular social layer in the eleventh-century Hungarian kingdom, the group of ecclesiastical serfs: the *exsequiales* (Hungarian: *torlók, dusnokok*), who were obliged to render special services to the Church. They were to provide the financial basis of the funeral feasts for the anniversary of their former lords, the patrons of their churches. They appeared in the charters as early as 1067, and the first disposition concerning them was issued in 1092.[36] Somewhat similar social groups are to be found both in Western and Central Europe; however, the Hungarian case differed in terms of the legal status involved and its consequences. It cannot be excluded that the convertors used the pattern of the Frankish category of *cerocensualis* in promoting the establishment of a similar Hungarian (semi-servile) group, but the local social basis for this was fundamentally different. On the other hand, the Bohemian *animatores* (Bohemian: *dusniki*) probably also followed the same pattern, and the Hungarian name for the same group was derived from the Bohemian denotation. However, some historians have argued that there was no direct relation between their emergence.[37]

(7) Last but not least, one can, by chance, find charters speaking of the actual conditions of the early ecclesiastical hierarchy or the density of parish churches in a way reflecting the spread of Christianity and pastoral care in a given area or country. This, for example, is the case with two Hungarian charters from 1009. One of them is the interpolated foundation charter of the Pécs bishopric,[38] which puts the boundaries of the bishopric in writing; while its pair describes the belongings of the Veszprém bishopric.[39] The significance of these privileges is that we are not only informed about the state or development of these bishoprics but about the neighbouring Church organization as well. Hungarian scholars have deduced many important and far-reaching statements from these documents, trying to fill in the enormous white spots in the picture of the eleventh century drawn on the basis of the written materials.

István Monok, and Judit Nyerges, 3 vols (Budapest, 1998), II, 486–87.

[36] See the foundation charter of Százd monastery (1067), *Diplomata Hungariae Antiquissima*, I, 182–85; the decrees of the Szabolcs Synod, c. 1092, *Decreta Regni Medievalis Hungariae*, I, 55–61.

[37] Compare László Solymosi, 'Hozott-e Szt. István törvényt a torlókról?' [Did St Stephen Decree on the Exsequiales?], in *Doctor et apostol: Szent István-tanulmányok*, ed. József Török (Budapest, 1994), pp. 229–73.

[38] *Diplomata Hungariae Antiquissima*, I, 54–58.

[39] *Diplomata Hungariae Antiquissima*, I, 49–53.

Finally, it is worth emphasising once again that all the data listed may only indicate or indirectly reflect the process and results of conversion or, rather, the spread and acceptance of Christianity. Although these elements are irreplaceable pieces of early Hungarian history, including the conversion to the Catholic faith, they are useless out of their own context or without source criticism.

Signs of Conversion in
Central European Laws

JÁNOS M. BAK

I t is surely a commonplace that legal enactments, be they royal ordinances, synodal statutes, or conciliar canons, offer evidence for intentions and programmes, in a word, for norms that are set to be observed and enforced. Naturally, the fact that written laws, statutes, or simply texts that record legal decisions exist—and the form in which they were written and transmitted—offers in itself evidence for the state of social order, for concepts of justice and conflict solution, and for more or less commonly held values. In order to learn whether these norms were actually accepted and observed, we need to look to other types of evidence. Nevertheless, it may be worth looking at some laws issued in the period of christianization, for they may offer insights into the process of conversion. They may contain evidence both for the formal introduction of values and institutions of the Catholic Church and the acceptance and gradual internalization of these values by the population. The attempt at codification of some sort is in itself a 'sign' of a given society's (people's)—or at least its elite's—intention to join the Christian world. It was the Christian part of medieval Europe that inherited from its Roman past the tradition of written law in contrast to the oral transmission of communal norms, characteristic for gentile (tribal, pagan) populations. Thus, the mere existence of written law can be taken as a 'sign of conversion'.

In Central Europe the legal documents of the Kingdom of Hungary offer the most suitable object for such a study, as no comparable collection of laws, secular or ecclesiastical, survived from the neighbouring countries that can be dated in the early decades or even centuries of christianization. Therefore, if in the following I concentrate on these, it is not local patriotism that guides me, but rather the regret that I could not find appropriate comparative material elsewhere in the region.[1]

Six 'books of law' survived in one form or another from eleventh to early twelfth-century Hungary: two of St Stephen (dated to c. 1020–38), three of St Ladislas (one of which may have been enacted or compiled before his reign, thus they should be dated as c. 1060–90) and three of King Coloman (issued between 1105 and 1116). Only one of these (Book 1 of Stephen's laws) has come down to us in a near-contemporary copy,[2] one synodal statute in a medieval liturgical codex,[3] while all the others are known only from sixteenth-century or later copies. A few of them are formally called synodal statutes, the others are formulated as emanating from the king and his council, but this distinction does not seem to be particularly relevant, as matters lay and clerical are treated in all of them without distinction.[4] In addition to these texts, I shall include a

---

[1] The so-called decree of the Czech Duke Břetislav I Přemysl (1034–55), as summarized by Cosmas of Prague (*Chronica Boemorum*, ed. by B. Bretholz, *Monumenta Germaniae Historica, Scriptores rerum Germanicarum,* new ser., 2 (1923; repr. Berlin, 1980), pp. 86–88), seems to reflect an authentic enactment of the duke and Bishop Severus, enunciated at the grave of St Adalbert. A fairly similar text was found in a thirteenth-century manuscript of the chapter of Olomouc; cf. V. Vaněček, 'Nový text (varianta) dekretů Břetislavových z r. 1039' [New Text-Variant of the Decree of B. of 1039], *Slavia Antiqua,* 3 (1951–52), 131–35. Its occasional parallels to the Hungarian laws will be noted. For Poland only the short references of Thietmar of Merseburg to legal practices under Boleslaw the Brave (*Chronicon,* ed. by W. Holtzmann and W. Trillmilch, Ausgewählte Quellen zur deutschen Geschichte des Mittelalters, 9 (Darmstadt, 1957), p. 440) are known from the early period. I had no chance to study in any detail the legislation of Kievan Rus', esp. the ecclesiastical one (e.g. *Kirchenrechtliche und kulturgeschichtliche Denkmäler Altrusslands nebst Geschichte des russischen Kirchenrechts. Pamiantniki drevnie-russkogo kanonicheskogo prava,* ed. and trans. by L. K. Goetz (Stuttgart, 1905), which, even though derivative of Byzantine codices, reflect the attempts at codifying Christian tenets in a newly converted east-central European country. The general early legislation of Kievan Rus' (such as the *Russkaia pravda*) does not seem to contain any reference to christianization, treating almost exclusively matters of what we would call criminal law.

[2] In the Codex Admont (Cod. 712), presently in the Széchényi National Library, Budapest, Clmae 433, from the twelfth century.

[3] In the Codex Pray, presently in the Széchényi National Library, Budapest, Nyelvemlékek, MS 1 from 1192–95.

[4] For the history of the 'legislation' under the early Árpádian kings, see the preface in *The Laws of the Medieval Kingdom of Hungary. Decreta regni mediaevalis Hungariae,* 2 vols, ed. by J. M. Bak, G. Bónis, J. R. Sweeney, and L. S. Domonkos, 2nd edn (Idyllwild, CA, 1999) (henceforth *DRMH*), I, xxvi–lix. There the dating of the laws is also discussed with relevant bibliography (e.g. pp. 83, 88, 123; page numbers of the 2nd edition are in some cases off by one or two pages from the first, faulty, edition). The posthumously published fine study of M. Jánosi,

charter containing something of a contract between the king of Hungary and a number of recently settled and baptized Cuman leaders of 1279. This document—sometimes called the Cuman Law—refers to the early stage of christianization of these nomads, even though it originates in a later century.[5]

I intend to briefly survey these enactments for evidence on the form and content of enunciating and enforcing basic Christian tenets from devotion to the religion to the observance of its moral and liturgical prescriptions; the modes of establishing an 'infrastructure' for the Christian Church and ordering its upkeep; handling the problem of pagan remnants, feigned conversion, and apostasy; and the reception of certain Christian propositions in the light of legal and administrative measures implicitly built upon such a 'conversion'.[6]

The very first paragraph of Stephen, 1 enunciates the preeminence of matters clerical, buildings and persons alike, but it was borrowed verbatim from the synod of Mainz 847, and may have been added to the laws a generation later. But paragraph 13—the ascription of which to the founding king is not being questioned—entrusts the chastisement of those who neglect Christian observance to the bishops to be judged according to canon law, thus making trespass against the new values a punishable offense. What this 'Christian observance' entails is detailed in paragraphs 9–12: no work but attendance of service on Sunday,[7] keeping the fast on the Ember Days and Friday,[8] and the obligation of the family or the lord of the deceased to call a priest to the dying.[9] Essentially the same basic commands are contained in canon 25 of the Synod of Szabolcs at the end of the eleventh century.[10] Moreover, there is extensive discussion

---

Törvényalkotás a korai Árpád-korban [Law Making in the Early Árpád-Age] (Szeged, 1996) on the details of textual transmission of the laws remained, alas, fragmentary.

[5] *DRMH*, I, 67–70.

[6] These aspects, which could be called more or less 'direct' signs of conversion, could be augmented by a number of issues that belong to the project of changing pagan (gentile) cultural habits, above all, rules of marriage, adultery, and so on. As is well known, these issues played an important part in establishing a Christian society, as witnessed in both the famous letter of Pope Gregory to Archbishop Augustine of Canterbury or the letter of Pope Nicholas to Tsar Boris of the Bulgarians. A discussion of these aspects would need a much wider-cast net—and more space than this short report.

[7] Compare Cosmas, *Chronica*, pp. 87f., where the confiscation of the tools of the Sunday-worker is prescribed, just as in Stephen, 1, 8 (*DRMH*, I, 3).

[8] Transgressions against rules of fast were punished in a peculiar way (if one can trust Thietmar) in Poland: the culprit's teeth were broken out; cf. *Chronicon*, p. 440; however, it is unclear, whether this had been prescribed by an edict of the ruler or was an indigenous practice of the people, maybe transferred from some similar pagan practice. No specific punishment or penance is prescribed in the Hungarian laws.

[9] Stephen, 1, 12; *DRMH*, I, 4–5.

[10] *DRMH*, I, 57.

about those who mutter and chatter (*murmurant vel locuntur*) during Mass (Stephen, 1, 19).[11] That some other trespasses may also endanger the salvation of the soul is implied in some paragraphs, such as the one about the warrior who 'with disregard to his soul' kills his wife (for which he has both to pay composition (*wergeld*) and do penance, Stephen, 1, 15), or about those who enslave freemen in spite of 'it [being] worthy of God' that everyone live in liberty.[12] In several other cases (in some other types of homicide, and so on) the traditional (gentile?) legislation about retribution, which is in no way specifically 'Christian', was augmented by the aspect of sin, for which ecclesiastical punishment, penance, usually a fast, was to be meted out. In these passages the new religion was intended to strengthen attempts at keeping the peace and avoiding blood feuds.

A special aspect of 'religious' legislation—if this is the right word—refers to witches and sorcerers. It has often been argued that the Christian prosecution of the *strigae* and *malefices* (as in Stephen, 1, 33–34)[13] was in fact aimed at priests or priestesses or other cultural representatives (shamans, medicine-men) of pre-Christian beliefs or even pagan religion. This may have been implied, but the text does not hint at it. There is no reference whatsoever to these persons being connected to paganism. The punishments are mainly aimed at 'marking them out' so that they cannot do incantations and other harmful deeds—the efficacy of which is not questioned.[14] The witch is to be instructed in the faith and punished in the church by flagellation for the first offense, by branding for the second offense, and by 'being handed over to the judge' (I presume, secular justice) for the third. King Coloman, however, followed another tradition in this matter, namely—if we may say so—the more Christian one, when he declared that *de strigiis que non sunt nulla questio fiat*. This passage was for a long time seen as a proof of enlightened modernity on the part of the learned king; in fact, it belongs to that type of anti-witch legislation which denies the existence of the form-changing creatures or vampires, strictly according to Christian belief (with parallels in Lombard and other laws). Maybe this law could be seen as implementing a Christian attitude, in which supernatural qualities and feats are associated only with God and his saints and thaumaturges. That is why the king refuses to have cases of *strigae* handled in his courts.[15]

---

[11] *DRMH*, I, 5.

[12] *DRMH*, I, 4 and Stephen 1, 22; *DRMH*, I, 6.

[13] *DRMH*, I, 7–8.

[14] In can. 34 of the Synod of Szabolcs (*DRMH*, I, 58) witches (*strigae*) are mentioned together with whores (*meretrices*)—both to be punished by the bishop at his discretion—thus seen as immoral persons, but hardly as pagans or particularly dangerous.

[15] See our discussion of Coloman, 57 (*DRMH*, I, 29 with n. 48 on p. 92); cf. also J. B. Russell, *Witchcraft in the Middle Ages* (Ithaca, NY, 1972,) p. 97, who sees in the canon a 'reversal of policies', but seems to have overlooked the problems in the meaning of the word *striga*, as sorcerers, *malefici*, are to be punished by secular and clerical justice according to the

The establishment of an ecclesiastical infrastructure started with the foundation of the bishoprics by St Stephen, for which little written evidence survives, none in the laws.[16] The parish system, however, was decreed by the founder-king. In Stephen, 2, 1 the king prescribed that every group of ten villages should build a church which he will supply with vessels and the bishops with books.[17] In the late eleventh century several decisions were taken in order to bind the village to its church. The Synod of Szabolcs (canon 19) prescribed that villagers shall 'not abandon their church and wander away'.[18] True, the same synod acknowledged the possibility that a village is too far from the church (which is likely if ten settlements were members of one parish!) and allowed that in this case one person should come to service 'on behalf of all' and bring offerings to the altar (canon 11).[19] Another command in the same direction is that the dead be buried in the churchyard.[20] This obligation rests on the family, the lord of a servile person, and

---

same law. The punishment of sorcery 'according to the canons' is (repeated?—depending on the date of the synod) also in Synodus Strigoniensis, can. 49 (*DRMH*, I, 63).

[16] See G. Györffy, 'Zu den Anfängen der ungarischen Kirchenorgansiation auf Grund neuer quellenkritischer Ergebnisse', *Archivum Historiae Pontificiae*, 7 (1969), 79–113.

[17] *DRMH*, I, 9. Unfortunately, none of these *Urpfarren* left any archaeological or documentary evidence: the wooden churches were either replaced by stone buildings as the communities grew or the Mongol invasion of 1241 destroyed them. A century later the Synodus Strigoniensis (can. 17) repeated that no church be consecrated unless properly endowed (ibid., I, 63), which may have something to do with the problem of 'proprietary churches', an issue too complicated to be discussed here.

[18] *DRMH*, I, 56, repeated in Synodus Strigoniensis, can. 85 (ibid., I, 65), there with a fine of ten gold *solidi* and the obligation to return. The exact meaning of this paragraph is highly debated. Some read it as evidence for nomadic (or at least semi-nomadic) lifestyle of eleventh and twelfth-century Hungarians, some rather as that for a kind of primitive slash-and-burn agriculture, in which 'villages' moved to fields farther afield, once the ones near the settlement were exhausted. It is also possible that the measure refers to limited transhumance to summer pasture from winter quarters. Whichever the case may be, the aim of the canon is to reduce nomadism of any sort.

[19] *DRMH*, I, 55.

[20] Synod of Szabolcs, can. 25 (*DRMH*, I, 57). However, the matter of Christian vs. pre-Christian cemeteries is not a simple one. The 'old' view that all serial graves are pagan while all graves around churches are Christian, cannot be proven from archaeology; see J. Laszlovszky, 'Social Stratification and Material Culture in 10th–14th-Century Hungary', in *Alltag und materielle Kultur im mittelalterlichen Ungarn*, ed. by A. Kubinyi and J. Laszlovszky, Medium Aevum Quotidianum, 22 (Krems, 1991), pp. 32–68. Moreover, according to the *Vita S. Gerhardi* (*Legenda S. Gerhardi episcopi. Legenda maior,* cap. 11, ed. by E. [I.] Madzsar in E. [I.] Szentpétery, *Scriptores rerum Hungaricarum tempore ducum regumque stirpis Arpadianae gestarum,* 2 vols (Budapest, 1938), II, 495) the missionary bishop sent out his canons to 'Christianise' existing cemeteries and have churches built next to them, thus 'ex post' baptising non-Christian burial sites.

on the reeve (*villicus*) with regard to the poor. It belongs to the enforcement of Christian duties in general and has its parallels in the Bohemian legal tradition.[21] However, I believe, it may also have been issued in order to bind the people to their church, taking into account the communities' age-old tradition in which the living were anxious to stay close to their dead. In a semi-pastoral society this was a significant step towards settlement, and settlement seems to have implied christianization, or vice versa—as we shall see in the example of the Cumans.

The most significant issue for the upkeep of the new religion's institutions was, of course, the command to pay the tithe. In a few words, with Biblical overtones, this was commanded by St Stephen (2, 20) with a punishment of those who 'steal' the bishop's tithe.[22] It is interesting that canon 40 of the Synod of Szabolcs (if the rubrics are authentic) is entitled 'Those who refuse the tithe', which may point to resistance against ecclesiastical taxation, probably during the so-called pagan uprisings in the 1040s. The canon actually regulates in quite some detail the mode of tithing based on the oath of the 'owner of the grain', which, if challenged, had to be verified by royal and episcopal officials. Those not willing to render the tithe are also mentioned as to be punished by ecclesiastical censure. This enactment, referred to as 'the institution of the holy kings', was cited for centuries as the basic regulation for tithing (which is also an implicit proof of the authenticity of this, otherwise poorly authenticated, text).

Obviously on the insistence of the clergy, the early laws contain measures about grants to churches. We do not know how old that Hungarian inheritance custom was which regarded landed property as belonging to the entire clan and thus inherited by its male members as long as there was one. The right of any landowner to make pious donations to churches from his property may have contradicted this custom, but was enacted repeatedly and, indeed, practised by the great families as far back as we have records of it.[23] The origin of the so-called clan-monasteries as cultic and burial centres of early medieval noble families is a debated issue as one of those connected with the assumed transformation of gentile sanctity into Christian religiosity. But founded they were from early on, and well endowed by aristocrats, following the king's example.

There are very few references in the surviving Hungarian corpus of laws to the survival of paganism, and they are rather general. One synodal statute from 1092 sets the punishment for 'making sacrifices next to wells or giving offering to trees, fountains and stones according to heathen rites'—a trespass which was mentioned in laws and

---

[21] According to Cosmas, *Chronica*, p. 88, the duke and bishop prohibited burial 'in fields and woods' and ordered, besides heavy fines, re-burial in Christian ground. This measure may have aimed at actual pagan practices of burial in non-Christian sacred places and was perhaps not merely an attempt at connecting the community to its church.

[22] *DRMH*, I, 11.

[23] From Stephen, 1, 6 (*DRMH*, I, 3) to the Synod of Szabolcs, can. 5 (ibid., 1, 55). However, the latter contains sanctions about unfulfilled pledges to churches, perhaps suggesting resistence on the part of the families to hand over land bequeath by deceased members.

penitentials everywhere in Christendom—at one ox. (In earlier laws a young ox, *iuvencus*, is equalled to one golden Byzantine coin. Since for beating a man who is trying to recover a fugitive slave the culprit has to render ten steers, this does not seem to have been a very high fine.) A decade or so later, another synod differentiates between the young and the old 'celebrating anything taken from heathen rites': the former do forty days penance, the latter only seven days with flogging.[24] No detailed measure against heathen rites can be found in the fairly extensive royal legislation beyond these generalities.

There is, however, much more about Muslims who accepted Christianity— probably under some kind of pressure—but who may have secretly adhered to their ancestral religion. The laws of King Ladislas and Coloman deal in several paragraphs with the control of the conversion of people called Ishmaelites and aim at their assimilation.[25] According to these, the converted Muslims had to stop circumcision, marry Christian girls, abandon their habits of fast and ablutions, and eat only pork whenever they received guests.[26] Trespassers were to be denounced to the bishop. As far as we can ascertain, these measures were successful, for Muslim travellers in Hungary noted in the twelfth century that they met former co-religionists who had forgotten Arabic and the teachings of Islam.[27] Somewhat similar is the law about the Cumans who settled in Hungary in the 1250s, having been expelled from their steppe homeland by the advancing Mongols. Apparently, the presence of an at least partly pagan population—that seems to have held Christians captive—caused concern to the Church, and a papal legate intervened in settling the disputes between them and their Christian neighbours. In a royal decree, which was in fact an agreement between Cuman leaders and King Ladislas IV (whose mother was a Cuman princess), the newcomers had to promise to allow that those not yet baptized be converted to the Catholic faith and observe all the teachings of the Roman church. We are told that the preaching of

---

[24] Synod of Szabolcs, can. 22 (*DRMH*, I, 56) and Synodus Strigoniensis (c. 1105–16), can. 7 (ibid., 60). The Latin text is equivocal: the two kinds of punishments may refer to major and minor pagan practices or older and younger trespassers. It is interesting, however, that can. 8 (ibid.) punishes the person (implicitly: priest) who does not celebrate the prescribed feasts, with the same punishment, equating thus commission with omission.

[25] It should be noted that no similar laws were passed about Jews. The legislation of Coloman and his predecessors aimed at separating them from Christians, restricting their activities while securing their right to trade, but no legal attempt is made to assimilate them; see e.g. *Capitula Colomani Regis de Iudeis, DRMH*, I, 66, with notes and lit. on p. 130.

[26] Synod of Szabolcs, can. 9; (*DRMH*, I, 55); Coloman, 46–49 (ibid., 28). The synod ordered baptized Ishmaelites who relapsed through practising circumcision, to be removed from their village, but allowed them to prove their innocence by ordeal. It is peculiar, however, that the incriminating fact was not to be established by autopsy.

[27] See S. Balić, 'Der Islam im mittelalterlichen Ungarn', *Südost-Forschungen*, 23 (1964), 10–35.

the legate moved the Cuman leaders 'thoroughly to abandon the cult of idols and all heathen rites'. In this case of mass conversion we have additional evidence that the acceptance of Christianity implied more than new religious observance, rather an entire 'way of life'. For the decree stipulates that 'in particular, from now on they [the Cumans] shall settle down and leave their tents and houses made of felt. They shall reside and remain in villages in a Christian way [more Christianorum] with buildings and houses attached to the ground. They shall conform to all Christian customs, except that of shaving their beards, cutting their hair,[28] and wearing their form of dress'.[29] These compromises were permitted graciously by the papal legate not wanting, as the record tells us, to force the newly converted to do things against their will. Adding these measures to the aforementioned prescriptions of the eleventh-century laws about binding the village to its church, we can see that in the case of nomadic or semi-nomadic peoples the change to settled, village life was part and parcel of the conversion project. I believe, this is an interesting insight, among others, into the possible causes of failure of the mission on the Eurasian steppe, where many more nomadic peoples chose to embrace Islam (or earlier, in the case of the Khasars, Judaism) than Christianity.

And finally, there are several paragraphs in the laws of the eleventh and twelfth centuries that imply the widespread acceptance of certain Christian tenets. It seems logical to assume that recourse to oaths or clergy-administered ordeals is based on the assumption that people in general believe in the eternal punishment of the perjurer in the afterworld or in the active intervention of the divine in establishing guilt. Otherwise these modes of proof would not have worked, and the 'legislator' would not have counted on their efficacy. Reference to ordeal (as iudicium legale) can be found in the law of St Stephen, and more explicitly in those of Ladislas and Coloman, where ordeal by fire and water is specified and the major ecclesiastical centres as the sole locations for its administration are defined.[30] There are several references to oath-taking and the punishment—secular as well as 'otherworldly'—of perjury. Even more indirect are those clauses in the laws, which assume actions motivated by Christian piety, such as the manumission of bondmen/women (slaves, serfs?).[31]

Unfortunately, it is not clear, what kind of gathering is meant by the word kalendas (Synod of Szabolcs, canon 14 and 39, Synodus Strigoniensis, canon 47), where,

---

[28] It is characteristic of the multisemic meaning of hairdo that among Hungarians the opposite counted as pagan custom: the chronicles record that the rebels against the new order in 1046 shaved their head as a sign of returning to paganism; Legenda S. Gerhardi, cap. 15, in Szentpétery, Scriptores rerum Hungaricum, II, 501.

[29] Charter of 10 August 1279, DRMH, I, 67–70, esp. p. 67.

[30] Stephen, 1, 22 (DRMH, I, 6); Ladislas, 2, 4 (ibid, p. 13), Coloman, 22 (ibid, p. 26), Synodus Strigoniensis, 44–45 (ibid, p. 62).

[31] Stephen, 1, 18 (DRMH, I, 5): Si quis misercordia ductus servos et ancillas libertate feriaverit. [. . .]

apparently, priests and laymen sat and drank together. These associations or confraternities, named after the date of their regular meeting, may have consisted in the early stages of clergy alone but it is more likely that they were mixed companies. If they really existed in the eleventh and twelfth centuries, this would suggest that certain forms of 'social life' were connected to the church as early as that.[32]

Lastly, a few measures, introduced in the course of the—admittedly limited and belated—reception of Gregorian reform in the Hungarian church, hint at the possibility that people in the eleventh and twelfth centuries found it efficacious to obtain access to Christian rituals for their own (or their relatives') sake. The prohibitions of 'making deals with the mass in return for a gift' or of 'selling the feasts' (Synodus Strigoniensis, can. 40, 43, 86)[33] suggest that there were laymen who wished to use ecclesiastical rites for the salvation of their souls, above and beyond the legitimate request for prayer for the dead or similar liturgical events. The prohibition would not have made sense, had those 'buying feasts' not found it important to gain personal access to the sacred power of the church. It offers, thus, implicit proof of their belief in Christian ritual.

All in all, the laws, even if offering only normative evidence, do hint at some important aspects of christianization in the region. The limited set of demands on the newly converted, the close connection between lifestyle (sedentarization) and conversion, and the few references to the implicit acceptance of Christian values during the first century of Christian mission can be established from them, beyond the many pious wishes of the legislators and their clerical advisors. Whether ladykillers ([. . .] *qui uxores occidunt*, Stephen, 1, 15)[34] would have perceived the murder of their wives as 'neglecting their salvation' (as the law formulates) or warrior lords respected the fact that the priests whom they hired to celebrate the necessary rituals for their families and peasants 'work more than any one of you' (Stephen, 1, 5)[35] we know not. But that many a powerful family founded monasteries on the king's prodding and these grants were

---

[32] *DRMH*, I, 56, 58, 62. In most cases the proper behaviour at these banquets is stipulated for the clergy; but can. 14 of the Synod of Szabolcs implies that priests and other 'brethren' constituted the association, for if someone was absent, he had to excuse himself from *presbiteri sui et fratrum*. Writing about such early guilds, S. Reynolds (*Kingdoms and Communities in Western Europe 900–1200*, 2nd edn (Oxford, 1997), pp. 67–73) suggests that their 'main activity' was drinking, which may be a slight overstatement. Little is known about these 'Kalends' in Hungary—or, for that matter, elsewhere (see E. Hoffmann, 'Kaland', in *Lexikon des Mittelalters*, V, 864–65)—before the fourteenth and fifteenth centuries, but see now A. Kubinyi, 'Vallásos társulatok a későközépkori magyarországi városokban' [Religious Fraternities in Late Medieval Towns of Hungary], in idem, *Főpapok, egyházi intézmények és vallásosság a középkori Magyarországon* [Prelates, Ecclesiastical Institutions and Religiosity in Medieval Hungary], (Budapest, 1999), pp. 341–52.

[33] *DRMH*, I, 62 and 65.

[34] *DRMH*, I, 4.

[35] *DRMH*, I, 3.

protected by law, that the prohibition of ritual ablutions forced Muslims to become Christians, and that by c. 1200 people wished to protect themselves from evil not only by traditional charms and amulets, but also by 'buying a mass', suggest that the project had considerable success. Thus, even these clerically inspired texts of the elite, these announcements of intent, do contain signs of the progress of conversion, and not merely of its institutional aspect.

Signs of Conversion
in *Vitae sanctorum*

ANNA KUZNETSOVA

T he purpose of this paper is to explore what kind of information we can gain from missionary saints' *Lives* for the history of christianization. In the last decades conversion histories of all genres and types have attracted much scholarly attention. I have decided to profit from this fact by quoting others rather than wasting time in reinventing the wheel. Birgit Sawyer, who wrote about Scandinavian conversion, considered (inter alia) that the saints' *Lives* among her sources were 'works of propaganda that tell us far more about the intentions and claims of their creators than about the course of events as experienced by others'.[1] Although she makes this statement in a more general context, this is also true for missionary hagiography in particular: the *Vitae* aimed at glorifying what the missionaries did, and at inspiring their disciples to accomplish what they did not. The *Vitae* were thus tools in the building of political and educational programmes.

To continue with generalities: hagiography as a genre is in itself a sign of conversion. Laws, histories, and epistles are known in the non-Christian world as well,

I am grateful to participants in the session at Leeds, in particular to its moderator Ian Wood and my senior colleague János Bak, for their comments and suggestions, some of which I was able to incorporate in this article.

[1] Birgit Sawyer, 'Scandinavian Conversion Histories', in *The Christianisation of Scandinavia: Report of a Symposium Held at Kungälv, Sweden, 4–9 August 1985,* ed. Birgit Sawyer, Peter Sawyer, and Ian Wood (Alingsås, 1987), p. 108.

but saints' *Lives* appeared only with Christendom.[2] In fact, the appearance of certain types of *Vitae* may be a sign of conversion—in the sense of Christianity having been accepted as the people's religion. For example, in medieval Russia during the first period of Christianity, hagiography consisted of *Lives* of rulers and princes and founders of monasteries. *Lives* of Holy Fools, protectors of the common believers and in a way representatives of popular belief, appeared only later. It would be interesting to elaborate how the different types of *Vitae*—not only those of missionaries, but also of early martyrs, rulers, and monks, whether closer to or further from the actual events of christianization—reflect this process.

However, in order not to overgeneralize about hagiography as a source for conversion, I have selected four *Vitae* of saint-missionaries who were active in Central and Eastern Europe.[3] The first two are the *Lives* of Cyril, otherwise known to us as Constantine, the inventor of the Slavic alphabet, and of Methodius, his brother and assistant, who after Constantine/Cyril's death became archbishop of Moravia. Both brothers are known as the teachers of the Slavs, whose missionary activity took place in the mid-ninth century in the principality of Moravia. Their *Vitae* were written in the late ninth century in Old Church Slavonic.[4]

My third source is the *Legenda maior* of Gerhard, missionary in Hungary and bishop of Marosvár (d. 1046). There are two *Vitae* of this saint: the *Legenda minor* and the *Legenda maior*, both written in Latin. Both of these have caused extensive debates, primarily over the time of their composition, but the present consensus leans towards placing the *Legenda minor* in the eleventh to twelfth centuries. As for the *Legenda maior*, the majority of scholars consider it a fourteenth-century compilation, although some are of the opinion that it too was written in the twelfth century.[5]

My fourth *Vita* is that of Stephen of Perm, written soon after his death, at the end of the fourteenth or the beginning of the fifteenth century in Russia. It was written by Epiphanius the Most Wise, who was also known for his *Vita* of Sergij of Radonezh and

---

[2] Here I consider only Christian *Vitae*, though genres similar to hagiography existed in other religions as well (eg. Buddhism and Islam).

[3] Some of the saints I am dealing with in this essay (Sts Cyril and Methodius, St Gerhard) were active among the people who had already formally converted to Christianity. Yet, I consider the use of the term 'missionary' as being appropriate in the present context since those saints still had to teach Christian norms to the newly converted and fight many of the old beliefs that had survived among them.

[4] There are several editions and translations of these *Vitae*. The most accessible English translation I am using here is *The Vita of Constantine and the Vita of Methodius*, trans. with commentaries by M. Kantor and R. S. White, introd. by A. Dostal (Ann Arbor, 1976). In the following, I refer to these texts by chapter.

[5] *Legenda S. Gerhardi episcopi*, in *Scriptores rerum Hungaricarum tempore ducum regumque stirpis Arpadianae gestarum*, ed. by Emericus [Imre] Szentpétery, 2 vols (Budapest, 1938–39), II, 464–506. In the following I shall refer to the *Legenda maior* by chapter.

other works. Stephen of Perm is one of the best known missionary saints of Russia; he christianized the pagan Zyrians, now called the Komi, and translated the liturgy and the gospel into their vernacular.[6]

All four *Vitae* are those of missionary saints, and report on the efforts of their heroes to christianize pagans or, in case of St Cyril, even Muslims and Jews. However, the reliability of these sources is a highly debatable issue. In the first place doubts are raised by the very character of the missionary *Vita*: it is in a way a sermon that aims at glorifying the missionary saint, educating the flock and strengthening Christian belief among the converted. Thus these *Lives* are more programmes for conversion, or panegyrics of the saint-missionary, than true and authentic pictures of conversion.

The least trustworthy data from the *Vitae* are their numbers. The results of missionary activity, as reflected in the *Vitae*, are sometimes presented in terms of exact numbers of converted people. But this is merely an attempt to make the information offered look authentic. The most effective method of demonstrating the success of a missionary was to show how the number of those he converted grew. In a way this follows the method of the *Acts of the Apostles,* where we are given the exact numbers of the enlarging Christian community; the first meeting is recorded as having numbered 120 people (Acts 1. 16), later about 3000 were converted (Acts 2. 41), and, finally, almost the whole city had gathered to listen to the apostles' preaching (Acts 13. 44). A similar pattern can be observed in the *Vita* of Stephen of Perm as well as in that of Gerhard. At first, Stephen of Perm is surrounded by a very few followers; only after time, when the missionary demonstrates the advantages of his religion does their number grow.[7] Thirty freshly converted men are the first to bring their sons to St Gerhard to be taught by him (Chapter 10); on the feast-day of St John the Baptist, however, one hundred people came to listen to his sermon (Chapter 10). The *Vita Constantini* gives us a precise number of converted Khazars: two hundred (Chapter 11).[8]

Because of their desire to present the missionary saint in the most advantageous light, hagiographers frequently introduce disputations between their heroes and non-Christians. These disputations took different forms. In the *Vita Constantini* there are extensive discussions between Constantine on the one hand and Muslims and Jews on

---

[6] There is a recent edition of this *Vita: Svjatitel' Stefan Permskij. K 600-letiju so dnja prestavlenija* [St Stephen of Perm. On the 600th anniversary of his assumption], ed. by Gelian M. Proxorov (St Petersburg, 1995). Here, as elsewhere when possible, I use the summary and partial translation of the *Vita* into English in George Fedotov, *The Russian Religious Mind*, 2 vols (Cambridge, MA, 1966), II, 230–45.

[7] Fedotov, *The Russian Religious Mind*, II, 236–37.

[8] However, as it has been argued, this number could have been used in the *Vita* due to its special symbolic meaning. Vladimír Vavřínek, 'Staroslověnské Životy Konstantina a Metoděje' [Old Slavonic *Lives* of Constantine and Methodius], in *Rozpravy Československé Akademie Věd, Řada společenských věd,* 73.7 (1963), 61.

the other, on such subjects as the Trinity, the veneration of icons, and circumcision (Chapters 6–11). This is a dialogue in which both parties are matched, being representatives of sophisticated religions with their own holy books as their foundations.

However, another type of a dialogue is that between the missionary and the pagan shaman called Pam in the *Vita* of Stephen of Perm.[9] We are informed by the hagiographer that Pam and St Stephen 'were arguing day and night'. An important part of the competition is Pam's formulation of three major arguments against Christianity. The first is that the numerous pagan gods are patrons of different types of hunting, which makes the Zyrians very successful at collecting the furs of many different animals, which then can be sold to Constantinople, Germany, and Lithuania. The second of Pam's arguments is that his traditional faith helps the bear hunter: the shaman maintains that as few as one or two Zyrian men can kill a bear, while hundreds of Christians could not hunt down even one. Finally, Pam appears to refer to clairvoyance among shamans: he argues that the Zyrian faith is better because news is rapidly disseminated, and that 'whatever happens in a far-off country, in a foreign town—the complete news of it reaches us at the same hour. And you, Christians, cannot learn it'. These three arguments give us a hint of what pagans considered to be the main strengths of their religion. On the other hand, one can argue that, as we are dealing with the Christian author of a Christian *Vita*, these three tenets could be seen rather as the Christian perception of the heathen Zyrian faith. What gives the reader more confidence in the hagiographer's knowledge of paganism is the description of the 'practical' part of the disputation between Pam and Stephen. Stephan proposes that Pam agree to an ordeal by fire and water, to pass through a burning hut and to throw himself into an opening in the ice on the Vichegda river.[10] Such trials by fire and water are well known in challenges between shamans, and Stephen of Perm seems to have been aware of that. He knew exactly what would convince the heathens of Christian superiority. At first Pam agrees but then loses his courage, and when Stephen drags him by the hand into the fire, he acknowledges his defeat. He is convinced that the Christian had learned from childhood how to conjure fire and water, whereas he, Pam, does not possess this gift.[11] The people demand Pam's death according to their custom, but the saint rescues him. He condemns Pam to exile and forbids the shaman to eat and drink with the newly converted Christians.

---

[9] For the following, see Fedotov, *The Russian Religious Mind*, II, 238–40.

[10] Ephanius does not clearly tell us who was the initiator of this ordeal. Although later Stephen asked Pam why he proposed what he could not accomplish, it was Stephen himself who had a burning hut prepared for passing through and who had an opening made in the ice on the Vychegda river to jump into. See Proxorov, *Svjatitel'*, pp. 148–53.

[11] It may be that what the shaman meant by considering Stephan to be experienced in passing through a burning hut and jumping into an opening in the ice was that Russians have a special way of washing themselves in a hot steam-bath and then cooling off in a cold river even in winter.

In the *Legenda maior* of St Gerhard (Chapter 10) we come across another interesting example of missionary methods. On the day of St John the Baptist some one hundred people came to listen to Gerhard's sermon. The saint was moved by so much interest in his preaching, and he immediately ordered a big banquet for his audience. After the feast the guests left Bishop Gerhard extensive presents: horses, cattle, sheep, carpets, and women's golden rings. 'Why do you do that?', asked the surprised bishop, 'do you think you are obliged to bring me presents in return for my invitation?' 'No', was the answer. 'But you preached to us about giving alms, alms that extinguish sins'. This gesture of the people reciprocating Gerhard's invitation by bringing presents may have had its roots in the gentile custom of gift exchange. What the *Vita* seems to teach in this passage is the (purportedly successful) reinterpretation of pre-Christian traditions within the Christian system of values. This story can be seen as both a sign of missionary practice and a didactic example.

One of the most important aspects of missionary activity appears in all four *Vitae*: the use of the vernacular language in the process of christianization. All four *Vitae* present their saints as concerned with this issue. All four saints used it differently and all four were successful. Hagiographers emphasise that the missionaries' ability to address people in their own language was one of the main reasons for their success—yet the degree of importance of this ability is seen differently in the four *Vitae*. The *Vitae* of Constantine, Methodius, and Stephen of Perm tell us that the saints not only knew the vernacular of those to whom they came with their mission but even invented alphabets (Slavic and Zyrian) for their converts. The legends of St Gerhard admit that the holy bishop did not know Hungarian himself and used interpreters in his activities, but he nevertheless encouraged the use of that language among his disciples. His *Legenda maior* (Chapter 9) tells us that out of ten monks Gerhard selected the seven who knew Hungarian to be archdeacons and even lists their names. Whereas St Gerhard was content to use the Latin liturgy and the Vulgate for his purposes, St Cyril with the help of his brother Methodius translated Holy Scripture and the liturgy into Slavonic. St Stephen of Perm did the same for the Zyrians. However, Epiphanius, the author of St Stephen's *Vita*, does not pay as much attention to this as the hagiographer or hagiographers of *Vita Constantini* and *Vita Methodii*. Whereas the most important factor in Stephen's victory over the heathen Zyrians was his ability to demonstrate spiritual power over the shaman, the *Vita Constantini* and the *Vita Methodii* emphasise that the strength of the Cyrillo-Methodian mission was that both missionaries knew Slavonic. We know from contemporary sources that one of the problems associated with the activity of the two Thessalonian brothers was that they were conducting their mission in areas that belonged to the missionary field of Salzburg, Passau, and Regensburg and, moreover, the Moravians had been already christianized. The Cyrillo-Methodian *Vitae* attempted to explain why Cyril and Methodius were needed in Moravia and why they were so successful among the Slavs there. So hagiography, as we can observe in this case, sometimes reveals a hint of a debate or competition regarding conversion.

One very important missionary method, also known to us from sources other than *Vitae* (for example from the *Chronicle* of Helmold of Bosau) was aimed at proving that the Christian god was far more helpful in military operations than pagan deities were. It is reflected in the *Vita Methodii* (Chapter 11) where the recently christianized Moravian prince Svatopluk fought pagans without any success close to St Peter's Day. Methodius addresses him saying that if he and his men spent the feast of St Peter in church, then Svatopluk would be victorious. And so it happened, the hagiographer tells us. This story could serve as a didactic example, intended to teach rulers both Christian discipline and church attendance.

If we want to know what pagan practice was in the areas of missionary activity of the saints we will not find much on this topic in the *Vitae*. Hagiographers are mainly interested in describing such pagan practices when their missionary has to fight them. Thus there do exist certain descriptions of objects and customs relating to pagan rites. However they are not very elaborate. So St Stephen's *Vita* portrays the saint smashing the head of an idol without giving any more detail about the object itself. Similarly, the destruction of pagan shrines was a practical proof of the weakness of the heathen gods. In the majority of cases, however, it is enough for the hagiographer merely to report their destruction or, vice versa, to inform us that they were re-erected during pagan uprisings. In the *Vita* of St Stephen of Perm, however, we meet with a more elaborate description of pagan shrines, which was included on purpose by his hagiographer. Epiphanius wished to stress the simplicity and primitiveness of pagan shrines in contrast to the beauty of Christian churches in order to show another advantage that conversion would bring. Zyrian pagan shrines were simple huts hung with precious furs as offerings to the gods. When Stephen built Christian churches, the Zyrians were as impressed as the envoys of Prince Vladimir had once been with Hagia Sophia in Constantinople.[12]

One of the clearest descriptions of what was considered to be pagan behaviour is contained in the *Vita Gerhardi* (Chapter 15, probably taken from a chronicle).[13] The chapter describes the pagan uprising lead by Vata in 1046 and refers to those pagan customs which the rebel re-instituted: Vata shaved his head, his people started to eat horse-meat,[14] killed priests, destroyed churches, and began to venerate idols again. The hagiographer's detailed description of what was supposed to be pagan may have been seen as useful for readers who were no longer contemporary to the christianization

---

[12] Fedotov, *The Russian Religious Mind*, II, 236.

[13] Compare *Chronici Hungarici comp. saec. XIV,* cap. 80, in Szentpétery, *Scriptores,* I, 336.

[14] A connection between non-Christian behaviour and the eating of certain kinds of food can be traced in some other narratives. One of the legends on St Stephen of Perm contains an interesting description of the return to paganism in the village of Gom, where its inhabitants were both venerating idols and 'eating squirrels'; see Deacon S. Otradinskij, *Svjatoj Stefan, Prosvjatitel' Zyrjan i pervyj episkop Permskij. Po povodu 500-letija so dnja ego končiny* [St Stephen, the Teacher of Zyrians and the First Bishop of Perm. To the 500th Anniversary of his Assumption] (Moscow, 1896), p. 33. For the Western material, see, e.g. Rob Meens, 'Pollution in the Early Middle Ages: The Case of the Food Regulations in Penitentials', *Early Medieval Europe*, 4.1 (1995), 3–19.

process. As mentioned before, the dating of the *Legenda maior* is highly problematic. If it was written in the fourteenth century its description of pagan practices would really be designed to inform a much later audience. However, if it was written closer to the actual events of christianization, this example may very well have had an educational purpose, giving guidance for both priests and their flock about what was permissible for Christians and what was not.

We also learn about pagan practices or rather about the aims of conversion when missionaries indicate what should not be done, or, in other words, when hagiographers are educating converts about which of their social practices should be abandoned. For example, adultery occupies one of the most prominent places amongst descriptions of non-Christian practices in both the *Vita Constantini* and *Vita Methodii*. A large part of the *Vita Constantini* is taken up with an extensive sermon against adultery, complete with biblical quotations (Chapter 15). In the *Vita Methodii* the saint prophesied a miserable end for an adulterous couple (Chapter 11). Adultery is also listed among those sins that were allegedly allowed by the missionaries previous to Cyril and Methodius. Of course, what is called adultery in the *Vitae* may very well be a reflection of different rules for endogamous and exogamous marriage, a subject of great interest and discussion throughout this period, as demonstrated by the correspondence between Augustine of Canterbury and Gregory the Great, or the *Responsa* of Pope Nicholas to the Bulgarians.

Coming back to the 'polemical' character of hagiography, there are some interesting passages in the *Vita Constantini* (Chapter 15) where the hagiographer speaks about advantages of 'his' saint in comparison with previous (Western) missionaries to Moravia. He tells us that they taught that 'underground there live people with huge heads; and all reptiles are the creation of the devil and if one kills a snake, he will be absolved of nine sins because of this. If one kills a man, let him drink from a wooden cup for three months and not touch one of glass'. Clearly, the 'missionary-competition' is presented in terms which are almost as superstitious as that between Stephen and the pagan shaman.[15] Actually, this particular passage from the *Vita* may be a sign (unique in written sources of the time) of Irish missionary activity in the lands of Moravia. The reference to 'people with huge heads, who live underground' has been connected with the theory of the antipodes and suggested to indicate the presence of disciples of St Vergil of Salzburg in Moravia.[16] This hypothesis could be also supported by the sentences about drinking from a wooden cup, which may be a reflection of Irish penitential tradition.

---

[15] As a matter of fact, there are hints at a missionary competition in St Gerhard's legends as well because there had been a Greek mission in eastern/southeastern Hungary before his arrival, but I cannot go into this issue here.

[16] J. [Ivan] Dujcev, 'Un episodio dell' attività di Constantino Filosofo in Moravia', *Ricerche slavistiche,* 3 (1954), 90; Zdenek R. Dittrich, *Christianity in Great-Moravia* (Groningen, 1962), pp. 42–45.

There are many other aspects of conversion that would be worth exploring with the help of hagiography, such as the problem of the relationship between missionaries and local rulers, or their motivation for embarking on their often dangerous mission. But these would be subjects for another paper.

I should like to conclude in the same way as I began, by quoting, this time a student of the *Vita Anskarii* who stated that this work 'cannot be plundered for facts without some attention to the author's intention'.[17] I believe that this insight should be adopted in the study of other hagiographic sources as well.

---

[17] Ian Wood, 'Christians and Pagans in Ninth-Century Scandinavia', in *Christianisation of Scandinavia*, p. 41.

Conversion in Chronicles:
The Hungarian Case

LÁSZLÓ VESZPRÉMY

Sources

S ince then, strangers, who were the equals of the Hungarians in nobility came into the country at that time, it must be asked why this should have been so, since the Hungarians would have been sufficient in number to people Pannonia. Advised by a divine oracle, Duke Geysa among others began to convert the Hungarian people to the Christian faith. And since he could not convert them by his admonitions, for they were devoted and dedicated to their pagan rites, it was necessary to subdue some of them by force of arms, and since those fought against the faith outnumbered those who adhered to it, he considered that he must make his desire known to the Christian kings and princes. They, having heard his desire, not only sent help but appeared in person, for the cruelty of the Hungarians was both hurtful and hateful to them.

The Clan of Hunt and Paznan. In those days there also came Hunt and Paznan, who in the river Goron had girded his sword upon King St Stephen in accordance with Teuton custom. Their clan bears their names without change. Duke Geysa and King St Stephen, his son who trusted to the help of these counts, and even more in God, inspired in the rebels such terror of their arms and some out of fear submitted to baptism; others were converted and accepted it of their own free will. Duke Geysa as well as his son rewarded these counts for their services with gifts of broad, rich lands to them and their heirs, as it can be seen today. Through the contraction of marriages they became in the course of time intermingled with the Hungarians. It was by their advice and with their help that a king was set up over the Hungarians, and that many Hungarian nobles who adhered to Duke Cupan and rejected baptism and the faith, were degraded into shameful servitude. He was considered the more noble and the more fit for the conduct of affairs who had been the more prompt to accept the faith of Christ.

The excerpts quoted are from the earliest extant manuscript of the Hungarian Chronicle. The Chronicle originated in the mid-eleventh century; the excerpts are taken from the fourteenth-century Chronicle Composition.[1] They assumed their present form in the thirteenth century. Even taking into account the excerpts to be cited below, the number of chapters devoted to conversion is a small proportion of the total 212 chapters. They are in striking contrast with the information, however fragmentary, of eleventh-century Hungarian history. The following picture of conversion emerges from the Hungarian Chronicle: in the decades around the year 1000, Prince Géza, and later his son King Stephen fight against the rebellious warlords, including Koppány mentioned

---

[1] The Hungarian Chronicon Composition of the fourteenth century, chs 37, 41.

Ch. 37: 'Cum ergo quidam sint hospites isto tempore nobilitate pares Hungaris, inquirendum est, quare istud esse habuit / undeque processit /, cum Hungari numero ad implendam Pannoniam suffecissent. Geycha namque dux inter alios divino premonitus oraculo convertere cepit Hungarorum gentem ad fidem Christianam. Et dum monitu illos convertere non posset paganismis ritibus deditos et intentos, oportebat quosdam armis edomare, ad quod faciendum, quia plures fuere fidei repugnantes, quam quippe adherentes, necessarium habuit desiderium suum divulgare regibus et principibus Christianis. Quo audito huiusmodi desiderio non solum iuvamen transmiserunt, sed etiam personaliter adierunt, quibus fuerat Hungarorum crudelitas nociva / plurimum / ac exosa'.

Ch. 41: 'Generatio Hunt et Paznan. Adierunt etiam istis diebus Hunt et Paznan, qui Sanctum Stephanum regem in flumine Goron gladio Theutonico more accinxerunt. Istorum namque generatio ab istis nominibus distare non videtur. Istorum itaque comitum dux Geycha fretus auxilio et sanctus rex Stephanus suus filius, et divino potius, quosdam rebelles armorum terroribus, nonnullos voluntarie converterunt ad baptismum. Quos quidem comites tam dux Geycha, quam filius suus latis et amplis hereditatibus, pro ipsorum servitiis ditavere, prout apparet nunc manifeste. Qui quidem temporis in processu Vngaris per contractus matrimoniorum sunt immixti. Istorum etiam consilio et auxilio super Hungaros rex est constitutus, pluresque nobiles Hungari duci Cupan adherentes, baptismum fidemque respuentes ad turpia servitia sunt detrusi. Illis namque in gerendis / rebus / iudicatus erat nobilior, qui fidei Christi citius adhesisset'.

For general information see György Györffy, *King Saint Stephen of Hungary* (New York, 1994); Marianne Sághy, 'La christianisation de la Hongrie', in *Gerbert l'Européen*. Actes du colloque d'Aurillac, 1996, ed. by Nicole Charbonnel and Jean-Eric Iung (Aurillac, 1997), pp. 255–62; Richard Marsina, 'Christianization of the Magyars and Hungary between the East and the West', *Studia Historica Slovaca,* 19 (1995), 37–52. The standard chronicle edition is by Sándor Domanovszky in *Scriptores rerum Hungaricarum*, ed. by Imre Szentpétery (Budapest, 1937), I, 219–505; mentioned chapters are on pp. 294–95, 297. For an English translation of the Chronicle Composition see *The Illuminated Chronicle*, ed. by Dezső Dercsényi (Budapest, 1969); László Koszta, 'L'Organisation de l'église chrétienne en Hongrie', in *Les Hongrois et l'Europe conquête et intégration*, ed. by Sándor Csernus and Klára Korompay (Paris, 1999), pp. 293–311.

in Chapter 41 (and 64) and Gyula named in Chapter 65, sticking to paganism, and in opposition to the ruler. Then, in the middle of the century (1046, 1060–61) a nationwide revolt against the Germans combined with anti-Christian sentiment (Chapters 81–84). Its force is aptly illustrated by the number of leading ecclesiastics killed in the strife, including Bishop Gerhard, who was canonized together with King Stephen.[2]

Chapters 37 and 41 include information which in part can be read in the late eleventh-century legend of King St Stephen, and in a subsequent chapter of the Chronicle (64).[3] That this was tackled several times warns that a delicate historical theme is at issue. Typically enough, in St Stephen's legend it is not Géza but his son Stephen who asks for foreign aid, and those who are sent into the country are not soldiers but priests and monks.[4] By contrast, the chronicle tradition, closer to the historical fact, says that it was Géza who required military aid for himself and his son. It also slants the accounts to please the distinguished clans of foreign origin: in this interpretation, the foundation of the kingdom and victory over the pagans must be attributed to them. These chapters aptly reveal a peculiarity of the Hungarian historical tradition. Notably, the events are discussed in two parts: in a chronological and in a personal, biographical one. In the chronological section, there is a laconic mention of the country's conversion to Christian faith, while the biographical sections are more detailed (Chapters 37, 41).

That is why Simon of Kéza, who worked between 1282 and 1285, mentions casually in his chronicle, à propos the last Hungarian raids in the late tenth century, that 'it was the last loot of the Hungarians living in paganism' (Chapter 42), and in the next chapter, Stephen, the first king of the Hungarians founds churches.[5] Simon of Kéza also relates what the cited Chapters 37 and 41 contain about the battles against the heathen in the biographical sections of prominent foreigners.

The account of missionary fights also focuses around the figures of noble foreigners who become the real heroes of these conflicts, instead of the King Stephen. This goes so far as to attribute the girding of the young king before a battle—quite anachronistically—to foreign newcomers, although it is seriously questioned by historical evidence. There is nothing of the kind documented in the German empire between 936 and 1065. A later chapter (64) of the Hungarian Chronicle, which associates the same event with another noble German incomer, Vecellin, is ignorant of the girding by Hont and Pázmány.[6]

---

[2] *Scriptores rerum Hungaricarum*, I, 336–42.

[3] *Scriptores rerum Hungaricarum*, I, 312–14; Legends of St Stephen are edited by Emma Bartoniek in *Scriptores rerum Hungaricarum*, II, 365–44.

[4] Greater Legend, *Scriptores rerum Hungaricarum*, I, 382; Hartvik's Legend, *Scriptores rerum Hungaricarum*, I, 410.

[5] Simon of Kéza's Chronicle is ed. by S. Domanovszky in *Scriptores rerum Hungaricarum*, I, 131–94. For a new edition see Simonis de Kéza, *Gesta Hungarorum*, in *The Deeds of the Hungarians*, ed. by L. Veszprémy and Frank Schaer (Budapest and New York, 1999).

[6] L. Veszprémy, 'The Girding of St Stephen' [in Hungarian], *Hadtörténelmi Közlemények*, 102 (1989), 3–13; for the German empire see Wilchelm Erben, 'Schwertleite und Ritterschlag.

Chronicles and Legends

The first Hungarian canonization, that of King Stephen and Bishop Gerhard, took place extremely early, in 1083, at the same time when the first chronicles were drafted. An intricate web of influences evolved between chronicle and legend; from that moment on, the legends were enriched with account of newer descriptions of Christian conversion, so the authentic tale of conversion became the legend. The chronicles themselves refer to that: if the reader should want to learn more, he should consult the legend.[7]

As the Christian conversion and Church organization carried out by St Stephen became the basis of the state ideology with the help of the legends by the end of the eleventh century, the historical character of the canonized king, who converted the people and founded the state gradually faded. This is most obvious in the relegation of the achievements of the king's father, Géza, into the background and in the emphasis on Stephen as the apostolic king. The legends claim that a celestial apparition prohibited Géza from laying the foundations of Christian Hungary and the Church because his hands were smeared with human blood, a point mentioned by Thietmar of Merseburg (1018).[8] According to this tradition, the bloody actions of conversion took place during the period of Géza. King Stephen had no conflict with his people over faith; he only confronted some rival noblemen whose defeat automatically ensured the victory of the faith in the country.

Heavenly apparitions, however, were not only characteristic of the legend as a genre, but could also be used to veil over the external circumstances of conversion, its international implications, and above all of the role of the German emperor who initiated the conversion. This is certainly not insignificant, because the act earned him certain rights of suzerainty over the converted area, or legitimized his dominion. This fact continued to be mentioned by political polemic literature centuries later as well.[9]

The emphasis on Stephen as the state and Church founder and apostolic king gained

---

Beiträge zu einer Rechtsgeschichte der Waffen', *Zeitschrift für historische Waffenkunde,* 8 (1918–20), 105–67.

[7] See, for example, in the Chronicle of Zagreb, ed. by Imre Szentpétery in *Scriptores rerum Hungaricarum,* I, 197–215, 207: 'Dux Geycha filius [that is Géza] Thoxon [. . .] nutu tactus divino cepit cogitare de / ritibus / paganismi destruendis et de cultu divino augmentando, / seque fecit / baptizari et tandem in sancto proposito et statu mortuus est, / prout / hec plenius in legenda beati regis Stephani eius filii sunt descripta'.

[8] Greater Legend, *Scriptores rerum Hungaricarum,* I, 379: 'Non tibi concessum est, quod meditaris, quia manus pollutas humano sanguine gestas.' Thietmar of Merseburg, VIII, 3, *Monumenta Germaniae Historica, Scriptores* (henceforth *MGH, SS*), 3: 'Huius [that is Stephen I] pater erat Deviux [that is Géza] nomine, admodum crudelis et multos ob subitum furorem suum occidens. Qui cum Christianus efficeretur ad corroborandam hanc fidem contra reluctantes subditos sevit et antiquum facinus zelo Dei exestuans abluit'.

[9] See Arnold Angenendt, *Kaiserherrschaft und Königstaufe. Kaiser, Könige und Päpste als geistliche Patrone in abendländischen Missionsgeschichte* (Berlin, 1984), pp. 313–14.

a special topicality in the Hungary of the latter half of the eleventh century, when the country was in the cross-fire of papal, Gregorian, and German imperial power interests. It was the legends of the late eleventh to the turn of the twelfth century that made the pope and contemporary Europe recognize the apostolic right of the Hungarian king. It was on the basis of these legends that the pope's acknowledgement of Stephen's achievements was requested by the Hungarian kings, and that later Pope Innocent III approved as canonical the Legend of St Stephen by Hartvik, after the omission of certain passages most offensive to the papacy.[10]

Legend writers usually relied on the Hungarian Chronicle; when one comes across some philological correspondence, it is usually the chronicle that preserves the earlier or better reading, since legends were more directly exposed to daily political and ideological polemics, incorporating changes whenever deemed necessary. For a legend writer, the chronicle provided the raw material which he elaborated, at times, upsetting the chronology as well. The legend of St Stephen offers an adequate example: the author relates a shrewd Hungarian victory over the Germans attributed to divine intervention, in connection with the German campaign led against Hungary in 1030. The source is the description in the Hungarian Chronicle of a later victory over the Germans won in 1051. Contemporary readers possibly overlooked the duplication, or if they did not, they took the similarity of the two stories for a confirmation of their reality.[11]

Continuity or Break?

Conversion is addressed by Hungarian narrative sources reticently, which itself indicates that they did not want to treat conversion to Christianity as a radical change.[12] They date the history of the Hungarian people from far before the Christian era, hence

---

[10] József Gerics, *Church, State and Mentality in Medieval Hungary* [in Hungarian] (Budapest, 1995), pp. 144–64. Even the papal charters followed the Hartvik version of Stephen's legend as a model, because that was the oldest written evidence for papal-Hungarian connections of St Stephen's reign. Géza Érszegi, 'The Privileges of the Blessed Virgin's Church in Fehérvár' [in Hungarian], in *A székesfehérvári Boldogasszony bazilika történeti jelentősége*, ed. by Gábor Farkas (Székesfehérvár, 1996), pp. 115–42.

[11] The campaign of Emperor Henry III in 1051, mentioned in the Chronicle, *Scriptores rerum Hungaricarum*, I, 347–49; the same by the Greater and the Hartvik Legend, *Scriptores rerum Hungaricarum*, II, 389–90, 423–24; evaluated by Gerics in *Church, State and Mentality*, pp. 16–19. This passage on Stephen's miracle was repeated in the medieval Hungarian breviaries for the first time in the thirteenth century.

[12] A recent overview by Norbert Kersken, *Geschichtsschreibung im Europa der Nationes. Nationalgeschichtliche Gesamtdarstellungen im Mittelalter* (Cologne, 1995), pp. 814–16. According to Kersken the least is written on conversion in Spanish, Norwegian, and Hungarian historiography. These chronicles usually mention the place, date, and the baptizer's name. This is missing in the Polish works too, undoubtably for political reasons.

a sharp dividing line between the pagan and Christian ages would have questioned the justification of discussing Hungarian prehistory at length. Paradoxically enough, legends and chronicles are at one in this regard. For one thing, both genres belonged to court literature in Hungary, and the client who commissioned the work expected the authors to apply the ideological and legal arguments prevalent in the court. The Greater Legend of St Stephen bears out continuity just as the chronicles do. The former makes explicit mention of the fact that imperial Rome also became Christian after paganism just as the pagan Hungarians ravaged Christian Europe upon divine *afflatus* before their conversion.[13] This statement was meant to prove that the German emperors, who claimed continuity with the Roman Empire, had no grounds to reproach the Hungarians for their pagan past.

The acme of this position is the *Gesta Hungarorum,* written by an anonymous chronicler around 1200, which is devoted exclusively to the prehistory of the Hungarians.[14] Of course, already at that time, the pagan Hungarians—as *flagellum Dei* —were governed by the Holy Spirit, even in their raids against the Christians and in the seizure of the land where they settled. The author, a fan of Roman law, consciously searched for links in Hungarian history before and after the settlement. This he found in the person of Attila, king of the Huns, whom he inserted in the family tree of the Hungarian kings. He laid the foundations of a view prevalent up to the nineteenth century. It said that the occupation of the Carpathian Basin by the Hungarians in 896 was preceded by the first capture of the area by Huns which legalized and justified the Hungarian settlement. Attila as the scourge of God could thus be more easily transferred to the pagan Hungarians.

The final version of the continuity of pagan and Christian Hungarian history was created by Simon of Kéza in the 1280s: the Huns and Magyars were not merely related but identical, so the settlement of the Hungarians in 896 was none other than the second Hun settlement. The author derives the origin of the *communitas* of noblemen, the roots of popular sovereignty from pagan, Hunnish times. He is at a loss to explain the origin of social inequality, of servitude, in Chapter 41 of the Chronicle. If the Hungarians were guided by the Holy Ghost from the beginning, the difference between noblemen and non-nobles could simply not depend on the embracing of Christianity; he argues that those who failed to turn up when the duke had summoned them to take up arms were cast into subjugation.[15] What explains Simon of Kéza's view is, for one thing, the

---

[13] Greater Legend, *Scriptores rerum Hungaricarum,* II, 378: '[. . .] etiam ipsa mundi totius metropolis Roma, cum monarchia dignitatis imperatorie Christi fidei colla submittens vanitatum erroribus renunciavit'. Discussed by Gerics, *Church, State and Mentality,* pp. 158–60.

[14] Recent edition by Gabriel Silagi with L. Veszprémy, *Die Gesta Hungarorum des anonymen Notars* (Sigmaringen, 1991).

[15] Jenő Szűcs, *Theoretical Elements in Simon of Kéza's Gesta Hungarorum,* Studia Historica, 96 (Budapest, 1975). Its new version is published as an introduction to the edition of Simon's chronicle, ed. by L. Veszprémy and Frank Schaer, *The Deeds of the Hungarians,* pp. xxix–cii.

serious controversy between the king of the period, Ladislas IV, and the pope. The king's court priest probably wanted to prove that Hungarian history was guided by divine will even before the conversion, and that insisting on the charge of heathendom against such a people and their ruler was senseless. Even in 1279 the papal legate to Hungary reminded the Hungarian king, Ladislas IV, that St Stephen subordinated his country to St Peter, that is to the Apostolic See, repeating the well-known Gregorian argumentation which was entirely rejected by Hungarian *literati*. This argument appeared for the first time in Gregory VII's letter to Salomon, king of Hungary, albeit some modern historians assume that King Stephen himself offered the country to the Virgin Mary, in opposition to hegemonic efforts.[16]

However, the main motive for stressing continuity must have been defence against foreign accusations already made in the eleventh century. Both papal and the imperial propaganda questioned several times—rightly at the time of the pagan revolts—the completion and thoroughness of the Hungarians' conversion, as in Poland. In the eleventh-century German-Polish historiographical polemics, the German writers identify the Poles' disobedience to the German emperor with rebellion against the Christian Church, bringing up their recent and superficial Christianity as proof.[17] Thietmar of Merseburg, called Boleslav the Bold, revolting against the Germans, the foe of all believers, just as Gerhoh of Rechersperg and Otto of Freising, found correlation between the Hungarians' infidelity and anti-German sentiments in the twelfth century.[18] The latter even doubted the sainthood of King Stephen, who was already widely revered as a saint at the time. These Germans emphasised a certain continuity in Hungarian history as well, that of their pagan and barbaric traditions. The argumentation of the Hungarian chroniclers and legend writers must have been provoked by an existing ideological accusation. That is why they stressed the continuity of Hungarian history, its character as salvation history, and the rapid and complete success of conversion by St Stephen.

---

[16] *Das Register Gregors VII*, ed. by Erich Caspar (Berlin, 1920), nr. II, 13, p. 145, cited by Gerics, *Church, State and Mentality*, p. 150.

[17] For the problems about 'fidelis Dei et regis' concept, see Angenendt, *Kaiserherrschaft und Königstaufe*, p. 313; Gerics, *Church, State and Mentality*, pp. 162–63.

[18] These citations are collected in Gerics, *Church, State and Mentality*; Gerhoh, *Commentarius in psalmum LXIV*, caput 58 (Libelli de lite, 3, 463): '[. . .] in terra Hungarica et barbarica vix nomine tenus Christianorum principum dominio subdita', labelling the Hungarian king, Géza II, as 'rex licet immitis et barbarus'; Otto of Freising, *Chronica*, VI, 27, ed. by A. Hofmeister (1912): 'Sorore quoque sua [that is Henry II] Gisila Stephano Ungarorum regi in uxorem data, tam ipsum quam totum eius regnum ad fidem vocavit. Hunc Stephanum Ungari hactenus fidem Christianam servantes velut principium fidei suae inter sanctos colendum dignum ducunt'. The German argumentation is quite similer with regard to the age of the First Crusade, when the first looting crusaders were defeated by the Hungarian king, Coloman. According to Ekkehardus Uraugiensis and Annalista Saxo, *MGH, SS*, 6, anno 1096: 'Fama quippe Colomanni iam premonuerat aures, inter paganorum et Ungarorum nil aput Teutonicas differre mentes'.

Who Was the Converter?

The Hungarian raids hitting tenth-century Europe were put to an end by the political reconciliation between Germans and Hungarians. The process began with the Hungarian legation to the German emperor's court in Quedlinburg in 973, and ended with the Hungarian ruler Géza's son marrying Gisela, the sister of the German emperor and saint to be Henry (II), sometime in the 990s. It is a well-established view that in Emperor Otto III's Evangeliarium of Aachen (1001–1102) there are two princes admitted by the emperor into the family of European Christian peoples: Boleslav the Bold and Stephen of Hungary.[19] It is clear from historical circumstances that conversion must have been carried out with German assistance, probably with the substantial support of Stephan's German wife and her surroundings. While, however, medieval Hungarian historiography acknowledged the role of German warriors in consolidating Géza's and Stephen's power, they would not hear of such assistance in the sphere of Church organization. The country, it is claimed, was converted by the first king, Stephen, a real apostle as it were, who also founded an archbishopric and a chain of bishoprics. Not even his father was allowed a role in this work, and there is still no factual information about how far Géza got in converting the people to Christianity.

It is a telling sign that no single precise date or place associated with the early phase of conversion is recorded in Hungarian works, including the year of Stephen's baptism or wedding. It is most likely that historiography of that time deliberately shunned the subject, reckoning Hungarian history from the year of the coronation in 1000 or 1001. Typically enough, the Bavarian version of the St Venceslav legend (*Crescente fide*) also distorts the facts when describing the very first phase of conversion, keeping silent about the fact of Moravian-Slavic evangelization.[20] Nor did the names of German missionaries survive in Hungarian sources, except for Adalbert, mentioned as the bishop of Prague, who paid to Hungary a fleeting visit in 995(?) but became the co-patron saint of the first Hungarian archbishopric.[21] There will be no knowing how true the content

---

[19] Johannes Fried, *Otto III und Boleslaw Chrobry* (Stuttgart,1989), pp. 21–64.

[20] Marvin Kantor, *The Origins of Christianity in Bohemia. Sources and Commentary* (Evanston, IL,1990), pp. 143–54, 271 n. 10, 288 n. 1.

[21] It is rather obscure what Adalbert did in Hungary. The baptism of Géza's son, Stephen, is too late; perhaps, his presence had something to do with the wedding preparations of Stephan and Gisela. Tamás Bogyay, 'Adalbert von Prag und die Ungarn—ein Problem der Quellen-Interpretation', *Ungarn-Jahrbuch,* 7 (1976), 9–36; idem, *Stephanus Rex* (Vienna, 1976). The tradition of Adalbert as performer of the wedding ceremony is attested for the first time in the fourteenth century in Scheyern (Bavaria). For Adalbert see also L. Veszprémy, 'Der hl. Adalbert im wissenschaftlichen Geschpräch ungarischer Historiker', in *Bohemia*, 40 (1999), 87–102. Rychard Grzesik, 'Die Ungarnmission des hl. Adalberts', in *The Man of Many Devices, Who Wandered Full Many Ways . . . : Festschrift in Honor of János M. Bak*, ed. by Balázs Nagy and Marcell Sebők (Budapest and New York, 1999), pp. 230–40.

of the undoubtedly interpolated lines of the chronicler Ademar de Chabannes (d. c. 1035) is, but his account clearly conforms to the general practice of the age: the emperor who promoted conversion, Otto III, adopts the baptized duke, Géza, as his godson, symbolically yielding rule over the country to him.[22] Adopting a newly baptized duke as godson was so common[23] that in the years prior to the Mongolian invasion of 1241–42 the baptized Coman duke also became the godson of the Hungarian King Andrew II, represented by his son, Prince Béla, at the baptism ceremony.[24] If the ceremony of the royal baptism was missing in the Hungarian historical tradition, it had to be reconstructed. By the end of the eleventh century, St Adalbert became the only converter who baptized the young Stephen, and by the thirteenth century a fictitious godfather was invented.[25]

Nevertheless, the organization of the Church did not become the subject of an open historiographic controversy because, unlike the bishopric of Lund in Scandinavia or Prague in Bohemia, Esztergom, the Hungarian ecclesiastic centre, was raised to the rank of an archbishopric parallel to Gniezno in Poland (1000) at an early phase of the conversion, and was thus freed from German dependency, causing much polemic later.[26] The only moot question remained whether Stephen converted his people of his own will or upon his wife's encouragement.

Several foreign analogies can be cited to exemplify the 'converting royal spouse' derived from Merovingian tradition.[27] In the Polish chronicles Princess Dobrava, the daughter of the Bohemian Duke Boleslav I, helped the work of evangelizers in Poland. In 965 she married Mieszko, the duke of the Poles, and the next year the duke's baptism followed. Contemporary German historiographers including Thietmar (IV, 56) emphasise that 'the poison of inborn heathendom left him upon the frequent urging of his beloved wife'. The missionary role of the royal spouse was accepted in Poland, because her kinship with the German imperial court was not so close.

This widespread argumentation was also used by German chroniclers in connection

---

[22] Ademar, ch. 31, quoted by Angenendt, *Kaiserherrschaft und Königstaufe*, pp. 305–9. According to Ademar the converter was Bruno of St Gallen, who really was a missionary in Hungary in Géza's time. Thietmar of Merseburg's statement, IV, 59, in *MGH, SS*, 3, is accepted by modern scholars: 'Imperatoris predicti [that is Otto III] gratia et hortatu gener Heinrici, ducis Bawariorum Waic [that is Stephen I of Hungary] in regno suimet episcopales cathedras faciens coronam et benedictionem accepit'.

[23] Angenendt, *Kaiserherrschaft und Königstaufe*, pp. 91–162.

[24] Nicolaus Pfeiffer, *Die ungarische Dominikanerordensprovinz* (Zürich, 1913), document 34, pp. 178–79.

[25] Hungarian Chronicle Composition, ch. 38, *Scriptores rerum Hungaricarum*, I, 295–96.

[26] For Scandinavian parallels see Birgit Sawyer, 'Scandinavian Conversion Histories', in *The Christianisation of Scandinavia*, ed. by Birgit Sawyer, Peter Sawyer, and Ian Wood (Alsingsås, 1987), pp. 88–110.

[27] An overview is in Kersken, *Geschichtsschreibung*, p. 815.

with Hungarians. Chroniclers of the mid-eleventh century, Wipo (d. c. 1046) and Herimannus Augiensis (d. 1054), make the pointed remark that Gisela converted her husband Stephan, and through him, the entire Hungarian nation, by marrying him.[28] Medieval Hungarian historiography ignored Gisela's alleged missionary role. Quite the contrary, the Hungarian chronicle makes quite unfavourable mentions of Gisela, attributing cruel deeds to her.[29] Underlying this was a deliberate wish to blur or discredit her role, rather than reality itself.

Gisela's favourable portrait abroad is most often based on the work of Sigibertus Gemblacensis (d. 1112), who noted Gisela's evangelizing role in an entry for 1010 in his *Chronographia*. The liturgical sources, the readings and prayers the feast of St Henry, also disseminated this view. His *vita* composed for his canonization in 1146 called the German emperor 'apostolus Ungarorum', who converted the Hungarians with the help of his sister. One can easily spot foreign sources already of the eleventh century which, quite exceptionally, drew on Hungarian sources or information. Thus, Leo Marsciannus's Chronicle of Monte Cassino, Bonizo, the bishop of Sutri, and the monk Albericus of the thirteenth century put down both Hungarian and foreign recollections of Gisela, noting of the former: *'Ungari dicunt'*.

As a result of the historiographical dispute on the significance of the converter, some chronicles in Poland also carry information about evangelizing in Hungary. Upon the model of Dobrava's converting role, they present the conversion of the Hungarians as stemming from them. They may have received some encouragement from the missionary role of St Adalbert, whose activity in Hungary during the period of Géza and Stephen was preserved by Hungarian legends and chronicles alike. He features in twelfth- to fifteenth-century Czech and Polish sources as the converter of both *Hungaria* and *Polonia*. The Hungarian-Polish chronicle compiled in Galicia in the early thirteenth century assigns a Polish wife, a fictitious Polish Princess Adelaid, to Duke Géza.[30] As with innumerable other invented Hungarian-Slavic relations which the chronicle abounds in, the purpose is simply to historically justify Hungarian sovereignty over the territory

---

[28] Gerics, *Church, State and Mentality*, pp. 71–76, quoting Wipo, II, 24: 'Nupta Stephano regi Ungarorum causa fuit Christianitatis primum in gente Pannonica' and Herimannus 'Gisela Stephano regi Ungarorum cum se ad Christi fidem converteret, quisi vere iuxta nomen suum fidei obses in coniugium data'. On Gisella, see János M. Bak, 'Roles and Functions of Queens in Árpádian and Angevin Hungary', in *Medieval Queenship*, ed. by John Carmi Parsons (Wolfeboro Falls, 1994), pp. 14–15.

[29] Medieval sources on Gisella collected and reprinted in András Uzsoki, 'The Tomb of Gisela, the First Hungarian Queen' [in Hungarian], *Publicationes Museorum Comitatus Vesprimiensis*, 16 (1982), 125–68. György Györffy, 'Gisela', in *Bayerisch-ungarische Frauengestalten*, ed. by György Györffy, Ilona Sz. Jónás, and Emil Niederhauser (Augsburg, 1996), pp. 4–13.

[30] Ryszard Grzesik, 'Adelhaid, an Alleged Polish Princess on the Hungarian Thone' [in Hungarian], *Aetas*, 3 (1995), 114–25.

above Galicia, which, however, was a temporary affair. For people of the period, it was again a tendentious account of conversion that seemed suited to represent a political ambition.

St Stephen and St Ladislas

Several examples can be adduced from European historiography to illustrate that a king who oversaw conversion to Christianity and suffered a martyr's death for the faith became the perennial patron saint, *rex perpetuus,* of a country, with a stock of myths centering around his person. Fine examples are that of Olaf, king of Norway who died in 1030, and Venceslav of Bohemia, who was killed for his faith in 929. The events from the life of St Stephen described in the chronicles and legends would have been apposite ground for twelfth- to fourteenth-century elaboration and formulation, as was fashionable in the literature of the age. Stephen's life was teeming with dramatic turns, fights, and a bit of misinterpretation could even have attributed to him a pilgrimage to Rome and Jerusalem, a journey to the Holy Land on the pattern of Charlemagne. The fact that it failed to come about suggests that Stephen's story became petrified and discoloured because it featured the law-giver, the guarantor of the country's secular and ecclesiastic independence, which was further delimited by the passages selected from the legends for the liturgical books (missals, breviaries).

At any rate, when at the end of the twelfth century Béla III, the new king acceding to the throne of Hungary from faraway Byzantium, wished to lay the ideological foundations of his rule after decades of domestic and external hostilities, he had his predecessor Ladislas I canonized in 1192. He had his legend written, and had the Hungarian chronicle extended with the rewritten story of St Ladislas. What especially touched the people of around 1200 in St Ladislas's story were his fights against the pagans attacking the country in which his miraculous valiance sent the raiders fleeing and freed the abducted virgins. From this moment onwards, the symbol of Christian Hungary was St Ladislas, blurring even the memory of the converting King Stephen.[31]

Another justification for all this is Béla being the first king of Hungary to pledge a crusade to the Holy Land, and who was only prevented from taking up the cross by his old age and death. During Stephen's reign pilgrims proceeded peacefully through the country to Jerusalem. Ladislas I, by contrast, died in 1095, the year prior to the declaration of the First Crusade, so it was not too hard to promote him as the leader of the crusade. Ladislas I's campaign left deep marks on Hungarian historical thinking. In

---

[31] On Ladislas see Kornél Szovák, 'The Image of the Ideal King in Twelfth-Century Hungary. Remarks on the Legend of St Ladislas', in *Kings and Kingship in Medieval Europe,* ed. by Anne J. Duggan (London, 1993), pp. 241–64. Ernő Marosi, 'Der heilige Ladislaus als ungarischer Nationalheiliger', *Acta Historiae Artium Academiae Scientiarum Hungaricae,* 33 (1987), 210–55; L. Veszprémy, 'Dux et praeceptor Hierosoliminatorum. König Ladisclaus als immaginärer Kreuzritter, in *The Man of Many Devices,* pp. 470–77.

the seventeenth century, for instance, the Hungarians were fired to fight the Ottomans with Ladislas' crusading oath, and on the one thousandth jubilee of the Hungarian settlement in the country, in 1896, Ladislas was also given a place on the monuments as a fighter against pagans.

The core of this story was again preserved by the chronicle.[32] It says that envoys of the French, Hispanian, and English monarchs appeared before him as he was celebrating Easter in his court. He was asked to lead the crusading army, and he consented. Spinning on this thread, the legend of Ladislas speaks about the rulers themselves seeking Ladislas out. The apparently legally educated author of this chronicle section emphasises his narration by often quoting Gratianus's book of law word for word and by evoking the spirit, and a few details, of the legend of Charlemagne.

Let it be added that by the end of the twelfth century, the chronicles and legends about the conversion of Hungarians did not only contain closed, canonized historical source material but also attached to it an excessively pious, ascetic image of King Stephen. This image failed to tally with the age's ideal of a valiant king or knight. For contemporaries, the vision of conversion was too peaceful and eventless. Stephen put down his domestic rivals sticking to paganism without serious resistance and settled his external rivals, such as the Pechenegs, peacefully in the country. That was not what people wanted to read at the end of the twelfth century when, for example in the work of Jocundus on St Servatius, Charlemagne fought like a lion against the heathen. Chroniclers were looking for historical material which combined the biblical David and Charlemagne in the figure of the king. This they found in the events of St Ladislas' time, not in that of St Stephen.

Conclusion

Historical information about the conversion of Hungarians is very sparse in the narrative sources. This is because the sources were heavily influenced by the external—political and ideological—expectations related to conversion and the foundation of the Church already demonstrable in the eleventh century. The role of the Byzantine and then of the German imperial courts, which initiated the conversion, had to be suppressed; the image of King Stephen expected in Hungary was that of a basically peaceful Church-organizer and ruler who was independent of the pope and the emperor alike, and only resorted to arms in the last instance. The problem is compounded further by the fact that the sporadic historical information which survives made its way into the chronicles through the filter of the immigrant German clans' tradition exaggerating their own role.[33] The diversity of expectations eventually made the figure of the converting

---

[32] Chapter 139 of the Chronicle Composition, in *Scriptores rerum Hungaricarum*, I, 417–18; Ladislas's Legend, ch. 7, in *Scriptores rerum Hungaricarum*, II, 521–22.

[33] For the different stages of these insertions see, for example, in ch. 37 the words 'Duke Geysa *among others* [. . .]' reducing the historical role of Geysa, or in ch. 41, 'who trusted to the

king so rigid that from the late twelfth century the up-to-date literary genres had to look elsewhere for a ruler to symbolize the Christian country. Him they found, not in Stephen the converter, but in Ladislas I, who completed the conversion and fought against external pagan invaders. The efforts of contemporaneous Hungarian chroniclers and legend writers to deceive the outside world were so successful that what they present is source material for the study of the art of deception rather than of the history of Hungarian conversion.

---

help of these counts and *even more in God* [. . .]', and '[. . .] they were converted and accepted it of their *own free will*' reducing the role of the Germans.

Mission to the Heathen in Prussia and Livonia: The Attitudes of the Religious Military Orders toward Christianization

MARIE-LUISE FAVREAU-LILIE

The subjugation of heathen tribes in the west Baltic, primarily the Livs and the Prussians, and the integration of their territory into the Christian Occident was basically the work of two military religious orders: the Livonian Sword-Brothers and the Teutonic Order, although early attempts for a peaceful and nonviolent mission by the Cistercians are evidenced in the 1180s.

'Brothers of the Knighthood of Christ in Livonia' (*fratres milicie Christi de Livonia*) was the name of the order founded in 1202 shortly after the end of the first crusade against the Livs. Its mission was not only to protect the missionaries but also to conquer heathen territory. Albert of Bekeshoevede, bishop of Riga from 1199 until 1229,[1] was able to establish spiritual authority in the bishopric of Livonia with the help of these knights, who demanded a share of the booty and became lords in their part (one third) of the conquered regions.[2]

---

[1] Gisela Gnegel-Waitschies, *Bischof Albert von Riga. Ein Bremer Domherr als Kirchenfuerst im Osten (1199–1229)*, Nord- und osteuropaeische Geschichtsstudien, 2 (Hamburg, 1958).

[2] Friedrich Benninghoven, *Der Orden der Schwertbrueder. Fratres Milicie Christi de Livonia*, Ostmitteleuropa in Vergangenheit und Gegenwart, 9 (Koeln, 1965); Sven Ekdahl, 'Die Rolle der Ritterorden bei der Christianisierung der Liven und Letten', in *Gli inizi del christianesimo in Livonia-Lettonia. Atti del colloquio internazionale di storia ecclesiastica in occasione dell' VIII centenario della chiesa in Livonia (1186–1986), Roma, 24–25 Giugno 1986*, Pontificio comitato di scienze storiche, Atti e documenti, 1 (Città del Vaticano, 1989), pp. 203–43, 221–23.

The Teutonic Order had acquired experience in frontier war against the pagans in Hungary and had tasted territorial rule years prior to the launch of its campaign against the Prussians. However, these knights would first learn in Prussia the problems that arose when self-interest in securing lordships in conquered heathen territory collided with the missionary policies of the papacy.

Called to the aid of the duke of Mazovia in 1225 or 1226, the Teutonic Knights began their crusade against the Prussians in 1231 after years of meticulous preparation.[3] Emperor Frederick II, Duke Conrad of Mazovia himself, and others as well as the papacy had to make concessions that enabled the Teutonic Order to establish an autonomous lordship in *Kulmerland* and in the conquered regions.[4]

A crusade against the heathen: in Livonia and later in Prussia, this meant the military conquest of pagan settlements, the subjection and if necessary forcible baptism of the defeated Balts. Neither in Livonia nor in Prussia was it deemed sufficient to baptize the clan and tribal leaders in order to win over the entire population. It was necessary to indoctrinate even after mass baptism as many Livs and Prussians as possible, so that the uninitiated would voluntarily adopt Christianity and ask for baptism. It was necessary to follow up the hurried baptisms with careful instruction in the faith and to explain the significance of the sacraments and the importance of church-building. Qualified clergy were needed to carry out missionary and general spiritual welfare work among the Livs and the Prussians;[5] clergy were also required to establish an ecclesiastical organization in the mission regions.

Were the two religious military orders in Livonia and Prussia at all interested in a peaceful mission in their conquered territories? Who made decisions about the type of missionary work and about the organization of the church in these territories? The knight-brothers themselves as lords, the bishops, or the pope?

The example provided by the Cistercian mission to the Livs and the Prussians[6] was

---

[3] Compare William Urban, *The Prussian Crusade* (New York and London, 1980).

[4] *Preußisches Urkundenbuch, Politische Abtheilung,* vol. I, parts 1–2 (henceforth PUB, I, 1–2); I, 1 ed. by R. Philippi (henceforth PUB, I, 1) (Koenigsberg, 1882); I, 2 ed. by August Seraphim (Koenigsberg, 1909); see PUB, I, 1, nos 56, 72–80, 94, 108, 357.

[5] For the organization of missions, see a letter of Pope Gregory IX addressed to missionaries (probably Dominicans) evangelizing the defeated Prussians and trying to enlarge the missionary districts allotted to them on their own authority (PUB, I, 1, no. 97).

[6] For the Cistercians' principles of mission with the Livs and Prussians that even Pope Gregory IX initially decided to patronize (PUB, I, 1, no. 61), see in particular, Fritz Blanke, 'Die Missionsmethode des Bischofs Christian von Preussen', *Altpreussische Forschungen*, 4.2 (1927), 20–42; idem, 'Die Entscheidungsjahre der Preussenmission (1206–1274)' (1928), later printed in *Heidenmission und Kreuzzugsgedanke in der deutschen Ostpolitik des Mittelalters*, ed. by Helmut Beumann (Darmstadt, 1963), pp. 389–416; idem, 'Die Preussenmission vor der Ankunft des Deutschen Ordens', in *Deutsche Staatenbildung und deutsche Kultur im Preussenland*, ed. by Landeshauptmann der Provinz Ostpreussen (Paul Blunk) (Koenigsberg, 1931), pp. 40–49;

unacceptable to the Teutonic Knights and to the Livonian Sword-Brothers before them.[7] The principle of a mission based solely on preaching and patient example that worked toward the voluntary conversion of the individual was irreconcilable with their idea that only forcible mass baptism of the subjugated pagans could spell a clear victory for Christendom.

The military orders were also keen on exploiting the subjected and baptized peoples materially. This brought them into conflict with the missionary policies of the papacy, which above all wanted to safeguard the liberties of the converted populace. The papacy believed that the conversion to Christianity should not go hand-in-hand with a lowering of social status of new converts, nor with a diminishing of freedom.[8]

Had this fundamental principle of the Church been upheld, the monastic knights would not have been able to consolidate their rule in Livonia and Prussia as quickly as they thought necessary. The necessary castle-building and the garrisoning of the captured regions could only be accomplished by exacting labour service from the conquered peoples. Hence the religious military orders had little interest in cursorily baptizing all Livs and Prussians seeking conversion, because exploiting pagans as labourers was much easier than exploiting converts, for the church did not concern itself with the predicament of infidels.[9]

Urban, *Prussian Crusade*, pp. 75–78; Kaspar Elm, 'Christi cultores et novelle ecclesie plantatores. Der Anteil der Mönche, Kanoniker und Mendikanten an der Christianisierung der Liven und dem Aufbau der Kirche von Livland', in *Gli inizi del Cristianesimo in Livonia*, pp. 127–70; Manfred Hellmann, 'Die Anfänge christlicher Mission in den baltischen Ländern', in *Studien über die Anfänge der Mission in Livland*, ed. by idem, Vorträge und Forschungen, 37 (Sigmaringen, 1989), pp. 7–36; Reinhard Schneider, 'Strassentheater im Missionseinsatz. Zu Heinrichs von Lettland Bericht über ein grosses Spiel in Riga 1205', in *Studien über die Anfänge der Mission in Livland*, pp. 107–22.

[7] Fritz Blanke, 'Die Stellung der Ritterorden zur Preussenmission', in *Deutsche Theologie. Bericht über den Theologentag zu Eisenach, Herbst 1927*, ed. by Arthur Titius (Göttingen, 1928), pp. 114–21; Erich Maschke, *Der deutsche Orden und die Preussen. Bekehrung und Unterwerfung in der preussisch-baltischen Mission des 13. Jahrhunderts*, ed. by Emil Ebering, Historische Studien, 176 (Berlin, 1928); Karol Górski, 'Probleme der Christianisierung in Preussen, Livland und Litauen', in *Die Rolle der Ritterorden in der Christianisierung und Kolonisierung des Ostseegebietes*, ed. by Zenon Hubert Nowak, Universitas Nicolai Copernici. Ordines militares, Colloquia Torunensia Historica, 1 (Toruń, 1983), pp. 9–34.

[8] PUB, I, 1, no. 54, *sub beati Petri et nostri protectione suscipimus, ut in libertate vestra manentes nulli alii sitis quam soli Christo [. . .] et obedientie ecclesie Romane subiecti.* Cf. Hartmut Boockmann, 'Die Freiheit der Prussen im 13. Jahrhundert', in *Die abendländische Freiheit vom 10. zum 14. Jahrhundert. Der Wirkungszusammenhang von Idee und Wirklichkeit im europäischen Vergleich*, ed. by Johannes Fried, Vorträge und Forschungen, 39 (Sigmaringen, 1991), pp. 287–306.

[9] PUB, I, 1, no. 134, pp. 100–101. Only in 1260 did the Curia consider it admissible to

Did the religious military orders effect a change in the mission in Prussia and Livonia to suit their own interests? In neither order was the mission the responsibility of its own priests. Apart from this fact, the situation in Livonia and in Prussia differed considerably.

The 'Brothers of the Knighthood of Christ in Livonia' had no influence on the mission in their territory. They never broke away from the bishop of Riga, whose missionary authority also extended into that part of Livonia that had fallen to the Sword-Brothers as booty. The Livonian monastic knights hindered the Cistercian mission installed and supported by the bishop of Riga whenever it threatened their own interests as territorial lords. This led to conflict, to repeated intervention by papal legates, and finally to compromise.[10] The Sword-Brothers did not have the same free hand with the Livs that the Teutonic Knights enjoyed in Prussia.

The Teutonic Order itself was in charge of the spiritual welfare and mission for its entire territory, though it was also held accountable to the papacy. First the Teutonic Order set about forming a clergy that could also speak the local tongue.[11] Apparently only very few qualified clerics came to Prussia from the German Empire; so the Teutonic Order probably began even in the thirteenth century to recruit young Prussians for religious vocation in order to enlist them as clergy in their native land.

In the territory of the Teutonic Order, it was not a simple matter to establish a training centre for young Prussian clergy. Except for probably one school which the Livonian Sword-Brothers had been allowed to establish in Riga in 1226,[12] in the thirteenth century there were no schools in either Livonia or Prussia at which Letts, Livs, Estonians, and Prussians—and not infrequently hostages of different tribes—could be educated for a clerical life and perhaps missionary work later on. Only after the Teutonic Order had finished consolidating its power did it achieve its goal of building its own school for priests in Prussia.[13]

---

compel, at least in the case of home defence, the Prussian subjects of the bishop of Prussia to military service and participation in erecting strongholds (PUB, I, 2, no. 86).

[10] Benninghoven, *Orden der Schwertbrueder*, pp. 77–80, 113–16, 194–206, 312–13, 408–12.

[11] Maschke, *Der deutsche Orden und die Preussen*, p. 95 n. 196.

[12] Benninghoven, *Orden der Schwertbrüder*, pp. 202, 230. Years before Bishop Christian of Prussia had recognized the importance of establishing schools amongst the Balts (PUB, I, 1, no. 23; Blanke, 'Missionsmethode', pp. 39, 41). Bishop William of Modena, who probably had learned the native tongue of the Prussians in order to evangelize them, published a Prussian translation of a widely spread Latin grammar (*Donato*) in order to facilitate the education of a native clergy: Albricus Triumfontium, *Chronica*, ed. by Paul Scheffer-Boichorst, *Monumenta Germaniae Historica, Scriptores,* 23 (Hannover, 1874), p. 921. Cf. Maschke, *Der deutsche Orden,* p. 62; Urban, *Prussian Crusade,* p. 108.

[13] Blanke, 'Missionsmethode', p. 40; Marjan Tumler, *Der Deutsche Orden im Werden, Wachsen und Wirken bis 1400* (Montreal and Wien, 1955), p. 476.

The only alternative was to send young Balts to schools in the German Empire, to some convent schools, for example, situated in the archbishopric of Bremen.[14] Not just unconditional supporters of the Teutonic Order's rule received an education; this is evidenced in the person of Henry of the Mountain, *Henricus de Monte*, the leader of the large-scale Prussian uprising from 1260 to 1274, who probably had once studied at the endowed school attached to the cathedral of Magdeburg. He was remembered even in the fourteenth century.[15]

The Teutonic Order was indeed very concerned with stocking the parishes of Prussia with clergy who had knowledge of both the language and the region. But the idea of someday being able to trust solely Prussian clergy with the spiritual welfare of the Prussians was illusory. At first parishes were located only in the few cities founded by the Teutonic Order and centred around several clans of converted Prussians. Missionary work devoted to founding parishes and building churches in Prussia had probably begun at the earliest after the first Prussian rebellion, for the treaty signed in Christburg in 1249 required the Prussians to build a total of twenty-one churches in Warmia, Pomesania, and Natangia.[16] The Prussians did not hurry to accomplish this task, as eleven years later only about half of these churches had been built. The development of rural parishes in the other regions dominated by the Teutonic Order (in Livonia and Curonia) likewise progressed at a none too impressive pace.

Cooperation between the Teutonic Knights and the experienced Cistercian missionaries, and not least with Bishop Christian of Prussia, foundered chiefly due to the extremely divergent missionary attitudes of the Cistercians and the Teutonic Knights.[17] Whereas the Bishop of Prussia extolled the principle of voluntary baptism, the Teutonic Knights were not averse to forcible mass baptism. Whereas the bishop demanded thorough catechizing of new converts after baptism, the Teutonic Knights were less than

---

[14] H. Gruener, 'Missionsmethode und Erfolg bei der Christianisierung Livlands', *Allgemeine Missionszeitschrift*, 41 (1914), 156–57, 211–12; Blanke, 'Missionsmethode', pp. 40–41; Elm, 'Christi cultores', p. 149. For hostages transferred to the German Empire and educated there for a clerical life in their native land, see Heinricus, *Chronicon Livonie*, 4.4–5; 10.7, 30.5, ed. by Leonid Arbusow and Albert Bauer, *Monumenta Germaniae Historica, Scriptores rerum Germanicarum*, 31 (Hannover, 1955), pp. 14, 15, 37, 220.

[15] Peter of Dusburg, *Chronicon terrae Prussiae*, 3.91, 3.167, ed. by Max Toeppen, Scriptores rerum Prussicarum, 1 (Leipzig, 1861), pp. 101, 128. Cf. Reinhard Wenskus, 'Der Deutsche Orden und die nichtdeutsche Bevölkerung des Preussenlandes mit besonderer Berücksichtigung der Siedlung', in *Die Deutsche Ostsiedlung des Mittelalters als Problem der europaeischen Geschichte*, ed. by Walter Schlesinger, Vortraege und Forschungen, 18 (Sigmaringen, 1974), p. 420.

[16] PUB, I, 1, no. 218, pp. 158–65; esp. p. 162. In Livonia, however, churches of stone had been erected by the Sword-Brothers before 1237; Benninghoven, *Der Orden der Schwertbrueder*, pp. 228–29.

[17] PUB, I, 1, no. 134, pp. 100–101; see also ibid., nos 62, 65, 149.

thorough. Whereas the bishop was adamant that every voluntary request for baptism by a heathen be immediately granted, the Teutonic Knights seemed a bit deaf to these requests. Whereas the bishop, in accordance with papal missionary policy, called for upholding the liberties of new Prussian converts, the Teutonic Knights tended to neglect these rights and whenever possible to disregard them entirely. The Teutonic Order had no interest in cooperating with Bishop Christian of Prussia, and was disinclined to any and all cooperation with the Cistercians.

The Livonian Sword-Brothers and the Teutonic Order ignored the principles of the Cistercian missionaries, the missionary agenda of the Curia, as well as canonical laws dealing with the treatment of new Christians, wherever these conflicted with the orders' own aims. The military orders believed that their rule in the conquered territories could only be adequately established if they exacted labour and extraordinary taxes from the new Christians, a demand that was at complete odds with the beliefs of the orders' ideological foes. This conflict of interest surfaced in Livonia earlier than it did in Prussia,[18] but the subjects of the Sword-Brothers were not exasperated in the same way as were the Balts in the State of the Teutonic Order later on.

The Teutonic Order had similar problems with the mission and with the status of converted Prussians, who it ruthlessly employed in castle-building and arbitrarily recruited for military service. The actions of the order prompted a severe reproof from Bishop Christian of Prussia.[19] The Teutonic Order undoubtedly had no objections when the Curia decided to replace the Cistercians as standard-bearers of the mission in Kulmerland and in all territories awarded the order by Pope Gregory IX in 1234 as eternal and free property under papal protection.

The Cistercians were at first succeeded by the Dominican Order.[20] The Dominicans had probably begun their missionary work among the Prussians by 1227 from their base in Danzig before the crusade against the Prussians had been launched.[21] The Teutonic Order itself recommended to the pope that the Dominicans be entrusted with the preaching for the planned crusade.[22] The Teutonic Knights could also trust in the

---

[18] Benninghoven, *Der Orden der Schwertbrueder*, pp. 113–16, 121–26, 179–86; Ernst Pitz, *Papstreskript und Kaiserreskript im Mittelalter*, Bibliothek des Deutschen Historischen Instituts in Rom, 36 (Tübingen, 1971), pp. 41–44; Ekdahl, 'Rolle der Ritterorden', pp. 235–38, 239–40.

[19] Johannes Voigt, *Geschichte Preussens,* 3 (Koenigsberg, 1828), pp. 590–91 n. 2; PUB, I, 1, no. 134, pp. 100–102.

[20] For what follows, see Berthold Altaner, *Die Dominikanermissionen des 13. Jahrhunderts. Forschungen zur Geschichte der kirchlichen Unionen und der Mohammedaner-und Heidenmission des Mittelalters* (Habelschwerdt, 1924), pp. 160–67. Fritz Blanke, 'Der innere Gang der ostpreussischen Kirchengeschichte', in *Bilder aus dem religioesen und kirchlichen Leben Ostpreussens. Festschrift zum Koenigsberger Evangelischen Kirchentag in Koenigsberg vom 17.–21. Juni 1927*, ed. by Carl Flothow (Koenigsberg in Preussen, 1927), pp. 22–23.

[21] Altaner, *Dominikanermissionen*, pp. 162–63.

[22] For the Dominicans' preaching the crusade against the Prussians since 1230/1231 see

Dominicans' qualification in missionary work: during the crusade against the Prussians begun in 1231, as in later campaigns, the Dominicans showed that they had no reservations against forcible baptism. They baptized the elite Prussians and forced the collective conversion to Christianity of entire clans and tribes, who would not have been granted peace in any other manner. From their base in Livonia, where they had arrived in the initial stage of the Prussian Crusade, settling in Riga in 1234,[23] the Dominicans lent similar support to the Teutonic Order in the late thirteenth century during the campaigns against the Curonians and other east Baltic tribes.[24]

Thanks to donations from the Teutonic Order especially, the Dominicans were able to build some convents from the 1230s to the 1260s in the cities of Chelmno (1233), Elbing (after 1237) and Torun.[25] These convents also served as centres for missionary work among the Prussians. However, a thorough conversion of the Prussians never succeeded, although there were doubtless some Dominican missionaries who were also competent in the language.[26] No details are known about the Dominicans' work, but they must have acted in accordance with the wishes of the Teutonic Order and the Curia, for this would explain the appointment of Dominicans to most of the missionary bishoprics founded in the Order's territory in 1243.[27]

The Dominicans were greatly indebted to the Teutonic Order; probably for this reason they were not emphatic in upholding the papal promises to the newly converted Prussians. The Dominicans were unable to mitigate the rage felt toward the Teutonic Knights by the subjugated Prussian populace, which equated Christianity with the order's domination. As the Prussians in Pomesania, Warmia, and Natangia dared an open revolt for the first time in the 1240s to protest their poor social, legal, and material position, the Dominicans were doubtless indirectly to blame for the bad conditions.

The Teutonic Order initially did not support a Franciscan mission to the Prussians, but the Franciscans became active in Prussia no later than after the first rebellion.[28]

PUB, I, 1, nos 85, 87, 89. The Dominicans started their missions in the conquered Prussian territories by 1233 (ibid., nos 98, 101) whereas they had been busy in Pomesania at least since 1231 (ibid., no. 84).

[23] Altaner, *Dominikanermissionen*, pp. 164, 190; Elm, 'Christi cultores', p. 164.

[24] Altaner, *Dominikanermissionen*, p. 191. For the Dominicans' crusade preaching against Livonians (since the 1240s) and Curonians (since 1260), cf. PUB, I, 1, nos 146, 148, 151, 255, 275, 326; PUB, I, 2, nos 23, 30, 103, 111, 112, 147, 158, 199–201, 205, 234, 235. *Livlaendische Reimchronik*, ed. by Ludger Meyer (Paderborn, 1876), vv. 4235–42, 9625; cf. Elm, 'Christi cultores', pp. 167–68.

[25] Altaner, *Dominikanermissionen*, pp. 176–78.

[26] Altaner, *Dominikanermissionen*, pp. 167, 179–80; Werner Roth, *Die Dominikaner und Franziskaner im Deutsch-Ordensland Preussen bis 1466* (unpublished doctoral thesis, Koenigsberg in Preussen, 1918), p. 25; PUB, I, 2, no. 65, p. 61.

[27] Altaner, *Dominikanermissionen*, pp. 167–76.

[28] The Franciscans established a convent at the city of Torún in 1239: Roth, *Dominikaner*

Since 1255 at the latest, they joined the crusader armies not only preaching during the campaign but also cooperating in the hostilities against the heathen Balts.[29] The Franciscans were in any case first called upon to support the missionary crusade waged by the Teutonic Knights when there was need of more crusade preaching and missionary activities than the Dominicans were able to accomplish.[30] There was no dispute or competition between Franciscans and Dominicans when they commonly joined a crusade. But when the Teutonic Order wanted to direct the crusade into adjacent heathen territories, and the help of crusade preachers was needed to recruit crusaders, the preaching of the crusade directed to these territories was transferred to the Franciscans: since 1255 the Franciscans alone preached the crusade against the Lithuanians and Jatwingians.[31] Nevertheless, for the Teutonic Order the conquest of Lithuania would remain a dream, and a mission to this region would never come about.

I now come to the conclusion: after 1249 neither the Dominicans nor the Franciscans could effect a change in the behaviour of the Teutonic Knights towards the once-pagan population in Prussia and Livonia, and complete the mission. The large-scale Prussian uprising in 1260 erased any and all progress made by the mendicant orders up to that time. After the revolt had been quashed, which for most Prussians —according to the treaty of Christburg—meant the loss of freedom, the Teutonic Knights no longer pursued a peaceful mission to the now mostly disenfranchised Prussians. With the conquest of the frontier regions in the campaign against Lithuania at the end of the thirteenth century, the subjugation of forcibly baptized Baltic tribes came to an end; however, their christianization would remain incomplete until the Reformation of the sixteenth century.[32] The rapid conversion to Christianity of large numbers of people during the armed land-grab of the religious military orders should not be misunderstood. For the Livonian Sword-Brothers and the Teutonic Order, the mission was in fact only worthwhile if it helped secure their territorial rule.

---

und Franziskaner, p. 89. In 1252 (ibid., p. 24) or 1253 (Altaner, *Dominikanermissionen*, p. 174 n. 20) for the first time a member of the order of St Francis was elected bishop of a Prussian see (Samland).

[29] *Livlaendische Reimchronik*, vv. 4238–40; cf. Altaner, *Dominikanermissionen*, p. 191; Elm, 'Christi cultores', pp. 167–68.

[30] See, for instance, PUB, I, 2, nos 103, 111, 112, 127, 141, 147, 160, 198–201, 205, 234, 235; Elm, 'Christi cultores', p. 167 n. 179.

[31] PUB, I, 1, no. 322; PUB, I, 2, nos 21, 28, 29.

[32] For this, see Blanke, 'Der innere Gang', pp. 28–35; idem, 'Entscheidungsjahre der Preussenmission', p. 414; Dieter Heckmann, 'Koenigsberg und sein Hinterland im Spätmittelalter', in *Die preußischen Hansestaedte im Nord- und Ostseeraum des Mittelalters*, ed. by Zenon Hubert Novak (Torún, 1998), pp. 79–89, esp. 83–84. See also *Berichte der Generalprokuratoren des Deutschen Ordens*, 4.2 (1433–1436), ed. by Kurt Forstreuter and Hans Koeppen (Goettingen, 1976), no. 713. It goes without saying that Marjan Tumler as grandmaster of the Teutonic Order (Tumler, *Der Deutsche Orden*, p. 477 n. 7) had to refuse this verdict.

The Conversion of the Jews

The Forced Baptism of
Jews in Christian Europe:
An Introductory Overview

BENJAMIN RAVID

O ne of the major threats to the peace and tranquillity of the Jewish communities of pre-emancipation Europe, indeed perhaps the most serious after physical attacks and expulsions, was that of forced baptism.[1] What was to become the generally accepted policy of the medieval and early modern Catholic Church with regard to the forced baptism of Jews was set forth by Pope Gregory I (590–604). In a letter written in 591 to the Bishops of Arles and Marseilles, Gregory praised the intention of those who converted Jews by force, but expressed his fear that doing so would either have no effect or, worse, would lead to the loss of the very souls whose

---

This article constitutes a greatly expanded version of the introduction to my detailed study of the forced baptism of Jewish minors in early-modern Venice, to appear in *Italia*, 13–14, *Studies in Honor of Prof. Giuseppi Sermoneta,* ed. by Robert Bonfil.

[1] In view of the important and traumatic effects of forced baptisms of Jews in general and especially of Jewish minors against the will of their parents, it is remarkable that there is no comprehensive study of the problem. See the brief remarks in Salo W. Baron, *A Social and Religious History of the Jews,* 2nd edn, 18 vols (Philadelphia and New York, 1952–87), IX, 12–17, XIV, 140–41; also Solomon Grayzel, *The Church and the Jews in the XIIIth Century* (Philadelphia, 1933), I, 13–15, 100–103, 226–29; and Solomon Grayzel, 'Popes, Jews, and Inquisition from "Sicut" to "Turbato"', in *Essays on the Occasion of the Seventieth Anniversary of Dropsie College,* ed. by Abraham Katsch and Leon Nemoy (Philadelphia, 1979), pp. 151–88, reprinted in Solomon Grayzel, *The Church and the Jews in the XIIIth Century,* II, ed. by Kenneth R. Stow (New York, 1989), pp. 3–45, see also pp. 102–6, 113–15, 165–67, 209, 264–66, 290.

salvation was being sought, for 'when any one is brought to the font of baptism, not by the sweetness of preaching but by compulsion, he returns to his former superstition, and dies the worse from having been born again'. Accordingly, he proposed that the Jews rather be stirred up by the sweetness of frequent preaching so that they might genuinely desire to convert and not, as he put it, return to their former vomit (cf. Proverbs 26. 11).[2]

The question of the forced conversion of Jews was taken up some three decades after Gregory by the Fourth Council of Toledo, which met in 633 under Isidore of Seville. In two oft-cited and generally accepted canons, that Council provided that Jews should not be converted by force, for just as the fall in the garden of Eden had been an act of free will, so too ought salvation to be voluntary. Nevertheless, since those who had been converted by force had partaken of the holy sacrament and received the grace of baptism, they should be required to remain Christian, lest the name of God be blasphemed and the faith that they had assumed be considered worthless and despicable. Moreover, the Council declared, those who after converting then practised Jewish ceremonies and did not 'amend of their own accord, may be compelled by sacerdotal correction'.[3]

Either as a result of the Rhineland massacres during the First Crusade or of a specific incident that affected the Jews of Rome, Pope Calixtus III (1119–24), in response to a request of the Jews of Rome, set forth the official attitude of the Papacy toward the forced conversion of the Jews in his Bull, known, after its opening words, as *Sicut Judeis*. He ordered that

> no Christian shall use violence to force them into baptism while they are unwilling and refuse, but that [only] if any one of them seeks refuge among the Christians of his own free will and by reason of faith, his willingness having become quite clear, shall he be made a Christian without subjecting himself to any opprobrium. For surely none can be believed to possess the true Christian faith if he is known to have come to Christian baptism unwillingly and even against his wishes.[4]

---

[2] The text of the letter of Gregory is readily available in Jacob Marcus, *The Jew in the Medieval World* (Cincinnati, 1938), pp. 111–12.

[3] See Jean Juster, 'The Legal Condition of the Jews under the Visigoth Kings', brought up-to-date by Alfredo M. Rabello, *Israel Law Review*, 11 (1976), 216–87, 391–414, 563–90, and published in book form with the same title and pagination (Jerusalem, 1976), pp. 264–65 n. 18, p. 410 n. 150.

[4] On the *Sicut Judeis* Bull, see Solomon Grayzel, 'The Papal Bull *Sicut Judeis*', in *Studies and Essays in Honor of Abraham A. Neuman*, ed. by Meir Ben-Horin, Bernard D. Weinryb, and Solomon Zeitlin (Leiden, 1962), pp. 243–80 (reprinted in *Essential Papers on Judaism and Christianity in Conflict*, ed. by Jeremy Cohen (New York, 1991), pp. 231–59); and also Grayzel, 'Popes, Jews, and Inquisition', and especially on forced conversions, pp. 3–5, 7–8, 18.

Obviously, a clear, unambiguous, and universally accepted definition of what constituted baptism undertaken with violence and force, and therefore not valid, was very necessary, yet it was never forthcoming. Generally, it was felt that only imminent loss of life really constituted grounds for invalidating baptism.[5] Accordingly, zealous Christians did not refrain from using force of varying degrees, up to the final ultimatum of conversion or death—or on the part of governments, more frequently conversion or exile—in their attempts to convert the Jews. Thus, despite the formal stance of Catholicism against forced baptism, nevertheless, generally, following the Council of Toledo, once performed, all baptisms, whether forced or not, were considered not only valid but also irreversible, since baptism constituted an indelible sacrament, and consequently to allow converts to Christianity to revert to Judaism would be dishonourable to Christianity. The characteristic papal stance was that articulated by Innocent III (1198–1216), who in 1201 affirmed that

> one who is drawn to Christianity by violence, through fear and through torture, and receives the sacrament of Baptism in order to avoid loss, he (like one who comes to Baptism in dissimulation) does receive the impress of Christianity, and may be forced to observe the Christian Faith as one who expressed a conditional willingness, though, absolutely speaking, he was unwilling. [. . .] He, however, who never consented, but wholly objected, accepted neither the impress nor the purpose of the Sacrament, for it is better expressly to object, than to give the least consent.[6]

Eventually, Clement IV (1261–68) established the papal policy in his Bull *Turbate corde* of 1267. Asserting that he was deeply disturbed by reports that many Christians —presumably he was referring to individuals who had formerly been Jews rather than ones who had been born into Christianity—had adopted Judaism, which he considered an insult to the name of Christianity that could only result in the subversion of the Christian faith, he empowered all Dominican and Franciscan friars who were deputized by the papal authorities as inquisitors of heresy, or would so be in the future, to seek out the guilty by using both Christian and Jewish witnesses. Christians who were found guilty were to be treated as heretics, while Jews who had induced Christians to adopt their rites were to be appropriately punished. Anyone standing in the way of the inquisitors was to be subjected to ecclesiastical punishment, and if necessary the aid of the secular powers was to be invoked.[7] In this spirit, a decretal issued sometime before 1298 by Boniface VIII (1294–1308) as an instruction to inquisitors, advised that

---

[5] See the general discussion in Baron, *Social and Religious History*, IX, 13–15; also the excerpts from Raymond of Penaforte and Alexander of Hales in Robert Chazan, *Church, State and Jews in the Middle Ages* (New York, 1980), pp. 38, 48–49; and Grayzel, *Church and the Jews*, II, 166–67 nn. 3 and 4, p. 209 n. 3.

[6] See Grayzel, *Church and the Jews*, I, 101–3 and II, 166 n. 3.

[7] See Grayzel, *Church and the Jews*, II, 102–4; also pp. 15–16, 122–23, 147, 171–72, 181.

one must proceed against Christians who adopt or revert to the rites of the Jews, even
if they were originally baptised as infants or under fear of death—although they were
not absolutely or precisely compelled to baptism—as one would proceed against
heretics who had confessed or been convicted on the testimony of Christians or Jews.
One should proceed against abettors, receivers, and defenders of these people as one
proceeds against abettors, receivers, and defenders of heretics.[8]

Obviously, these papal pronouncements basically nullified the protection provided
for in the *Sicut Judeis* Bulls. Consequently, only infrequently were secular authorities,
and even more rarely popes, willing to allow forced converts or their descendants to
revert to Judaism. One outstanding occasion of such permission granted by the secular
authorities, who were motivated primarily by economic considerations, occurred after
the First Crusades, when the Holy Roman Emperor Henry IV allowed Jews converted
to Christianity by force to return to Judaism.[9]

The great medieval theologian and scholastic Thomas Aquinas (1225–74)
summarized the approach of the Catholic Church on the issue of converting the Jews
in his *Summa theologia*.[10] Aquinas distinguished very carefully between two types of
unbelievers. On the one hand

there are some who have never received the faith, such as heathens and Jews. These are
by no means to be compelled, for belief is voluntary. [. . .] However, there are other
unbelievers who at one time accepted and professed the faith, such as heretics and
apostates of all sorts, and these are to be submitted to physical compulsion that they
should hold to what they once received and fulfill what they promised.[11]

Accordingly, Aquinas specified, 'Jews who have not accepted the faith should in no
way be coerced into it'. But nevertheless, he added, not unexpectedly, 'Those however
who have accepted it should be compelled to keep it'.

One specific type of conversion especially bothered the Jewish community and was
the subject of much controversy, and that was the issue of the conversion of Jewish
minors to Christianity against the wishes of their parents. In such cases, the attitude of

---

[8] See Grayzel, *Church and the Jews*, II, 209.

[9] See Grayzel, *Church and the Jews*, II, 166 n. 3.

[10] Aquinas dealt with the question of whether infidels should be compelled to believe in his
Summa theologia (henceforth *ST*), 2a2ae, q. 10, a. 8, available in the Latin original with English
translation in Aquinas, *Summa Theologia*, ed. by Thomas Gilby (New York and London, 1964),
XXXII, 60–65. On the views of Aquinas regarding the conversion of the Jews, see John Y. B.
Hood, *Aquinas and the Jews* (Philadelphia, 1995), pp. 88–92; also Hans Liebeschutz, 'Judaism
and Jewry in the Social Doctrine of Thomas Aquinas', *Journal of Jewish Studies*, 12 (1961),
57–81.

[11] See *ST*, 2a2ae, q. 4, a. 8; Latin and English text in Gilby, XXXII, 63.

medieval Catholicism was more divided. On the one hand, Aquinas adopted a liberal approach that was often cited by the Jews.[12] He argued against the practice on two grounds.

> One, the danger to faith. For if they are baptised before coming to the use of reason, such children when they grow up might easily be persuaded by their parents to renounce that which they had unknowingly embraced. And this would be detrimental to the faith. The other reason is that the practice would be repugnant to natural justice. For by origin the child is part of the father; at first, when still in the womb, he is not indeed separate from his parents, and later on when he is born and until he has reached the age of freedom, he is enfolded in the care of his parents, which is like a spiritual womb. In fact, so long as he has not the use of reason, he is like a non-rational animal. So that even as according to civil law an ox or a horse belongs to the owner who can use them when he chooses as his own instruments, so is it according to natural law that a child until he comes to the age of reason is under the charge of the father. [. . .] Hence, it would be contrary to natural justice for him to be taken away from the care of the parents or have any arrangements made for him against their wishes. As soon, however, as he begins to have the use of free will, then he begins to be his own master and to provide for himself in matters of divine and natural rights. Then he may be brought to the faith, not by compulsion but by persuasion; he can even consent to the faith and be baptised, but not before he enjoys the use of reason.[13]

Aquinas even objected to the generally accepted position that Jewish minors about to die could be baptized against the wishes of their parents.[14]

However, not all of the medievals shared the views of Aquinas. The opposite approach, expressed by Duns Scotus (1265?–1308), found many adherents. Scotus claimed that rulers had a moral obligation to convert all Jewish minors, for the rights of God over children were superior to those of parents. He additionally warned that newly baptized children should immediately be taken away from their parents and raised in Christian homes in order to avoid any relapses to Judaism and to assure that their offspring would become genuine believers.[15]

In Rome, it became the scrupulously observed practice not to baptize Jewish children under the age of twelve or thirteen without the explicit consent of both their parents, or at least the father, or should both parents be dead, then that of the grandfather or grandmother; exceptions were made only in two cases: if a child had been baptized because it had been presumed to be in danger of death, or if it had been

---

[12] See *ST*, 2a2ae, q. 4, a. 12; Latin and English text in Gilby, XXXII, 75–79.

[13] See *ST*, 2a2ae, q. 4, a. 12; Latin and English text in Gilby, XXXII, 76–79.

[14] Gilby, p. 79.

[15] For further details, see Baron, *Social and Religious History,* IX, 16–17; and Grayzel, *Church and the Jews,* II, 14–15.

abandoned by both parents or by whomever had custody over it. On the other hand, if those responsible for the child had not given their consent or if the situation was unclear, then the child was returned to the Jews with the obligation to present itself again to the appropriate Christian authorities for re-examination at the end of its twelfth year.[16] The above-related two exceptions were recognized in the papal Bull *De baptismo Judeorum* (1747) of Benedict XIV (1740–58), which, however, also reaffirmed the validity of a properly performed baptism even if it were not authorized, although it asserted that those who performed it should be punished.[17]

The most remarkable developments in the long history of the phenomenon of the forced conversion of Jews, in both theory and practice, occurred at the end of the Middle Ages. The year 1391 marked the watershed in the history of the Jews of Castille and Aragon. Conversion, which previously had affected only a relatively small minority, became more frequent as inflamed mobs gave the Jews the choice of conversion or death, or at least so intimidated them that conversion appeared attractive. Subsequently, in the following decades, more Jews converted to Christianity as a result of the combined effects of conversionist pressures and the long-standing restrictive legislation enacted against them. The number of Jews who converted cannot be ascertained, but clearly their proportion was unprecedented. Many of them really abandoned Judaism and became bona-fide Christians. Others regretted their conversion and wanted to revert to Judaism. However, they faced the negative Christian attitude toward reverting to Judaism, and if they secretly practised Judaism, were referred to derogatorily as *Marranos,* a word that meant 'pig', which is why modern scholarship prefers the term crypto-Jews.[18]

Additionally, socio-economic tensions soon developed between Old Christians and New Christians, the latter the designation by which all new converts were known. Many Old Christians resented the New who, liberated from all restrictions, were free to compete as equals. It was as if they were suddenly confronted by a huge immigration. Furthermore, they suspected, not without validity, that many of the New Christians were secretly judaizing. The complaints against the New Christians, motivated by a combination of religious fervour and socio-economic jealousy, gained in intensity. Finally, in 1478, at the urging of Thomas Torquemada, the confessor of Queen Isabella, the pope authorized the establishment of the Spanish Inquisition. Five years later, Torquemada was appointed Inquisitor General.

The Inquisition had no direct jurisdiction over professing Jews who did not overtly challenge Christianity, because the observance of Judaism was legal since the Jews were

---

[16] See Attilio Milano, *Il Ghetto di Roma* (Rome, 1964), pp. 285–91.

[17] See Piero C. Ioly Zorattini, *Battesimi di fanciulli Ebrei a Venezia nel Settecento* (Udine, 1984), pp. 10–12.

[18] For further details on the course of events on the Iberian Peninsula, see Benjamin Ravid, 'An Introduction to the Economic History of the Iberian Diaspora', *Judaism*, 41 (1992), 268–85.

regarded not as heretics but as tolerated infidels. However, the crypto-Jews were considered heretics who had to be punished and then reconciled with the Church. Accordingly, the aim of the Inquisition was to obtain a confession, and then to impose the appropriate penance in order to reconcile the accused with the Church and save their immortal soul. If a confession were not forthcoming, then torture could be employed to obtain it. The penalty could be death in the absence of a confession—either because the individuals charged were contumacious and acknowledged unrepentantly the charge or else were *negativos* who refused to confess because they were really innocent or hoped that they would be acquitted. The death penalty could also be imposed for alleged serious second offences which would make the individual a relapsed heretic. Since it was not proper for the Church to put people to death, the Inquisition would hand the individuals in question over to the secular authorities. Then, to avoid the literal shedding of blood, the condemned were burned alive at the stake at the *auto-da-fé*. A last-minute confession at the stake might lead to being mercifully garrotted before the pyre was lighted. While the pogrom, to borrow a term from the later experience of the Jews in nineteenth-century Russia, was not legitimate in the eyes of the Church or of the state, the *auto-da-fé* was. Obviously, as long as Judaism was permitted in Spain, those New Christians who wished to maintain their ties to Judaism as crypto-Jews could find spiritual, material, and institutional support and encouragement from the numerous and widespread organized Jewish communities. Therefore, it was deemed necessary to eliminate totally the open observance of Judaism in Spain. Consequently, in March 1492, following the fall of Granada, the last Moorish bastion in Spain, Ferdinand and Isabella issued a decree requiring all the Jews of Spain to leave within four months.

The number of places to which Jews could emigrate was limited. The majority took the easiest option of overland routes, mainly to Portugal. Far fewer embarked upon the more perilous sea voyages, fraught with the dangers of pirates, shipwreck, and drought, to North Africa, to those few places on the Italian peninsula which would accept them, and especially to the mainland of the eastern Mediterranean and its islands. That area was being consolidated in the hands of the Ottoman sultan, and he welcomed the Jews in anticipation of what he thought they could do for his realm.

The fate of the exiles in Portugal was complex. King John of Portugal authorized six hundred wealthy families to stay in return for a large sum; others, upon payment of an entrance fee, were allowed to remain for eight months, by the end of which they were to depart or else become royal slaves. But the king did not provide adequate ships for them to leave, and those who remained without converting were enslaved. Fortunately for them, John died shortly afterwards, in 1495, and was succeeded by his brother Emmanuel. Emmanuel was very concerned with developing the economy and commerce of Portugal and, accordingly, freed the Jewish slaves so that they could become productive members of society. However, he wished to marry the daughter of Ferdinand and Isabella, and the princess was unwilling to consent unless the Jews were eliminated from Portugal.

Emmanuel allowed the dynastic consideration of uniting Spain and Portugal under his heirs to prevail, and, in December 1496, he ordered all Jews to leave Portugal by the end of October 1497 under penalty of death. However, since he really wanted them to remain because they were useful for the economy, he exerted pressure upon them to convert, even baptising all children between the ages of four and fourteen and having them returned to their parents only if the latter also converted. Then, after limiting the ports of embarkation to three, he required all the Jews to gather in Lisbon, where the available shipping was not sufficient, and as soon as the deadline for departure passed, all those who remained were converted by force. Accordingly, while reference is frequently made to 'the expulsion of the Jews from Portugal in 1497', often together with that from Spain, in reality no actual expulsion took place in Portugal.

However, as of 1497, Judaism was indeed completely proscribed on the Iberian Peninsula. No longer were Jews confronted with the choice of conversion or exile, but rather New Christians had the option either of practising only Catholicism or else risk burning at the stake if caught Judaizing.

In order to placate the new converts, Emmanuel promised them immunity from persecution on religious grounds for twenty years, and later this was extended. As in Spain, the Old Christians greatly resented the New Christians because of their economic success in various areas from which previously they had been excluded as Jews, and also out of a not-unjustified sense that many were secretly judaizing. Tensions increased, finally erupting in a major riot in Lisbon in 1506. The king severely punished the perpetrators and allowed New Christians to depart, but subsequently they were forbidden to leave. They were needed, since they were not only the predominant element in the international commerce of Portugal in a period of great colonial expansion, but also to a great extent they assumed the role of the 'middle class' in that underdeveloped country and especially helped with the royal finances and administration.

Despite the concerted efforts of the New Christians to prevent the establishment of the Inquisition in Portugal, it was finally authorized in 1536. Understandably, over the decades, the pressure of the two Inquisitions of Spain and Portugal induced many New Christians, and obviously especially those who were secretly judaizing, to leave the Iberian peninsula, legally or illegally. A major place of refuge continued to be the Ottoman Empire, whose Sultan was completely indifferent to the issue of whether the sacrament of baptism when imparted under compulsion—or even undertaken voluntarily—was indeed indelible and irreversible or not. Rather, concerned with the well-being of his country, he welcomed both Jewish immigrants and also those of Jewish descent.

Meanwhile, the Italian peninsula had not been as attractive a place of refuge for the Spanish exiles of 1492 or for crypto-Jews in the early sixteenth-century, because only a very few places were willing to receive them. However, the situation changed greatly during the course of the sixteenth century. The establishment of the Inquisition in Portugal gave an additional impetus to the desire of New Christians to leave the Iberian Peninsula just at the time when various Italian authorities, realizing that Iberian New Christian merchants were very active in international maritime commerce, adopted a policy of *raison d'état* which led them to offer liberal terms as they endeavoured— indeed, even competed—to attract merchants to their own domains.

The reason for this competition is to be sought in the general economic circumstances of the times. Certain Italian port cities, especially Venice and Ancona, had enjoyed an active trade with the East, and with the consolidation of the eastern Mediterranean in the hands of the Ottoman Turks, Ottoman subjects began to play a more significant role in this maritime commerce. Their ranks included Jews, and increasingly Jews of Iberian origin, either exiles of 1492 and their descendants or else former New Christians who had later travelled from the Iberian peninsula eastward to assume Judaism in the safety of the Ottoman Empire and then returned to Catholic Europe as Ottoman subjects. In 1514, Ancona began to offer favourable terms to attract Levantine merchants. Then, after Ancona became a part of the Papal States in 1532, the popes maintained a policy of attracting foreign merchants. Pope Paul III (1534–49), undertook a major step in 1547, as he issued a safe-conduct inviting 'all merchants of whatever nation, faith or sect, even if Turks, Jews or other infidels' to settle with their families in Ancona, reiterating that it was to be valid for all persons coming from Portugal, even if 'they were of Jewish origin, called New Christians [. . .] or of the Jewish nation of whatever origin', and moreover no official was to bother them with charges of heresy, apostasy, or blasphemy, or to investigate their practices during the time that they had previously lived as Christians. In short, he was assuring New Christians that they could assume Judaism with impunity in the Papal States. Five years later, in 1552, Pope Julius III (1550–55) reconfirmed that safe-conduct and other privileges.[19]

Presumably, the legal basis for these permissive actions was a Bull of Clement VII (1523–34) of 1533, asserting that those who had been baptized by force were not to be considered Christians and would have every right to complain of being punished in violation of the principles of justice and equity. However, this leniency was supposed to apply only to those individuals who had been converted by force in Spain and Portugal and not also to their descendants, who are usually also referred to somewhat ambiguously as 'New Christians', while actually the term 'descendants of New Christians' would be more accurate and precise, since they had been baptized at birth— or should have been. It should be noted that the Papal States was not the only area to invite foreign merchants, including New Christians who were allowed to assume Judaism with impunity. Other states issued such invitations, including Ferrara (1538), Florence (1551), and Savoy (1572).

In the interim, clouds were gathering on the Italian horizon. Inquisitions were established on the Italian peninsula, starting with the Roman Inquisition in 1542 at the urging of Cardinal Caraffa, later Pope Paul IV (1555–59), and then followed by

---

[19] For a more detailed presentation of the developments related in this paragraph and the following four, see B. Ravid, 'Venice, Rome, and the Reversion of New Christians to Judaism: A Study in *Ragione di Stato*', in *L'identità dissimulata: Studi e ricerche su Conversos e Giudaizzanti in Europa e nell'area mediterranea nell'età moderna*, ed. by P. C. Ioly Zorattini.

independent local Inquisitions in other jurisdictions. However, these Italian Inquisitions came into being for a reason completely different from that which had led to the Iberian Inquisitions; for they were set up not to deal with judaizing New Christians but rather with the new presence and diffusion of Protestantism which the Catholic world perceived as heresy. Still, clearly the Jews were better off where there was no Inquisition, for it was accepted that the Inquisition could reach out into the Jewish world if the Jews were suspected of deliberately undermining Christianity, a charge which was easy to level and difficult to disprove, while New Christians who had assumed Judaism were always potentially vulnerable to accusations of heresy.

The situation underwent a fundamental and far-reaching change with the Counter-reformation and its new harsh papal attitude toward the Jews, which also had ram-ifications for the attitude toward the reversion of New Christians to Judaism. In 1556, the year following his Bull *Cum nimis absurdum*, Pope Paul IV suddenly reversed the economically motivated policy of his predecessors to grant safe-conducts to former New Christians. Instead, he issued a Bull which declared that anyone born in Portugal who subsequently had lived as a Jew in the Italian peninsula was to be considered a Christian heretic, even if under torture they denied ever having received baptism or having lived as a Christian, on the grounds that Judaism had been illegal in Portugal since 1497. Immediately afterwards, reversing the previous, tolerant papal policy not only in theory but also in practice, the pope had twenty-six Jews, including at least one woman, burned in Ancona on the grounds that they had relapsed from Christianity. *Bona fide* Ottoman Jewish merchants continued to be welcome in Ancona, but Jews of New Christian descent were well-advised to stay out of the Papal States. Elsewhere in the Italian peninsula, as a rule the background of those who openly and unambiguously professed Judaism was not checked, and relatively few Jews were harassed by the Inquisition, let alone subject to the *auto-da-fé*.

Although the very brief period of papal disregard of the traditional policy regarding the efficacy of the sacrament of baptism was over, it continued in the two maritime centres of Venice and Livorno, which greatly desired the presence of Jewish merchants with their wide-spread kinship networks to meet the increasing competition of English, French, Spanish, Portuguese, and Dutch merchants in the Mediterranean, and the threat of the new trade routes to the East around the Cape of Good Hope. Indeed, a generation after the Holy League in which the papacy organized Venice and Spain against the Ottoman Empire in the campaign that culminated in the Battle of Lepanto, the papacy sharply criticised the Venetian government for allowing Iberian New Christians to assume Judaism. The Venetians not only responded that it was in the interest of Christianity, for otherwise those individuals would go to enrich the Ottoman Empire, its traditional enemy, but also asserted that since popes, including Paul III, had previously permitted such reversions, to permit them could not be wrong in principle.

Thus, while commercial considerations of *raison d'état* temporarily induced the papacy to modify its traditional religious position on the efficacy of the sacrament of baptism upon converts from Judaism to Christianity, ultimately the medieval papal attitude was reaffirmed. Then, when the briefly held, more permissive papal attitude was invoked by a major Catholic Italian state, it was explicitly condemned by the papacy as the traditional papal attitude continued to be maintained well into the modern period, as the sensational Mortara affair was to demonstrate in the 1850s.[20]

---

[20] On the Mortara affair, see now D. Kertzer, *The Kidnapping of Edgardo Mortara* (New York, 1997).

Living in Limbo:
The Experience of Jewish
Converts in Medieval England

REVA BERMAN BROWN & SEAN MCCARTNEY

T he Jewish community of medieval England came into existence when Jews were invited to immigrate after the Norman Conquest,[1] as part of a policy of stimulating commercial development, and came to an end when the Jews were expelled by Edward I in 1290. A section of the Rouen community seems to have followed William the Conqueror's path across the Channel to London, the only place in England were Jews are definitely known to have lived before the middle of the twelfth century. As a nationwide minority, the Jewish community dates only from Henry II's reign (1154–89).[2]

Initially, the king borrowed from 'his' Jews, then he taxed them, not only on their financial activities, but on marriage, on death—and on conversion. The prevailing ethos of the times required that Jews should embrace Christianity, and the king was in no position to oppose this pious purpose. Yet, once Christian, the ex-Jew could no longer

---

[1] This is the view of most historians, although it is not undisputed. See Cecil Roth, *A History of the Jews in England* (Oxford, 1949), who cites William of Malmesbury, *Gesta regum Anglorum*, IV, 317, as stating that the Jews of London had been brought there by William the Conqueror. Also, H. G. Richardson, *The English Jewry under Angevin Kings* (London, 1960), pp. 1–3; and Robert C. Stacey, 'Jewish Lending and the Medieval English Economy', in *A Commercialising Economy*, ed. by Richard H. Britnell and Bruce M. S. Campbell (Manchester, 1995), pp. 78–101.

[2] Paul R. Hyams, 'The Jewish Minority in Medieval England, 1066–1290', *Journal of Jewish Studies*, 25.2 (1974), 270–93, 271.

undertake the financial activities which were essential for the economy of England, because of the ban on usury for Christians.[3] So official policy paradoxically aimed simultaneously at defending the religious integrity of the kingdom by the conversion of the Jews, and at maintaining a flourishing Jewish community to stimulate commercial activity in general, and to increase the revenue of the Crown in particular. In the final analysis, the king was usually more interested in converting the Jews into cash than into Christians. This ambiguity continued with the treatment of those (few) Jews who did convert: their integration into Christian society (theoretically assured if their conversion was accepted as genuine) was in practice very difficult, and frequently impossible. The purpose of this paper is to explore the ambiguities in this position, with especial reference to the *Domus Conversorum* (House of Converts).

During the two centuries that they lived and worked in England, the Jews' status was unique. They were outside the feudal system, protected by and 'belonging to' the Crown. They were literally the king's Jews. The Statute of Jewry of Henry III (1253) makes this explicit: 'All Jews, wherever in the realm they are, must be under the King's liege protection and guardianship, nor can any of them put himself under the protection of any powerful person without the King's licence, because the Jews themselves and all their chattels are the King's. If therefore anyone detain them or their money, the King may claim them, if he so desire and if he is able, as his own'.[4] What is significant about the above proclamation is the overt financial claim; it is 'all their chattels' and 'their money' which is at the root of things.

This status seems to have been a peculiarity of English Jewry, at least in the Angevin period. Langmuir points out that the concept of the Jews as the king's property develops later in France: even towards the end of the twelfth century, the rule that a magnate had the right to prevent Jews who resided in his lands from leaving and placing themselves under the protection of another was by no means generally accepted in France.[5] It is possible, if by no means certain, that the royal monopoly in England reflected the unusually powerful position of the English kings compared to their French

---

[3] Stacey, 'Jewish Lending and the Medieval English Economy', p. 89, refers to Christian financiers operating in the mid-twelfth century—the Fleming William Cade, William Trentegeruns of Rouen, the London merchants William fitz Isabel and Gervase and Henry of Cornhill—though these had disappeared by 1200, and 'for the next half-century, wide-scale moneylending in England seems to have been left almost entirely to Jews' (p. 90). Why Jews maintained their dominant position in finance is, of course, beyond the scope of this paper.

[4] Paul R. Hyams, 'The Jews in Medieval England, 1066–1290', in *England and Germany in the High Middle Ages,* ed. by Alfred Haverkamp and Hanna Vollrath (Oxford, 1996), pp. 173–92. Hyams suggests (p. 182) that possessives like 'mine', 'his', and 'the king's' denote relationships, in the first instance, and not property or possession, and that therefore a chattel-ownership reading of this is an anachronism.

[5] Gavin Langmuir, '"Judei nostri" and the Beginning of Capetian Legislation', *Traditio,* 16 (1960), 203–39.

counterparts in the twelfth and thirteenth centuries and the peculiar conditions of the Jews who had recently immigrated to a conquered England.[6] Thus there is a connection between the strength of the central government in England and the position of the Jews.[7]

The Jews were outside, but alongside, the feudal hierarchy in which land was given in return for military service. Allegiance was owed directly to the Crown which had allowed them into England, and moreover, they were only tolerated in the country as long as it suited the Crown to allow it. This is made explicit in Henry III's 1233 Statute of Jewry which demanded that Jews who are not profiting the Crown (*qui nichil habent vnde regi seruiant*) leave the realm (*exeant de regno*) by a specified date or face imprisonment (*detrudantur in carcerem*).[8]

While the role of money was growing throughout the period, it was the land and its produce which constituted wealth. Feudal government was designed rather to hamper than to assist commercial activity.[9] Moreover, the public opinion of all classes, albeit in varying degrees, continued to look upon the trader as a parasite, a speculator, a usurer, and moveable wealth as a fruit of fraud and rapine, rather than of labour,[10] despite the fact that most people needed to trade by this period, at least locally, if not abroad. In itself, being rich in moveables did not command respect; on the contrary, the merchant with plenty of assets, who used money to make more in commercial or money-lending operations, awoke all sorts of emotions in the medieval breast—hate, envy, scorn, fear—but not respect.

Wealth as seen by the aristocracy was not an end in itself, nor was it something that should be accumulated or used for economic improvement or development. The landowner who sought to increase his income did not do so with a view to stepping up production; it was simply a way of widening his circle of friends and retainers, allies and vassals, among whom he would then distribute his largesse of money and goods.[11]

It was within this antagonistic milieu that the king's Jews were required to operate, excluded from legitimate wealth by the non-possibility of owning land, and consigned to money-lending as the reason for their presence in the kingdom.

---

[6] This point is made by Gavin Langmuir in 'The Jews and the Archives of Angevin England', *Traditio*, 19 (1963), 183–224, 199. The paper contains an extended review of Richardson, *The English Jewry under Angevin Kings*.

[7] See R. Chazan, *Medieval Jewry in Northern France* (Baltimore, 1973); and Gavin Langmuir, '"Tanquam Servi": The Change in Jewish Status in French Law about 1200', in *Les Juifs dans l'histoire de France*, ed. by M. Yardeni (Leiden, 1980).

[8] Text in Richardson, *The English Jewry under Angevin Kings,* p. 294.

[9] See R. H. Hilton, *English and French Towns in Feudal Society* (Cambridge, 1992). Hilton challenges traditional views of the urban character of medieval towns and takes issue with the perception that they were the harbinger of capitalism.

[10] See Edward Miller and John Hatcher, *Medieval England: Towns, Commerce and Crafts 1086–1348* (London, 1995).

[11] See N. J. G. Pounds, *An Economic History of Medieval Europe,* 2nd edn (London, 1994).

Jewish Life in the Christian Community

What was it like to be one of the king's Jews? Firstly, the Jews were a minority within a minority—they lived in towns, and town-dwellers were a small percentage of the total population, who owned, worked, and lived on the land. Villeins formed more than three-quarters of the population of England from the eleventh to the thirteenth centuries.[12] (A villein was a labourer owning a pair of oxen and fifteen to thirty acres of land, according to the Domesday Book of 1086.) Secondly, the Jews lived among their Christian neighbours. There were no Jewish ghettos in medieval England, although there were neighbourhoods, called 'the Jewry', with a density of Jews, living among non-Jews, in a society which did not yet value privacy highly. Within the towns, the Jews tended to live close to a market place and the royal castle, if there was one.

The town communities were always used as centres from which to cover the local countryside—none of the major seaports apart from London had an important community.[13] The Jewish communities appear to have spread out from London during the first half of the twelfth century, and by 1159 prosperous communities were well established in Norwich, Lincoln, Cambridge, Winchester, Oxford, Northampton, Thetford, and Bungay,[14] and probably also at Bury St Edmunds, with smaller communities in Gloucester, Worcester, and Newport, Essex.[15]

The average community is unlikely to have comprised more than 50 to 100 people. The Jewry in Norwich, which in its heyday was one of the most prosperous in England, was never more than 200, of whom half would be children.[16] This suggests a close-knit community, in which everybody knew everybody else; despite living among their Christian neighbours, the Jews were isolated by their own religious and community traditions. Moreover, the typical family unit was small. Dobson argues that 'in the great majority of documented medieval Jewish families, it seems difficult to find incontrovertible evidence that a Jewish father and mother had more than two living children; whilst it is even more noticeable that the copious records of the Jewish plea rolls are more or less totally devoid of references to extant grandparents or even to uncles, aunts and cousins'.[17] As a consequence, the Jews were observers of the Christian life lived around them—the churches occupied

---

[12] Edward Miller and John Hatcher, *Medieval England: Rural Society and Economic Change, 1086–1348* (London, 1978).

[13] Stacey, 'Jewish Lending and the Medieval English Economy', pp. 85–86.

[14] Richardson, *The English Jewry under Angevin Kings*, p. 13, notes that, exceptionally, Thetford and Bungay, which were impermanent, were under the private lordship of Hugh Bigod, earl of Leicester.

[15] Stacey, 'Jewish Lending and the Medieval English Economy', pp. 85–86.

[16] Vivian D. Lipman, *The Jews of Medieval Norwich* (London, 1967).

[17] R. B. Dobson, 'The Role of Jewish Women in Medieval England', *Studies in Church History*, 29 (1992), 145–68, 153.

prominent places even in the streets of the Jewry, so that it was not possible to ignore the bells, the processions on feast days, and the ceremonial marking of (parish) boundaries.

Urban life (both public and private) was lived out in communal actions and activities, so that the Jewish community was in the larger society, not of it. For instance, Jews were forbidden to appear on the streets during the Christian Holy Week because their presence was considered likely to inspire violence. In Western Europe, and also in England, fear and misunderstanding from Jewish and Christian communities alike led to the growing attitude of Jewish exclusivity on the part of the rabbinic commentators on the law, an exclusivity specifically directed at minimising contact between Jews and Christians, and thus minimizing potential violence from Christians towards their Jewish neighbours.[18]

In the life the converts had left behind, religious and social activity centred about the synagogue (*beth knesset*). This was a house of prayer (*beth tefilah*) and of study (*beth midrash*). Synagogues were mostly small establishments, often maintained by wealthy magnates in their own houses, it being regarded as a duty incumbent upon the wealthy members of each community to provide a synagogue and its embellishments.[19] Here communal meetings would be held, excommunications fulminated, and announcements made. The synagogue formed the channel of communication with the civil authorities, necessary proclamations being made in it both in Latin and Hebrew on two or three Sabbaths in succession. This would indicate that there was at least one synagogue in all Jewish communities and that all members attended at least once every two to three weeks.

Jewish communities would have required a communal oven for baking the Passover *mazot*, a slaughter house for the ritual slaughtering of meat, together with a *shohet* or ritual butcher,[20] and the women of the community would have need of a *mikvah* for the ritual baths required after menstruation and childbirth.[21] The synagogue would have a cantor or *hazan* to read the Law during services, a sexton, and a *gabbai*, the synagogue's treasurer. The professional rabbi had barely made his appearance, though 'masters of the Jewish law' were to be found in most places. The authority they exercised was principally moral. England had its representatives of the German mystical

---

[18] See Langmuir, 'The Jews and the Archives of Angevin England'; and J. Katz, *Exclusiveness and Tolerance: Studies in Jewish-Gentile Relations in Medieval and Modern Times* (New York, 1961).

[19] Joe Hillaby, 'Beth Miqdash Me'at: The Synagogues of Medieval England', *Journal of Ecclesiastical History*, 44.2 (1993), 182–98, 187. This provision can be traced back from dedicatory inscriptions of founders' names in fourth-century Tiberias, and medieval Spain and Portugal and Germany.

[20] Hillaby, 'Beth Miqdash Me'at: The Synagogues of Medieval England', p. 197, cites Statute 51, Henry III, c. 6, which enacted that no one should buy 'meat from the Jews and sell again to Christians or meat [ritually] slaughtered for Jews and by them rejected'.

[21] T. Noble and T. Gardiner, 'Brief History of Jacob's Well', *Bristol Templar*, 5.1 (Spring, 1989), 8–10, discuss the possible *mikvah* in Bristol.

school of Hasidim, but the average English Jew followed the path of normal observance; the synagogue ritual was very similar to that followed in France, whence most
of the English Jews had come.

The Issue of Conversion

Running parallel with the political and economic policies of the Norman and
Angevin kings towards 'their' Jews, was the religious issue of their conversion. While,
demographically speaking, the medieval Jewish population was a relatively incon-
spicuous one,[22] in the financial sphere, the Jewish presence was distinct, and from 1194,
their transactions were governed by a special organ of government, the Exchequer of
the Jews.[23] And the Jews were all the more noticeable because they remained insistently
loyal to their Jewish identity, and thus were a source of enormous social anxiety in a
society which was otherwise religiously homogeneous. Their loyalty to Judaism, as
medieval people interpreted it, intrinsically challenged Christianity's truth.[24] This view
created a degree of ambivalence about encouraging missions to convert the Jews. On
the one hand, Augustine of Hippo (d. 423) had argued that Jews were useful to
Christians in that they bore witness to the truth of Christianity (*testimonium veritatis*).
Jews did this because they had in their possession the holy books in which Christians
found the prophecies concerning the coming of Christ. Without the continued presence

---

[22] The question of numbers is obviously important, but unfortunately assessment remains
little more than guesswork. The geography of settlement shows that there was steady expansion
during the twelfth century and confirms other evidence that numbers were falling during the
thirteenth. V. D. Lipman, 'The Anatomy of Mediaeval Anglo-Jewry', *Transactions of the Jewish
Historical Society*, 21 (1962–67), 64–77, puts the total population at about 4000 to 5000 in 1200.
This would be perhaps 0.25 per cent of the total for England as a whole, 1.25 per cent for the total
urban population. By the expulsion in 1290, the numbers had dropped to between 2500 and 3000.
These figures are very rough indeed, but the impression they give of a very small group in terms
of total numbers is probably justified.

[23] Here the Jews were unique in that they were assigned a special royal court for external
relations, and especially to settle disputes between Jews and Christians. See Richardson, *The
English Jewry under Angevin Kings,* pp. 149–53, for an account of Jewish transactions and the
role of the Jewish Exchequer. The jurisdiction of the Exchequer, though comprehensive, was not
exclusive. One can find cases involving Jews on the rolls of other courts, including those of the
'Great Exchequer' and the court *Coram Rege* (the King's Bench), itself the origin of the later
Court of Common Pleas. For French administrative practice of the time see R. Chazan, *Medieval
Jewry in Northern France* (Baltimore, 1973); J. Baldwin, *The Government of Philip Augustus*
(Berkeley, 1986); and W. C. Jordan, *The French Monarchy and the Jews: From Philip Augustus
to the Last Capetians* (Philadelphia, 1989).

[24] K. Stow, *Alienated Minority. The Jews of Medieval Latin Europe* (Cambridge, MA,
1992), p. 7.

of Jews, pagans could easily argue that Christians had made up the prophetic texts themselves. With Jews at hand, Christians could prove that this was not so. Because Jews performed this useful function, they should not be persecuted or compelled to convert to Christianity.[25] On the other hand, Church doctrine explicitly linked the end of days, and the Last Days/Second Coming, with the conversion of the Jews. In the meantime, their freedom of action had to be restrained for fear of the harm they might otherwise do in sowing doubts, by mockery, or by all-too-informed argument.[26] Besides which, there was the uneasy fear that if, after conversion *en masse*, the Second Coming did not happen, this doctrine would quite literally have been shown as untrue.[27]

The popular mistrust of the Jews had three main roots: it stemmed from the religious identification of medieval Jews with the New Testament killers of Christ; it also derived from the fear of the strange and the stranger (in this the Jews were not alone —for example, the Flemings were also mistrusted, despite being fellow Christians); and Jewish moneylending incurred resentment.[28]

Serious theological discussion about Jewish conversion did not begin until the twelfth century, and it was not until the thirteenth century that theological arguments began to be developed and employed in organized campaigns aimed at converting large numbers of Jews to Christianity, a cause which the friars in particular took up strongly.[29] Where conversion was concerned, the Christian attitude regarded baptism as irrevocable, even if it was coerced under threat of death, and the Church was determined to retain converts. It was prepared to punish apostates who reverted to Judaism after baptism, and was also determined to punish those who aided them to relapse.[30] A convert from Judaism to Christianity was as much an apostate in Jewish eyes as was a baptized Christian who returned to Judaism an apostate in the eyes of the Church. The two religions regarded apostasy differently, however. The Christian view was provided by John Pecham, archbishop of Canterbury—although Jews cannot be forced to profess the Christian faith, nonetheless, once they have been converted to it, and baptized into it, they are to be forced, by every means, spiritual and secular, to keep to the faith and to live according to it for the rest of their lives.[31] Jewish law recognized that forced conversions might occur, and rabbinic tradition allowed Jews to accept baptism, while exercising a mental reservation which

---

[25] A. S. Abulafia, *Christians and Jews in the Twelfth-Century Renaissance* (London, 1995), p. 65.

[26] Hyams, 'The Jews in Medieval England, 1066–1290'.

[27] Stow, *Alienated Minority*, p. 264.

[28] Hyams, 'The Jews in Medieval England, 1066–1290', p. 174.

[29] R. C. Stacey, 'The Conversion of Jews to Christianity in Thirteenth-Century England', *Speculum*, 67 (1992), 263–83.

[30] Stow, *Alienated Minority*, p. 119.

[31] F. Donald Logan, 'Thirteen London Jews and Conversion to Christianity: Problems of Apostasy in the 1280s', *Bulletin of the Institute for Historical Research*, 45 (1972), 214–29, esp. p. 215.

allowed them to remain as secret Jews, if the only alternative to baptism was death. According to Jewish law, even the voluntary, sincerely committed convert did not cease to be a Jew, albeit an apostate one.[32] But suspicion remained, and the reality was not always congruent with the principle that conversion did not sever a Jew's ties to Judaism. Forced converts who wished to be reconciled with Judaism in this world—not only 'after death'—found the return path strewn with obstacles.[33]

The general Christian populace did not take converts (forced or voluntary) to its heart. The derision that even voluntary converts encountered is epitomized by the complaint of the convert known as Master Andreas who mentions that while some people might greet him with goodwill, others suspect that he, like other converts, will go 'to a place where they are not recognized, and there they will return to their Jewish origins'.[34]

The story of Benedict of York illustrates this ambivalence. Richard I had issued a proclamation prohibiting women and Jews from admittance to his coronation on Sunday, 3 September 1189. A deputation from the Jewish communities presented itself at the gateway of Westminster Hall, bearing rich gifts—probably in the hope of obtaining a renewal of the charter of privileges granted originally by Henry I. Some of the delegation, eager to see the magnificence, perhaps, took advantage of a momentary disorder to slip in and were driven out by a zealous doorkeeper with unnecessary brutality. This aroused the crowd at the palace gates, and several members of the deputation were beaten or trampled to death before they could escape. The wealthy Benedict, who had come as one of the representatives of the community of York, saved his life by consenting to embrace Christianity and was immediately baptized and given the name William.

The day after the riot, Richard sent for Benedict of York, who admitted that he had adopted Christianity only in order to escape death. Richard turned to the archbishop of Canterbury and asked how Benedict/William should be dealt with. The archbishop is said to have responded contemptuously, 'If he will not serve God, let him serve the devil', and Richard allowed Benedict to return to Judaism—a not-altogether altruistic act because, while the king would presumably have made an immediate 'killing' if he had ruled that the baptism must stand, since Benedict's property would have been forfeit to the Crown, it was presumably financially better to have a solvent Jew, continuing to conduct the business from which Richard would derive revenue, than a destitute convert.[35]

---

[32] Hyams, 'The Jewish Minority in Medieval England, 1066–1290', citing Rashi (p. 276): 'although he has sinned, he remains a Jew'.

[33] R. I. Moore, *The Formation of a Persecuting Society: Power and Deviance in Western Europe, 950–1250* (Oxford, 1987).

[34] Stow, *Alienated Minority*, p. 228.

[35] Roth, *A Short History of the Jewish People*, p. 20.

Benedict died in Northampton, but the Pipe Roll records that he was not buried in the Jewish cemetery.[36] The two reasons given create a puzzle. These are: 'both because he had been made a Christian' (from the Jewish point of view, Benedict's conversion was forced and therefore not genuine, so he was still a Jew), 'and because, like a dog to his vomit, he had returned to his Jewish depravity' (which, from the Jewish perspective would be adequate grounds for a Jewish burial).

There is a postscript to Benedict's story. The Rotuli Carti (16 April 1200) states that King John grants 'two messuages in Northampton with their appurtenances, which belonged to Benedict, Jew of York, and which are our escheats to Simon de Pateshull and his heirs'.[37] So the king (though in this case, Richard's successor) obtained Benedict's property in the end.

In 1278, Pope Nicholas III issued the papal bull, *Vineam sorec*, to promote missionary sermons, and after 1280, Jews throughout England were compelled to attend conversion sermons, preached by the Dominicans, which were to be heard 'without tumult, contention, or blasphemy' from their audience,[38] although they appear to have had little practical effect, nor did they allay the social and religious unease created by the presence of the Jews.

To encourage conversions, Edward waived for a seven-year period his legal claim on the property of those who left their faith. From now on, they might retain one-half of what they previously owned, though it had been amassed in sin, the remainder (with certain other income from Jewry, including the proceeds of the recently instituted poll-tax) being devoted to the upkeep of the *Domus Conversorum* (the House of Converts) in London, of which more below.

Edward's support of compulsory sermons had little practical effect, however. His father, Henry III, had been more successful. From the 1240s to the 1260s, a period of savage taxation, about 300 of England's 5,000 Jews (6 per cent) converted. These converts included the notables Elias l'Eveske and Isaac of Norwich. They appear to have been persuaded less by reason than by the threat of capital punishment or by Henry's financial soakings.[39] Nevertheless, this number of converts is clearly connected

---

[36] Pipe Rolls (henceforth PR), 1 Richard I, vol. III, 12, published along with Pipe Rolls 31 Henry I and 2–5 Henry II by the Record Commission. All others published by the Pipe Roll Society.

[37] Rotuli Carti, i. 52, 55^b.

[38] Calendar of Patent Rolls, 6 vols, for the reign of Henry III (London, 1895–1913), 1272–81, p. 256 (henceforth CPR; this and all subsequent citations are referenced by year and page, and not volume). See R. Cha, *Daggers of Faith: Thirteenth-Century Christian Missionizing and Jewish Response* (Berkeley, 1989); and J. Cohen, *The Friars and the Jews: The Evolution of Medieval Anti-Judaism* (Ithaca, NY, 1982), for an analysis of the accelerating pressures mounted against thirteenth-century European Jewry, the development of an anti-Jewish ideology, and the Jewish response.

[39] Stacey, 'The Conversion of Jews to Christianity in Thirteenth-Century England'.

to the existence of a place—the *Domus Conversorum*—where converted Jews could live in safety.

Why Did the Jews Convert?

In the main, they converted for three reasons: poverty, what one could call the threat of immediate and unpleasant circumstances, and genuine conviction. There was an upsurge of conversion between 1240 and 1260, the period during which Henry III's excessive taxation drove many Jews into poverty, if not destitution. The Jewish community's ability to look after the financial needs of its destitute members was diminished just at the time when the number of the destitute was increasing rapidly. As a result, orphans, widows, and parents who had lost a spouse must have found themselves to be a burden on their relatives' charity that the relatives were unable to sustain. Conversion in such cases might have been the only alternative to starvation.

In many instances, the threat of immediate and unpleasant circumstances involved imprisonment in the Tower of London. From the Calendar of Patent Rolls,[40] we have the story of the Lincoln Jew, awaiting execution for the alleged ritual murder of Hugh of Lincoln (1255), who was suddenly convinced of the truth of Christianity. He adopted the name of the king's confessor, and the converted John of Lincoln was released from the Tower and the prospect of certain death. In a similar case in 1252,[41] Isaac of Norwich also converted to Christianity while awaiting trial (and probably execution) for coin clipping.

Forced conversions took place during the Barons' Wars of 1263–65 when Simon de Montfort's forces sacked the Jewries of London, Canterbury, Winchester, and Northampton, presenting Jewish women in particular with the alternatives of baptism or death.

Of course, it is difficult to discriminate between those whose immediate stimulus to convert was poverty or fear of death, but who became genuine believers in their new religion, and those who maintained their inner reservation and whose Christianity was only skin deep. It is even more difficult to identify those whose contact with Christianity was the stimulus to convert for spiritual, rather than material, reasons, and who genuinely preferred the new truth of Christianity to the religion into which they had been born. There is no equivalent document from genuinely-convinced converts in England to that of the converts Peter Alfonsis, Pablo Christiani, or Hermann of Cologne, whose writings on his conversion were widely distributed.[42]

---

[40] CPR, 1247–58, p. 457.

[41] CPR, 1247–58, p. 224.

[42] See Jeremy Cohen, 'The Mentality of the Medieval Jewish Apostate: Peter Alfonsis, Hermann of Cologne, and Pablo Christiani', in *Jewish Apostasy in the Modern World*, ed. by Todd M. Endleman and Jeffrey Gurock (New York, 1987).

The Establishment of the Domus Conversorum

Henry III issued an Order in Council on 16 January 1232 to the effect that he desired 'for the health of his own soul and for the souls of his ancestors and heirs, to the honour of God and of the glorious Virgin' to found a home for destitute Jews who had converted to Christianity.[43] The statement can be taken as largely pious cant. In the first place, the property of any Jew who converted automatically escheated to the Crown, so that even if a Jew was not destitute before conversion, he or she certainly was afterwards. The king was seizing the property of converts, and then generously offering them a bare subsistence 'for the health of his soul'. If Jewish converts were already destitute (which might itself be a stimulus for conversion), they quite likely had become so as a result of the taxes the same king had levied on them. For such Jews, the alternative to conversion was not appealing.

The *Domus Conversorum* (*Le Converse Inn* in Norman-French; the House of Converts in modern English) was established in what was then called 'the street called New Street, in the suburbs of London, running between the Old Temple and the New',[44] and which later was called Chancery Lane. Seven hundred years later, the site of the *Domus* was to be occupied by the Public Record Office.

The two bishops whose signatures are appended to the Order are Peter des Roches, bishop of Winchester, the favourite of Henry III, and William, bishop of Carlisle. In April 1233, a further Order was issued to the bishop of Chichester which details the sources of income for the *Domus* from certain confiscated lands and from fines. The king fixed an endowment of the establishment at 700 marks (£470) a year,[45] but as with many of Henry's financial promises, the *Domus* rarely received more than a third of the promised sum.

Soon after the foundation of the *Domus,* Matthew Paris, the monk of St Albans, tells us that Henry III 'built a decent church,[46] fit for a conventual congregation, with other buildings adjoining, at his own expense, in the place where he had established a House of Converts,

---

[43] Michael Adler, 'History of the "Domus Conversorum"', *Transactions of the Jewish Historical Society of England 1899–1901*, 4 (1903), pp. 16–75. The Latin text is reproduced in Appendix I, 'Order of Henry III, for the Foundation of the Domus Conversorum' (1232), p. 51.

[44] The first Temple, or Old Temple of the Knights Templars was founded in Holborn, and was removed to its site in Fleet Street in 1185.

[45] The grant will be found in the Calendar of Charter Rolls, 6 vols (London, 1903–27) (henceforth C.Ch.R), 1226–57, p. 143; full text in *Foedera, Conventiones, Litterae, et Cujuscunque Gerneris Acta Publica,* ed. by Thomas Rymer and Robert Sanderson, rev. by Adam Clarke and Frederick Holbrooke (London, 1816), 1, 1, p. 201.

[46] This 'decent church' became the Rolls Chapel and was much modernized over the centuries. The *Domus* itself was annexed by Edward III and Richard II to the Mastership of the Rolls. The *Domus* remained, with various repairs and additions until it was pulled down by Colin Campbell when he built the Rolls House on its site between the years 1717 and 1724, and the old materials were sold.

for the ransom of his soul and that of his father, King John, and all their ancestors, in the seventeenth year of his reign, that is to say, in London, not far from the Old Temple. To this house, converted Jews retired, leaving their Jewish blindness, and had a home and a safe refuge for their whole lives, living under an honourable rule, with sufficient sustenance without servile work or the profits of usury. So it happened that in a short time, a large number were collected there. And now, being baptized and instructed in the Christian law, they live a praiseworthy life under a Governor specially appointed.'[47]

Fifty-eight years after its foundation and eight years into his reign, on 3 June 1280, Edward I issued precise regulations for the management of the *Domus*.[48] Included among the sources of income was the *chevage*, a poll-tax levied on the Jews, from the age of twelve, for the support of the *Domus*. The officials appointed to collect the *chevage* had authority to summon such Jews as did not render true returns of their wealth before a Justice, and if any Jews refused to pay the *chevage*, the officials were empowered to distrain upon their goods or to imprison them. Thus, the king's pious generosity was being subsidized by the Jewish community.

If the bishops considered that the substantial 'bribes' of a free home and maintenance would effect a conversion *en masse* of the English Jews, they were mistaken. The *Domus* had been in existence for 68 years in 1290, when the Jews were expelled from England at Edward I's edict, and at that point, there were 80 converted Jews living there, out of a possible 3000 Jews expelled.[49]

Life in the Domus

The *Domus* was conceived and organized as a monastery. The inmates were called brothers, notwithstanding the presence of many women. They ate at common tables and lived a form of common life, referred to as *contubernio* in the sources, from which dissentient converts could be excluded[50]—a great contrast to the small family units in which they had lived as Jews.

Although converts' chattels were forfeit to the Crown, the royal bounty which the converts received amounted to 1½d. a day for a man and 1d. for a woman. Was this enough to live on, rather than merely to exist? The daily penny formed 1/160th of a mark, and for much of this period was considered to be sufficient recompense for day-labour. Hardship and serious privation arose when the stipend was not paid, or was paid late. A 1282 petition from

---

[47] Matthew Paris, *Chronica majora*, III, 262.

[48] CPR, 1272–81, pp. 371–72. Adler, 'History of the "Domus Conversorum"', provides the Latin text in Appendix II, 'Rules for the Government of the Domus (1280)', pp. 52–53.

[49] CPR, 1290, p. 19.

[50] Close Rolls of the Reign of Edward I, 5 vols (London, 1900–1908) (henceforth Cl.R), 1234–37, p. 78; Calendar of Liberate Rolls, 6 vols (London, 1917–64) (henceforth CLR), p. 165. For a comparison with Christian confraternities, see R. N. Swanson, *Religion and Devotion in Europe, 1215–1515* (Cambridge, 1995).

the warden to the king spoke of his 'starving, shivering converts', who were forced to beg their bread from door to door, because their wages were so far in arrears.[51] The records reveal that similar conditions existed in 1272 and 1290, when the response was 'Rex cogitabit cum viderit tempus' (The king will think about it when he can find the time).[52]

Religious services were celebrated daily, presided over by a pair of chaplains, who were themselves supposed to be converts from Judaism, although such convert priests were not always available.[53] The chapel was dedicated to the Holy Trinity; within it was an altar to the Virgin Mary, the patron saint of the *Domus*, whose name, however, was taken by only a single converted Jewess during the entire thirteenth century—a Maria of Lincoln, who appears among the converts sent for support in 1255 to religious houses. As Stacey suggests, as the human mother of God, Mary may have been a particularly problematic figure for Jewish converts to Christianity.[54]

The *Domus* was also a school, intended to teach new converts the doctrines of faith and perhaps also an employable skill. The house was headed by a keeper or warden, who was sometimes referred to as *doctor conversorum* or *custos*; the chaplains were also known as keepers. The *Domus* was also a kind of halfway house, a *converso* world that must have retained a Jewish flavour, despite the Christian symbolism of its monastic organization. Although the converts could pass in and out of the *Domus*, many inmates lived their entire Christian lives there.

There was nothing in the contemporary Jewish experience remotely like the quintessential Christian institution of the monastery. The monastic atmosphere of the *Domus* probably served a socialization function in acclimatizing the convert to his or her new faith, but it would not have helped the converts to learn to live as Christians in the world outside the *Domus*. Indeed, their children and grandchildren could be found still residing in the *Domus*. Although after 1280, Edward I emphasised, in his reforms, the importance of teaching the inmates employable skills in order to move them out into the world, there is no sign that these measures had any appreciable effect in shortening the length of time most inmates resided in the *Domus*. This was one reason why the king did not succeed in shutting down the *Domus* in the fourteenth century, after the expulsion of the entire Jewish community from England in 1290.

The story of one convert, Claricia of Exeter, is illustrative of this, although the story varies in the Adler and Stacey interpretations.[55] Claricia was admitted to the *Domus* at some

---

[51] C. Johnson, 'The Keeper of Papal Bulls', in *Essays in Medieval History Presented to Thomas Frederick Tout*, ed. by A. G. Little and F. M. Powicke (Manchester, 1925), p. 136.

[52] *Rotuli Parliamentorum*, I, 49a, cited in Stacey, 'The Conversion of Jews to Christianity', p. 275.

[53] CPR, 1266–72, p. 55; CPR, 1272–81, pp. 371–72.

[54] Stacey, 'The Conversion of Jews to Christianity', p. 273.

[55] Adler, 'History of the "Domus Conversorum"', pp. 16–75; Adler, *The Jews of Medieval England*, pp. 307–21; and Stacey, 'The Conversion of Jews to Christianity'.

date prior to 1280.[56] She was the daughter of Jacob Copin, the richest Jew of Exeter. There are two versions of what happened to him. According to Adler,[57] Jacob surrendered his wealth as required by the expulsion order and left England with the majority of his co-religionists in 1290, leaving his daughter behind in the *Domus*. According to Stacey,[58] Jacob Copin was executed for coin clipping in 1278. If that is the correct version, it perhaps explains why Claricia, now destitute, became a convert—if nothing else, she would have a roof over her head. While an inquiry into the *Domus* in 1308 records Claricia in the list of those inmates 'Alive in 1280, but Since Dead',[59] according to Stacey, Claricia had left the *Domus* by 1308 to return to Exeter, where she married and raised a family. In 1330, she returned to the *Domus*, followed six years later by two of her children, Richard and Katherine, who may not have lived full time in the *Domus*. Before entering the *Domus*, Richard and Katherine had been in receipt of the allowance as if they themselves were converts. Adler has the very old Claricia resident in 1353, as 'the sole representative of converted Judaism in England, sixty-three years after the Expulsion'.[60] To minister to her spiritual needs, the same establishment of two chaplains and one clerk, in addition to the master of the rolls (as the keeper was now called), was maintained. The master of the rolls received 20 marks a year (just over £13), the two chaplains 5 marks (around £3.35p each), and the clerk, an annual salary of 2 marks (about £1.33p). Adler records that Claricia died in 1356, the sole inhabitant of the *Domus*, and the last representative of converted Judaism in England, sixty-six years after the expulsion. If Adler is correct, then Claricia would have been a very old woman. Whatever age she was in 1280 when she is first recorded as being in the *Domus*, there are seventy-six years between that date and 1356.

Recorded payments from the exchequer to the *Domus* during the 1240s averaged about 180 marks per year (£120).[61] If one presumes an equal number of male and female converts, this would provide support for about sixty inmates per year. The House had other resources, however, beyond its direct receipts from the Crown, including rentals from London property.[62] It would be naive to think that either Henry or Edward limited residence in the *Domus* to the number of inmates whom they could fully support.[63]

Henry's bestowal of garments for the use of the inmates gives some indication of the numbers of inmates in the mid-1250s. For instance, the Close Roll for 1255–56 orders the king's almoner to deliver cloth for 150 robes for the converts before Christmas, in the next

[56] Adler, 'History of the "Domus Conversorum"', p. 53.

[57] Adler, 'History of the "Domus Conversorum"', p. 18, gives no source for this statement.

[58] Stacey, 'The Conversion of Jews to Christianity', p. 273, where he cites Close Rolls of the Reign of Edward I, 5 vols (London, 1900–1908) (henceforth C.Cl.R), 1330–33, p. 64.

[59] Adler, 'History of the "Domus Conversorum"', p. 53.

[60] Adler, 'History of the "Domus Conversorum"', p. 31.

[61] Discussed in Stacey, 'The Conversion of Jews to Christianity', p. 267 n. 22.

[62] Stacey, 'The Conversion of Jews to Christianity', p. 267.

[63] Ibid.

year, cloth for 171 tunics for Easter, and 164 for Pentecost, and in the following year, cloth for 150 tunics at command of the king and queen, and 21 at command of their children.[64]

The upsurge in conversions between 1240 and 1260 reflects the effect of Henry III's excessive royal taxation of the Jews and a resulting breakdown in the internal solidarity and cohesion of the Jewish community. This crisis may also have undermined the internal charitable mechanisms by which the Jewish community had previously cared for its own destitute members.

Why Did the Converts Stay in the Domus?

Viewed in a positive light, the converts might have preferred the limbo of the small world they had made for themselves, perched as it was between both Jewish and Christian society. Monks, nuns, and the Jewish converts were people without family, even though it could be said that they had voluntarily given up being members of their blood kinship. And having no family ties meant having no communal ties either. The *Domus* might well have replaced these lost bonds and enabled the converts to forge new ones of their own choosing from among their colleagues.

Choosing to convert meant rejecting the totality of their Jewish pasts and all that they had once been. We have insufficient knowledge of the psychology of thirteenth-century converts to do more than speculate on the impact of such a rejection on their psyches, but it must be remembered that they were not just rejecting Judaism and all that it stood for, but embracing Christianity, and practising it in a society that viewed Jews and converts from Judaism alike with scorn, dislike, and suspicion.

Viewed negatively, the reluctance of converts to leave the *Domus* could indicate the difficulties they faced in trying to integrate themselves into the mainstream of Christian society. There seem to have been three routes into the wider society: the one, which would achieve complete social integration, was to enter holy orders and become a priest or monk, though this seems to have been rarely done. A convert cleric, totally accepted by the Church, is likely to have blended in with his fellow clerics. There is one who stands out, however. Theobald, the monk of Norwich who played a key role in the 1140s in medieval Europe's first accusation of ritual murder of the boy who became St William of Norwich, claimed to be a convert from Judaism,[65] and there is mention of a monk at Westminster who was a convert.[66] The second route was to obtain service in the royal household, again not often achieved. Several converted Jews did become royal sergeants at arms. Three stand out: Roger the Convert,[67] who was in the service of Henry III and Edward I for twenty years; his son, John the Convert, who followed his father into the king's

---

[64] William J. Hardy, *Middlesex and Hertfordshire Notes and Queries*, 2.8 (1896), 49–68, 51.

[65] Gavin I. Langmuir, 'Thomas of Monmouth: Detector of Ritual Murder', *Speculum*, 59 (1984), 835–37.

[66] Richardson, *The English Jewry under Angevin Kings*, p. 31.

[67] Adler, *Jews of Medieval England*, pp. 294–96.

household; and the most prominent, Henry of Winchester, who was knighted and in 1252 was appointed the king's notary at the Jewish exchequer, where he was charged with writing the Hebrew inscriptions on the deeds and plea rolls.[68] The third route to integration was to marry a Christian, even more fraught with potential problems. We have the record of Alicia the convert who married Gilbert de Northbrook and left the *Domus*,[69] and of one male convert who married the Christian Susanna of Lincoln.[70] And an instance of the widow of a convert admitted to the *Domus*, although she herself had always professed Christianity.[71] Considering the difficulty of achieving acceptance, let alone integration, to stay in the safety of the *Domus*, despite its social isolation must have appeared to be the most advantageous course of action.

What We Know of the Inmates of the Domus

We know little more than their names from the lists of inmates between 1280 and 1308,[72] divided into those alive in 1280, but dead before 1308—17 men and 17 women—and living at the time of the enquiry—23 men and 28 women. The names give a good idea of their physical attributes—Johannes le Bel and Juliana la Bossue (the Hunchback)—and what we have is new baptismal names very different from their former Jewish names—Agnes, Anne, Christina, Elena, Matill' (Matilda) in place of such names as Duzelina, Gentilia, Pucella, and Precieuse, or Reginald, Henri, Willemus, Ricardus and Hugo in place of the male names which used the French equivalents of their Hebrew names—Deuleben or Benedict (Berechiah or Baruch), Bonevie or Vives (Hayyim or Hagin), Deulesault (Isaiah), and Deudone (Nathaniel). We know that they had gathered together in the London *Domus* from a variety of other towns, because their names give their places of origin—Bartholmeus de Wynton (Winchester) and Johanna de Norwych.

All of which amounts to hardly anything, compared with what we do not know about the inmates. Were they sincerely convinced of the truth of Christianity? Were they happy in their new lives, or did they put up with their lives in the limbo of the *Domus* because it was the least worst alternative to death or destitution? Did they 'take to' the communal life after having lived in small, individual family groups? How difficult was it to adjust to being dependent on 'income support' after having been masters and mistresses of their own financial affairs? Why did they leave the *Domus* and then return to it, sometimes more than once? We know about the inmates as a category, and we have glimpses of the occasional individual; the rest is silence.

---

[68] Cl.R, 1253–54, p. 148.

[69] Cl.R, 1247–51, p. 565.

[70] Cl.R, 1242–47, p. 376.

[71] Cl.R, 30 Henry III, m. 38.

[72] Adler, 'History of the 'Domus Conversorum'', p. 53.

Life outside the Domus

Under Edward I, the *Domus* housed between 80 and 100 converts at any given time.[73] While we have no such reliable censuses for Henry III's reign, the level of financial support the king was providing to the *Domus* makes it unlikely that it could have housed many more converts than this, even in the peak years during the 1250s. It would therefore seem that throughout the 1200s, more converts probably lived outside the *Domus* than in it, if Stacey's estimate of 300 conversions between the 1240s and 1250s is correct.[74]

The information that we have about the lives of converted Jews tends to be mainly from the *Domus* records, although one can patch together stories from the various Pipe and Calendar Rolls which allow some idea of who the Jewish converts were. The Pipe Rolls are a source of information about named converts whose activities had attracted official attention, even though these references cannot cover more than a fraction of the cases of conversion. The Pipe Rolls record the result of the judicial examination of Crown debtors, principally sheriffs who were called upon to account for the revenues that passed through their hands. The balance of receipts, after the deduction of authorized local expenditure, was required to be paid into the Treasury. The Pipe Rolls therefore reveal only a part, and not the most important part, of the king's financial affairs. What they tell us of the king's credit transactions is accidental and merely incidental to an inquiry that has nothing to do with the larger aspects of royal finance.

We have little information about converts for the first hundred or so years of the Jewish settlement. A convert called Pedro Alfonso, who died in 1110,[75] was personal physician to Alfonso VI of Castile, and later became court physician to Henry I of England.[76] The more than thirty tales attributed him were translated into many languages and were drawn on as plot material by Chaucer, Shakespeare, and other European writers. Under John, and during the minority of Henry III, we can trace a few converted Jews in royal service as cross-bowmen,[77] and the previously mentioned Roger the Convert, who was Edward I's sergeant at arms.[78]

We find the following information—again bare statements, with little background information or explanation as to consequences:[79]

---

[73] Adler, *The Jews of Medieval England*, p. 288.

[74] Stacey, 'The Conversion of Jews to Christianity', p. 269.

[75] F. Heer, *The Medieval World: Europe from 1100 to 1350*, trans. by Janet Sondheimer (London, 1962), pp. 254–66, 257.

[76] The Jews and medicine is a well-studied area; see, for example, Joseph Shatzmiller, *Jews, Medicine, and Medieval Society* (Berkeley, 1994), for an analysis of the social and economic forces that allowed Jewish medical professionals to survive and thrive in the otherwise hostile climate of thirteenth- and fourteenth-century Europe.

[77] Stacey, 'The Conversion of Jews to Christianity', p. 266.

[78] CPR, 1272–81, p. 74.

[79] Richardson, *The English Jewry under Angevin Kings*.

1180:   Isabelle, a converted Jewess appears in the Pipe Rolls because Jeremiah of
        Dunstable was fined one mark for imprisoning her. Converts Nicholas, John, and
        Peter are mentioned because, for eighteen months, Henry II was paying them alms
        through the sheriffs of Essex and Surrey.[80]

1198:   Converts Richard and Henry appear as informers against the Jew Deulesalt of
        London, and Thomas of Canterbury is assessed at one mark for tallage.[81]

1199:   The convert John of Gloucester is associated with a number of Jews in an appeal
        against Elias the Jew.[82]

1199:   The convert Constance, who had married Gerin the tailor, applied to obtain, on
        preferential terms, her father's property in York, which had escheated to the
        Crown.[83]

1234:   Chera, a Jewess, widow of Augustine the convert, sued for her dower and was
        denied.[84] In this case, we have the story behind this judgement: Augustine of
        Canterbury had become a Christian, and was permitted by Henry III to retain his
        house, which he then donated to St Augustine's Abbey. The Abbey, in turn, sold
        the house to another Jew, Isaac of Canterbury. Augustine's wife, Chera, had
        remained a Jew, and presumably she had to leave the house when her husband
        gave it to the Abbey. When Augustine died, Chera sued the new owner of the
        house, Isaac, for one-third of the value of the house as dower, due from her late
        husband. Henry ordered the justices of the Jews not to hear the case, declaring that
        Chera ought to have followed her husband into Christianity.

1245:   Emma, widow of Reiner son of Viel, had a dispute regarding her dower with
        Chera, wife of Isaac the chirographer (who was prominent in the previous reign of
        John) and Chera's son by a former marriage. The property in dispute consisted of
        six messuages in Winchester, which Emma claimed as dower by her husband's
        gift.[85]

1246:   Deulebeneie of Winchester's wife left him in 1246 to convert to Christianity. In
        this case, Henry III enforced her dower claim, awarding her 34 marks from
        Deulebeneie's estate.[86] Stacey provides the end of this story: 'In the end, the king
        wound up paying the dower directly; he then credited Deulebeneie with the 34-
        mark payment against his debts, a peculiar arrangement which cost Deulebeneie
        nothing at all and cost the king 34 marks in cash'.[87]

---

[80] PR, 26b Henry II, p. 129.

[81] PR, 3 Richard I, p. 208.

[82] PR, 1 John I, p. 32.

[83] Memoranda Roll 1 John I (henceforth MR), p. 24.

[84] Cl.R, 1231–34, p. 555.

[85] Curia Regis Rolls (henceforth CRR), VII, 70.

[86] Cl.R, 1247–51, p. 70.

[87] Stacey, 'The Conversion of Jews to Christianity', p. 272.

1249:   Josce, son of Sampson, of Canterbury took back the gift of 30 marks which he had given to his daughter in dowry when she and her husband converted to Christianity. Henry ordered the gift restored from Josce's chattels.[88]

1272:   Isaac l'Eveske, son of Henry the convert, is present in the tallage roll.[89] Henry, the baptismal name presumably bestowed by the king, may well conceal the Jewish name of Elias, and Matthew Paris mentions the 1259 conversion of Elias l'Eveske and two other Jews.[90] Elias/Henry was a man of wealth who had been archpriest, and he appears to have lost all his landed property upon conversion—it was only eight years later that Edward allowed retention of one-half of the Jew's estate upon conversion.[91]

Most converts living outside the *Domus* seem to have remained in the towns where they had lived as Jews. Sometimes they even lived in the same houses. After 1280, when Edward began allowing converts to retain a half of their former property, they almost invariably did so.[92] One must remember that aside from London, with between 500 and 700 Jews, the Jewish communities of England probably contained only between 50 and 100 persons each.

We have no idea of the extent to which family relationships and friendships were maintained when the convert stayed within the Jewish community. The resulting social tensions must have been difficult to negotiate on both sides. If the converts maintained familial contact and friendships, they would open themselves up to accusations of backsliding or apostasy. Because they appear in the official records, we have reports of incidents where Jewish children were 'rescued', by abduction, from convert parents by relatives or fellow Jews.[93] The question of the religion of the children born to a Jew before his or her conversion to Christianity was difficult to solve in practice. In 1236, a convert complained to the king that the Jews of Northampton had abducted his children; the complaint was solved by allowing the children to choose to follow their father into Christianity or to remain '*in errore suo*', if they so wished.[94]

We can get an inkling of the marital and familial tensions that must have arisen. There are cases of one spouse converting, where the other remained Jewish. A wife so deserted would need her dower (one third of her husband's estate) to maintain herself and her children. Because the convert's assets escheated to the Crown, she would need to appeal to the king to enforce her dower claim. If she left the marriage in order to convert, she could

---

[88] Cl.R, 1247–51, p. 194.

[89] PRO, E. 401/1567.

[90] Matthew Paris, *Chronica majora*, v. 730, cited in Richardson, *The English Jewry under Angevin Kings*, p. 32.

[91] H. P. Stokes, *A Short History of the Jews in England* (London, 1921).

[92] Stacey, 'The Conversion of Jews to Christianity', p. 279

[93] Cl.R, 1234–37, pp. 264, 323.

[94] Cl.R, 1234–37, p. 358.

also argue for her dower, even though her husband had remained Jewish and in possession of his assets.

Besides living in the community, converts could become corody holders in a monastery.[95] In 1247 and again in 1255, with his finances in crisis, Henry III sent at least 150 converts to various religious houses around the kingdom, each one bearing a special royal letter requesting the house to provide the convert with food and lodging for two years, or failing that, with 3d. per day in maintenance.[96] This is likely to indicate the splitting up of families, not only converts from their Jewish families but convert family members of different ages or genders from each other—a wife or husband without the spouse who had remained Jewish, brothers and sisters without their parents or orphaned, single parents with dependent children. We are unlikely to know how often siblings left behind living parents, or whether a converted woman took her children with her, if her husband remained Jewish. Perhaps this was one of the appeals of the *Domus*, that family members who had converted together could continue to live together, as it would seem Claricia and her children did.

Apostasy

Apostasy—the reversion of the convert to Judaism—was seen as 'bad publicity' detrimental to conversion. On a spiritual level, it was tragic perfidy harmful to the souls of the apostates. Edward's 1280 letter to his sheriffs ordering them to induce the Jews to hear the preaching of the Dominicans forbade the Jews from taking action to impede their fellow Jews from converting.[97]

In 1274, nine Jews were accused of having abducted two recent converts, Juliana and Roesia. Juliana claimed that she was threatened with death if she failed to abjure Christianity and return to Judaism, and that, when she refused, her captors tried to transport her overseas (to France), but a storm drove her ship ashore at Sandwich.[98]

Edward's solution to the problem of apostasy was pragmatic. In 1279, he issued orders that relapsed converts should be punished 'according to what is wont to be done in such

---

[95] Corody was the provision of an allowance for maintenance, originally the right of free quarters due from a vassal to a lord on his circuit, and later applied to certain contributions of food and provisions paid annually by religious houses. A corody holder was also a person who had given his or her estate to an abbey in exchange for maintenance for life. W. H. Bliss, ed., *Calendar of Entries in the Papal Registers Relating to Great Britain and Ireland* (London, 1893), mentions this practice being applied to converts, stating that in 1199, a religious community was ordered to accept a Jewish convert into their house as a corody holder.

[96] PRO, C 60/52, dorse.

[97] CPR, 1272–81, p. 356.

[98] This is related in Logan, 'Thirteen London Jews', who cites the Calendar of the Exchequer of the Jews, II, 209–10, and says that the fate of Roesia does not appear in the plea rolls of the Exchequer, so we know no more about her. Calendar of the Plea Rolls of the Exchequer of the Jews, II, ed. by J. M. Rigg (London, 1905–10).

cases'.[99] Two cases before 1279 reveal what was 'wont to be done' during the reign of Henry III, which was having recourse to the secular arm to enforce a solution to the religious problem of apostasy: on 6 April 1245, a royal writ was sent to the sheriff of Oxfordshire ordering him to capture and imprison at Oxford a man who was not only a relapsed Jewish convert, but also a cleric and acolyte as well. The cleric was to remain imprisoned until the bishop of Lincoln, Robert Grosseteste, determined otherwise. We have no further information of his fate.[100] The sheriff of Wiltshire received a royal writ of 18 July 1247 instructing him to deliver the apostate Solomon to the keeping of the constable of the Tower of London.[101]

What Happened to the Domus after the Expulsion?

Officially, all Jews were banished from England in 1290.[102] The claim that in ordering the Jews expelled, Edward singled out apostasy—along with usury—as a fundamental reason for expulsion must be weighed seriously.[103] Edward clearly hoped that the necessity for the existence of the *Domus* would very shortly cease, but instead the *Domus* continued to receive baptized Jews.

Adler traces the history of the *Domus Conversorum* from the expulsion in 1290 up to 1891.[104] For a period of 319 years, during the very years that no Jew was permitted by law to enter England, the documents of the *Domus Conversorum* tell us of a regular succession of Jews landing in England. In all, there were 38 men and 10 women admitted into the royal institution at Chancery Lane after the Expulsion of 1290. These figures account only for the Jews who abjured their faith and accepted the royal pensions. There must have been numbers of Jews who lived in England and succeeded in concealing their belief, or were even courageous enough to profess it openly.[105]

---

[99] C.Cl.R, 1272–79, p. 565.

[100] Cl.R, 1242–47, p. 298.

[101] CLR, 1245–51, p. 133.

[102] The Expulsion has been explained in terms of the Jews' economic role, or of the authority of the centralized monarchy with its concentration of wealth and patronage, or some combination of both these factors.

[103] Hyams, 'The Jewish Minority in Medieval England, 1066–1290,' *Journal of Jewish Studies*, 25.2 (1974), 270–293; Logan, 'Thirteen London Jews'.

[104] Adler, 'History of the "Domus Conversorum"'.

[105] Adler, 'History of the 'Domus Conversorum'', p. 50, mentions Nathanael Menda who lived openly as a Jew in London for six years prior to conversion, and Johanna and Alice who had been living as Jews in Dartmouth for some time before entering the *Domus* in London. Lucien Wolf, 'The Middle Age of Anglo Jewish History', *Anglo-Jewish Historical Exhibition*, 1 (1887), 53; and Sidney Lee, *Jewish Chronicle*, 26 January, 16 February, 27 April, 15 June, 1883, have produced further evidence to the same end.

The smallness in number of the inmates of the *Domus* (a total of 48 in the 319 years after 1290) is in itself 'an eloquent testimony to the fidelity with which Jews, as a whole, adhered to their ancestral faith, in spite of royal bounties, and in the face of incessant persecution'.[106]

The yearly grant, originally intended for the converts and the staff, was, in 1837 by Act of Parliament, set apart for the salaries of the preacher, the reader, and the clerk of the Rolls Chapel. When Sir John Romilly was appointed Master of the Rolls as late as 1851, his patent of appointment still granted him, for life 'the custody of the House, or Hospital, of Converts for the habitation of the Keeper or Master of the Rolls, Books, Writs and Records of the High Court of Chancery'.

Although the records end in 1609, so that it is impossible to know whether any converts entered the *Domus* after that, the Master of the Rolls continued to receive his salary as keeper of the *Domus* up to the early years of the twentieth century, and it was only in 1891 that the post of preacher of the Rolls Chapel was abolished by Act of Parliament, and the last traces of the *Domus* were removed. The buildings formerly occupied by the converts were used as storehouses for the rolls of Chancery—even the chapel was filled with these legal documents. Until its move to its new premises in Kew, the Public Record Office stood on the site of the houses and the chapel of the *Domus Conversorum*.

Conclusion

The *Domus Conversorum* served various purposes. In the first place, it symbolized the king's pious wish to see all the Jews in his realm converted, as was right and proper. Of course, having set up the *Domus*, the king's policy of continuing to insist on his right to seize a convert's property was not conducive to its success. Overall, the king's revenues from the Jews far exceeded his expenditure on the *Domus*. Indeed after 1280, the *Domus* was supported by a further poll-tax levied on the Jews themselves. In theory, therefore, the *Domus* was thus largely self-supporting: an arrangement that suggests that no serious hope was entertained that all the Jews might be converted.

Was the *Domus* more political symbolism than pious action? As symbolism, it demonstrated a marked change in the attitude towards Jewry. The eleventh-century story of Eadmer the monk of Canterbury of a disputation between Jews and Christians in the presence of William Rufus, who swore by the Holy Face of Lucca to become a Jew if the Jews had the best of the argument is only a story.[107] But, whether genuine or not, it is not one that could be told about later kings. Rufus would never have set up a home for converts. He accepted the Jews as a permanent and potentially beneficial part of the economic and political landscape. Later kings, increasingly, did not.

---

[106] Adler, 'History of the "Domus Conversorum"', p. 50.

[107] Richardson, *The English Jewry under Angevin Kings*, p. 24.

By the mid-thirteenth century, Henry III had set up a home for converted Jews; by the late thirteenth century, Edward, his son, compelled Jews to listen to sermons, and the friars made strenuous efforts to win them over. At the same time, Christian pressure on the Jews increased. The Jewish *tabula* was decreed by the Lateran Council of 1215, for example, although for a long time English kings refused to enforce it, typically allowing the Jews to buy themselves exemptions. But the Jews did not convert, not even when allowed to keep a portion of their property, although this only happened when the Jews had become so impoverished by oppressive taxation that the sacrifice the king made was not, in fact, that large. The setting up of the *Domus*, was thus, paradoxically, a form of persecution, a symbol of society's non-acceptance of the Jews. It was a solution to the medieval Jewish Problem. When it did not work, another needed to be found because the Jews stubbornly and insensately refused to convert, and were no longer of economic benefit. The decision is simple and drastic—if they won't convert, they might as well be expelled.

Note: Calculating the current values of medieval transactions in a meaningful way is clearly impossible. Adler, in *Jews of Medieval England*, p. 12, suggested equivalents to thirteenth-century prices. He based these 1939 values on Jacobs's, *The Jews of Angevin England*, published in 1893, giving them an index number/multiplication value of 30 (p. 316).

The increase in the Retail Price Index from 1939 to 1997 gives an overall factor of approximately 800. Applying this factor to the 1½d. per day which male converts received, gives a figure of £5. The lowest paid employee in the *Domus*, a clerk, received rather less than this, only 2 marks per year, which would give a modern equivalent of just £1000. This seems too low. Nevertheless, simply to give some idea of the scale of the sums involved (and not making any claims for precision), we have shown some translations.

		ADLER	BROWN/MCCARTNEY
1 mark =	13/4	£25	over £500
100 marks =	£67	£2010	over £50,000
500 marks =	£333		over £¼m

Thus, the 700 marks which Henry III fixed as the endowment of the *Domus* is worth £470 in medieval money and, using our index number of 800, nearly £400,00 in 1997.

Crusade and Conversion
in the Mediterranean Region

Marriage As a Means of
Conversion in Pierre Dubois's
De recuperatione Terre Sancte

MICHAEL R. EVANS

I n c. 1305–7, Pierre Dubois wrote the treatise, *De recuperatione Terre Sancte* (*The Recovery of the Holy Land*).[1] Although the first part was dedicated to Edward I, the treatise as a whole was a call to the kings of Western Christendom—in particular, Philip IV of France, for whom the second half of the treatise was intended—to regain the Holy Land from Islam, and a suggestion as to the methods that could be employed to accomplish this end. Dubois was once seen as a radical or 'modern' thinker; Powicke, writing in 1907, called him a 'mediaeval radical' and wrote of Dubois's schemes for French foreign policy as being 'worthy of the days of Louis XIV', and of his military thought as showing 'startling anticipation of modern military organisation'.[2] In fact, Dubois was far from unique; the *De recuperatione Terre Sancte* theme was so popular in the early fourteenth century that it has been described by Sylvia Schein as 'a new literary genre'.[3] The fall of Acre in 1291 was a fairly recent memory, and contemporaries did not see this as a full stop to the period of Christian rule in *Outremer*. Other fourteenth-century writers produced similar treatises, such as Ramon Llull, Mario Sanudo, and Philip IV's minister Guillaume de Nogaret. Schein further remarks that

---

[1] Pierre Dubois, *The Recovery of the Holy Land*, ed. and trans. by Walther I. Brandt (New York, 1956).

[2] F. M. Powicke, 'Pierre Dubois, a Mediaeval Radical', in *Historical Essays*, ed. by T. F. Tout and J. Tait (Manchester, 1907), p. 178.

[3] Sylvia Schein, *Fideles Crucis: The Papacy, the West, and the Recovery of the Holy Land, 1274–1314* (Oxford, 1991), p. 91.

Dubois's theories 'are of little interest [. . .] [while] the practical opinions he presented were precisely those he plagiarised',[4] while even Dubois's modern translator, Brandt, remarks that 'he was not an original thinker [. . .]'.[5]

However, his thesis is remarkable in one aspect that has often attracted comment. He advocated the education of young men in the West for the purpose of spreading the faith, but also suggested that the more attractive and intelligent young women and girls receive an education, especially in 'medicine and surgery'.[6] These women would then be sent to the East, where they would be adopted by the local nobility and would become eligible marriage-partners among the princes of the East, and even the clerics for that matter. Dubois observed that 'it would be an excellent thing for the eastern prelates and clergy to have such wives; it is their custom to marry', a custom that the author seems to have approved of.[7] Once these marriages were achieved, this feminine fifth-column was to be brought into action:

> Wives with such education, who hold the articles of faith and the sacraments according to Roman usage, would teach their children and husbands to adhere to the Roman faith and to believe and sacrifice in accordance with it. They would employ arguments and opportunities far more effective than those by which the wiles of his wives led Solomon, the wisest of men, into idolatry.[8]

Dubois has often attracted attention as an advocate of the use of marriage to convert Muslims. However this particular passage has a rather different purpose; Dubois is clearly advocating marriage with eastern Christians in order to advance Catholicism and generally bolster the Latin Christian presence in the East. His references to 'Roman usage', 'Roman faith', and so on clearly show that he is talking about converting non-Roman Christians, in particular the Greeks. His comments on marrying prelates and clerics makes perfect sense in this context, as the eastern churches generally allow married clergy. However, as with many of Dubois's ideas, there is a contradiction at the heart of it. Why should a married cleric wish to accept the religion of his wife when that religion would require him to either cast her aside or cease to be a priest? He may be advocating uniate status for these clerics, but his stress on 'Roman usage' suggests that he wanted the Greeks to give up their own rite as well as their schismatic doctrinal practices.

There is nothing in this passage to suggest that he advocates marriage to Muslims. The reference to the wives of Solomon may suggest marriage to non-Christians, but it is more likely that this is a rhetorical device; if pagan women could lead astray the

---

[4] Schein, *Fideles Crucis*, p. 208.

[5] Dubois, *The Recovery of the Holy Land*, introduction, p. 62.

[6] Dubois, *The Recovery of the Holy Land*, p. 118.

[7] Dubois, *The Recovery of the Holy Land*, pp. 118–19.

[8] Dubois, *The Recovery of the Holy Land*, p. 119.

epitome of wisdom, how much more effective would educated Catholic girls be in converting presumably less wise Orthodox clerics. The only other reference that could be interpreted as suggesting marriage to Muslims is to be found in Dubois's belief that 'princes [. . .] of the Holy Land and of other lands adjacent' would marry these women. This would seem to refer to princes of the Muslim world, but is suitably vague as to whom Dubois is actually referring. Nor is his reference to 'princes, prelates, and other wealthy easterners' any more helpful.[9] The princes could be Armenian Christians, wealthy Christians living under Muslim rule in Syria, or Greek Christians in the Catholic territories of Cyprus and Greece.

The only reference to marriage to Muslims occurs later in the work. Dubois suggests that

> perhaps girls trained in the proposed schools may be given as wives to the Saracen chiefs, although preserving their faith lest they participate in their husbands' idolatry. By their efforts, with the help of God and the preaching disciples so they may have assistance of Catholics—for they cannot rely on Saracens—their husbands might be persuaded and led to the Catholic faith.[10]

Dubois goes on to argue that the Christian faith could easily be spread among the wives of Saracen rulers, who would prefer monogamy to polygamy. He does not address the question of why these wives should wish to abandon the certainties of marriage to a wealthy man for the uncertain future of being a cast-off concubine holding to a minority faith. This passage reads as something of an afterthought to his main reason for wishing to train women in theology, namely the conversion of Orthodox clergy. Furthermore, the precedents for Christian-Muslim marriages were not good. The nearest historical parallel for the use of such a marriage to further crusading ambitions occurred in the Third Crusade. In 1191 Richard I of England had proposed that his sister Joanna should marry Saladin's brother al-Malik al-'Adil (Safadin), with whom Richard was on good terms.[11] Richard's proposal would have granted Joanna the Christian-controlled lands in Palestine; in turn, Saladin would grant his brother all of his lands in Palestine, and al-'Adil and Joanna would then be crowned king and queen of Jerusalem. According to one Arab chronicler, the terms were approved by Saladin, 'knowing quite well that the King of England would never agree to them and they were only a trick and a practical joke on his part'.[12] The plan came to nought as Joanna refused to consider it, declaring

---

[9] Dubois, *The Recovery of the Holy Land*, p. 118.

[10] Dubois, *The Recovery of the Holy Land*, p. 124.

[11] *The Itinerary of King Richard I*, ed. by L. Landon, Pipe Roll Society, new ser., 13 (London, 1935), pp. 56–58; Bahā' ad-Dīn ibn Shaddād, 'Anecdotes et Beaux Traits de la Vie du Sultan Youssof', *Recueil des historiens des croisades, historiens orientaux*, 5 vols (Paris, 1872–1906), III, 273–74.

[12] Bahā' ad-Dīn, *Recueil des historiens des croisades*, III, 278.

that she would not marry an infidel. Richard suggested to Saladin that the difficulty might be overcome if al-'Adil became a Christian, but the scheme never came to fruition.[13]

There were, however, precedents for Dubois's ideas about marriage as a means of conversion. He may have been familiar with the examples in late Roman or early medieval times of Christian women marrying and helping to convert pagan kings, such as Queen Clotilda, the wife of Clovis, and the Frankish princess Bertha, wife of King Ethelbert of Kent. More recently, the theologian Thomas of Chobham had addressed the question in his *Summa confessorum* of c. 1215. This addressed the problem of whether a Jewess who converted to Christianity should remain married to her Jewish husband. Chobham concluded that she should, as she could lead him in turn to the true faith.[14] This was part of a more general view on the part of Chobham that, in Sharon Farmer's words, wives 'should employ persuasion, feminine enticements, and even deceit in their attempts to influence and correct the moral and economic behaviour of their husbands'. In Chobham's words, 'in imposing penance, it should always be enjoined upon women to be preachers to their husbands, because no priest is able to soften the heart of a man the way his wife can'. A wife should 'even in the bedroom, in the midst of their embraces [. . .] speak alluringly to her husband' in order to persuade him to mend the errors of his ways.[15]

Chobham's views are of particular interest to us in that they foreshadow Dubois's views on the question of conversion. Around the time of the Fourth Lateran Council of 1215, there was a great deal of interest among theologians in questions of marriage; to quote Farmer again, 'one of the issues that they examined concerned mixed marriages— those between newly converted believers and unbelievers (presumably Jews and Moslems) and those between Christian women and usurers, who were virtually equated with unbelievers'.[16] The reference to usurers as wayward Christians also finds an echo in Dubois's ideas about converting the Orthodox, as it demonstrates that Christians as well as non-believers could be subject to conversion.

Theologians drew on Paul's advice in his *Letter to the Corinthians* that Christians who were married to unbelievers should not divorce their husband or wife.[17] Augustine's interpretation of this advice was that a husband should keep an unbelieving wife 'so that perchance she could thus become a believer' as 'some wives are coming to the faith through believing husbands and some husbands are coming to the faith through believing wives'.[18] However, Augustine did not advocate a conscious attempt

---

[13] Bahā' ad-Dīn, *Recueil des historiens des croisades,* III, 278–79.

[14] Sharon Farmer, 'Persuasive Voices: Clerical Images of Medieval Wives', *Speculum,* 61.3 (1986), 517–43.

[15] Farmer, 'Persuasive Voices', p. 517.

[16] Farmer, 'Persuasive Voices', p. 527.

[17] I Corinthians 7. 12–16.

[18] Farmer, 'Persuasive Voices', pp. 527–28.

at proselytizing in the marriage bed, rather suggesting that the believing spouse should influence his or her partner 'by a good mode of life and conduct'.[19] Thomas went one step further than saying that a Christian could remain with a non-believing partner in the hope that he or she might be converted; he argued that the justification for such a marriage remaining intact was precisely in order that the Christian partner should *actively* seek to convert the non-Christian.[20] We do not know if Thomas influenced Dubois, but as a Paris-trained lawyer, who attended lectures by such theological luminaries as Thomas Aquinas and Siger de Brabant, it is not unreasonable to suppose that Dubois was aware of Chobham's ideas. However, it must be noted that Dubois took Chobham's ideas one step further in arguing that Christian women should actively seek husbands among schismatics and non-believers, a notion that is surely contrary to Paul's original intentions.

To return to the argument raised at the start of this paper, Dubois was not primarily advocating marriage of Christian women to Muslims, and it is difficult to envisage circumstances in which such a venture could possibly have been considered a viable proposition. There were, however, those among Dubois's contemporaries who advocated active campaigns to convert the Infidel. Ramon Llull advocated conversion of Muslims through reason, and even devised a plan whereby he intended to go to Muslim countries and challenge Islamic scholars to debates, promising to convert to Islam if he felt their arguments had defeated his own. He persuaded the king of Mallorca in 1275 to found a Franciscan monastery dedicated to training Arabic-speaking missionaries. Dubois also advocated the teaching of Arabic,[21] but betrays an ignorance of Islam in dubbing the Muslims 'idol worshippers', a popular slander against Islam which would not have been repeated by somebody like Llull who understood that religion.[22]

I would argue that Dubois was at least as interested in Constantinople as in the reconquest of Jerusalem, and his desire to convert the Greek Orthodox clergy should be seen in the light of his interest in re-establishing the Latin Empire in the East. Dubois wrote two other works on the affairs of the East, the *Summaria brevis* of 1300, and *Pro facto Terre Sancte* of 1308. These works embody two of the principle themes of Dubois's thinking; a glorification of France and the Capetian Monarchy, and an interest in the affairs of Constantinople. In the *Summaria brevis*, Dubois invoked the memory of Charlemagne to argue that the king of France (Philip IV) should invade Italy, take over the temporal powers of the pope, then make himself emperor of Germany and of Byzantium, a set of ideas repeated in the *De recuperatione*.[23] Dubois advocated the training of westerners to speak the Greek language in order to reconcile them to Latin

---

[19] Farmer, 'Persuasive Voices', p. 528.

[20] Farmer, 'Persuasive Voices', p. 530.

[21] Dubois, *The Recovery of the Holy Land*, p. 128.

[22] Dubois, *The Recovery of the Holy Land*, p. 77.

[23] Dubois, *The Recovery of the Holy Land*, p. 211.

rule after the projected reconquest of Constantinople. He used the language of preaching in his advocacy of this political conversion of the Greeks. In order to 'gain the love of the Greeks', westerners had to follow the example of the Apostles: 'How could they have preached and taught the Gospel of God intelligibly to all barbarian nations, except God Himself had granted them the use of all languages?'[24] Dubois was a great believer in learning languages, and one of his criticisms of Pope Boniface VIII—against whom he was a propagandist for Philip—was that, unlike the apostles, he knew no languages, so was not fit to be head of the Universal Church.[25]

In the now-lost work *Super abreviatione guerrarum et hujusmodi provisionibus* of 1304, Dubois first advocated that Philip IV's brother Charles of Valois should become emperor of Constantinople.[26] This treatise is probably summarized in chapter 117 of *De recuperatione*, where Dubois advocates that Charles, alongside King Charles II of Sicily, attack the Greeks after the conquest of Jerusalem had been assured.[27] In his *Pro facto Terre Sancte* of 1308, Dubois advocated that the king of France take control of the western Empire, the throne of which was vacant following the assassination of Albert I, with papal assistance (the Frenchman Clement V now being pope). The resources of Germany and Italy could then be used to conquer the Byzantine Empire and the Holy Land, and their people could be used as colonists to secure these lands for France and western Christendom.[28]

Dubois was not alone among writers of the *De recuperatione* genre in also advocating the conquest of Constantinople. Ramon Llull, in his *Liber de acquisitione Terrae Sanctae* of 1309 advocated the conquest of Constantinople as a prelude to the recovery of the Holy Land. Likewise, the Dominican William Adam advocated a land-based crusade to the Holy Land, conquering Constantinople *en route*, in his treatise *De modo Sarracenos extirpandi* of 1312.[29] However, Dubois was remarkable in the stress he placed on the quasi-imperial mission of France, in *Romania* as in Germany.

If we set aside the grandiose designs for Capetian domination, it is possible to see that some of Dubois's ideas were rooted quite firmly in the politics of the eastern Mediterranean. The Byzantine recapture of Constantinople from the Latins in 1261, and the failure of the Greek recognition of papal supremacy at the Council of Lyons in 1274 to hold, led to many schemes for the conquest of Byzantium by Catholic powers, and the restoration of the titular Latin emperor. These schemes received intermittent papal

---

[24] Dubois, *The Recovery of the Holy Land*, p. 177.

[25] Dubois, *The Recovery of the Holy Land*, pp. 212–13.

[26] Dubois, *The Recovery of the Holy Land*, p. 213.

[27] Dubois, *The Recovery of the Holy Land*, pp. 175–77.

[28] Dubois, *The Recovery of the Holy Land*, p. 215.

[29] Norman Housley, *The Later Crusades, 1274–1580: From Lyons to Alcazar* (Oxford, 1992), pp. 28–29.

support, and initially centred on the king of Sicily Charles of Anjou,[30] who arranged a marriage between his daughter Beatrice and Philip, son and heir of the ex-emperor Baldwin II. By the time of Dubois's writings, Philip IV's younger brother, Charles of Valois, had become titular emperor through his marriage to Catherine de Courtenay, who was the offspring of the marriage between Philip and Beatrice. Charles II of Sicily, who Dubois proposed as an ally for Valois, had inherited his father's interest in the Balkans, although not any direct claim to the imperial throne.[31]

These ambitions were coming to a head around the time that Dubois was writing the *De recuperatione*. Charles of Valois made careful preparations to build a coalition for the conquest of Constantinople, forming alliances with Venice in 1306, the Catalan Grand Company in 1307, and Serbia in 1308. However, all his plans came to nought, as the Catalans, the main enemies of Capetian ambition in the Mediterranean, broke ranks to conquer Attica for themselves. The death of his wife in 1308 deprived Charles of his claim to the imperial throne, and the Venetians made their own truce with the Byzantine emperor Andronikos in 1310. An attempt was made to revive the Valois-Angevin alliance in 1313, when Catherine, daughter of Charles of Valois and Catherine de Courtenay, married Philip, a son of Charles II of Sicily, but by this time the Angevin rulers in southern Italy lacked the resources to mount a serious challenge in the Balkans.[32]

Although related to the specific aim of restoring a Latin emperor in Constantinople, these schemes were part of a more general Angevin expansionist policy in the Balkans. Charles of Anjou had already shown ambitions in that direction, capturing the Albanian port of Durres (Durazzo) and the island of Corfu, and establishing an overlordship over the Latin princes of southern Greece. These ambitions were themselves inherited from his predecessors; Charles's intervention in the Balkans mirrored that of the Norman rulers of Sicily in the eleventh century, while his empire-building across the eastern Mediterranean was not dissimilar to that of Frederick II, with whom he shared an ambition to make himself king of Jerusalem.

To conclude, Pierre Dubois's ideas should be viewed firmly in the context of his interest in the French conquest of the Byzantine Empire. His schemes for this conquest were not as visionary as has often been supposed, reflecting the contemporary attempts by the Capetians and their Angevin cousins in Naples to recapture Constantinople for Latin Christendom. The particular matter of Dubois's advocacy of marriage as a means of conversion should be viewed primarily in a Greek rather than Muslim context, as part

---

[30] By the time Dubois wrote his works on the affairs of the East, the Angevins had lost control of Sicily itself to the Aragonese, but retained their possessions on the mainland, and the title 'king of Sicily'. This Angevin rump kingdom is often referred to as the Kingdom of Naples, to distinguish it from the Aragonese Kingdom of Sicily.

[31] Housley, *The Later Crusades, 1274–1580*, pp. 51–55.

[32] Housley, *The Later Crusades, 1274–1580*, pp. 54–55.

of the scheme to recapture Byzantium. The particular ideas expressed were not so radical as might be supposed, as the example of Thomas of Chobham's concept of woman as preachers to their husbands provides a clear precedent. Nevertheless, Dubois's treatise remains a fascinating insight into the views of a fourteenth-century propagandist and thinker.

Mission et frontière dans l'espace Méditerranéen: Tentatives d'une société guerrière pour la propagation de la foi

LUDWIG VONES

L 'histoire des royaumes chrétiens dans la Péninsule Ibérique est caractérisée par le phénomène de la frontière ou plus précisément par une suite complexe de régions frontalières se succédant et changeant continuellement, séparant les pays chrétiens des territoires musulmans et formant pendant certaines périodes des larges zones tampon désertes et dépeuplées, des 'no man's lands', exposés à des raids militaires des deux côtés. Et dans le cadre de la reconquête les chrétiens tentèrent dès le IXe siècle de franchir ces frontières ou de les déplacer vers le sud.[1] Les progrès de la

---

[1] Pour une vue d'ensemble et l'abondante littérature sur ce point voir L. Vones, *Geschichte der Iberischen Halbinsel im Mittelalter 711–1480. Reiche—Kronen—Regionen* (Sigmaringen, 1993). Sur le phénomène de la frontière cf. C. Sánchez-Albornoz, *Despoblación y repoblación del Valle del Duero* (Buenos Aires, 1966); M. González Jiménez, 'Frontier and Settlement in the Kingdom of Castile (1085–1350)', dans *Medieval Frontier Societies*, ed. R. Bartlett et A. MacKay (Oxford, 1989), pp. 49–74; une vaste synthèse proposa récemment R. Bartlett, *The Making of Europe. Conquest, Colonization and Cultural Change, 950–1350* (1993; repr., London, 1994). L'étude de N. Housley, 'Frontier Societies and Crusading in the Late Middle Ages', *Mediterranean Historical Review*, 10 (1995), 104–19, s'occupe d'avantage de la situation en Orient pendant le bas Moyen-Âge. Sur les différentes intérpretations de la reconquête présentées récemment cf. O. Engels, 'Die Reconquista', dans le même, *Reconquista und Landesherrschaft. Studien zur Rechts—und Verfassungsgeschichte Spaniens im Mittelalter* (Paderborn, 1989), pp. 279–300; et A. P. Bronisch, *Reconquista und Heiliger Krieg. Die Deutung des Krieges im christlichen Spanien von den Westgoten bis ins frühe 12. Jahrhundert* (Münster i. W., 1998);

reconquête, qui fut d'abord avant tout une entreprise politique, rendaient pendant certaines périodes des prises de contact serrées entre les camps adversaires plus faciles. Mais cela ne changeait rien à l'état de guerre permanent et au refus catégorique d'une entente quelconque de cette société chrétienne de la Péninsule Ibérique, qu'on a à juste titre caractérisée comme 'A Society Organized for War'.[2] L'imposition de tributs favorisa les pactes d'alliance politique entre les chefs maures et les seigneurs chrétiens en dépit de tout antagonisme religieux, tandis que l'existence des mozarabes—des chrétiens vivant sous la domination arabe—encourageait toujours à la poursuite d'efforts missionnaires pour le réconfort de ces croyants, dont la situation religieuse restait toujours précaire. Mais ces tentatives n'étaient tolérées que dans un cadre assez restreint et entraînaient des réactions violentes, dès qu'elles visaient à la conversion des musulmans ou à une attaque ouverte contre l'Islam.[3] Une certaine détente se fit sentir au XIe siècle après la désintégration du Califat de Cordoue, en présence d'évidents signes de dissolution des royaumes arabes de *taifas*. Mais déjà vers la fin de ce siècle le pendule oscilla de nouveau de l'autre côté: des partisans fanatiques de mouvements fondamentalistes de l'Afrique du Nord passaient en Espagne—d'abord les Almoravides et cinquante ans plus tard les Almohades—et ranimaient les antagonismes dans le sens d'une guerre sainte, le Gihâd.[4] Le même effet se produit du côté chrétien. Les croisades, destinées à promouvoir la reconquête, prirent dès lors une orientation religieuse

---

pour un survol de l'ensemble des recherches voir J. M. Mínguez, *La Reconquista* (Madrid, 1989).

[2] E. Lourie, 'A Society Organized for War: Medieval Spain', *Past and Present*, 35 (1966), 54–76 (repris dans La même, *Crusade and Colonisation. Muslims, Christians and Jews in Medieval Aragon* (London, 1990), no. 1); J. F. Powers, *A Society Organized for War. The Iberian Municipal Militias in the Central Middle Ages, 1000–1284* (Berkeley, CA, 1988).

[3] Un exemple significatif offrent les soi-disants 'martyrs de Cordoue', qui défièrent le sort en protestant publiquement de leur foi chrétienne, en diffamant Mahomet comme l'antichrist et en s'attaquant au Coran. Voir sur ce sujet R. Franke, 'Die freiwilligen Märtyrer von Cordova und das Verhältnis der Mozaraber zum Islam', *Spanische Forsch. der Görresgesellsch. Ges. Aufsätze zur Kulturgesch. Spaniens*, 13 (1958), 1–170; E. P. Colbert, *The Martyrs of Córdoba (850–859)* (Washington, 1962); et K. B. Wolf, *Christian Martyrs in Muslim Spain* (Leiden, 1988).

[4] Sur la situation politique de l'al-Andalus pendant cette période cf. D. Wasserstein, *The Rise and Fall of the Party-Kings. Politics and Society in Islamic Spain, 1002–1086* (Princeton, 1985); A. Huici Miranda, *Historia política del imperio almohade*, 2 vols (Tetuán, 1956–1957); R. Le Tourneau, *The Almohad Movement in North Africa in the Twelfth and Thirteenth Centuries* (Princeton, 1969). À propos du Gihad, ses racines et ses répercussions voir A. Noth, *Heiliger Krieg und Heiliger Kampf in Islam und Christentum* (Bonn, 1966); D. Urvoy, 'Sur l'évolution de la notion de Gihad dans l'Espagne musulmane', *Mélanges de la Casa de Velázquez*, 9 (1973), 335–71; ainsi que du même, 'Une étude sociologique des mouvements religieux dans l'Espagne musulmane de la chute du Califat au milieu du XIIIe siècle', *Mélanges de la Casa de Velázquez*, 8 (1972), 223–93; A. Morabia, *Le Gihâd dans l'Islam médiéval. Le 'combat sacré' des origines au XIIe siècle* (Paris, 1993).

prononcée.[5] Ce changement de cap cadrait assez bien avec l'attitude de la papauté, qui depuis le XIe siècle avait de plus en plus pris l'offensive vis-à-vis des musulmans de la partie ouest de la Méditerranée—de la Péninsule Ibérique en passant par la Sardaigne jusqu'en Italie du Sud. Empreinte d'une spiritualité nouvelle, issue du mouvement de la réforme de l'Église, la papauté considérait alors la conversion des hétérodoxes comme un acte d'amour agissant,[6] et commençait même à jeter ses visées sur l'Afrique, sans toutefois arriver à y prendre pied.[7] Il ne peut pourtant pas être question—au moins jusqu'à la fin du XIIe siècle—d'un sérieux effort du côté chrétien de propager la foi en al-Andalus. Si les musulmans opposèrent un refus catégorique à toute tentative de conversion, l'Église elle-même se montra plutôt réservée et—en vue d'éventuels contacts—élabora des normes de droit canonique soulignant davantage ce que divisait les deux religions. On ne possédait d'ailleurs que peu d'informations précises sur l'Islam et le prophète Mahomet et se contentait de clichées diffamatoires.[8] Pendant les longues années de luttes on avait cultivé de génération en génération une certaine idée de l'ennemi, qui maintenant s'avérait être un obstacle insurmontable à une compréhension mutuelle et à une vraie entente en matière religieuse.[9] De toute façon le contact direct avec les musulmans ne pouvait être établi qu'après la reconquête d'une ville, d'une région ou d'un royaume. Et cette reconquête impliquait d'abord des mesures restrictives telle que la transformation de la mosquée en cathédrale, l'établissement d'une administration chrétienne et la formation d'une communauté civile et religieuse. Les rapports entre chrétiens et mudéjares, c'est-à-dire les musulmans demeurant sous domination chrétienne, étaient réglés par des contrats, fixant d'avance les droits des colons à s'installer à un certain endroit et les redevances à payer. Assez souvent on se souciait moins d'établir un programme pour obtenir leur conversion au christianisme, que de fixer les conditions leur permettant de garder leur foi actuelle.[10] Et ce fut

---

[5] Sur la situation dans la Péninsule Ibérique cf. J. Goñi Gaztambide, *Historia de la Bula de la Cruzada en España* (Vitoria, 1958); C. Erdmann, *Die Entstehung des Kreuzzugsgedankens* (Stuttgart, 1935; repr. Darmstadt, 1965); B. Z. Kedar, *Crusade and Mission. European Approaches toward the Muslims* (Princeton, 1984).

[6] J. Riley-Smith, 'Crusading as an Act of Love', *History,* 65 (1980), 177–92.

[7] A. Hettinger, *Die Beziehungen des Papsttums zu Afrika von der Mitte des 11. bis zum Ende des 12. Jahrhunderts* (Köln, 1993).

[8] R. W. Southern, *Western Views of Islam in the Middle Ages* (Cambridge, 1962); N. Daniel, *Islam and the West. The Making of an Image* (Edinburgh, 1960); Du même, *The Arabs and Mediaeval Europe,* 2nd edn (London, 1981); W. M. Watt, *The Influence of Islam on Medieval Europe* (Edinburgh, 1972); P. Sénac, *L'image de l'autre. L'Occident médiéval face à l'Islam* (Paris, 1983).

[9] R. Barkai, *Cristianos y musulmanes en la España medieval (El enemigo en el espejo)* (Madrid, 1984).

[10] Cf. J. F. O'Callaghan, 'The Mudejars of Castile and Portugal in the Twelfth and Thirteenth Centuries', dans *Muslims under Latin Rule, 1100–1300,* ed. J. M. Powell (Princeton, 1990), pp.

justement l'insertion juridique des musulmans qui empêcha non seulement leur christ-ianisation, mais aussi toute tentative en ce sens. La Couronne et les autres institutions concernées n'avaient aucun intérêt à perdre de par leur conversion les redevances et services dus, qui constituaient dans ces régions frontalières peu peuplées des rentrées et rendements importants, et les seigneurs fonciers tenaient à garder à leur disposition cet important réservoir de main d'œuvres ou même d'esclaves. On craignait aussi le danger de contacts trop intenses, comportant le risque de contagion et d'un embrouil-lement d'idées religieuses—un problème qui s'était déjà posé à propos des juifs.[11] Du point de vue du droit canonique on faisait d'ailleurs d'importantes réserves quant à l'intégration sociale d'éventuels convertis. Il s'avérait difficile de trouver une solution adéquate pour régler la cohabitation des convertis avec leur parents pas encore gagnés à la nouvelle foi. L'intégration des familles converties, dont la situation préalable était peu compatible avec le droit matrimonial et l'éthique chrétienne, posait quantité de problèmes d'autant plus, qu'on n'avait cessé d'interdire tout contact direct entre chrétiens et musulmans en vue d'une séparation rigoureuse des deux communautés religieuses.[12] C'est pourquoi on renonça même à l'intérieur de la zone d'influence chrétienne à toute propagation active de la foi, resta dans l'expectative et se résigna à émettre des normes restrictives touchant les rapports et les contacts directs avec les partenaires commerciaux musulmans.[13] Même la croissance proportionnelle de la

---

11–56; J. M. Powell, 'The Papacy and the Muslim Frontier', *Muslims under Latin Rule*, pp. 175–203.

[11] Powell, 'The Papacy and the Muslim Frontier', pp. 185 sqq.

[12] P. Herde, 'Christians and Saracens at the Time of the Crusades. Some Comments of Contemporary Medieval Canonists', *Studia Gratiana*, 12 (1967), 359–76; E.-D. Hehl, *Kirche und Krieg im 12. Jahrhundert. Studien zu kanonischem Recht und politischer Wirklichkeit* (Stuttgart, 1980), pp. 159 sqq.; R. I. Burns, 'El Dret Canònic i la Reconquesta: convergència i simbiosi', dans Le même, *Jaume I i els Valencians del segle XIII* (València, 1981), pp. 53–100; H. Gilles, 'Législation et doctrine canoniques sur les Sarrassins', dans *Cahiers de Fanjeaux 18: Islam et chrétiens du Midi (XIIᵉ–XIVᵉ s.)* (Fanjeaux, Toulouse, 1983), pp. 195–213; B. Z. Kedar, 'Muslim Conversion in Canon Law', dans *Proceedings of the Sixth International Congress of Medieval Canon Law*, ed. S. Kuttner et K. Pennington (Città del Vaticano, 1985), pp. 320–32; Le même, 'De Iudeis et Sarracenis. On the Categorization of Muslims in Medieval Canon Law', dans *Studia in Honorem Eminentissimi Cardinalis Alphonsi M. Stickler*, curante R. I. Castillo Lara (Roma, 1992), pp. 207–13.

[13] Herde, 'Christians and Saracens', pp. 371 sqq.; Gilles, 'Législation et doctrine canoniques sur les Sarrassins', pp. 205 sqq.; Kedar, 'Muslim Conversion in Canon Law', pp. 326 sqq. Voir aussi J. Trenchs Ódena, '*De Alexandrinis*. El comercio prohibido con los musulmanos y el papado de Aviñón durante la primera mitad del siglo XIV', *Anuario de Estudios Medievales*, 10 (1980), 237–320; Du même, 'Les "Alexandrini", ou la désobéissance aux embargos conciliaires ou pontificaux contre les Musulmans', dans *Cahiers de Fanjeaux 18: Islam et chrétiens du Midi*, pp. 169–93; D. Abulafia, *Italy, Sicily and the Mediterranean, 1100–1400* (London, 1987); Du

population mudéjare dans la péninsule Ibérique ne changea rien à cette attitude. Les recommandations du IVe concile du Latran en 1215 relatives à la séparation entre chrétiens et juifs et le port de vêtements spécifiques, furent maintenant appliquées aux musulmans.[14] Mais leur mise en pratique fut souvent moins rigoureuse, puisqu'on ne pouvait reprocher aux musulmans la crucifixion du Christ[15] et que—contrairement aux juifs—ils n'entraient pas en concurrence avec les chrétiens dans la course aux fonctions publiques.[16]

Les problèmes ébauchés ici prirent une toute autre importance au XIIIe siècle, au moment de l'effondrement définitif de la domination almohade dans la Péninsule Ibérique et en Afrique du Nord. Imbus de l'esprit de croisade les royaumes chrétiens avaient remporté la grande bataille de Las Navas de Tolosa en 1212 et s'apprêtaient à reconquérir les petits États arabes restant dans la péninsule—en Estrémadure, Andalousie, Valence et Murcie—et dans les Iles Baléares. A l'exception du royaume des Nasrides, centré autour de Grenade, ils ne restaient donc plus que quelques dynasties arabes au Maghreb nord-africain, tels que les Mérinides au Maroc autour de Marrakech et Fès, les Banu 'Abd al-Wad en Alger autour de Tlemcen et les Hafsides dans l'Ifriqiyya (proprement dit) autour de Tunis et Bougie.[17] L'immense succès de la conquête chrétienne, qui mit l'Islam dans la partie ouest de la Méditerranée sur la défensive pour le reste du Moyen-Âge, ne provoqua alors pas seulement un simple déplacement des zones frontalières vers le Sud ou de l'al-Andalus vers le Maghreb, mais contribua à rendre ces frontières de plus en plus abordables jusqu'à leur disparition totale.

Cela ouvrit des perspectives nouvelles pour une action missionnaire dans les autres pays musulmans, bienqu'on ne réussît que très rarement à obtenir la conversion tant

---

même, *Commerce and Conquest in the Mediterranean, 1100–1500* (Aldershot, 1993).

[14] *Conciliorum oecumenicorum decreta,* ed. J. Alberigo et al., 3rd edn (Bologna, 1973), p. 266, § 68; *Constitutiones Concilii quarti Lateranensis una cum Commentariis glossatorum,* ed. A. García y García (Città del Vaticano, 1981), pp. 107–8, § 68. Cf. A. Cutler, 'Innocent III and the Distinctive Clothing of Jews and Muslims', *Studies in Medieval Culture,* 3 (1970), pp. 92–116.

[15] Les différences les plus significatives sont relevées par M. de Epalza, *Jésus otage. Juifs, chrétiens et musulmans en Espagne (VIe–XVIIe s.)* (Paris, 1987).

[16] *Conciliorum oecumenicorum decreta,* pp. 266–67, § 69; *Constitutiones Concilii quarti Lateranensis,* ed. García y García, pp. 108–9, § 69.

[17] R. Brunschvig, *La Berberie orientale sous les Hafsides. Des origines à la fin du XVe siècle,* 2 vols (Paris, 1940); C.-E. Dufourcq, *L'Espagne catalane et le Maghrib au XIIIe et XIVe siècles. De la bataille de Las Navas de Tolosa, 1212, à l'avènement du sultan mérinide Aboul-Hassan, 1331* (Paris, 1966); Du même, *L'Ibérie chrétienne et le Maghreb (XIIe–XVe siècles)* (London, 1990). Voir d'une manière générale H.-R. Singer, 'Der Maghreb und die Pyrenäenhalbinsel bis zum Ausgang des Mittelalters', dans *Geschichte der arabischen Welt,* ed. U. Haarmann, 2nd edn (München, 1991), pp. 264–322.

souhaitée d'un prince.[18] Il restait toujours une grande faveur, si un tel prince permettait à ses sujets de se convertir officiellement au christianisme ou de bâtir une église.[19] En même temps l'idée d'une mission chrétienne reçut une forte poussée par l'essor des ordres nouveaux. Porteurs d'une spiritualité nouvelle, les ordres mendiants professaient l'idée d'une action missionnaire en dehors de la zone d'influence chrétienne et jouissaient bientôt du soutien des rois de Castille et d'Aragon. Ils étaient secondés par les *viri redemptores*, les trinitaires aux activités concentrées avant tout en Orient, et les mercédiaires, originaires de la Catalogne, dont le fondateur Pere Nolasc récueillit des aumônes à Barcelone. Ces ordres n'étaient pas spécialisés dans l'évangélisation, mais plutôt concernés du sort des prisonniers chrétiens dans les pays sous domination arabe. Leur tâche ne se limitait pas uniquement à la rédemption des prisonniers de guerre ou au payement de leur rançon, mais s'étendait aussi aux soins à prodiguer aux esclaves chrétiens et aux mercenaires castillans ou catalano-aragonais entrés dans les services des princes musulmans.[20]

Mais la réalisation d'une conception plus progressive dans la partie ouest de la Méditerranée de ce 'Thirteenth-Century Dream of Conversion', dont parle Robert Ignatius Burns,[21] fut d'abord l'œuvre des franciscains et dominicains. Leurs actions ne se limitaient pourtant pas à une propagation active de la foi dans les pays sous

---

[18] Voir Burns, 'Christian-Islamic Confrontation in the West: The Thirteenth-Century Dream of Conversion', *American Historical Review*, 76 (1971), 1391–94; J. Muldoon, *Popes, Lawyers, and Infidels. The Church and the Non-Christian World, 1250–1550* (Philadelphia, 1979), pp. 40sq.; Kedar, *Crusade and Mission*, p. 144.

[19] Cf. Kedar, *Crusade and Mission*, p. 138.

[20] Sur la fondation de ces ordres voir maintenant G. Cipollone, *Cristianità—Islam. Cattività e liberazione in nome di Dio. Il tempo di Innocenzo III dopo il '1187'* (Roma, 1992); Du même, 'Les Trinitaires, rédempteurs des captifs (1198)', dans *La guerre, la violence et les gens au Moyen Âge.* I: *Guerre et Violence*, sous la direction de Philippe Contamine et Olivier Guyotjeannin (Paris, 1996), pp. 311–20; J. W. Brodman, *Ransoming Captives in Crusader Spain. The Order of Merced on the Christian-Islamic Frontier* (Philadelphia, 1986); Le même, 'Ransomers or Royal Agents: The Mercedarians and the Aragonese Crown in the Fourteenth Century', dans *Iberia and the Mediterranean World of the Middle Ages. Essays in Honor of Robert I. Burns*, II: *Proceedings from 'Spain and the Western Mediterranean'* (Leiden, 1996), pp. 239–52.

[21] R. I. Burns, 'Christian-Islamic Confrontation in the West', pp. 1386–1434; Du même, 'Christian-Muslim Confrontation: The Thirteenth-Century Dream of Conversion', dans Du même, *Muslims, Christians, and Jews in the Crusader Kingdom of Valencia. Societies in symbiosis* (Cambridge, 1984), pp. 80–108, 310–12. Les thèses avancées par Burns, dont l'œuvre principale: *The Crusader Kingdom of Valencia: Reconstruction on a Thirteenth-Century Frontier*, 2 vols (Cambridge, MA, 1967), est maintenant disponible en español dans une version complétée: *El reino de Valencia en el siglo XIII (Iglesia y sociedad)*, 2 vols (Valencia, 1982), sont discutées dans la *Revista d'Història Medieval*, 1 (1990), 215 sqq. Cf. aussi note 36 infra.

domination arabe. Ils élaboraient en même temps une nouvelle base théorique de la mission chrétienne.[22] Saint François d'Assise lui-même était animé d'un authentique zèle missionnaire. Ne citons qu'à titre d'exemple que son projet de prêcher en personne la parole de Dieu devant les princes païens, pour les convertir au christianisme ou pour souffrir peut-être le martyre. Il le tenta par trois fois. Deux fois il échoua—1212 au cours de son voyage en Orient et 1214 sur le chemin du Maroc—mais la troisième fois il réussit enfin. Lors de la croisade de Damiette (1220) il rencontra le sultan Melek al-Kamil pour disputer avec lui—sans grand succès d'ailleurs—sur la vraie foi.[23] Sur ses traces cinq franciscains ingénus tentèrent une autre entreprise missionnaire, dont le résultat fut moins satisfaisant: leur polémique publique contre Mahomet et l'Islam occasionna—si l'on peut se fier à une source peu sûre—en 1220 leur exécution au Maroc et fournit tout de suite matière à légende.[24] Quelques-uns de leurs frères furent expulsés de Séville ou du Maroc pour des délits analogues mais moins graves. Deux franciscains italiens par contre furent encore en 1228 exécutés à Valence.[25] Ce fut la papauté qui encouragea pendant toute cette période les contacts avec l'Afrique du Nord, pour rétablir l'organisation ecclésiastique dans ces régions. Innocent III avait déjà en 1198/99 soutenu les actions des trinitaires au Maghreb.[26] Ses successeurs immédiats, Honorius III, Grégoire IX, Innocent IV et Alexandre IV ne réclamèrent pas seulement le libre exercice de la religion chrétienne, mais surtout l'érection d'un évêché à

---

[22] B. Altaner, *Die Dominikanermissionen des 13. Jahrhunderts. Forschungen zur Geschichte der kirchlichen Unionen und der Mohammedaner—und Heidenmission des Mittelalters* (Habelschwerdt, Schles., 1924); O. van der Vat, *Die Anfänge der Franziskanermissionen und ihre Weiterentwicklung im nahen Orient und in den mohammedanischen Ländern während des 13. Jahrhunderts* (Werl, Westf., 1934), notamment pp. 60–123; E. R. Daniel, *The Franciscan Concept of Mission in the High Middle Ages* (Lexington, KY, 1975); J. Webster, *Els Menorets. The Franciscans in the Realms of Aragon. From St. Francis to the Black Death* (Toronto, 1993).

[23] Voir maintenant le résumé de H. Feld, *Franziskus von Assisi und seine Bewegung* (Darmstadt, 1994), pp. 295 sqq., ainsi que C. T. Maier, *Preaching the Crusades. Mendicant Friars and the Cross in the Thirteenth Century* (Cambridge, 1994), pp. 8 sqq. Sur ses tentatives en Égypte voir L. Lemmens, 'De Sancto Francisco Christum Praedicante coram Sultano Egypti', *Archivum Franciscanum Historicum,* 19 (1926), 559–78; F. Cardini, 'Nella presenza del Soldan superba: Bernardo, Francesco, Bonaventura e il superamento spirituale dell'idea di crociata', *Studi francescani,* 71 (1974), 199–250; J. M. Powell, 'Francesco d'Assisi e la Quinta Crociata. Una Missione di Pace', *Schede medievali,* 4 (1983), 68–77.

[24] *Passio sanctorum martyrum [. . .] in Marochio martyrizatorum,* dans *Analecta Franciscana,* 3 (Quaracchi, 1897), pp. 584–90.

[25] Held, *Franziskus von Assisi,* pp. 296 sq.; Burns, 'Christian-Islamic Confrontation', pp. 1396 sq.

[26] Cf. K.-E. Lupprian, *Die Beziehungen der Päpste zu islamischen und mongolischen Herrschern im 13. Jahrhundert anhand ihres Briefwechsels* (Città del Vaticano, 1981), pp. 20 et 106–7, no. 1.

Marrakech. Ce fut en raison de son pouvoir primatial qu'on chargea l'archevêque de Tolède, Rodrigo Jiménez de Rada, de choisir des candidats qualifiés parmi les franciscains et dominicains. Le premier évêque, qui monta sur ce siège sous l'ancien titre d'un évêque de *Baetica*, fut Dominique de Ségovie, un frère prêcheur. En 1246 il fut relayé par le franciscain Lope Fernández de Ayn, qui devait plus tard transférer son siège à Ceuta. Et même à Fès—au sein du règne almohade—l'existence d'un évêque franciscain est attestée pour un certain temps.[27] Quand Lope Fernández résigna vers 1257 son siège d'évêque du Maroc, d'autres franciscains, tels que Blanco et en 1290 Rodrigo de Gudal prirent la relève, remplissant en même temps les fonctions de légat apostolique.[28]

En principe la papauté avait tendance à eximer les évêchés missionnaires et à les soumettre directement au Saint-Siège, coupant ainsi court aux querelles des métropoles hispaniques sur la question des obédiences. Tel fut le cas du diocèse du Maroc, que les archevêchés de Tolède et de Séville—nouvellement érigés—se disputaient comme suffragant, mais aussi du siège de Majorque, érigé en 1232 et réclamé comme suffragant par Tarragone aussi bien que par Barcelone.[29]

L'influence croissante des ordres mendiants sur la propagation de la foi dans les pays islamiques, et les plus grandes facilités d'accès des missionnaires aux régions musulmanes jadis fermées, annoncent déjà une des tendances de ce siècle: un désamorçage progressif de l'attitude belliqueuse à l'égard de l'Islam, comme conséquence d'une désintégration du règne almohade et de l'affaiblissement de l'idée de croisade, malgré toutes les campagnes guerrières dans le cadre de la reconquête. L'effritement des courants fondamentalistes dans les deux camps devait permettre l'ouverture d'un dialogue.[30] Une plus grande flexibilité, dont un des signes caractéristiques fut la volonté

---

[27] Lupprian, *Die Beziehungen der Päpste*, pp. 21–26, 128–29, no. 13, pp. 176–81, no. 28–31; A. López, 'Obispos en el Africa Septentrional desde el siglo XIII', *Archivo Ibero-Americano*, 14 (1920), 397–502; Altaner, *Die Dominikanermissionen*, notamment pp. 98 sqq.; J. M. Coll, 'San Raymundo de Peñafort y las Misiones del Norte Africano en la Edad Media', *Missionalia Hispanica*, 5 (1948), 417–57, spécialement 422 sqq.; W. R. Thomson, *Friars in the Cathedral. The First Franciscan Bishops, 1226–1261* (Toronto, 1975), pp. 28–34; Maier, *Preaching the Crusades*, pp. 82 sq. Sur la situation à Ceuta au XIIIe siècle voir maintenant M. del Carmen Mosquera Merino, *La Señoría de Ceuta en el siglo XIII* (Ceuta, 1994).

[28] Cf. L. Pellegrini, 'Le missione francescane sotto Alessandro IV (1254–1261)', *Studi francescani*, 64.1 (1967), 91–118, notamment pp. 102 sqq.

[29] Cf. D. Mansilla Reoyo, *Geografía eclesiástica de España. Estudio histórico-geográfico de las diócesis*, 2 vols (Roma, 1994), II, 275–77, 288–90.

[30] Sur la naissance d'un dialogue dans la Péninsule Ibérique voir le tour d'horizon de R. Barkai, 'Diálogo filosófico-religioso en el seno de las tres culturas ibéricas', dans *Diálogo filosófico-religioso entre Cristianismo, Judaísmo e Islamismo durante la Edad Media en la Península Ibérica*, ed. H. Santiago-Otero (Turnhout, 1994), pp. 1–27; et I. Willi-Plein et T. Willi, *Glaubensdolch und Messiasbeweis: Die Begegnung von Judentum, Christentum und Islam im 13. Jahrhundert in Spanien* (Neukirchen-Vluyn, 1980).

expresse de certains princes musulmans de se convertir au christianisme, relaya au moment politique opportun la confrontation implacable. Dans ce contexte il est important de tenir compte d'un changement d'attitude vis-à-vis des gentils—y inclus les musulmans—occasionné par l'influence de la philosophie aristotélicienne, dont les écrits—jusqu'alors inconnus au Moyen-Âge et transmis par la tradition arabe et les commentaires d'Averroès—ont été progressivement rendus accessibles depuis le milieu du XIIe siècle, surtout par les activités de l'école de traduction de Tolède. La nouvelle conception, qu'on s'était fait de l'homme, permettait de reconnaître aux païens le droit à une existence propre en se référant au droit naturel et au *ius gentium*. Toute action guerrière basée uniquement sur des raisons religieuses devenait ainsi contestable. C'est surtout grâce aux efforts d'Innocent IV que l'idée missionnaire revêtait au XIIIe siècle une forme plus modérée. Pour lui les mécréants étaient—en dépit de leur statut de gens non baptisées—placés sous le droit naturel et détenaient ainsi certains droits strictement limités. Il n'était donc plus admissible de partir en croisade contre eux uniquement en raison de leur foi, mais il fallait avancer d'autres motifs, tels que les injustices perpétrées vis-à-vis des chrétiens, pour prouver, qu'il s'agissait bel et bien d'une guerre juste.[31] C'était surtout aux universités et écoles de droits qu'incombait la tâche de développer les normes de droit naturel et par conséquence une nouvelle conception de l'homme. Là les érudits franciscains et dominicains jouaient un rôle important dans l'élaboration et la diffusion des thèses propagées, mais aussi dans les discussions et

---

[31] Cf. à ce propos R. C. Schwinges, 'Kreuzzugsideologie und Toleranz im Denken Wilhelms von Tyrus', *Saeculum*, 25 (1974), 367–85, resp. Du même, 'Wilhelm von Tyrus: Vom Umgang mit Feindbildern im 12. Jahrhundert', dans *Spannungen und Widersprüche. Gedenkschrift für František Graus* (Sigmaringen, 1992), pp. 155–72; Du même, 'Die Wahrnehmung des Anderen durch Geschichtsschreibung. Muslime und Christen im Spiegel der Werke Wilhelms von Tyrus (†1186) und Rodrigo Ximénez‛ de Rada (†1247)', dans *Toleranz im Mittelalter*, hg. v. A. Patschovsky et H. Zimmermann (Sigmaringen, 1998), pp. 101–27, et surtout Du même, *Kreuzzugsideologie und Toleranz. Studien zu Wilhelm von Tyrus* (Stuttgart, 1977), notamment pp. 227sqq., 241sqq., qui ne présente pas seulement une étude sur l'univers de Guillaume de Tyre (environ 1130 à 1186) mais y ajoute aussi une bibliographie. Les idées d'Innocent IV sont analysées par A. Melloni, *Innocenzo IV. La concezione e l'esperienza della cristianità come 'regimen unius personae'* (Genova, 1990), pp. 177sqq. À propos de la notion complexe de tolérance et de son application à la situation au Moyen-Âge voir K. Schreiner, 'Toleranz im Mittelalter und in der beginnenden Neuzeit', dans *Geschichtliche Grundbegriffe,* 6 (Stuttgart, 1990), pp. 445–94, 523–605; Le même, ' "Tolerantia'. Begriffs- und wirkungsgeschichtliche Studien zur Toleranzauffassung des Kirchenvaters Augustinus', dans *Toleranz im Mittelalter*, pp. 335–89; A. Patschovsky, 'Toleranz im Mittelalter. Idee und Wirklichkeit', dans *Toleranz im Mittelalter*, pp. 391–402; pour le domaine islamique: C. Colpe, 'Toleranz im Islam', dans *Mit Fremden leben* (München, 1995), pp. 81–92; H. Houben, 'Möglichkeiten und Grenzen religiöser Toleranz im normannisch-staufischen Süditalien', *Deutsches Archiv*, 50 (1990), 159–98.

disputes qui s'ensuivaient.[32] Et c'était avant tout pour cette raison que les ordres mendiants, spécialistes de la prédication, optaient pour une propagation de la foi basée sur la persuasion et le recours au pouvoir de la parole prêchée. Pour eux la croisade ne constituait plus un moyen pour obtenir une conversion forcée des mécréants dans le sens d'un *compellere intrare* inconditionnel, mais plutôt un instrument d'évangélisation, destiné à faciliter aux ordres missionnaires l'accès au monde musulman pour y préparer les cœurs à l'annonce de la parole de Dieu. Il est évident que ce furent surtout les ordres mendiants, bien insérés dans les villes, qui propagèrent cette conception modérée de la croisade, d'autant plus qu'ils comprenaient fort bien les implications économiques pour les intérêts commerciaux des bourgeois.[33] La croisade armée—critiquée de plus en plus âprement sous sa forme et ses objectifs traditionnels[34]—devait à leurs yeux servir uniquement comme moyen de pression au service de la propagation de la foi et faciliter ainsi aux souverains musulmans la tâche de prendre une décision, permettant aux missionnaires d'établir le contact indispensable avec une population susceptible mais peu encline à être convertie et d'établir à long terme les bases pour des rapports commerciaux paisibles. Pour justifier les croisades contre les musulmans, il suffit de leur reprocher entre autre que l'Islam contestait la nature divine de Jésus, qu'il manifestait clairement son intention de propager ses idées dans le monde entier et qu'il avait l'intention de passer à l'attaque contre le christianisme.[35] Il ne peut pas surprendre, qu'une telle conception trouvât un écho favorable et continu dans la Péninsule Ibérique, où la situation de frontière avait jusqu'alors fortement marquée une perception avant tout religieuse de la reconquête. Après les événements du XIIIe siècle cette situation perdura en Espagne uniquement vis-à-vis du royaume de Grenade. Une nouvelle frontière face aux royaumes musulmans africains s'établit en Afrique du Nord, où la conversion de la population au christianisme n'impliquait pas d'inconvénients pour les souverains hispaniques. Dans la Péninsule Ibérique par contre l'exploitation de la population musulmane s'aggrava encore, puisqu'on ne cessa d'encourager l'immigration en provenance d'autres pays musulmans pour supplier au manque de colons

---

[32] Cf. d'une manière générale M. Grabmann, 'Das Naturrecht der Scholastik von Gratian bis Thomas von Aquin', dans Du même, *Mittelalterliches Geistesleben. Abhandlungen zur Geschichte der Scholastik und Mystik*, 1 (München, 1926), pp. 65–103; M.-D. Chenu, *La théologie comme science au XIIIe siècle*, 3rd edn (Paris 1957); R. Weigand, *Die Naturrechtslehre der Legisten und Dekretisten von Irnerius bis Accursius und von Gratian bis Johannes Teutonicus* (München, 1967); Fernand Van Steenberghen, *La philosophie au XIIIe siècle*, 2nd edn (Louvain, Paris, 1991).

[33] Maier, *Preaching the Crusades*, passim.

[34] P. A. Throop, *Criticism of the Crusade. A Study of Public Opinion and Crusade Propaganda* (Amsterdam, 1940); E. Siberry, 'Missionaries and Crusaders, 1095–1274: Opponents or Allies', *Studies in Church History*, 20 (1983), 103–10; La même, *Criticism of Crusading, 1095–1274* (Oxford, 1985).

[35] Kedar, *Crusade and Mission*, pp. 156 sq.

chrétiens.[36] Ce fait provoqua plus d'une fois des troubles sociaux, où les ressentiments contre les convertis et les mudéjares éclatèrent au grand jour.[37] Le processus d'acculturation et d'assimilation se trouvait ainsi ralenti,[38] et quand on réussit enfin, grâce à des mesures royales, à augmenter la densité de la population chrétienne, il s'ensuit une confrontation acharnée entre chrétiens et musulmans, peu favorable au maintien d'une autonomie musulmane[39]. Cette situation fut à peu près la même dans les domaines de la Couronne de Castille, où les tensions aboutirent au sein du royaume de Murcie à une grande révolte,[40] qu'aux pays de la Couronne d'Aragon, où on retrouve même aux Iles Baléares des communautés musulmanes indépendantes.[41] Les rois par contre furent

---

[36] R. I. Burns, 'Journey from Islam. Incipient Cultural Transition in the Conquered Kingdom of Valencia (1240–1280)', *Speculum,* 35 (1960), 337–56 (repris dans Du même, *Moors and Crusaders in Mediterranean Spain. Collected Studies* (London, 1978), no. 12); Le même, 'Immigrants from Islam: The Crusader's Use of Muslims as Settlers in Thirteenth-Century Spain', *American Historical Review,* 80 (1975), 21–42 (repris dans Du même, *Moors and Crusaders*, no. 2); Le même, *Islam under the Crusaders: Colonial Survival in the Thirteenth-Century Kingdom of Valencia* (Princeton, 1973); Le même, *Medieval Colonialism: Postcrusade Exploitation of Islamic Valencia* (Princeton, 1975); Le même, 'The Muslim in the Christian Feudal Order: The Kingdom of Valencia, 1240–1280', *Studies in Medieval Culture,* 5 (1976), 105–26 (repris dans Du même, *Moors and Crusaders*, no. 11); Le même, 'Muslims in the Thirteenth-Century Realms of Aragon: Interaction and Reaction', dans *Muslims under Latin Rule, 1100–1300,* ed. J. M. Powell (Princeton, 1990), pp. 57–102.

[37] R. I. Burns, 'Social Riots on the Christian-Moslem Frontier: Thirteenth-Century Valencia', *American Historical Review,* 66 (1960–61), 378–400 (repris dans Du même, *Moors and Crusaders,* no. 3).

[38] Cf. R. I. Burns, 'Spanish Islam in Transition: Acculturative Survival and its Price in the Christian Kingdom of Valencia, 1240–1280', dans *Islam and Cultural Change in the Middle Ages,* ed. S. Vryonis Jr. (Wiesbaden, 1975), pp. 87–105 (repris dans Du même, *Moors and Crusaders,* no. 13).

[39] Cf. D. Menjot, 'Chrétiens et Musulmans à Murcie sous la domination castillane: Un exemple de confrontation Islam-Chrétienté au bas Moyen Âge', dans *Ier Colloque franco-polonais, Nice-Antibes* (Nice, 1982).

[40] Cf. J. Torres Fontes, 'Los mudéjares murcianos en el siglo XIII', *Murgetana,* 17 (1961), 57–90; Le même, *La reconquista de Murcia en 1266 por Jaime I de Aragón,* 2nd edn (Murcia, 1987); D. Menjot, 'Les Mudéjares du royaume de Murcie', dans *Revue du Monde Musulman et de la Méditerranée, 63–64: Minorités religieuses dans l'Espagne médiévale* (Aix-en-Provence, 1992), pp. 165–78.

[41] Cf. E. Lourie, 'Free Moslems in the Balearics under Christian Rule in the Thirteenth Century', *Speculum,* 45 (1970), 624–49 (repris dans La même, *Crusade and Colonisation. Muslims, Christians and Jews in Medieval Aragon,* no. 6); La même, 'Anatomy of Ambivalence: Muslims under the Crown of Aragon in the Late Thirteenth Century', dans La même, *Crusade and Colonisation,* no. 7.

bientôt gagnés à l'idée de contraindre les mudéjares à servir comme les juifs de cible
aux efforts missionnaires des frères prêcheurs, et les forcèrent à venir assister à leurs
prêches notamment lors des principales fêtes religieuses.[42] Au sein des ordres religieux
une discussion d'un haut niveau théorique[43] portait tout au long du siècle sur la croisade,
la propagation de la foi et la conversion. Les franciscains surtout furent fortement
influencés par les conceptions eschatologiques des spirituels, inspirés eux-mêmes par
Joaquim de Flore, sur la 'conversion apocalyptique'. Au moment prévu pour la fin du
monde on projetait une dernière grande croisade, susceptible d'amener la conversion
en masse des musulmans et des juifs.[44] Il s'en suit une modification profonde de la
conception chrétienne de la propagation de la foi, bien que la motivation déjà ébauchée
chez Saint François d'Assise, d'agir uniquement par l'amour de Dieu et le désir de subir
le martyr, ne perdît rien de son attrait.[45] Parmi les représentants des divers ordres
spécialement engagés dans ce domaine, il faut d'abord citer les dominicains Raymond
de Penyafort, *le zelator fidei propagandae inter Sarracenos*,[46] qui participa à
l'organisation de la conquête de Majorque et à l'érection de son évêché, élabora un
vaste programme de christianisation des juifs et musulmans et fonda ensuite une
véritable 'école missionnaire';[47] Humbert de Romans et son *Opus tripartitum*;[48]
Raymond Martin, continuateur de l'œuvre de Raymond de Penyafort, et son traité peu
connu *Capistrum judaeorum,* son manuel sur l'assistance spirituelle des chrétiens
vivants sous la domination des maures *Explanatio simboli Apostolorum ad institutionem
fidelium,* sa *Pugio fidei adversus mauros et iudeos* et son traité anti-islamiste récemment
redécouvert *De Seta Mahometi*;[49] et enfin Thomas d'Aquin, longtemps en liaison

---

[42] Kedar, *Crusade and Mission*, pp. 137, 196.

[43] Kedar, *Crusade and Mission*, passim.

[44] Daniel, *The Franciscan Concept of Mission in the High Middle Ages*, pp. 12 sq., 76 sqq.;
Le même, 'Apocalyptic Conversion: The Joachite Alternative to the Crusades', *Traditio,* 25
(1969), 142 sqq.

[45] Cf. par exemple Daniel, *The Franciscan Concept of Mission*, pp. 40–49; Le même, 'The
Desire for Martyrdom: A *Leitmotiv* of St. Bonaventure', *Franciscan Studies*, 32 (1972), 74–87.

[46] *Monumenta Ordinis Praedicatorum Historica*, ed. B. M. Reichert (Romae, 1897), I, 332
(chronique de l'ordre par Girard de Fracheto).

[47] Sur Raymond de Penyafort et son école voir Altaner, *Die Dominikanermissionen*, pp.
89 sqq.; J. Cohen, *The Friars and the Jews. The Evolution of Medieval Anti-Judaism* (Ithaca,
1982), pp. 103 sqq., 129 sqq.

[48] Throop, *Criticism of the Crusade*, pp. 147–213; B. Roberg, *Das Zweite Konzil von Lyon
[1274]* (Paderborn, 1990), pp. 106–26; E. T. Brett, *Humbert of Romans. His Life and Views of
Thirteenth-Century Society* (Toronto, 1984).

[49] Altaner, *Die Dominikanermissionen*, notamment pp. 95 sqq.; J. M. March i Batlles, 'En
Ramón Martí i la seva "Explanatio Symboli Apostolorum"', *Anuari de l'Institut d'Estudis
Catalans*, 2 (1908), 443–96; A. Berthier, 'Un maître orientaliste du XIIIe siècle: Raymond Martin
O.P.', *Archivum Fratrum Praedicatorum*, 6 (1936), 267–311; Cohen, *The Friars and the Jews,*

fructueuse avec Raymond Martin, qui écrivit une *Summa contra gentiles* et un véritable manuel de missionnaire *De rationibus fidei contra Saracenos, Graecos et Armenos.*[50] Parmi les franciscains il faut d'abord nommer Roger Bacon[51] et surtout le courtisan, philosophe et poète majorquin Raymond Lulle, qui entra sur le tard dans le tiers ordre de Saint-François, et composa une multitude d'œuvres,[52] dont nous n'allons citer que les plus importants comme le *Llibre de Contemplació en Déu* (1271/73), le *Llibre del*

---

pp. 129 sqq.; J. Hernando i Delgado, 'Ramón Martí (s. XIII), *De Seta Machometi o de origine, progressu et fine Machometi et quadruplici reprobatione prophetiae eius.* Introducción, transcripción y notas', *Acta Historica et Archaeologica Medievalia*, 3–4 (1982–83), 9–63; Le même, 'Le "De Seta Machometi" du Cod. 46 d'Osma, œuvre de Raymond Martin (Ramón Martí)', dans *Cahiers de Fanjeaux, 18: Islam et Chrétiens du Midi (XII*ᵉ*-XIV*ᵉ *s.)*, pp. 351–71; A. Cortabarría Beitía, 'La connaissance des textes arabes chez Raymond Martin, O.P., et sa position en face de l'Islam', ibid., pp. 279–300; A. Robles Sierra, *Fray Ramón Martí de Subirats, O.P., y el diálogo misional en el siglo XIII* (Caleruega/Burgos, 1986); E. Colomer, 'La controversia islamo-judeo-cristiana en la obra apologética de Ramon Martí', dans *Diálogo filosófico-religioso entre Cristianismo, Judaísmo e Islamismo*, ed. Santiago-Otero, pp. 229–57.

[50] M. Grabmann, 'Die Schrift: De rationibus fidei contra Saracenos Graecos et Armenos ad Cantorem Antiochenum des heiligen Thomas von Aquin', *Scholastik*, 17 (1942), 187–216.

[51] Cf. D. Bigalli, 'Giudizio escatologico e tecnica di missione nei pensatori francescani: Ruggero Bacone', dans *Espansione del Francescanesimo tra Occidente e Oriente nel secolo XIII.* Atti del VI Convegno Internazionale, Assisi, 12–14 ottobre 1978 (Assisi, 1979), pp. 151–86.

[52] De la littérature surabondante sur Raymond Lulle ne citons qu'à titre d'exemple: E. W. Platzeck, *Raimund Lull. Sein Leben – seine Werke. Die Grundlagen seines Denkens (Prinzipienlehre)*, 2 vols (Rome, 1962–64); A. Llinares, *Raymond Lulle, philosophe de l'action* (Paris, 1963); *Vida de Ramon Lulle: Les fonts escrites i la iconografia coetànies*, ed. M. Batllori et J. N. Hillgarth (Barcelona, 1982); A. Bonner et L. Badia, *Ramon Llull: Vida, pensament i obra literària* (Barcelona, 1988); sur sa conception de la mission voir notamment B. Altaner, 'Glaubenszwang und Glaubensfreiheit in der Missionstheorie des Raymundus Lullus. Ein Beitrag zur Geschichte des Toleranzgedankens', *Historisches Jahrbuch*, 48 (1928), 586–610, pp. 596 sqq., 602 sqq.; M. Batllori, 'Teoria ed azione missionaria in Raimondo Lullo', dans *Espansione del Francescanesimo*, pp. 187–211; Cohen, *The Friars and the Jews*, pp. 199 sqq.; R. Sugranyes de Franch, 'L'apologétique de Raimond Lulle vis-à-vis de l'Islam', dans *Cahiers de Fanjeaux, 18: Islam et Chrétiens du Midi (XII*ᵉ*-XIV*ᵉ *s.)*, pp. 373–93; Kedar, *Crusade and Mission*, pp. 189 sqq.; V. Servera, 'Utopie et histoire. Les postulats théoriques de la praxis missionnaire', dans *Cahiers de Fanjeaux, 22: Raymond Lulle et le Pays d'Oc* (Fanjeaux, Toulouse, 1987), pp. 191–229; ainsi que récemment P. D. Beatie, '*Pro exaltatione sanctae fidei catholicae*: Mission and Crusade in the Writings of Ramon Lull', dans *Iberia and the Mediterranean World of the Middle Ages: Studies in Honor of Robert I. Burns*, ed. L. Simon (Leiden, 1995), I, 113–32; et M. D. Johnston, 'Ramon Llull and the Compulsory Evangelization of Jews and Muslims', dans ibid., tout comme d'une manière générale, Le même, *The Evangelical Rhetoric of Ramon Llull. Lay Learning and Piety in the Christian West Around 1300* (Oxford, 1996).

gentil e los tres savis (avant 1277), la *Disputatio fidelis et infidelis* (1288/89), le *Liber predicationis contra Judeos*, qui visait aussi les musulmans, le *Liber de fine* (1305) et la *Disputatio Raymundi Christiani et Hamar Sarraceni* (1308).[53] On peut en effet constater chez Lulle, que ses premiers écrits, influencés peut-être comme la *Ars iuris* (composée entre 1275 et 1281 à Montpellier) par la pensée d'Innocent IV,[54] sont imprégnés d'une volonté de compréhension et de respect vis-à-vis des infidèles, qui—après maintes enseignements et sermons—ne devraient recevoir le baptême que de leur libre choix, tandis sur le tard, ses écrits composés après 1294/96, recommandent de nouveau l'emploi de mesures de force pour obtenir des conversions.[55] Vers 1299 enfin il demanda au roi Jacques II d'Aragon dans son *Dictat de Ramon* d'obliger les juifs et les musulmans à assister à des disputations officielles et requérit du roi de faire enfin la conquête de Jérusalem. Vers 1311 il exigea dans sa *Petitio in concilio generali ad acquirendam Terram sanctam* adressée au concile de Vienne, que des sermons fussent régulièrement prononcés les vendredis et samedis dans les synagogues et mosquées pour engager les infidèles à se convertir.[56] Son intention était avant tout d'ébaucher une théologie métaphysique basée sur les résultats d'une nouvelle philosophie, pour pouvoir faire face à une confrontation avec les dignitaires religieux de l'Islam, très experts en philosophie grecque et arabe. Pour être préparé à soutenir avec succès les disputations tant souhaités, il fallait disposer d'arguments propres à repousser toute attaque aux vérités essentielles de la doctrine chrétienne. Et malgré quelques déformations polémiques les œuvres de Lulle, réprouvées par les scolastiques de Paris en raison de leur disposition à proposer des solutions rationnelles à des problèmes religieux, s'avéraient utiles à la diffusion de ces arguments.[57] Pour arriver à une propagation pacifique de la foi, il ne fallait pas non plus négliger des aspects plus pratiques comme

---

[53] Johnston, *The Evangelical Rhetoric*, pp. 167 sqq.

[54] Ainsi le postule Kedar, *Crusade and Mission*, pp. 191 sqq.

[55] Altaner, 'Glaubenszwang und Glaubensfreiheit', pp. 605 sqq.; Kedar, *Crusade and Mission*, pp. 195 sq.; Johnston, 'Ramon Llull and the Compulsory Evangelization of Jews and Muslims', passim.

[56] Altaner, 'Glaubenszwang und Glaubensfreiheit', pp. 603 sqq.; E. Müller, *Das Konzil von Vienne 1311–1312. Seine Quellen und seine Geschichte* (Münster i.W., 1934), pp. 610 sq., 693–97; Kedar, *Crusade and Mission*, p. 196. Cf. *Raimundi Lulli opera Latina*, ed. H. Harada, Corpus Christianorum Continuato Mediaevalis, 34 (Turnholti, 1980), VIII, 239–45; J. Perarnau i Espelt, 'Un text català de Ramon Llull desconegut: La *Petició de Ramon al Papa Celestí V per a la conversió dels infidels*. Edició i estudi', *Arxiu de textos Catalans antics*, 1 (1982), 9–46.

[57] C. Lohr, 'Ramon Lull and Thirteenth-Century Religious Dialogue', dans *Diálogo filosófico-religioso entre Cristianismo, Judaísmo e Islamismo*, ed. Santiago-Otero, pp. 117–29. Sur l'influence des écrits et des idées de Lulle voir surtout J. N. Hillgarth, *Ramon Lull and Lullism in Fourteenth-Century France* (Oxford, 1971); Le même, 'Vida i importància de Ramon Llull en el context del segle XIII', *Anuario de Estudios Medievales*, 26 (1996), 967–78; J. Rubió i Balaguer, *Ramon Llull i el Lul·lisme* (Montserrat, 1985).

l'établissement d'écoles pour l'étude de langues—tels que l'arabe, le grecque et l'hébreu—et l'acquisition de connaissances approfondies des conditions culturelles et spirituelles de la vie des autres, un savoir autant utile que la faculté de raisonner, à priori dispensée dans les universités. L'étude des fondements encore peu connus de l'Islam (une ignorance qui avait toujours constituée un obstacle majeur à la réussite d'efforts missionnaires),[58] et la traduction du Coran (entreprise pour la première fois vers le milieu du XIIe siècle sur l'instigation de Pierre le Vénérable, le célèbre abbé de Cluny, par un groupe de traducteurs) acquérirent maintenant une signification pratique pour toute activité missionnaire.[59] Ce fut surtout dans la Péninsule Ibérique et dans l'Ile de Majorque qu'on retrouva au XIIIe siècle les écoles de langue, de traduction et de disputations, qui avaient d'abord apparu en Palestine et Syrie[60] et délivraient souvent à la fin des études une *licentia disputandi* au lieu de l'habituelle *licentia docendi*.[61] Puisqu'ici le problème des barrières linguistiques—comme Burns l'a si bien démontré pour Valence—se posa quotidiennement aux autorités, obligées d'expédier les affaires administratives courantes d'une population fortement arabisée,[62] c'est sous l'égide des dominicains, surtout d'un Raymond de Penyafort, que de telles écoles furent d'abord fondées à Murcie et à Tunis, et plus tard à Barcelone, Valence et Jativa, avant que le plus célèbre d'entre eux, le collège d'étude à Miramar en Majorque ne fut réalisé par Raymond Lulle dans le cadre de son programme d'évangélisation.[63] Bien que le collège

---

[58] Cf. U. Monneret de Villard, *Lo studio dell'Islam in Europa nel XII e nel XIII secolo* (Città del Vaticano, 1944).

[59] Sur la traduction du Coran et le rôle joué par Pierre le Vénérable voir M.-T. d'Alverny, 'Deux Traductions latines du Coran au Moyen Age', *Archives d'histoire doctrinale et littéraire du Moyen Age*, 22–23 (1947–48), 69–131; C. J. Bishko, 'Peter the Venerable's Journey to Spain', dans *Petrus Venerabilis 1156–1956*, ed. G. Constable et J. Kritzeck (Roma, 1956), pp. 163–75; J. Kritzeck, *Peter the Venerable and Islam* (Princeton, 1964), pp. 10–36.

[60] Cf. B. Altaner, 'Sprachstudien und Sprachkenntnisse im Dienste der Mission des 13. und 14. Jahrhunderts', *Zeitschrift für Missionswissenschaft und Religionswissenschaft*, 21 (1931), 113–36.

[61] Cohen, *The Friars and the Jews*, p. 107.

[62] R. I. Burns, 'La muralla de la llengua: el problema del bilingüisme i de la interacció entre musulmans i cristians', dans *Jaume I i els Valencians del segle XIII* (València, 1981), pp. 303–30. Cf. à ce sujet A. Ferrando Francés, 'Les interrelacions lingüístiques en la València doscentista. Comentaris a les aportacions de Robert I. Burns', *Revista d'història medieval*, 1 (1990), 233–47.

[63] Altaner, *Die Dominikanermissionen*, pp. 93 sqq.; Le même, 'Sprachstudien und Sprachkenntnisse'; Le même, 'Die fremdsprachliche Ausbildung der Dominikanermissionare während des 13. und 14. Jahrhunderts', *Zeitschrift für Missionswissenschaft und Religionswissenschaft*, 23 (1933), 233–41; Le même, 'Zur Kenntnis des Arabischen im 13. und 14. Jahrhundert', *Orientalia Christiana Periodica*, 2 (1936), 437–452; J. M. Coll, 'Escuelas de lenguas orientales en los siglos XIII–XIV', *Analecta Sacra Tarraconensis*, 17 (1944), 115–38; 18 (1945), 59–87; 19 (1946), 217–40; B. Bischoff, 'The Study of Foreign Languages in the

de Miramar, protégé par le roi Jacques II de Majorque, fût érigé dans les environs du couvent des frères mineurs, il ne fut jamais totalement intégré dans l'ordre et s'en distingua toujours par une conception du travail missionnaire légèrement différente. La raison en était, comme l'on admet généralement, que son fondateur appréciait beaucoup la spiritualité dominicaine et qu'il se laissa en plus inspirer par les décisions correspondantes du chapitre provincial de Tolède en 1250.[64] Avec Raymond Lulle, dont la pensée fut influencée en la matière par Jacques de Vitry, Roger Bacon et Guillaume de Tripolis—ce dernier s'appliquant d'ailleurs autant que Raymond Martin à trouver une approche personnelle à la pensée islamique—la conception d'une christianisation pacifique des musulmans par le moyen de la *via disputationis* et le rejet de tout projet de croisade comme moyen approprié, atteignit à son apogée.[65] Mais pas pour longtemps. Le philosophe majorquin fit volte-face. Sous l'impression de la chute de Saint-Jean-d'Acre en 1291 ou plus vraisemblablement sous l'effet des attaques fanatiques des Mérinides dans la lutte pour la possession du détroit de Gibraltar,[66] il opta de nouveau pour la croisade et l'assistance obligatoire des infidèles aux prêches comme instrument adéquat d'une propagation de la foi. Il s'apprêta donc à la faire accompagner par ses prédicateurs instruits en théologie et savants en langue, pour prêcher la parole de Dieu aux musulmans prisonniers et vaincus—donnant ainsi la préférence à une sorte

---

Middle Ages', *Speculum*, 36 (1961), 209–24; P. Ribes Montané, 'San Ramón de Penyafort y los estudios eclesiásticos', *Analecta Sacra Tarraconensis*, 48 (1975), 85–142; A. Cortabarría Beitía, 'El estudio de las lenguas en la Orden dominicana', *Estudios filosóficos*, 19 (1970), 77–127, 359–92 (version française dans *Mélanges de l'Institut Dominicain d'Études Orientales*, 10 (1970), 189–248); Le même, 'San Ramon de Penyafort y los estudios dominicanos de lenguas', *Escritos del Vedat*, 7 (1977), 138 sqq.; S. Garcías Palou, *El Miramar de Ramon Llull* (Palma de Mallorca, 1977); D. Urvoy, 'Les Musulmans et l'usage de la langue arabe par les missionnaires', *Traditio*, 34 (1978), 416–27; Kedar, *Crusade and Mission*, notamment pp. 189 sqq.

[64] Cf. Daniel, *The Franciscan Concept of Mission*, pp. 73 sq.; Webster, *Els Menorets*, pp. 36 sqq.; La même, 'Conversion and Co-Existence: The Franciscan Mission in the Crown of Aragon', dans *Iberia and the Mediterranean World*, II, 163–76; J. Tusquets, 'Relación de Ramon Lull con Ramon de Peñafort y con la Orden dominicana', *Escritos del Vedat*, 7 (1977), 177–95; L. Robles Sierra, 'El 'Studium arabicum' del Capítulo dominicano de Toledo. Antecedentes del 'Miramar' de Ramon Lull', *Estudios Lulianos*, 24 (1980), 23–47.

[65] Cf. D. Urvoy, *Penser l'Islam: Les présupposés islamiques de l'Art de Lull* (Paris, 1980); S. Gracías Palou, *Ramon Llull y el islám* (Palma de Mallorca, 1981); A. Cortabarría Beitía, 'Connaissance de l'Islam chez Raymond Lulle et Raymond Martin O.P. Parallèle', dans *Cahiers de Fanjeaux, 22: Raymond Lulle et le Pays d'Oc*, pp. 33–55.

[66] Voir à ce propos A. Khaneboubi, *Les premiers sultans mérinides 1269–1331. Histoire politique et sociale* (Paris, 1987); M. A. Manzano Rodríguez, *La intervención de los Benimerines en la Península Ibérica* (Madrid, 1992); M. D. López Pérez, *La Corona de Aragón y el Magreb en el siglo XIV (1331–1410)* (Barcelona, 1995).

d'amalgame de croisade et d'évangélisation pacifique.[67] Cela ne l'empêcha d'ailleurs pas, de tenter vers la fin de sa vie de propager lui-même la foi en Afrique du Nord. Après avoir entrepris déjà en 1293, c'est-à-dire immédiatement après la catastrophe de Saint-Jean d'Acre, un premier voyage à Tunis pour réaliser ce projet, c'est uniquement par son expulsion forcée de la ville qu'il fut empêché de cueillir les fruits de ses entretiens paisibles et de caractère philosophiques—à savoir le baptême de ses premiers disciples musulmans.[68] En 1307 il entreprit un deuxième voyage, qui l'emmena cette fois à Bougie.[69] C'est alors qu'il essuya un échec total, en faisant preuve de présomption dans ses tentatives de convaincre ses auditeurs. Il fut battu, torturé, lapidé et jeté dans un cachot infect près des latrines (*reclusus est apud latrinam carceris latronum*). Ce ne fut que grâce à l'intervention de commerçants catalans et genevois, qu'il fut enfin libéré.[70] Il semble, qu'il ait alors décidé à subir le martyre, puisque sa manière d'agir ne permet guère d'autre explication plausible. Il se présenta au publique dans la grande place de Bougie et tenta de susciter une controverse avec les musulmans présents, en s'écriant à haute voix: '*Lex christianorum est vera, sancta et Deo accepta, lex autem Sarracenorum falsa et erronea; et hoc sum paratus probare*'.[71] Ce n'est qu'en 1314/15 qu'il retourna à Tunis, préférant apparemment cette fois d'avoir des rapports amicaux avec le maître de Tunis et son entourage cultivé et de ne pas rechercher la confrontation à tout prix. Il leur dédia les écrits composés dans ces lieux et échangea avec eux des arguments, qui portaient l'empreinte de son longue expérience.[72] Son prétendu martyre à la suite de son séjours à Tunis est à reléguer dans le domaine de la légende.[73] Son

---

[67] Kedar, *Crusade and Mission*, pp. 195 sq. Sur l'idée de croisade chez Lulle voir en plus de Kedar, *Crusade and Mission*, pp. 189 sqq.; A. Gottron, *Ramon Lulls Kreuzzugsideen* (Berlin, Leipzig, 1912); Altaner, 'Glaubenszwang und Glaubensfreiheit', pp. 586–610; R. Sugranyes de Franch, 'Un texte de Ramón Lull sur la croisade et les missions', *Nova et vetera,* 21 (1946), 98–112; Le même, *Ramón Lull, docteur des missions* (Schöneck, Beckenried, 1952); Le même, 'Els projectes de creuada en la doctrina missional de Ramon Llull', *Estudios Lulianos,* 4 (1960), 275–290 (version française dans *Nova et vetera,* 37 (1962), 92–107).

[68] *Vita beati Raymundi Lulli,* ed. B. de Gaiffier, *Analecta Bollandiana,* 48 (1930), 130–78, ici 161–63. Cf. Llinares, *Raymond Lulle,* pp. 106 sq.

[69] Cf. Platzeck, *Raimund Lull,* pp. 32, 39 sqq.; Llinares, *Raymond Lulle,* pp. 116 sqq.; C.-E. Dufourcq, 'La Méditerranée et le Christianisme: Cadre géopolitique et économique de l'apostolat missionaire de Raymond Lulle', *Estudios Lulianos,* 24 (1980), 5–22.

[70] *Vita beati Raymundi Lulli,* ed. Gaiffier, p. 170. Cf. Llinares, *Raymond Lulle,* pp. 116 sq., et plus spécialement Le même, 'Le dramatique épisode algérien de la vie de Raymond Lulle', *Revue de la Méditerranée,* 19 (1959), 385–397 (également dans: *Estudios Lulianos,* 4 (1960), 63–72); Le même, 'Raymond Lulle et l'Afrique', *Revue Africaine,* 105 (1961), 98–116.

[71] *Vita beati Raymundi Lulli,* ed. Gaiffier, p. 168 sq.

[72] Hillgarth, *Ramon Lull,* pp. 26 sqq.; Llinares, *Raymond Lulle,* pp. 123 sqq.; H. Daiber, 'Der Missionar Ramon Lull und seine Kritik am Islam', *Estudios Lulianos,* 25 (1981), 47–57.

[73] Hillgarth, *Ramon Lull,* p. 133 sqq.

attitude indécise se reflète aussi dans ses écrits théoriques. Peu avant, en mai 1314, il avait rappelé dans son traité 'De civitate mundi', composé à Messine, qu'il était du devoir de l'empereur de prendre l'épée pour la défense de l'Église romaine contre les infidèles et les schismatiques, contre les chrétiens injustes et les mécréants occupant la Terre Sainte,[74] et cela après s'être prononcé encore en 1312 dans son traité *De participatione Christianorum et Sarracenorum* nettement en faveur de disputations entre chrétiens et musulmans, *et forte per talem modum posset esse pax inter christianos et sarracenos habendo talem modum per universum mundum non quod christiani vadant ad destruendum sarracenos nec sarraceni christianos.*[75]

La situation spécifique de la frontière, où l'on se tenait toujours sur sa garde, avait d'abord paralysée toute volonté de compréhension mutuelle dans le domaine religieux, et avait ensuite—après le succès total de la reconquête—empêchée les souverains chrétiens à promouvoir de vraies tentatives d'évangélisation. C'est seulement grâce au changement culturel, qui se préparait dès le milieu du XIIᵉ siècle avec la réception des œuvres de la philosophie aristotélicienne et arabe jusqu'alors pratiquement inconnues et avec une nouvelle conception du droit naturel, qu'on arriva à un tournant décisif. De par cette nouvelle perception de l'homme, on cessa de considérer celui qui professait une autre foi comme un ennemi. On lui accorda le droit à sa propre sphère juridique et commença à voir en lui le prochain, dont le salut personnel devient matière à préoccupation. La version modérée du droit missionnaire permit, contrairement à l'attitude rigide observée jusqu'alors, non seulement une prise de position plus souple sur le plan politique et contractuel, mais facilita encore l'établissement de rapports commerciaux de plus en plus importants avec les musulmans nord-africains.[76] Quand les frontières communes avec l'Islam disparaissaient au fur et à mesure dans la Péninsule Ibérique, l'idée d'une évangélisation gagnait de plus en plus d'importance. Et ce furent les ordres mendiants nouvellement fondés et essaimant rapidement, qui se firent le porte-parole de ce mouvement, désireux d'obtenir la conversion des hétérodoxes par la conviction et la persuasion plutôt que par le moyen de la croisades, qui à leurs yeux n'était qu'un

---

[74] *Raimundi Lulli Opera Latina,* ed. J. Stöhr (Palma de Mallorca, 1960), II, 197. Cf. Kedar, *Crusade and Mission*, pp. 198–99.

[75] H. Wieruszowski, 'Ramon Lull et l'idée de la Cité de Dieu', *Estudis Franciscans,* 47 (1935), p. 110. Cf. Kedar, *Crusade and Mission*, p. 198; W. A. Euler, *'Unitas et pax'. Religionsvergleich bei Raimundus Lullus und Nikolaus von Kues* (Würzburg, 1990); Le même, 'Die Apologetik der christlichen Glaubenslehren bei Ramón Lull und Ramón Sibiuda', dans *Constantes y fragmentos del pensamiento luliano* (Tübingen, 1996), pp. 147–60; Le même, 'Religionsvergleich bei Ramón Lull und Nikolaus von Kues', dans *Anstöße zu einem Dialog der Religionen: Thomas von Aquin—Ramon Lull—Nikolaus von Kues* (Freiburg i. Br., 1997), pp. 71–91.

[76] Cf. à ce sujet notamment les études précitées de Dufourcq (voir note 17) et déjà d'une manière plus générale R.-H. Bautier, 'Les grands problèmes politiques et économiques de la Méditerranée médiévale', *Revue historique,* 234 (1965), 1–28.

instrument entre autres au service de la propagation de la foi. La réception et l'application de nouveaux principes se développa le plus rapidement à l'intérieur de ces ordres, qui étaient disponibles et prêts à prêcher la parole de Dieu. Ils étaient les mieux disposés à promouvoir une propagation rapide de la foi et se confinaient dans un champ d'action où la concurrence des anciens ordres et des évêques établis n'était pas à craindre. Après des débuts brillants, soutenu essentiellement par l'établissement d'écoles de langue comme preuve institutionnalisée de l'importance qu'on accordait à toute étude de l'autre et de sa façon de penser, l'élan de ce mouvement fut finalement brisé. La chute de Saint-Jean-d'Acre et la stagnation de la reconquête après l'intervention des Mérinides nord-africains dans la Péninsule Ibérique constitua un revers sérieux et provoqua le déclin définitif de nouvelles conceptions de la croisade et de la propagation de la foi.[77] Au cours du XIVᵉ siècle la mission dans les pays riverains de la Méditerranée s'éloigna de plus en plus de ses champs d'action traditionnels en Afrique du Nord et dans la Terre Sainte, et s'aventura sans grands succès dans les régions limitrophes de la chrétienté en Asie centrale et en l'Extrême-Orient.[78] La politique prit en même temps le pas sur la croisade, qui devint—après l'élaboration nécessaire des bases théoriques par Pierre Dubois ou Philippe de Mézières—un instrument de conquête militaire et de colonisation politique forcée et en conséquence un obstacle à toute propagation de foi promise au succès.[79] Même l'acquisition de connaissances linguistiques, qui s'était avérée un succès, fut de nouveau remise en question. Bien que le concile de Vienne, qui renforça encore la législation ecclésiastique contre les musulmans et leur religion,[80] rendît

---

[77] Sur une certaine décadence de l'idée de la croisade au bas Moyen-Âge voir en plus de Kedar, *Crusade and Mission*, pp. 199 sqq., surtout N. J. Housley, *The Later Crusades. From Lyons to Alcazar, 1274–1580* (Oxford, 1992; repr. London, 1995).

[78] Cf. J. Richard, *Orient et Occident au Moyen Âge: contacts et relations (XIIᵉ–XVᵉ siècle)* (London, 1976); Le même, *La papauté et les missions d'Orient au Moyen Âge (XIIIᵉ–XVᵉ siècles)* (Rome, 1977); Le même, *Les relations entre l'Orient et l'Occident au Moyen Âge. Études et documents* (London, 1978); F. Schmieder, *Europa und die Fremden. Die Mongolen im Urteil des Abendlandes vom 13. bis 15. Jahrhundert* (Sigmaringen, 1994). Sur les conceptions de Pierre Dubois et de Philippe de Mézières voir H. Kämpf, *Pierre Dubois und die geistigen Grundlagen des französischen Nationalbewußtseins um 1300* (Leipzig, Berlin, 1935); O. G. Oexle, 'Utopisches Denken im Mittelalter: Pierre Dubois', *Historische Zeitschrift*, 224 (1977), 293–339; N. Jorga, *Philippe de Mézières 1327–1405 et la croisade au XIVᵉ siècle* (Paris, 1896; repr. London, 1973); J. Williamson, 'Philippe de Mézières and the Idea of Crusade', dans *The Military Orders. Fighting for the Faith and Caring for the Sick*, ed. M. Barber (London, 1994), pp. 358–64; K. Petkov, 'The Rotten Apple and the Good Apples: Orthodox, Catholics, and Turks in Philippe de Mézières' Crusading Propaganda', *Journal of Medieval History*, 23 (1997), 255–70.

[79] P. Rousset, 'La croisade obstacle à la mission', *Nova et vetera*, 57 (1982), 137–42; M.-M. Dufeil, 'Vision d'Islam depuis l'Europe au début du XIVᵉ siècle', dans *Cahiers de Fanjeaux, 18: Islam et Chrétiens du Midi (XIIᵉ–XIVᵉ s.)*, pp. 235–58.

[80] *Conciliorum oecumenicorum decreta*, p. 380, § 25.

obligatoire l'établissement de deux chaires pour l'étude de langues orientales dans cinq universités occidentaux—non seulement à la curie romaine mais aussi à Paris, Oxford, Bologne et Salamanque—cette ordonnance demeura apparemment lettre morte pendant toute la période de la papauté d'Avignon.[81]

---

[81] *Conciliorum oecumenicorum decreta,* pp. 379–80, § 24. Cf. Müller, *Das Konzil von Vienne,* pp. 155 sq., 637–42; B. Altaner, 'Raymundus Lullus und der Sprachenkanon (can. 11) des Konzils von Vienne (1312)', *Historisches Jahrbuch,* 53 (1933), 190–219; R. Weiss, 'England and the Decree of the Council of Vienne on the Teaching of Greek, Arabic, Hebrew, and Syriac', dans Du même, *Medieval and Humanist Greek. Collected Essays* (Padova, 1977), pp. 68–79; E. Bellone, 'Cultura e studi nei progetti di reforma presentati al concilio di Vienne (1311–1312)', *Annuarium Historiae Conciliorum,* 9 (1977), 67–111.

Competing Faiths in Asia:
Muslims, Christians,
Zoroastrians, and Mongols

The Conversion Stories of Shaykh Abū Isḥāq Kāzarūnī (963–1033)

NEGUIN YAVARI

T he academic study of conversion has come full circle from the early twentieth century, when normative paradigms of spiritual conversion were outlined by William James and Arthur Darby Nock. Influenced by James's psychology of religion approach,[1] conversion was defined as an individual action of the will, the turning of a soul. Nock saw it as 'the reorientation of the soul of an individual, his deliberate turning from indifference or from an earlier form of piety to another, a turning which implies a consciousness that a great change is involved, that the old was wrong and the new is right'.[2] His concern was with conversion from paganism to Christianity, away from primitive religion, toward a higher truth. His model was that of St Paul, who chose Christianity because of spiritual conviction and moral decision. More importantly, the conversion happened in one decisive and self-conscious moment. Paul experienced a change of heart, a turning of the soul, and that altered the course of his life.

---

[1] James asserts, 'To be converted, to be regenerated, to receive grace, to gain an assurance, are so many phrases which denote the process, gradual or sudden, by which a self hitherto divided, and consciously wrong, inferior and unhappy, becomes unified and consciously right, superior and happy, in consequence of its firmer hold upon religious realities. This at least is what conversion signifies in general terms, whether or not we believe that a direct divine operation is needed to bring such a moral change about'. William James, *The Varieties of Religious Experience* (1902; repr. New York, 1997), p. 160.

[2] A. D. Nock, *Conversion* (Oxford, 1933), p. 7.

The relative (to Christianity) speed with which the message of Muhammad and the sword of Islam altered the religio-political order of the Near East and North Africa convinced modern scholars that conversion, of the individual, spiritual type, could not have happened in this context. Muhammad's first revelation is dated to about 610; he left his hometown to establish the first Muslim community in 622, and he died in 632, never naming a successor. More king than prophet, he was more interested in the spreading of the empire than of faith. Pillage and conquest, under the tutelage of Muhammad himself, substituted suffering for faith and martyrdom. Blood and booty thirsty, the Muslim armies established a vast empire in less than twenty years. Spirituality was apparently in short supply. Hence Alfred C. Underwood's celebrated characterization, '[h]ow superficial the conversion of the Arab tribes was is seen by the widespread apostasy that followed the prophet's death: while the subsequent conversion of millions of non-Arabs was the work not of the apostles, but of generals'.[3]

Most scholars of medieval conversions, including James Muldoon and Karl F. Morrison, have found Nock's model of 'peripety conversions' inadequate for explaining corporate conversions of the medieval period.[4] The problem, more than a definitional disagreement, lies also in that medievalists often find themselves with precious little in medieval chronicles and histories to illuminate the causes and conditions of conversions of entire peoples. Moreover, there are few individual accounts of a change of faith. The works of these scholars demonstrate that if narrative histories are to be read with empathy for medieval religiosity, then conversions are rarely represented by lightning events. Rather than a process of change, or an abrupt abandoning of one belief system, the conversion narrative represents, more accurately, a catalyst for change, or a metaphoric harbinger of the actual act of conversion. In other words, stunning spiritual conversions of the Pauline type,[5] or confessional autobiographical accounts such as St Augustine's,[6] or baptisms for that matter, do not encapsulate completed conversions. St Paul saw a vision but his conversion was only completed after it was explained to him. 'New research demonstrates that St Augustine was not only raised in a Christian milieu, but that he was probably born one himself. [. . .] His *Confessions* narrates changes of heart and mind of a sensitive and intellectually gifted young adult, but they do not directly explain Augustine's conversion to Christianity. So in effect his conversion in the garden at Milan can actually be seen as a reconversion, or as a series of connected

---

[3] Alfred C. Underwood, *Conversion: Christian and Non-Christian* (London, 1925), p. 15.

[4] On the inadequacy of these paradigms for the study of historical conversions, see Karl F. Morrison, *Understanding Conversion* (Charlottesville, 1992); *Varieties of Religious Conversion in the Middle Ages,* ed. by James Muldoon (Gainesville, 1997); Carole M. Cusack, 'Towards a General Theory of Conversion', in *Religious Change, Conversion and Culture,* ed. by Lynette Olson (Sydney, 1996), pp. 1–21.

[5] Morrison, *Understanding Conversion*, pp. xiii–39.

[6] James Muldoon, 'Introduction: The Conversion of Europe,' in *Varieties of Religious Conversion in the Middle Ages*, pp. 1–12.

events within his narrative'.[7] Far from describing a 'crisis', Augustine wrote the book as an apology, defending himself against enemies who denied the orthodoxy of his teaching and the legitimacy of his title as bishop.[8] Rather than a normative definition of an identifiable event, against which all conversions are measured, the new research focuses on the hermeneutics of conversion in the medieval period, which is protean and manifold. The task at hand is to uncover the truth of medieval conversions as opposed to unearthing instances of true conversions.

There is no thematic monograph on conversion in the corpus of medieval Islamic historiography. Modern scholars of Islam have combed through world or local histories and dynastic accounts to arrive at the 'historical truth' of the process of conversion in the conquered lands. They seem to agree that conversion to Islam was rarely forced, that the process was slow and varied, and that although the sources chronicle the execution of Zoroastrian priests and the destruction of fire-temples—in other words, of outward manifestations of the creed—social and economic considerations were more important than coercion in inducing significant numbers of conversions. Elton Daniel has further argued that it is clear from the sources that members of the Persian aristocracy— *dihqāns, marzubāns,* and the like—accepted Islam in order to preserve their social status and to avoid the stigma of paying certain taxes from which they had traditionally been exempted as a privileged class.[9] Jamsheed Choksy, too, agrees with Daniel that commoners converted simply to avoid taxation by the conquerors.[10] Touraj Daryaee has modified Choksy to claim that lower class Zoroastrians converted to Islam also to escape the burden of Zoroastrian ritual, priestly abuse, and a class-based society.[11] The social liberation theory is thwarted by evidence from the Bengal. In studying rural conversion to Islam in that region, Richard Eaton has observed that there is abundant evidence that Indian communities failed, upon Islamization, to improve their status in the social hierarchy. On the contrary, most simply carried into Muslim society the same birth-ascribed rank that they had formerly known in Hindu society. Paradoxically, and against the grain of conventional wisdom, Eaton found that large numbers of rural Muslims were not observed until as late as the end of the sixteenth century or afterward, whereas contact with Arab and Central Asian Muslims began in the late tenth century. Moreover, mass Islamization occurred under a regime, the Mughals (r. 1526–1858), that

---

[7] Frederick H. Russell, 'Augustine: Conversion by the Book', in *Varieties of Religious Conversion in the Middle Ages,* p. 14; see also, Nock, *Conversion,* pp. 259–63.

[8] Russell, 'Augustine: Conversion by the Book', pp. 14–15.

[9] Elton Daniel, 'Conversion II. Of Iranians to Islam', *Encyclopaedia Iranica* (1993), IV, 229–32.

[10] Jamsheed K. Choksy, 'Zoroastrians in Muslim Iran: Selected Problems of Coexistence and Interaction during the Early Medieval Period', *Iranian Studies,* 20 (1987), 17–30.

[11] Touraj Daryaee, 'Review of Jamsheed K. Choksy, *Conflict and Cooperation: Zoroastrian Subalterns and Muslim Elites'*, *International Journal of Middle East Studies,* 32 (2000), 158–60.

as a matter of policy showed no interest in proselytizing on behalf of the Islamic faith.[12]
What is important is that the study of conversion in the Islamic milieu, in its myriad
revelations, has focussed on the effects rather than the event, or more accurately, on
recovering the historical process of conversion.[13] What conversion meant for medieval
Muslims remains unexplained.

That modern Islamic scholarship is at a loss for chronicling definitions and
instances of conversion in the medieval sources is especially significant when we
remember that the Koran itself, rather than a biography of a chosen prophet or a history
of Arabs or Muslims, is primarily a call for conversion from idolatry and polytheism to
a previously pure monotheism. Not a history of a community of faith, or an elaborate
account of the faith and example of Muhammad, the Koran is a call for the abandoning
of polytheism and pseudo-monotheism for unmediated belief in the singular God of all
creation. The call for conversion is to be understood in a renewal of monotheism, rather
than its founding. The narrative is primarily addressed to believers, and non-believers
are subsumed under numerous appellations, including duplicitous hypocrites, idolaters,
and outright heretics. Against such a scriptural backdrop, is it not curious that true
belief, spiritual conversion, is allegedly not valorized in subsequent religious writings
of the medieval Islamic world?

In chronicling possible explanations for the paucity of conversion stories in the
medieval Islamic sources, Richard Bulliet has argued that in the earlier period, a convert
became a Muslim without understanding the language of the faith, and basically by
adopting customs, norms, and attire from the Arab community. Thus he separated
himself from his old religious community, espousing the values of the Islamic
community he had come into contact with. Conversion then, followed essentially a
bandwagon effect, the more Muslim communities in the midst of the conquered
territories, the more the number of converts. For Bulliet, then, a convert only learned
about Islam after his transformation, and 'this is why the personal conversion stories
that have been preserved say so little about preaching, studying, or intellectual or moral
transformation'.[14] Furthermore, and as evidenced in the conversion stories he has
chosen to study from al-Balādhurī's (d. c. 892) history of the Arab conquests, 'the initial
decision to join the religious community of the rulers had more to do with attainment

---

[12] Richard M. Eaton, *The Rise of Islam and the Bengal Frontier, 1204–1760* (Berkeley,
1993), pp. 113–37.

[13] Michael Morony has recently reviewed the various arguments on the nature and extent of
conversion to Islam; see his 'The Age of Conversions: A Reassessment', in *Conversion and
Continuity: Indigenous Christian communities in Islamic Lands, Eight to Eighteenth Centuries*,
ed. by Michael Gervers and Ramzi Jibran Bikhazi, Papers in Mediaeval Studies, 9 (Toronto,
1990), pp. 135–50.

[14] Richard Bulliet, 'Conversion Stories in Early Islam', in *Conversion and Continuity*, pp.
131.

or maintenance of status than it did with religious belief'.[15] Here, Bulliet is corroborated by a statement in a Zoroastrian religious text, *The Greater Bundahishn*, compiled in the ninth and tenth centuries, 'which emphasises that many noble families abandoned the faith in order to maintain their privileged life style'.[16] Bulliet goes on to argue that sometime in the tenth century, subsequent to the conversion of the majority of the conquered population, overt social markers such as language and dress lost their religious significance, and conversion became a matter of belief.

But how exactly did this happen, and what did medieval Muslims understand as a true conversion? To investigate this question, I have chosen to look at two typical examples of lightning, and hence superficial, conversion stories in medieval Islamic histories frequently cited in modern studies of conversion. Before we proceed, it should be noted that in these narrative sources, conversions to Islam, like other significant recantations, are typically presented in a particularly terse and matter-of-fact manner. Conversion scenes are short-lived with indirect discourse as a chief characteristic. Daniel Beaumont attributes the simplicity and terseness of the language describing the proclamation of Islam to the exigencies of the particular narrative form, known as the *akhbār* (sing. *khabar,* that is, news or account) tradition, in which early Islamic accounts of story-tellers were put into writing by the later historians in the ninth and the tenth centuries. In this transition from story-telling to *khabar*, 'there may have been a stage in which the core of the narrative was reduced to epitome—boiled down as it were, to *khabar* pith. This would consist either of transforming more mimetic narrative into more diegetic narrative, or of reworking the usage of diegetic narrative. In either case, the object is the same: to impose a singular meaning on an event with important theological considerations'.[17] Beaumont's argument for the possibility of a more customarily spiritual and elaborate presentation of individual conversions, primarily of notables and politically significant dignitaries, in a lost 'original' version, however, does not concern the communal conversions of the majority of Muslims.

The conversion of one such Persian luminary of the Sāsānid Empire is preserved in a tenth-century history of the Arab conquests. When the armies of Islam first approached the Iranian lands in the 640s, a certain prince by the name of Hurmuzān surrendered to the Arabs, whose victory was secured by the treachery of a Persian subject. The prince's one condition, that he be sent to the caliph 'Umar (r. 634–644) in Medina, was granted by the Arab general. When brought to 'Umar's presence, the caliph offered to spare the prince's life should he convert. The prince refused, and the caliph granted him a last wish. He asked for a jug of water, but did not drink, claiming

---

[15] Richard Bulliet, 'Conversion Stories in Early Islam', p. 131.

[16] *Greater Bundahišn,* ed. by Tahmuras D. Anklesaria, as *The Bundahishn* (Bombay, 1908), p. 1, l. 10; p. 2, l. 4; as quoted in Choksy, 'Zoroastrians in Muslim Iran', p. 26.

[17] Daniel Beaumont, 'Hard-Boiled: Narrative Discourse in Early Muslim Traditions', *Studia Islamica*, 83.1 (1996), p. 22.

that he was accustomed to drinking from bejewelled vessels. The attendants returned with a jug covered in precious stones. Again the prince refused to drink. The caliph asked him for an explanation, and Hurmuzan said he was not drinking for he feared the Muslims would kill him before he had quenched his thirst. The caliph swore not to kill him before he had drunk to his satisfaction. Upon hearing the caliph's vow, Hurmuzan spilled the water. 'Umar was impressed by the cunning prince, and prayed that he confess Islam. He turned to his people and asked them for guidance. 'Ali b. Abū Ṭālib (r. 656–661), 'Umar's main contender, and cousin and son-in-law of the Prophet himself, was present in the audience. 'Ali declared it unlawful for the caliph to go against his word and kill Hurmuzan. Instead, he suggested that the prince be allowed to remain in Medina and pay a poll tax. Hurmuzan objected, arguing that his standing in society would be compromised. 'Ali then decreed that should the prince be adamant in his refusal to either convert or to pay the tax, the caliph would have no choice but to execute him. 'Ali continued, 'I have done everything in my power to save the prince's neck, only to salvage such a promising and worthy life. Islam is the religion of truth, the best of religions, and its adherents are the closest people to God. Whoever professes to this faith shall be spared the fires of Hell'. Hurmuzan was awe-stricken. He said, 'Verily, it is so. I shall convert freely, for it would be a pity to deprive myself of such governance'.[18]

The above relates a conversion at the hands of a towering protagonist of early Islam, 'Umar b. al-Khaṭṭāb, companion, son-in-law, and father-in-law of the Prophet, the second caliph of Islam, commander of the faithful. Hurmuzan's spontaneous conversion is completely devoid of introspective ruminations. It is nonetheless significant. Ibn A'tham al-Kufi (d. 926) the historian, was a Shi'i, a follower of 'Ali, who considered 'Umar an illegitimate usurper of the caliphate. Written long after the death of both protagonists, and the ultimate prevalence of the Sunni alternative, the story is a testimony to 'Ali's justice, prudence, and effectiveness. When 'Umar falls silent, turning to his people for guidance, it is 'Ali whose acumen salvages the situation, making it historically significant. That is why the incident is remembered.

The Islamic sources also tell us that despite longstanding acrimonious relations, 'Umar frequently sought 'Ali's advice. Albrecht Noth has identified the seeking of consultation by the first caliphs of Islam to be a recurring topos in the early narrative sources. Its function is multiple: to idealize the Islamic past, when caliphs emulated the Prophetic tradition of seeking advice; to designate advice-seeking caliphs, especially when it is provided by companions of the Prophet, as justified ones; and to rationalize later legal practice by seeking the endorsement of early caliphs. In the case of the Shi'i Ibn A'tham, then, not only are we dealing with a legitimist or pro-'Alid bias, but 'of even more importance to our critique is the fact that this advising motif, like other

---

[18] Ibn A'tham al-Kūfī, *Kitāb al-futūḥ,* trans. by Muḥammad b. Aḥmad Mustawfī Harawī (d. 1200), ed. by Gholamreza Tabataba'i Majd, (Tehran, 1993), pp. 220–27.

narrative motifs we have examined, appears in reports which cannot be considered authentic'.[19]

The pro-'Alid bias, and the Koranic theme of the validation of the message of Islam by adherents of older monotheistic faiths, are manifested again in a conversion story found in the anonymous *Tā'rīkh-i Sīstān,* a local history from south-eastern Iran, dating most probably to the late tenth or early eleventh century. Following the massacre of the family of the Prophet, including his beloved grandson, Ḥusayn, outside Karbalā in 681 at the hands of the Umayyad (r. 661–750) armies, their severed heads were placed on spears and paraded through all the towns on the road back to Damascus. The procession arrived finally at a town in which there lived a Christian monk. Setting out to conduct his nocturnal prayers, a light emanating from the heavens stopped the monk in his tracks. He asked the Umayyad party who they were, and to whom the severed heads belonged. They responded that one belonged to Ḥusayn, the son of 'Alī, grandson of the Prophet. The monk was despondent. Had there been a progeny of Jesus left in this world, he thought, Christians would have held him more precious than their eyes. He then told the Umayyad party that should they leave him the head of Ḥusayn until the next morning, and, instead, he would give them 10,000 gold dinar. The Umayyads agreed. The monk cleaned Ḥusayn's head, performed all purifying rituals, and cried and prayed with the head at his side. At the crack of dawn he called on the head. 'O exalted head, I am sovereign over my soul'. He then converted to Islam, becoming a follower of Ḥusayn. He returned the head to the Umayyads, who set off for Damascus. Before approaching the city, they stopped to check on their booty. To their astonishment they found all the gold coins to have turned into clay. Imprinted upon them were Koranic verses admonishing usurpers and oppressors. Many of them wept and repented, threw the coins in the river, and dispersed in the desert.[20]

Here the primary theme is to discredit the Umayyad dynasty, and to point to the moral superiority of supporters of 'Alī and his sons. The righteous monk confirms the virtuosity of the religion of Ḥusayn. The conversion stories in question then, are not simply about conversion, but, more importantly, they reveal a secondary theme in the development of Islamic historiography, a later fabrication to aggrandize the companions of the Prophet and the early days of Islam.[21] Noth argues that the general topos of the

---

[19] Albrecht Noth, *The Early Arabic Historical Tradition: A Source-Critical Study,* 2nd edn, in collaboration with Lawrence I. Conrad, trans. by Michael Bonner (Princeton, 1994), p. 140.

[20] Anonymous, *Tā'rīkh-i Sīstān,* ed. by M. T. Bahār (Tehran, 1935), pp. 99–101.

[21] Al-Ṭabarī, the most prominent of all medieval Muslim historians, writing in the second decade of the tenth century, offers a variation of this story. In his recension, Hurmuzan converted only after he beguiled the caliph into pardoning him. When brought before the caliph 'Umar, the Persian prince inquired whether he should speak as one who will live or as one who is about to die. After 'Umar remarked that he should speak as one who will live, Hurmuzan alleged that 'Umar had in fact granted him clemency. The caliph, impressed by the cunning prince, then said that he either converts or dies. The prince converted, and 'Umar allocated a monthly stipend and

da'wa or call to Islam in the early conquest literature is, among other things, a representation, on the part of converts, especially Iranian ones, to legitimize their standing in Islam, and to elevate their position to an equal status with the conquering Arabs. The summons to Islam, and its acceptance or rejection, should not be held to account for the conversion of the vanquished population, 'for it is placed in material contexts in which it demonstrably does not belong, while it also appears in generalizing traditions which lack any relation whatsoever to actual events'.[22] It should be regarded rather, as a campaign on the part of the converts to gain recognition without regard to their origins or to the time of their conversion. Noth's assertion is further strengthened by his argument that the summons, in its literal expression preserved in the sources, could have enjoyed tangible effect in the time of the Prophet, when pagans in the Arabian deserts were addressed.[23] Its utility for the peoples the Muslims fought later is questionable, especially since they demonstrated little willingness to change their religion, choosing instead to submit and pay tribute.[24]

Although the medieval histories pay scant attention to the mass conversions of the conquered populations, conversion as a key to negotiating the parameters of political authority is an early feature of the Islamic corpus. Long before the conquests presented the Islamic polity with non-Arab and non-Muslim populations, conversion among the Arabs of Mecca and Medina was translated into a political asset, legitimating claims for leadership and authority in the aftermath of Muhammad's death. Shi'is and Sunnis have long disputed the first instance of male conversion to the new religion. Shi'is claim it was 'Ali, Muhammad's cousin and son-in-law, the man who in their view should have succeeded him in 632. Sunnis claim that 'Ali's youth at the time of conversion

---

a residence in Medina for him. This version is quoted in Jamsheed K. Choksy, *Conflict and Cooperation: Zoroastrian Subalterns and Muslim Elites in Medieval Iranian Society* (New York, 1997), p. 73. Choksy goes on to add that given the circumstances of Hurmuzan's conversion, his faith remained suspect, and later he was executed for allegedly playing a role in 'Umar's assassination. Choksy takes the story to tell an actual event, and uses it as an instance of motifs for Zoroastrian conversions to Islam. The story appears in varying recensions in numerous other sources, see for instance, Aḥmad b. Yaḥyā b. Jābir al-Balādhurī, *Futūḥ al-buldān*, ed. by Ṣ. Munjid (Cairo, 1957), II, 379–82.

[22] Noth, *The Early Arabic Historical Tradition*, pp. 166.

[23] G. R. Hawting has recently posited that the longstanding conviction in Islamic studies that the Koran itself was revealed in a polytheistic and largely pagan milieu needs to be reconsidered. Archaeological and textual evidence seem to indicate that monotheists, especially Jews and Christians, far outnumbered pagans in Arabia in the time of Muhammad. The numerous Koranic verses addressed to pagans then, should be understood as literary topoi, utilized for rhetorical and polemical purposes. G. R. Hawting, *The Idea of Idolatry and the Emergence of Islam* (Cambridge, 1999), esp. pp. 88–110.

[24] For patterns of Zoroastrian conversions to Islam, see Chosky, *Conflict and Cooperation*, pp. 69–109.

precludes legitimacy. The first adult male to convert to Islam is Abū Bakr (r. 632–634), who triumphed over ʿAlī to the caliphate and ruled as the first caliph of Islam. Noteworthy in this regard is the tendentious accounts surrounding the conversion of Muʿāwiya b. Abū Sufyān (r. 661–680), governor of Syria a few years after the death of Muhammad, who eventually defeated ʿAlī in battle in 660 and founded the Umayyad dynasty. Most histories of medieval Islam, albeit for different reasons, convey a negative image of the Umayyads to posterity. Muʿāwiya himself, although long recognized as an able administrator, is blamed for instigating rebellion, and engineering his son's advent to the throne once he passed away, this latter in blatant violation both of Muhammad's actual and ideological example. One of the most prevalent tools utilized to undermine the legitimacy of the Umayyad caliphate is the tardy conversion of Muʿāwiya to Islam. What is at stake here is that following the death of Muhammad, one of the most important criteria in establishing a share to political authority was the date of a person's or a clan's conversion. Those members of Muhammad's tribe, the Quraysh, who converted before the Muslim conquest of Mecca in 630, who jeopardized their lives and social standing before victory was apparent, are held superior to the rest who converted en masse following the imposition of the rule of Islam over their native city. Muʿāwiya's defenders, *inter alia,* argue that he had in fact converted before 630, as early as 628 or 629, but hid his true affiliation for a greater cause, filial loyalty. He did inform his mother, they claim, but she insisted that he hide his new faith for as long as his father was alive.[25]

That explicit conversion stories in medieval histories were never intended as documents of the actual process of conversion is perhaps best exemplified in the classic example of the fickle conversion of the paradigmatic other, the Ilkhānid (and Mongol) rulers of Persia (1256–1353). Uljāytū (r. 1304–16), the son of Ghāzān (r. 1295–1304), was a descendant of Qubilay, Hülegü's brother. Baptized as a child, he later became a Buddhist, then ruled according to the dictates of the Ḥanafī school of law until 1303 when he converted to the Shāfiʿī school. In 1310, he became a Shiʿi.[26] His father Ghāzān, as discussed in a separate study by Charles Melville, formally abandoned his shamanist or Buddhist beliefs in 1295, converting only after the majority of his army had adopted the Islamic faith. Melville draws on the various recensions of the conversion of Ghāzān preserved in the sources to designate the event as a turning point in the history of Iran, 'marking among other things a transition from the blatant exploitation of Iran by the Chingissid and Ilkhanid conquest states, to a more responsible attitude to government within the pre-existing Islamic ethos'.[27] Subsequent

---

[25] Isaac Hasson, 'La Conversion du Muʿāwiya ibn Abī Sufyān', *Jerusalem Studies in Arabic and Islam*, 22 (1998), 214–42.

[26] ʿAbd Allāh b. Luṭf Allāh Ḥāfiẓ al-Abrū, *Dhayl-i jāmiʿ al-tawārīkh-i Rashīdī*, ed. by Khanbaba Bayani (Tehran, 1971), p. 101 n. 1; as quoted in Sabine Schmidtke, *The Theology of al-ʿAllāma al-Ḥillī (d. 726/1325)*, (Berlin, 1991), pp. 23–25.

[27] Charles Melville, 'Pādshāh-i Islam: The Conversion of Sulṭān Maḥmūd Ghāzān Khān',

events contradict Melville's characterization. In that same year, news of Ghāzān's baptism was received with great jubilation in the Christian West, as his superficial conversion did not deter him from launching an attack on the Mamlūk state (1250–1517) in Syria and Egypt. 'The news of Ghāzān's invasion of Syria reached the West in greatly exaggerated form, as the story had been inflated to include the capture of Jerusalem and its return to the Latins, and in some variants, the conversion of Ghāzān to Christianity. [. . .] As Sylvia Schein has demonstrated, enthusiasm was widespread and quite genuine. So convinced was Ramon Llull that upon hearing news of Ghāzān's "conversion", he sailed to Cyprus hoping to meet with Ghāzān and personally undertake the conversion of the Il-khanid court and people'.[28] When Tamerlane defeated the Ottomans in 1402, his willingness to forge military alliances with the West, 'meant that he had pro-Christian sympathies if he was not already on the way to becoming a Christian himself'.[29] The Ṣafavid Shāh Ismāʿīl I (r. 1501–24), who established Shiʿism as the official religion of Iran, was, according to two contemporary and independent French and German reports, baptized by four Franciscan monks in 1508.[30] His great grandson, Shāh ʿAbbās I (r. 1587–1629), following his victories over the Turks, again according to contemporary Christian sources, was to have been converted by Jesuits, on Pentecost in 1605.[31] Adam Knobler goes on to conclude that conversion was one method of justifying alliances with Eastern princes, more so since the stories were never recorded in 'official' court archives, but circulated as 'popular tales', as well as a literary topos, as every single conversion story is linked with a Christian woman at the court. Following the centuries-old demonization of Islam, '"[c]onverts" or secret believers were to be found in the Muslim world, whose true faith would be revealed,

---

Pembroke Papers, 1 (1990), 159–77. Melville's contention is also questioned in a recent study by Reuven Amitai-Preiss, 'Ghazan, Islam, and Mongol tradition: A View from the Mamluk Sultanate', *Bulletin of the School of Oriental and African Studies*, 9.1 (1996), pp. 1–10. Amitai-Preiss concludes that far from integrating the Mongol apparatus of government with an Islamic ethos, 'Ghazan's reputation as a devout, orthodox Muslim is somewhat tarnished. We are left, then, with an inconsistent, even confused, but certainly more historically convincing convert to Islam', p. 10.

[28] Sylvia Schein, '*Gesta Dei per Mongolos 1300*: The Genesis of a Non-Event', *English Historical Review*, 94 (1979), 805–19; as quoted in Adam Knobler, 'Pseudo-Conversions and Patchwork Pedigrees: The Christianization of Muslim Princes and the Diplomacy of Holy War', *Journal of World History*, 7.2 (1996), 188.

[29] Knobler, 'Pseudo-Conversions and Patchwork Pedigrees', p. 191.

[30] Palmira Brummett, 'The Myth of Shah Ismail Safavi: Political Rhetoric and 'Divine' Kingship', in *Medieval Christian Perceptions of Islam: A Book of Essays*, ed. by John Victor Tolan (New York, 1996), pp. 331–59.

[31] Knobler, 'Pseudo-Conversions and Patchwork Pedigrees', pp. 194–95.

ensuring victory over a common enemy and the liberation of Christendom from the perceived Muslim threat'.[32]

In understanding conversions in the medieval period then, it is important to understand the various models as metaphors rather than axiomatic truth. What these narratives are attempting to do is to capture the experience of conversion in language. Medieval scholars wove the unknowable, the transcendental, into experiences, narrated in metaphors meaningful for their audience. The distance between what is called conversion and the actual process, to borrow from Morrison, between the text and the event, is the space which allows us to glimpse at the medieval understanding, the poetics, of conversion. Morrison goes on to add, 'There was an inescapable disequilibrium between empathy and poetics. What can be said about how theologians addressed the hermeneutic problems in Scripture can be applied also to their understanding of the difference between the supernatural experience of conversion, a thing felt, and writings about conversion, as things made. And it leads directly to their notions about the point at which the two intersected: that is, where empathy was reduced to form by poetics'.[33] The constraints of language for expressing spiritual experiences is further explored below, for as we shall see, one of the contributions of Sufism to the religion of Islam was the creation of a vocabulary and discourse for spiritual development. Writing about medieval history in particular necessitates a multiplicity of mimetic lenses, as what was written or what survives in written texts is only a part, or fragment, of history. What needs accommodation are the discrepancies between what was written and what was felt, and the exigencies of the audience to which the text was addressed.

Rather than historicized narratives of early pagan conversions to Christianity, what seems to have monopolized the discussion on conversion in the medieval Christian world, 'what came to be a major institution in European society—and for centuries the only one that with its teachings and presence permeated daily life in every region across the continent—was designed and formed for the express purpose of conversion, are the literary output of the monastic orders. The monastic life as St Benedict outlined it in his *Rule* is in fact a series of stages of spiritual development, "a school for the Lord's service", leading to the transformation of the individual. It is portrayed as a series of lesser transformations or conversions that, taken collectively, change the individual monk over a lifetime'.[34] Accordingly, I would agree with Bulliet that chronicles and dynastic histories may be the wrong sources for studying conversion in medieval Islam. I would, however, add personal and family histories to that list. Instead, I would, as

---

[32] Knobler, 'Pseudo-Conversions and Patchwork Pedigrees', p. 197. For medieval Christian examples of ephemeral conversions with political agendas, and the role of prominent females in their availing, see Rasa Mazeika, 'Bargaining for Baptism: Lithuanian Negotiations for Conversion, 1250–1358', in *Varieties of Religious Conversion in the Middle Ages*, pp. 131–40.

[33] Morrison, *Understanding Conversion*, p. 39.

[34] Muldoon, 'Introduction', p. 1.

scholars of Christian conversions have done for a long time, focus on saints' hagio-graphies. There, you would find references to supernatural or spiritual experiences, details of special charisma or spiritual gifts possessed by the Muslims who called non-Muslims to Islam, and notes of the convert's original religion. Before we embark on a comparative project, a few methodological observations are in order. In a recent study on manifestations of sainthood in world religions, and in an attempt to de-christianize the constitutive elements of the phenomenon, Richard Kieckhefer has come to define a saint as more than a holy man and less than a prophet, a model for veneration and emulation.[35] Following on Kieckhefer's model, what I am trying to establish here is not a Muslim equivalent for the Christian saint, the authenticity of the former,[36] or a universal definition of sainthood, but rather to draw on resemblances across religious traditions to illuminate the phenomenon in question.[37] In drawing analogies between medieval Christian saints and Sufi shaykhs, I am not postulating a universal category of sainthood, equally relevant to holy men of all times and cultural contexts. In a more limited sense, and in so far as conversion and piety are concerned, the function of monastic orders of the medieval West was roughly parallelled by Sufis of Islam, who

---

[35] Richard Kieckhefer, 'Imitators of Christ: Sainthood in the Christian Tradition', in *Sainthood: Its Manifestations in World Religions*, ed. by Richard Kieckhefer and George D. Bond (Berkeley, 1988), pp. 1–42. Noteworthy also is Ofer Livne-Kafri's study of the analogies between Christian monasticism and Islamic asceticism, wherein they are enumerated but not synthesized to form an argument; see 'Early Muslim Ascetics and the World of Christian Monasticism', *Jerusalem Studies in Arabic and Islam*, 20 (1996), 105–29.

[36] For such a plea, see Frederick M. Denny, 'Prophet and *Walī* Sainthood in Islam,' in *Sainthood: Its Manifestations in World Religions*, pp. 69–97. See also Carl Ernst's unjustified assertion: 'Humanity has always felt the need for mediators between the everyday world and the transcendent world of divinity. [. . .] Peter Brown has described several important characteristics of saints in Latin Christianity, much of which can only be seen, *mutatis mutandis*, in Islam. According to Brown, saints enjoy the special protection of God, they replace angels as the intermediaries between God and humanity, and their relationship with God reduplicates the patronage network of society, raising the possibility of their intervention with God to obtain favor for the believer. From the point of view of the history of religion, all these positions are found in the position of the Muslim *awliyā'*. So, leaving aside the juridical aspect of canonization, the term "saint" can be usefully applied to holy persons in Islam'. Carl W. Ernst, et. al., 'Introduction,' in *Manifestations of Sainthood in Islam* (Istanbul, 1993), pp. xi–xxviii. For a convincing refutation of this type of reductionism, see Peter Awn's study on Satan, who focuses on the diversity behind labels, both within the Christian tradition and in comparison to the Muslim one; Peter J. Awn, *Satan's Tragedy and Redemption: Iblīs in Sufi Psychology* (Leiden, 1983), pp. 1–6.

[37] Kieckhefer and Bond, 'Afterword: Toward a Comparative Study of Sainthood', in *Sainthood: Its Manifestations in World Religions*, pp. 243–54.

indulged in asceticism, piety, prayer, emulation of the Prophetic model, and living the good Muslim life. Sufi shaykhs mirrored their Christian counterparts in other activities: they too built communities, engaged in warfare, educated princes, wielded immense political power, threatened established religious norms, and perhaps most consequential of all, collaborated closely with wielders of the sword to form states from the fourteenth century onwards. The Ṣafavids (r. 1501–1732) originated as a Sufi order in the fourteenth century, the Chishtiyya collaborated closely with the Āl-i Kart (r. 1245–1389) in Herat in the same period. In North Africa, the Saʿdī state (r. mid-sixteenth century to c. 1659) competed and collaborated with the Sufi *zāwiyas* of the Jāzūliyya order in Morocco, and the Sānūsiya order founded in 1837 went on to create the Idrīsid confederation in 1905, leading ultimately to the formation of the modern state of Libya in 1963. The Bahmanids (r. 1347–1527) of northern India shifted their Sufi alliances several times from the fourteenth to the sixteenth centuries, starting with the Sunni Chishtiyya, followed by the Shiʿi Qādiriyya and finally settling on the Niʿmatullāhis.[38] In spite of these commonalities, common sense still prevents us from reducing medieval sainthood to a series of constitutive elements, enjoying fixed origins in one religious tradition and numerous cross-cultural permutations. Julian Baldick has, and in my view erroneously, traced occasional resemblances, sporadic affinities and common etymologies to argue that, '[i]n recent years more weight has been accorded to the view that Islamic mysticism, and in particular Sufism, grew out of Christian spirituality'.[39] The assertion is particularly misconstrued as Baldick fails to explicate the process and means by which this adaptation has occurred. Clearly, medieval monasticism and Sufism have discernible origins in their respective traditions, and their subsequent trajectories are best understood in relation to their specific and evolving historical contexts. Moreover, medieval Sufi shaykhs of the ninth century, with little in the way of organization and institutionalization, share perhaps simply in nomenclature with their fourteenth-century

---

[38] For the subversive role of Sufi shaykhs in the medieval period see my 'Niẓām al-Mulk Remembered: A Study in Historical Representation' (unpublished doctoral dissertation, Columbia University, 1992), chapter 5. On the Safavids, see Kathryn Babayan, 'Sufis, Dervishes and Mullas: The Controversy over Spiritual and Temporal Dominion in Seventeenth-Century Iran', in *Safavid Persia*, ed. by Charles Melville (London, 1996), pp. 117–38. The Āl-i Kart are discussed in Lawrence G. Potter, 'Sufis and Sultans in Post-Mongol Iran', *Iranian Studies*, 27.1–4 (1994), 77–103. For Morocco, see Francisco Rodriguez-Manas, 'Agriculture, Sufism and the State in Tenth/Sixteenth-Century Morocco', *Bulletin of the School of Oriental and African Studies*, 59.3 (1996), 450–71; and Vincent J. Cornell, *Realm of the Saint: Power and Authority in Moroccan Sufism* (Austin, 1998). For the Sanusiyya, see, Knut S. Vikor, *Sufi and Scholar of the Desert Edge, Muḥammad b. ʿAlī al-Sānūsī and his Brotherhood* (Norway, 1995). For the Bahmanids, see Muhammad Suleman Siddiqi, 'Sufi-State Relationship Under the Bahmanids, 1348–1538', *Revista degli studia Orientali*, 44.1–2 (1990), 71–96.

[39] Julian Baldick, *Mystical Islam* (London, 1989), pp. 15–24.

counterparts.[40] And, as we shall see below, primary sources for the study of Sufism in the ninth and the tenth centuries are generally products of later cultural milieus. In studying them, the researcher is persistently bound by the myriad ramifications of this hiatus. Representations present in these sources are of their own rather than those of their putative subject's historical circumstances. Later Sufi compilations do exhibit universalizing tendencies, organized to create a uniform past with common genealogies traced all the way back to the Prophet. But these remain anachronistic stereotypes, more revealing as rhetorical ploys than intellectual archaeologies.

It is already commonplace that outside the political boundaries of Islam, traders served as great agents of Islamization. Rather than propagating the faith themselves, these expediters usually had Muslim divine men in their midst. Nehemia Levtzion has argued that '[t]he frontiers of Islam were extended not through the work of the learned urban *'ulamā'*, but by the efforts of the rural rustic divines, many of whom were mystics and often also members of institutionalised ṣufī orders'.[41] This he says, occurred after the tenth century, and outside the political dominions of Islam. 'Mystics of different sorts carried the main burden of the spread of Islam in the further Islamic lands, but they also played an important role in promoting conversion to Islam in lands under Muslim rule, especially those conquered after the tenth century, such as Anatolia, India, or the Sudan'.[42] Within the confines of Islamic political authority, and as instigators of spiritual conversions of Muslims themselves, however, the active role of Sufi shaykhs has not been recognized.

That the earliest Muslim mystics of the eighth and the ninth centuries sought a spiritual renewal, a conversion to a dynamic and radical reorientation to God, is perhaps best exemplified in their creation of a new moral vocabulary, mostly by attributing new semantic functions to the familiar Koranic lexicon. In reference to conversion, Gerhard Bowering has argued that early Sufi movements, when faced with hostility from establishmentarian religious authorities, sought to overcome injustice and evil in this world

> by spiritual renewal, termed *tawba*, 'repentance and inner conversion'. Far from understanding *tawba* simply as conversion from one organized religion to another, the Sufis perceived it as a dynamic principle of radical reorientation to God that made them abandon the false ways of this world and follow the straight path to God. For this reason, they saw themselves as occupying a place similar to that of the Prophet, the

---

[40] Jürgen Paul has mapped the intellectual trajectory of Sufi shaykhs from individualistic movements in the ninth century to the full-fledged establishment of communities and *ṭuruq* by the Mongol period. Jürgen Paul, 'Au Début du genre hagiographique dans le Khurasan', in *Saints Orientaux*, ed. by Denise Aigle (Paris, 1995), pp. 15–38.

[41] Nehemia Levtzion, 'Toward a Comparative Study of Islamization', in *Conversion to Islam*, ed. by N. Levtzion (New York, 1979), pp. 16–18.

[42] Levtzion, 'Toward a Comparative Study of Islamization', pp. 16–18.

prototypical hearer of the Koranic word. Through this divine word the Sufis discovered in the symbolism of *tawba* a powerful paradigm to capture their unmediated encounter with God.[43]

Moreover, this particular understanding of *tawba* can be traced in early Sufi hagiographies, where it resonates with Nock's paradigm of peripety conversions. Resembling St Paul's experience on the road to Damascus,

> [i]n each of the five paradigmatic hagiographies the life change is embedded in a patterned scenario: an unforeseeable, sudden event shocks the individual; shaken by doubt or overcome by fear, he turns away from this world, abruptly abandons his accustomed way of life, repents and turns totally to God. [. . .] In each case, a symbolic figure marks the turning point. The legendary Ibrāhīm b. Adham (d. 777–778) happens upon a mysterious voice; an arrow pierces Fuḍayl b. 'Iyaḍ's (d. 803) heart; and Bishr al-Ḥāfī (d. 841) is visited by someone calling in a dream. Shaqīq al-Balkhī (d. 809) meets a clean-shaven monk in saffron robes in a Buddhist temple of Central Asia who, although an idolater, teaches him the true meaning of the divine Sustainer.[44]

The later metaphor of conversion as a profession of faith, approximating scripture and constructing the constitutive elements of holiness, is exemplified in Sufi hagiographies of the tenth and the eleventh centuries, and especially those of Iran. In contrast to a model of conversion which assumes a true and complete change of heart—usually from one belief system to another—achieved in a relatively short period, the medieval Islamic conversion story is symbolic of a spiritual transformation, a refocusing of one's moral life. If conversion in the eight and the ninth centuries was signalled by decisive moments, in the later periods, Sufi hagiographies provided 'paradigms of credibility'

---

[43] Gerhard Bowering, 'Early Sufism between Persecution and Heresy', in *Islamic Mysticism Contested*, ed. by Frederick de Jong and Bernd Radtke (Leiden, 1999), pp. 45–69. Here Bowering has refuted Josef Van Ess's simplistic nominalism when accounting for the absence of spiritual conversions in Islam, interestingly in a work on inter-faith dialogue. Van Ess has argued that, 'lacking a word for conscience, Arabic has no equivalent for the mysterious inwardness of change connoted by "conversion". To adhere to Islam is "to follow the right way", meaning formal observance. Consequently, nuances of doctrinal understanding, which shaped such narratives of conversion in western Europe as Bede's portrayal of the rivalry between Celtic and Roman practices, were for Muslims not indices of an unfolding apocalyptic between good and evil'. Van Ess is repeated in Morrison, who consequently goes on to deduce that conversion is seldom mentioned by Islamic historical writers, much less developed as an impelling and dominant current in world history. Josef Van Ess, 'Sunnites and Shi'ites: The State, Law, and Religion', in *Christianity and the World Religions: Paths of Dialogue with Islam, Hinduism, and Buddhism* (Garden City, NY, 1986), p. 46; as quoted in Morrison, *Understanding Conversion*, pp. 6–7.

[44] Bowering, 'Early Sufism between Persecution and Heresy', pp. 46–49.

drawn on the Koran and the life of Muhammad. The living example of Muhammad is what they represented, the Prophet as an idealized paradigm of piety. The divine is what they transported to their community. Living in an Islamic polity bereft of religious legitimacy by the mid-tenth century,[45] unsatisfied with the religiosity of a fully developed class of *ulamā* and traditionists who sought to monopolize religious interpretation through the elaborate and contrived mechanism of the Prophet's tradition (*sunna* and *ḥadīth*), the Sufi shaykhs sought to revitalize Muslim piety. The mid-tenth century also marks the completion of the historical process of conversion in Iran.[46] At this same time, textual representations of spiritual conversion became the blueprint for various Sufi hagiographies in medieval Iran.

Here I shall concentrate on the conversion stories preserved in the biography of a charismatic Sufi shaykh of this period, Shaykh Abū Isḥāq Ibrāhīm b. Shahriyār al-Kāzarūnī, who lived from 963 to 1033, in Kāzarūn, a district in the southwestern Iranian province of Fārs. The Arabs conquered Kāzarūn definitively in 647. The Persian biography of Shaykh Abū Isḥāq, entitled *Firdaws al-murshidiyya fī asrār al-ṣamadiyya*, was adapted from the Arabic original. Internal evidence shows that the original author, Imām Abū Bakr Muḥammad b. 'Abd al-Karīm b. 'Alī b. Sa'd, died in 1108. The Persian recension was produced by a certain Maḥmūd b. 'Uthmān in 1327.[47]

Kāzarūnī was probably the most prominent Sufi shaykh of his day in Fars.[48] He was born to a newly Islamized family; both his grandparents were Zoroastrian (again, the conversion topos). He founded a Sufi order, the Kāzarūniyya,[49] whose members were later instrumental in the conquest and Islamization of Anatolia. In this they followed the teachings of Kāzarūnī himself, who, at least metaphorically, apart from proselytization among the unconverted population of his native town, engaged also in frequent

---

[45] For a thoughtful account of the collapse of legitimate political order in Islam, and its representations in the medieval chronicles, see Tayeb El-Hibri, *Reinterpreting Islamic Historiography* (Cambridge, 1999).

[46] For a complete account of his methodology for establishing the chronology of conversion to Islam, see Richard W. Bulliet, *Conversion to Islam in the Medieval Period* (Cambridge, MA, 1981), pp. 16–63; and to corroborate Bulliet's dating of the process of conversion in Iran and Spain for Palestine, see Robert Schick, *The Christian Communities of Palestine from Byzantine to Islamic Rule: A Historical and Archaeological Study* (Princeton, 1995), pp. 139–58.

[47] Shaykh Abū Isḥāq's biography was first edited in 1948; see Maḥmūd b. 'Uthmān, *Die Vita des Scheich Abū Isḥāq al-Kāzarūnī*, ed. by F. Meier (Leipzig, 1948). A new edition with a long introduction on the various manuscripts and recensions of the text and an annotated bibliography of sources on Kāzarūnī was published several years later; see Maḥmūd b. 'Uthmān, *Firdaws al-murshidiyya fī asrār al-ṣamadiyya*, 2nd edn, ed. by Iraj Afshar (Tehran, 1979).

[48] For a complete biography, see H. Algar, 'Kāzarūnī, Shaykh Abū Ishḥāq Ibrāhīm b. Shahriyār', *Encyclopaedia of Islam* (1978), new edn, IV, 851–52.

[49] Denise Aigle, 'Un fondateur d'ordre en milieu rural. Le Cheikh Abū Isḥāq de Kāzarūn,' in *Saints Orientaux*, pp. 181–209.

'spiritual' raids along the Byzantine border, presumably to expand the domain of Islam.[50] Like Muhammad, the shaykh organized military expeditions against infidels. Like his companions, who with Muhammad are protagonists of the 'un-idyllic' idealized founding days of Islam, the shaykh rarely ever assumed personal command of the Muslim armies. Even back then, as Noth has demonstrated, the caliphs, and, especially, 'Umar, participated only symbolically in the initial conquests. The reports in the sources that pretend as if they actually partook in these expeditions, '[a]re more likely to have been apologetic in character: the somewhat painful fact that the Prophet's successors did not take part in the *futūḥ* would have been softened by traditions proclaiming that the caliphs had at least a desire to go to war'.[51]

Kāzarūnī was also responsible for a vast charity network in the region, building no less than sixty-five *khānqāhs* where the needy were fed each day. His earthly beneficence was accompanied by supernatural powers, miraculous feats, and divine oracles. Blessed for distinction since childhood, he is reported to have murmured religious chants, audible to those present, while still a foetus in his mother's womb. He was charitable from the very onset; he refused to suckle his mother before another child had done so to his heart's content. He was not a zealot either. The *Firdaws* tells us that he was remembered kindly by a contemporary Christian Abū al-'Alā', a notable at the Būyid (r. 932–1062) court.[52] Like Muhammad, he entered into treaties and negotiated compacts with peoples of the book. Moreover, he extended his hospitality indiscriminately, offering food and shelter to a dissimulating Jewish traveller, whose true confessional allegiance was known to the shaykh thanks to his supernatural powers.[53] And, unlike many of his peers and colleagues, he never married; in fact, he continuously shunned the company of women.[54] We are also told that later on in his life, he was in direct correspondence with the most illustrious Khurāsānī Sufi of the time, Shaykh Abū

---

[50] For an example of an erroneous reading of the shaykh's spiritual sojourns, taken literally as actual expeditions, see Algar's article, above. The shaykh encouraged such raids, and his disciples did actually engage in them, but he never participated in person. *Firdaws al-murshidiyya fī asrār al-ṣamadiyya*, pp. 180–82. In fact, the text explicitly states that the shaykh encouraged annual raids against the infidels, blessed the warriors, but stayed put in Kāzarūn: 'va Shaykh-i murshid har sāl tartīb-i nafaqāt-i īshān kardī va īshān rā bi ghazū firistādī va khawd dar vaṭan binishastī va bi himmat madad va mu'āvinat-i īshān kardī'. He was in spiritual contact with his warring devotees, interceding from Kāzarūn when he felt their fortune was running low.

[51] Noth, *The Arabic Historical Tradition*, pp. 140–41, 181.

[52] *Firdaws al-murshidiyya fī asrār al-ṣamadiyya*, p. 167.

[53] *Firdaws al-murshidiyya fī asrār al-ṣamadiyya*, p. 158.

[54] *Firdaws al-murshidiyya fī asrār al-ṣamadiyya*, p. 146. Some Muslim mystics did in fact adopt celibacy, although the Prophet, and the majority of the later *ulamā*, including Sufi shaykhs, forbade it, brandishing it as Christian in essence and practice. On this, see Livne-Kafri, 'Early Muslim Ascetics and the World of Christian Monasticism', p. 111.

Abū al-Khayr (967–1048). He was, like Kāzarūnī, a Shāfiʿī in law and Ashʿarī in theological outlook and, who in turn, claims to have been in correspondence with no less than Avicenna himself.[55]

Seven centuries after the death of Muhammad, four centuries after the completion of the conversion process in Iran, and three centuries after the death of the shaykh, his biography records his exploits against the Zoroastrian community of the region in great detail. The story of 24,000 Zoroastrians and Jews converting *en masse* at his hands is often cited and attributed to a wide range of mystics across an impressive spectrum of time. Most hagiographies of tenth-century Sufi shaykhs, including that of Shaykh Abu Saʿīd, recount similar feats.[56] How many Zoroastrians converted to Islam at the hands of the shaykh? His *vita* is replete with stories of his tireless efforts at promoting Islam. In one instance, we are told that the shaykh prophesied in the presence of his faithful disciples that a day would come when Zoroastrians would be the odd men out in a preponderantly Muslim Kāzarūn.[57] Should this be taken to indicate that Zoroastrians outnumbered Muslims in Kāzarūn around the year 1000? The story goes on to add that the prophecy was actually fulfilled in the shaykh's lifetime, and masses of Zoroastrians flocked to Islam at the hands of the shaykh. The narrative does not furnish any further explication as to the secret of his success.

Perhaps the most telling story of Zoroastrian conversions instigated by the shaykh concerns the construction of the first Friday mosque in Kāzarūn. The shaykh first built a small edifice pointing to Mecca, and the Zoroastrians destroyed it. He tried several times, only to meet the same fate. He even sought the intercession of the Buyid authorities in Fars, but good Shiʿis that they were, they failed to support the truly orthodox Sunni shaykh in his endeavour to spread the word of Islam. In defiance of the Buyid vizier's strict orders to avoid religious bloodshed, he started on the external wall of the mosque, and again the Zoroastrians demolished it. Throughout the ordeal, though, the shaykh never allowed his followers to confront the attackers. On one occasion, however, the shaykh's followers tried to protect the building, but were vanquished. They went to him in despair. In the true spirit of divine revelation, the shaykh preached patience. For a whole year in 981, the shaykh said his prayers in the fields. After some time, the Prophet appeared in his dream. Holding a rope in one hand, Muhammad was busily building a mosque. The shaykh rushed to greet the Prophet. Muhammad embraced him, and the shaykh carried the Prophet's scent on his body to the last day. The shaykh knew then, that the time had come for the building of his mosque. Its

---

[55] For a medieval biography of another roughly contemporaneous Sufi saint, Shaykh Abū Saʿīd Abū al-Khayr, see Muḥammad b. Munawwar b. Abū Saʿd b. Abū Ṭāhir b. Abū Saʿīd Miyhanī, *Asrār al-tawḥid fī maqāmāt al-Shaykh Abū Saʿīd*, 2 vols (Tehran, 1987).

[56] I am pursuing the subject of templates of credibility in Sufi hagiographies in a forthcoming paper on medieval piety, which traces conversion paradigms in several hagiographies of the tenth century.

[57] *Firdaws al-murshidiyya fī asrār al-ṣamadiyya*, p. 180.

construction was completed without a single incident within four years time. The author then proceeds to provide a variant of the account. Again, we see the shaykh intending to build a mosque. In the absence of any transgression on the part of the Muslims, the Zoroastrians initiated the hostilities. Finally, they took their grievances to their leader. The leader of the Zoroastrians decided to incarcerate the shaykh. The shaykh was captured and brought to him, but the Zoroastrian leader decided it imprudent to provoke the Muslims, and instead chose to reprimand him. He admonished the shaykh, and warned him of the consequences of his actions. The recalcitrant shaykh was not impressed. He attended to his daily prayers, and the Zoroastrians proved hopeless. Encouraged by their passivity, the shaykh decided to expand his mosque. Emulating the Prophet's precedence, he sought the advice of his confidants. Like their progenitors, they deferred to his judgement. The shaykh enlarged the mosque several times. The Zoroastrians, succumbing gradually to what appeared to be an irreversible trend, converted in due course. The shaykh, needless to say, continued to dazzle them with his miraculous feats.[58]

What are we to make of this story? Morony has read it to find that there were more rural Zoroastrians than urban ones in Iran. He has also read it to disprove Bulliet and Frye on conversion patterns in Iran.[59] The intended message of this story, and the reason for its remembrance, is not to furnish historical data on the number of Zoroastrian converts or details of their conversion. The message of this story is to recall the struggle the Prophet encountered against his stubborn, idolatrous kin from the tribe of Quraysh, and his eventual establishment of a Muslim community in Medina, epitomized in the construction of a mosque. Emulating the prophetic model, as we have seen, is an important element of the lives of saints and mystics in both the Christian and Muslim contexts. The account of the shaykh's building of the mosque is stylized and dramatized.[60] The elements of drama are all present: danger, conflict, and courage.[61] Conversion was subversive to authority, even if it is a Buyid vizier in Fars. For this re-enactment of the Prophetic story, infidel Zoroastrians are allied with a Christian vizier and the non-orthodox dynasty of the Shi'i Buyids. The substitution of real enemies by imaginary ones for polemical purposes is a salient feature of Islamic historiography. An interesting example is studied by Vera Moreen. In a saying attributed to the eleventh Shi'i imam, Ḥasan al-'Askarī (d. c. 874)—cited in the late tenth century and in wide circulation in the newly Shi'ified Iran of the seventeenth century—the Jews of Medina are called upon to espouse all Sunni positions in a debate allegedly attended by the Prophet himself. Obviously, the Jews-cum-Sunnis are defeated, and Muhammad strongly endorses the political claim of 'Alī and the Shi'i position on legitimate

---

[58] *Firdaws al-murshidiyya fī asrār al-ṣamadiyya*, pp. 27–29.

[59] Morony, 'The Age of Conversions: A Reassessment', pp. 145–50.

[60] *Firdaws al-murshidiyya fī asrār al-ṣamadiyya*, pp. 26–30, 487–91.

[61] This stylistic skeleton of conversion stories is drawn from Morrison, *Understanding Conversion*, pp. 14–65.

authority in Islam. Moreen concludes: 'It is fruitless to probe the historicity of this story. Who are the Jews in this tale? When and where did these incidents occur? We cannot answer these questions which are, as we have seen, beside the main polemical thrust of the tale. Nevertheless, one cannot help noticing the role assigned to these imaginary Jews'.[62] Similar to the conversion story above, the ḥadith contains no specifically Jewish position in the debate. Likewise, there is no theological component to the conflict with the Zoroastrians. The religious identity of the shaykh's enemies is tangential to the progression of events. They could be Jews, Christians, pagans, shamanists, etc. and that would have absolutely no bearing on the unfolding of the drama. The moral message of this story is not to document Zoroastrian opposition to Islam, but rather to construct supernatural and physical barriers to the mission of the shaykh, and to witness their crumbling when faced with steadfastness. What we have in the *vita* of our shaykh then is a combination of themes and topoi from the holy books of Islam, the Koran, as well as canonical biographies of Muhammad and collections of his sayings and actions. Emulating the style of the Koran, explanation is never offered through the provision of detail, but rather through repetition with subtle thematic variations. As scripture, the Koran manifests little concern for historical details, episodes, or actors. The shaykh's *vita* is an exegetical exercise, in that it interprets the Koranic topoi by representing them in actual episodes in the life of the shaykh. In the building of the mosque, he replicates a famous deed by Muhammad. He is opposed by Zoroastrians, who like the Jews and the Koran, subscribe to a distinct and quasi-legitimate belief system. His mission is justified when recognized as a threat by 'other peoples of the book'. Like Muhammad in the Koran, it is the adherents of other monotheistic faiths, namely Christians and Jews, who recognize his extra-human capacity and distinction from the onset.[63] He is also opposed by the hypocrites which figure so predominantly in the Koran, only this time, hypocrisy is represented by the Shi'i authorities in the provincial capital. The shaykh succeeds, not because he was courageous and dedicated, but by the grace of God. Reminiscent of the story of the conquest of Mecca in the Koran, the shaykh first engages in a series of inconclusive battles with the Zoroastrians, and the famous Koranic episode of the Battle of Badr where God for the first time reveals to the

---

[62] Vera Basch Moreen, 'Salmān Fārisī and the Jews: An Anti-Jewish Shī'ī Ḥadīth from the Seventeenth Century?' in *Irano-Judaica II*, ed. by Shaul Shaked and Amnon Netzer (Jerusalem, 1990), pp. 144–57. The debate above is led on the side of orthodoxy by the legendary Persian convert and companion of the Prophet, Salmān al-Fārisī. The association with a fictitious character enhances Moreen's proposed substitution. On Salmān, see Josef Horovitz, 'Salmān al-Fārisī', *Der Islam,* 12 (1922), 178–83; as quoted in Noth, *The Arabic Historical Tradition,* p. 157. See also, Louis Massignon, *Salman Pak and the Spiritual Beginnings of Iranian Islam,* trans. by J. M. Unvala (Bombay, 1955), where he argues for a historical Salmān, mythified to embody the Iranian nationalist aspirations for acceptance into the new religion, and as part of the same scheme, made into one of the first four Shi'i companions of 'Alī.

[63] Noth, *The Arabic Historical Tradition,* p. 167.

Muslims that he is on their side, is represented in a dream, itself a recurrent feature in almost every hagiography of the medieval period. The story is repeated with minor alterations throughout the text, drawing on stereotypical imagery from the Koran. It is their recurrence and uniformity in the *vitas* and in the different *vitas,* and across different religions that render credibility to lives of the saints and efficacy to their mission.[64] As Morrison has noted for the Christian context,

> The reading of scriptures and that of hagiographic writers were cognate enterprises; they were mutually reflective. Both were characterized by indifference to historical details and a zeal for apprehending the meanings hidden beneath the letter of the text. In sum, something far deeper than indifference to historical details was at work in this task of fictionalizing to reveal and actualize truth, something inherent in the history of conversion itself.[65]

We can take the metaphoric aspect of the story further if we see the mosque as Abdelkader Tayob has seen it in his recent study on negotiating sacred space in Medina in the early Islamic period. Tayob characterizes Muhammad's establishing of a mosque 'as part of the definition of the Muslim community in Medina. As the locale for prostration, it is linked inextricably with the monotheism of Muhammad's message'.[66] It also signals the creation of a community of faith, whose prevailing is ironically celebrated in the delineation of holy space dedicated to the expression of submission to the will of God. Semantically, as it implies a place for prostration, and as a gathering place for Muslims to express their *islām,* literally, it signifies submission to the religion of God. The conversion stories in the *vita* of Shaykh Abu Isḥāq do not shed any light on the spiritual transformation of infidels. It is, rather, the shaykh's charisma, and his revealed supernatural qualities that dazzle onlookers into submission. But that is not all. We find the shaykh to be primarily interested in propagating the Islamic way of life, not amongst infidels, but for the believers themselves. His policies *vis-à-vis* non-Muslims are overwhelmingly defensive in nature. In addition, the conversion stories are clearly meant to further aggrandise the shaykh, and not as an end in themselves. They are only one in a long series of accomplishments. In another story of this type, the shaykh is chastised by his Lebanese peers for not being a good ascetic pursuing solitary contemplation in isolation from the community. He responds by claiming that his mission—as a catalyst of conversion—compels him to live in the midst of common

---

[64] As mentioned earlier, I plan to develop this point further in a forthcoming study on medieval piety, which traces conversion paradigms in several hagiographies of the tenth century.

[65] Morrison, *Understanding Conversion,* p. 41.

[66] Abdelkader I. Tayob, 'Negotiating a Sacred Space in the *Sīrah*: Finding the *Masjid* for the Prophet', in *Literary Heritage of Classical Islam,* ed. by Mustansir Mir (Princeton, 1993), pp. 227–54, quote on p. 236.

people.[67] Peter Brown has recently revised his earlier understanding of the significance of the legends of saints for medieval Christians. Carrying the 'central value system' of the Christian church in their very persons, they exuded a sense of the possibility of the realization of the image of God in man that could bring Christ into the present.[68] 'To demonstrate the holiness of a person writers had to establish that the putative saint's life conformed in exact and literal detail to the rule of scripture'.[69] Like the Christians, most Muslims of the Iranian lands were only reading the religious texts for the first time in the ninth century, after the majority had already 'converted'. Again, like the compilers of Muhammad's traditions, Sufi saints appeared to explain the meaning of the Koran, and to avail the mission of Muhammad. Again, the stories are typically not linear, the piety of our shaykh, like Muhammad, never develops, he never becomes. From his birth, and even prior to it, he is marked by distinction, and selected by God. His personality and character do not evolve, and thus anecdotes of his life do not need to adhere to a temporal order.[70] The anecdotes reflect the struggle of Muhammad to build a community, strengthen the faith, and to live the righteous life. The Koran, like the shaykh's *vita*, calls for a renewal of a bygone Abrahamic monotheism, a redirection to the straight path. These are the poetics of conversion in the medieval Islamic period.

---

[67] *Firdaws al-murshidiyya fī asrār al-ṣamadiyya,* pp. 191–92.

[68] Peter Brown, 'The Saint as Exemplar in Late Antiquity', *Representations,* 1.2 (1983), 1–20.

[69] Morrison, *Understanding Conversion.* p. 41.

[70] For medieval spirituality and the reversibility of biographical time, see M. M. Bakhtin, *The Dialogic Imagination,* trans. by Caryl Emerson and Michael Holquist, ed. by Michael Holquist (Austin, 1981), pp. 132–43.

To Baptize Khans or to Convert Peoples?
Missionary Aims in Central Asia
in the Fourteenth Century

JAMES D. RYAN

T he conversion of unbelievers, bringing new peoples to the Christian faith, was highly esteemed in medieval Europe. Christ commanded his followers: 'Go, therefore, and make all nations your disciples: baptize them in the name of the Father and of the Son and of the Holy Spirit' (Matthew, 28. 19), and some in every medieval epoch left family and friends to become missionaries in uncertain, frequently dangerous circumstances. Those left behind praised them, extolling their zeal to save souls otherwise condemned, and missionaries frequently became great saints, venerated by descendants of those they had baptized. Europe's early missionaries were usually restless monks or courageous bishops, working as individuals or in small groups. They were often supported by expansionist lords, and sometimes worked in the wake of armed conquest, but only rarely was the bishop of Rome involved in despatching missionaries to heathen lands.[1] Another set of circumstances prevailed in the revival of missionary zeal in the thirteenth and fourteenth centuries. The later mission was far more organized, and many modern commentators see it as centrally directed, if not inspired, by the papacy.[2] This paper, which focuses on the mission to Asia, will demonstrate that there is ample reason to question that interpretation.

---

[1] For an overview of medieval mission activity, see K. S. Latourette, *The Thousand Years of Uncertainty*, II: *A History of the Expansion of Christianity* (New York, 1938).

[2] Such diverse authors as J. Richard, *La Papauté et les missions d'Orient au moyen age (XIIIe–XVe siècles)* (Rome, 1977); I. de Rachewiltz, *Papal Envoys to the Great Khans* (Stanford, 1971); and G. Soranzo, *Il Papato, l'Europa Christiana e i Tartari* (Milan, 1930), credit the papacy with a central role.

The papacy seems to have had central importance because mission history in the High Middle Ages is documented primarily by papal letters accrediting envoys, empowering missionaries, thanking rulers for their support, or urging conversion on those rulers and their subjects. Such documents give a strong impression of papal direction and control. That notwithstanding, close examination of papal documents in the context of mission activity in Asia argues that the papacy played a marginal role as that effort evolved. The Asian mission was inspired chiefly by the ardent commitment of Dominican and Franciscan friars who ventured forth to baptize unbelievers and, in some cases, by their desire to win heaven through death at the hands of those they strove to convert.

The mission of the High Middle Ages developed as the thirteenth century dawned. Major factors in this development were the rise of the mendicant religious orders, millenarian expectations which influenced the friars and which they helped excite, and novel opportunities for mission activity created by the rise of the Mongol empire. Papal support should not be included as a major stimulus for the revival of mission enthusiasm because, although the papacy was involved, it was neither initiator nor director. Rather, various popes played supporting roles by incorporating missionary activity into the evolving structure of the Roman Church. The limited nature of papal involvement will be seen in a brief review of the parts played by the mendicant orders, millenarian expectations, and the arrival of the Mongols in the unfolding of the Asian mission.

The mendicant orders were chiefly responsible for creating the new mission effort, and when papal attention was drawn to the mission, the mendicants became both generals and foot soldiers in campaigns of evangelization.[3] The Franciscans and Dominicans became involved in mission work because of their own sense of purpose, not on papal orders. The beginning of the Franciscan mission illustrates this. Francis saw himself as a missionary, and made mission activity an important part of Franciscan *religio*.[4] It was he who sent the protomartyrs, Berard of Carbio and his companions, to preach the gospel in the Iberian Peninsula in 1219.[5] After their arrest in Seville, when

---

[3] The most recent work on Asian missionaries is F. Schmieder, *Europa und die Fremden: Die Mongolen im Urteil des Abendlandes vom 13. bis in das 15. Jahrhundert* (Sigmaringen, 1994). See also N. Simonut, *Il Metodo d'Evangelizzazione dei Francescani tra Musulmani e Mongoli nei secoli XIII–XIV* (Milan, 1947); R. E. Daniel, *The Franciscan Concept of Mission in the High Middle Ages* (Lexington, 1975); L. von Auw, *Anglo Clareno et les Spirituels italiens* (Rome, 1979); B. Altaner, *Die Dominikanermissionen des 13. Jahrhunderts* (Habelschwerdt, 1924); and R. Loenertz, *La Société des frères pérégrinants: Étude sur l'Orient dominicain* (Rome, 1937).

[4] Francis himself attempted three missions to the Muslim world, and in 1219 he made his way to the court of the Egyptian Sultan al-Kamil; J. Moorman, *A History of the Franciscan Order from its Origins to the Year 1517* (Oxford, 1968), pp. 24–25, 48–49.

[5] Berard was accompanied by Peter, Odo, Accursio, and Adjutus. *Butler's Lives of the Saints*, ed. by H. Thurston and D. Atwater, 4 vols (New York, 1956), I, 103.

they attempted to preach in its main mosque, they were sent to Morocco for judgment because they constantly and loudly harangued their jailers about 'the wicked Muhammad and his damnable law'.[6] The sultan became infuriated because they were impertinent and refused to return to Europe, and he personally split open their heads on 16 January 1220. Their bizarre courtship of martyrdom in a vain attempt to make converts made them heroes to their confreres.[7] Longing for martyrdom remained a recurring theme in Franciscan missionary activities through the fifteenth century.[8]

Major papal involvement in the burgeoning mission effort did not come until fifteen years after the Franciscan protomartyrdoms, and after many friars had ventured far afield in search for converts. In 1235 Gregory IX (1227–41) issued *Cum hora undecima*, a mission Bull addressed to friars in and on their way to mission fields in western Asia.[9] When Innocent IV reissued this Bull in 1245, the list of mission lands included in its salutation indicated how far afield missionaries had already gone.[10] The Bull's opening lines also testify to the importance of millenarian expectations in the mission. 'Since the eleventh hour has come in the day given to mankind [. . .] spiritual men [. . .] must go forth again [. . .] to all peoples of every tongue and every kingdom to prophesy because [. . .] the remnant of Israel will not be saved until [. . .] the fullness of peoples first enter' the kingdom of heaven.[11] This echo of Joachim of Fiore's apocalyptic prophecy struck a particularly responsive chord with Franciscan missionaries.[12] Because they were preparing for the final days, the threat of martyrdom was

---

[6] From their cells they proclaimed 'multa turpia de Mahumeto & eius damnabili lege'; *Acta sanctorum*, January 16.

[7] Francis, learning of their martyrdom, exclaimed 'Now I can truly say I have five brothers'. *Analecta Franciscana*, III: *Chronica XXIV Generalium Ordinis Minorum* (Quaracchi, 1897), p. 593.

[8] Daniel, in his *Concept of Mission*, calls the desire to achieve martyrdom 'a central motivation' which 'compel[led] [. . .] them to go to Spain, North Africa and the Middle East to convert Muslims' (p. 41).

[9] Pontifica Commissio ad redigendum Codicem Iuris Canonici Orientalis, *Fontes*, ser. 3, [hereafter *Fontes*], III: *Acta Honorii III (1216–27) et Gregorii IX (1227–41)*, ed. by A. Tautu (Vatican City, 1950), p. 286, addressed to William of Monteferrato, OP, and his companions. It empowered them to preach, baptize, reunite churches, absolve excommunicates, dispense from irregularities, reconcile schismatics, and bless sacred vestments.

[10] *Fontes*, IV, t. 1: *Acta Innocenti PP IV (1243–54)*, ed. M. Wojnar (Rome, 1962), p. 36. A veritable gazetteer of actual and proposed mission fields, it listed twenty regions (such as 'terras Saracenorum, [. . .] Bulgarorum, Cumanorum, Ethyoporum, [. . .] Alanorum, Gazarorum, [. . .] Zicorum, [. . .] Nubianorum, [and] Nestorinorum'), and was enlarged when periodically reissued.

[11] *Fontes*, III, 286.

[12] See M. Reeves, *The Influence of Prophesy in the Late Middle Ages: A Study in Joachimism* (Oxford, 1969); and M. Reeves and B. Hirsch-Reich, *The Figura of Joachim of Fiore* (Oxford, 1969). For Joachim's influence on early Franciscans, see Daniel, *Concept of Mission*,

not a deterrent, but an encouragement, and the most dedicated among them did not shrink from attempting the patently impossible.

The continuous reissuing of mission Bulls creates a false impression of papal direction of missionary work. Bulls such as *Cum hora undecima* were certainly important because they incorporated mission work into the framework of emerging canon law and invested missionaries with the spiritual tools to carry out their work.[13] *Cum hora undecima* became, however, little more than a formulaic restatement of powers conferred as it was reissued by successive popes.[14] It and complimentary Bulls conferring faculties on missionaries were surely important to the friars, because such letters armed them, as they entered new territories, with extraordinary spiritual powers, some withheld even from bishops in Europe.[15] Beyond that the papacy did little for the new mission, however. Rather, by endorsing the mission and grafting it to the structure of the Roman Church, the papacy enhanced its own claim to worldwide authority. Thus, by the middle of the thirteenth century, mendicant activism, with papal blessings, had created a framework for the new mission, and by the early fourteenth century Franciscan and Dominican friars had reached the ends of the Asian world in their quest for converts.

The way was opened to them by the Mongols, who played a complex role in mission history. When the Mongols appeared on Europe's threshold, early in the thirteenth century, they were conquerors spreading devastation and terror.[16] To assess the threat they posed, Pope Innocent IV (1243–54) sent several ambassadors to the Mongols.[17] The best known of these, John of Plano Carpini, OFM, who travelled to the

---

pp. 20–22; and D. Burr, *Olivi and Franciscan Poverty: The Origins of the Usus Pauper Controversy* (Philadelphia, 1989).

[13] J. Muldoon, *Popes, Lawyers and Infidels* (Philadelphia, 1979), pp. 36–38, analyses *Cum hora undecima* in the context of canon law.

[14] For various editions of *Cum hora undecima*, with only minor changes, see *Fontes*, IV, t. 2: *Acta Alexandri PP IV (1254–61)*, ed. by T. Haluscynskj and M. Wojnar (Rome, 1966), p. 73; *Fontes*, V, t. 1: *Acta Urbani IV, Clementia IV, Gregorii X (1261–76)*, ed. by A. Tautu (Rome, 1953), pp. 26–28; *Fontes*, V, t. 2: *Acta Romanorum Pontificum ab Innocentio V ad Benedictum XI (1276–1304)*, ed. by F. Delorme and A. Tautu (Rome, 1954), pp. 142–44, 184–85, and 252–55.

[15] One such letter, *In apostolicae servitutis* (*Fontes*, V, 2, 134), from Nicholas IV to Franciscans in Tartar lands in 1288, gave authority to absolve those who laid violent hands on clerics, to dispense clerics from irregularities, and to reconcile heretics and schismatics.

[16] For Mongol history (with an excellent bibliographical study) see D. Morgan, *The Mongols* (London, 1986). For perceptions of the Mongols and their assaults on Europe, see J. Chambers, *The Devil's Horsemen: The Mongol Invasion of Europe* (London, 1979). Mongols overran both Poland and Hungary, and were about to attack Vienna in 1242 when Khan Ögödei's death caused them to abruptly withdraw.

[17] For Western contact with the Mongols, see Richard, *Papauté*; de Rachewiltz, *Papal*

camp of Khan Güyük (1246–48), returned with haughty letters demanding submission and tribute.[18] Even at this point mendicants were headed east to preach in Mongol territory, whether they were welcome or not. One of these, William of Rubruck, entered Asia as a missionary in 1253, but after almost two years concluded that it was 'inadvisable for any friar to make any further journeys to the Tartars', in large part because the Khan refused him permission to function as a missionary.[19]

In the next decade, however, the Mongols changed their attitude. After Hülegü (d. 1265) subdued Persia and Mesopotamia, his newly established Ilkhanate opened diplomatic contact with the pope and Western kings, and gave Western missionaries extensive privileges.[20] Even the khans of Kipchak, the Golden Horde, routinely gave or renewed *yarliqs*, grants of privilege, to missionaries. Möngke Temür (1267–80), for example, exempted 'Latin priests [. . .] called brothers' from military service and all taxes, and took their churches under his protection.[21] Qubilai Khan (1260–94) went further, inviting the papacy to send wise men and missionaries into China.[22] His requests

---

Envoys; Soranzo, *Il Papato*; J. Bentley, *Old World Encounters* (New York and Oxford, 1993), pp. 155–64; and J. R. S. Phillips, *The Medieval Expansion of Europe* (Oxford, 1988), pp. 57–140. For source collections, see *Sinica Franciscana*, ed. by A. Van den Wyngaert, I: *Itinera et relationes fratrum Minorum saeculi XIII et XIV* (Quaracchi, 1929) [hereafter *Sinica Fran.*]; *Biblioteca Bio-Bibliografica della Terra Santa e dell'Oriente francescano*, 4 vols, ed. by G. Golubovich (Quaracchi, 1906–29) [hereafter *BTS*]; C. Dawson, *Mission to Asia* (Toronto, 1980) (first published as *The Mongol Mission* (London, 1955)); and *Cathay and the Way Thither*, ed. by H. Yule and H. Cordlier, 2nd edn, 4 vols (London, 1913–16).

[18] Dawson, *Mission to Asia*, pp. 73–76, 85–86, gives the papal letters Plano Carpini carried to the Tartars, and Güyük's response.

[19] *The Mission of Friar William of Rubruck*, trans. by P. Jackson, with introduction and notes by P. Jackson and D. Morgan, Hakluyt Society, ser. 2, no. 173 (London, 1990), p. 278. J. D. Ryan, 'Conversion vs. Baptism? European Missionaries in Asia in the Thirteenth and Fourteenth Centuries', in *Varieties of Religious Conversion in the Middle Ages*, ed. by J. Muldoon (Gainsville, 1997), pp. 146–67, focuses on Rubruck's missionary activities.

[20] After the Mamluks defeated Hülegü's forces at 'Ayn Jalut, Syria (1260), he sought an alliance with Western crusaders against Egypt. Successive Ilkhans despatched at least eight embassies west between 1263 and 1291. See R. Grousset, *The Empire of the Steppes*, trans. by N. Walford (New Brunswick, NJ, 1970), pp. 353–71, 397–98; de Rachewiltz, *Papal Envoys*, pp. 150–59; K. M. Setton, *The Papacy and the Levant, 1204–1571* (Philadelphia, 1976), I, 112–18.

[21] This *yarliq* is preserved in a Latin translation of its 1314 reissue by Özbeg, a convert to Islam. M. Bihl and A. C. Moule, *Tria nova documenta de missionibus F M Tartariae Aquilonaris*, in *Archivum Franciscanum Historicum* (1924), XVII, 55–71, 65.

[22] According to Marco Polo, Qubilai requested 'a hundred men of learning, thoroughly acquainted with the principles of the Christian religion, [and] [. . .] the seven arts' in the late 1260s. *The Travels of Marco Polo*, ed. by M. Komroff (New York, 1926), p. 9 (revised from Marsden's translation).

were ultimately answered in 1294, when John of Montecorvino presented letters from Nicholas IV (1288–92) to Timür Öljeitü (1294–1307), Qubilai's successor.[23] By the last decade of the thirteenth century, Western missionaries were at work in all parts of the Mongol empire except Chaghatai Khanate, in Central Asia, where protracted civil wars and weak khans made the situation too dangerous for mission travellers. This rapid expansion of the mission in Asia was possible only because of Mongol support.

Although the opening up of the Mongol world presented unprecedented opportunities for evangelization, surviving records demonstrate only intermittent, reactive papal involvement. In the thirteenth century, with the exception of the embassies sent by Innocent IV, popes despatched friars to Asia only in response to the arrival of political emissaries from the East.[24] Similarly, fourteenth-century popes usually involved themselves in the mission only after wandering mendicants arrived at Avignon to report their exploits. When the mission and its needs were forcefully brought to their attention, the popes created a hierarchical framework for the mission in Asia. For example, news of Montecorvino's successes in China—thousands baptized, the construction of churches in Khan-baliq, and the conversion of an important Tartar vassal—reached Avignon in 1307.[25] Clement V (1305–14) immediately caused seven Franciscans to be consecrated as bishops to carry a pallium to Montecorvino and anoint him archbishop of the newly created see of Khan-baliq (modern Beijing), with authority to oversee and organize a hierarchy for the entire Tartar empire.[26] Clement thereby laid the foundation for a new mission strategy for Asia, upon which subsequent popes built during the following decades.[27] There was no systematic follow-up, however, and when John XXII (1316–34) created an additional archbishopric at Sultaniyya in 1318, it was a similarly ad hoc reaction to newly received reports from the East.[28] Wherever we have

---

[23] The pope's 1289 letter to 'cobla Chan' begins, 'Shortly after [. . .] our promotion we received [. . .] messengers [. . .] [who] earnestly begged [. . .] that we should send some Latin monks to your court'. A. C. Moule, *Christians in China before the Year 1500* (New York, 1926), pp. 168–69.

[24] de Rachewiltz, *Papal Envoys,* amply illustrates the reactive nature of papal embassies.

[25] Montecorvino's two letters from China (1305 and 1306) reported successes and begged for reinforcements. See *Sinica Fran.*, pp. 340–55; and Dawson, *Mission to Asia*, pp. 224–31. Thomas of Tolentino, OFM, carried these to Clement V's court, where he 'rehearsed in a wonderful speech before the lord Pope and the Cardinals [. . .] these wonderful works of our God so well begun'. Moule, *Christians in China*, p. 182.

[26] For documents attesting Clement's steps, see Moule, *Christians in China*, pp. 182–89.

[27] Richard, *Papauté*, pp. 123–24 and 144 ff., analyses the consequences of this transplantation of a Roman hierarchy into Asia. See also G. Fedalto, *La chiesa latina in Oriente* (Verona, 1973), I, 375–500.

[28] William Adam, OP, a missionary in Asia between 1312 and 1317, arrived at Avignon and told of Christian communities east of Muslim territory that might be enlisted in a crusade against the Mamluks. John XXII expressed fascination with this concept in the Bull *Redemptor noster*

documentation, a comparable story underlies the creation of other new sees, such as those erected in Central Asia and India in 1329 and 1330.[29] The papal court evidenced interest in Asia when mission travellers or ambassadors arrived from there, but the missions continued to grow, without ongoing papal oversight, through the efforts and enthusiasm of the friars. By 1330 an anonymous compiler could list forty mendicant convents in eastern lands: in Kipchak, Georgia, greater Armenia, Persia, Mesopotamia, and China.[30]

Part of that growth lay in Chaghatai Khanate, in Central Asia, which, because of its turbulent history, became a mission venue later than other khanates, and had fewer mission outposts. Partly for these reasons, surviving records concerning Mongol politics and the mission are extremely sketchy. Because papal documents are sometimes our only source of knowledge, even for Chaghatai's dynastic history, it is easy to over-emphasize the role of the popes. Nevertheless, a few unique documents survive, which, in conjunction with papal registers, provide vivid snapshots of mission activity in Chaghatai, and illuminate stratagems employed by missionaries trying to make converts in Central Asia.

Chaghatai Khanate, straddling the Silk Road, included all the territory between the western reaches of the Mongolian desert and the Amu Dar'ya River, a vast area Chingiz Khan had conquered in the second decade of the thirteenth century and bestowed upon his son, Chaghatai.[31] The great Central Asian trading centers of Bukhara, Samarqand, and Tashkent lay in its western regions, but Chaghatai and most of his successors avoided the urban areas and followed the traditional life of pastoral nomads. As a consequence, the khanate lacked formal political structure and had no real capital. Almalyq, a way station on the silk route near modern Yining, in Xinjiang, served as a rallying point for nomadic warriors who ruled Chaghatai. Over time, however, political and military power gravitated to the more densely populated areas in the west. *Ulus* Chaghatai evolved into a loose confederation of Turks, Uighurs, Qara-Khitais, Persians, and others under the leadership of a Mongol minority.[32]

---

which established the new archbishopric. Richard, *Papauté*, pp. 169–72; and R. Loenertz, *Société des frères pérégrinants,* pp. 137–41.

[29] John XXII erected an episcopal see for Quilon, India (*Columbum*), in 1329, after Jordan Catalan arrived at Avignon from extended Asia travels. See J. D. Ryan, 'European Travelers Before Columbus—the Fourteenth Century's Discovery of India', in *Catholic Historical Review,* 79.4 (October, 1993), 648–70, 660–61.

[30] *De locis Fratrum Minorum et Predicatorum in Tartaria, BTS,* II, 72, compiled about 1330.

[31] J. A. Boyle, 'Caghatay Khanate', *The Encyclopaedia of Islam,* new edn (Leiden, 1965), II, 3–4, summarizes the khanate's history.

[32] L. Kwanten, *Imperial Nomads: A History of Central Asia, 500–1500* (Philadelphia, 1979), pp. 249–50.

Chaghatai's descendants, like other Mongol khans, followed the *yasa*, Chingiz's law, and were generally tolerant of all religions.[33] Toleration allowed native, Nestorian Christians, who had suffered under Islamic domination, to become important again in Central Asia, and when European missionaries arrived in the fourteenth century they also enjoyed protection from Mongol rulers. Nevertheless, missionaries in Chaghatai worked in a dangerous, politically unstable environment. Central Asia was embroiled in civil wars from the election of Qubilai in 1260 until Du'a Khan (1282–1306) restored order and re-established peaceful relations with the other Mongol khans.[34] By that time, however, Chaghatai Khanate was being pulled apart by religious and ethnic differences, and Mongol custom worked against khans trying to create political stability. A khan's authority was seldom questioned in war, but in peace his powers were circumscribed, and by acting too independently he became a candidate for assassination by a potential rival.[35] In addition, the khanate usually passed to a senior male in the direct line, not just to an eldest son. This created many possible candidates for the khanate whenever Chaghatai's chief leaders, the emirs, became disgruntled. As it turned out, Du'a was succeeded by six of his sons between 1306 and 1334.

Despite this uncertainty, mission work was undertaken there, and two episcopal sees were created. One, at Almalyq, Chaghatai's traditional capital, was established sometime before 1328, but nothing is known concerning its foundation.[36] The second, at Samarqand, in western Chaghatai, was founded after Eljigidai, a son of Du'a who reigned briefly in 1326, sent two Dominican missionaries as envoys to Avignon. When they reported that the khan had been baptized, had given Dominicans licence to preach, and was building a church at Samarqand, John XXII enthusiastically created a bishopric for that city in 1329.[37] Long before its new bishop, Thomas of Mancasole de Plaisance, one of the khan's envoys, returned with papal greetings and gifts, the situation had changed dramatically. Eljigidai's reign had ended before his messenger reached Avignon. His brother, Tarmashirin (1326–34), embraced Islam after his accession,

---

[33] No copy of the *yasa* survives, but its contents are reported in Persian and Arabic sources. According to Gregorius Bar Hebraeus, it mandated that 'the pure, the innocent, the just, the learned and the wise of every people shall be respected and honored'. *Chronicon Syriacum*, ed. by P. Bedjan (Paris, 1890), pp. 411–12.

[34] A 1260–64 struggle between Qubilai and his brother, Ariq-böke, was largely fought in Chaghatai. After this Qaidu, a scion of the house of Ögedei, succeeded in dominating most of Central Asia and until his death in 1303 made war on Qubilai and his successors. Morgan, *Mongols*, pp. 117–19.

[35] Morgan, *Mongols*, pp. 39–40.

[36] A Carlino of '*Grassis*', bishop of Almalyq, died in Europe in 1328, perhaps when forced to flee his see. *BTS*, III, 343.

[37] John XXII's 1329 letter to Eljigidai, 'emperor of the Tartars in Khorassan, Turkestan and Hindoustan', accrediting Mancasole, recapitulated his report. See T. Ripoll and A. Bremond, *Bullarium Ordinis Fratrum Praedicatorum* [Rome, 1729], I, 187.

taking the name 'Ala al-Din, and ushered in a period of persecution for Christians and Jews. No word survives of Mancasole after 1330, or of the fate of the Dominican mission in Samarqand.

Rather more is known concerning the bishopric of Almalyq. In 1334 'Ala al-Din was displaced by a grandson of Du'a, Buzan, whose support came from the region of Almalyq, in eastern Chaghatai Khanate. In a reign that lasted only a few months, he forced Muslim emirs in Bukhara and Samarqand to give him homage, restored toleration, and authorized Christians and Jews to rebuild their houses of worship. His successor, Cangshi (1334–37), perhaps because he favored Christians too much, was not strong enough to bring Muslim emirs to heel, and withdrew to Almalyq. There he welcomed Nicholas, a friar appointed as archbishop of Khan-baliq, on his way to Cathay.[38] Cangshi encouraged Nicholas to stay long enough to strengthen the mission at Almalyq, and it appears that Nicholas installed another Franciscan, Richard of Burgundy, as its new bishop.[39] We know he enlarged the Franciscan establishment there from a letter of Benedict XII, thanking ministers of Cangshi's court for having donated land for a convent and Cangshi himself for giving Nicholas permission 'to construct and repair churches, as well as to preach freely'.[40] Unfortunately, although we have no word of Nicholas after he left Almalyq, it is clear that he never reached the Yüan court at Beijing.

Additional information concerning Almalyq is provided by Pascal of Victoria, who sent a letter west from there in 1338.[41] Pascal had entered the Mongol world in 1334, first spending a year in Kipchak (at Sarai) where he studied Turkic. He left there, accompanied by a native servant, and travelled with Armenian and Muslim merchants into Central Asia. When they arrived at Urgench, on the border of Chaghatai, rumours of disorder stopped caravan traffic and stranded Pascal in the Muslim quarter. These circumstances allowed him to spend twenty-five days preaching before the mosque on the 'cheats, falsehoods, and blunders' of Muhammad, whom he dubbed 'false prophet'.[42] Disorder notwithstanding, because he enjoyed licence to preach, he was

---

[38] In 1333 John XXII designated Nicholas to replace Montecorvino (d. c. 1329). Letters recommending him to the Great Khan and various Eastern rulers and peoples were drafted in October and November. *Annales Minorum*, 16 vols (Rome, 1731–36) [hereafter *Ann. Min.*], VII, 138–44; *Fontes*, VII, t. 2: *Acta Ioannis XXII (1317–1334)*, ed. by A. Tautu (Rome, 1952), pp. 255–57.

[39] Richard, *Papauté*, p. 163.

[40] *Laeti rumores Deo*, to 'Chansi' and *Laetanter de vobis*, to nobles at his court, both 1338, were sent after ambassadors from the Yüan court brought news of developments in Central Asia to Avignon. *Ann. Min.*, VII, 212–13. See n. 50, below.

[41] *Sinica Fran.*, I, 501 ff. Yule translates the letter, as printed in *Ann. Min.*, VII, 256–57, in *Cathay*, III, 81–88.

[42] Yule, *Cathay*, III, 86.

merely beaten, and continued on to Almalyq, still three months journey to the east.[43] Through those months, 'constantly alone among the Saracens [he wrote], by word and act and dress, I publicly bore the name of the Lord Jesus Christ'. His conduct was tolerated, and he arrived at Almalyq safely (probably in 1336) to join the convent of friars already there.[44] Pascal's narrative, a rare glimpse into the mind of a fourteenth-century missionary, vividly conveys his missionary zeal. His letter asked Franciscans at home for prayers, and promised he would stay in the East until his death. For Pascal it was a momentous undertaking: 'For [Christ] hath said that when the Gospel shall have been preached throughout the whole world, then shall the end come, and it is for me to preach among divers nations [. . .] to declare the way of salvation'. Pascal anticipated that, for 'the forgiveness of my sins, and that I may safely reach the kingdom of Heaven', he would 'suffer [for Christ's] name'.[45] Friars like Pascal hoped their preaching would result in the conversion of their auditors, but he apparently knew that it was more liable to promote his own translation into paradise, as a martyr. The events of the next year demonstrated that martyrdom was indeed a realistic prospect for missionaries in Central Asia.

According to a *relatio*, composed to commemorate the deaths of Bishop Richard and his companions, the mission at Almalyq flourished with the support of Khan Cangshi.[46] One of the friars, Francis of Alexandria, who removed a cancer from the khan 'more by prayer than by physic', was put in charge of the education of Cangshi's seven-year-old son, whom the friars baptized.[47] After Cangshi was poisoned in 1337, and his four sons killed, political chaos ensued.[48] In the following year the khanate was bestowed on Ali Sultan (1338–39), another convert to Islam, under whom a new wave of persecution began. Ali Sultan 'ordered that all Christians should be made Saracens, and that whoever should disobey [. . .] be put to death'.[49] The convent was sacked and burned, and seven who refused Islam, including Bishop Richard, Pascal, and their companions, were slaughtered.[50]

---

[43] According to Pegolotti, '*Description of Countries and Measures, etc.*', in Yule, *Cathay*, III, 147–48.

[44] Yule, *Cathay*, III, 88; *BTS*, II, 244.

[45] Yule, *Cathay*, III, 88.

[46] Various versions of the martyrs' suffering exist, all apparently based on reports circulated in Franciscan convents after their deaths. For an authoritative text, see *Sinica Fran.*, pp. 510–11.

[47] The martyrs' *passio*. Yule, *Cathay*, III, 32.

[48] Cangshi was deposed by Yesun Temür, who ruled for only a few months in 1337. See P. Pelliot, *Recherches sur les Chrétiens d'Asie centrale et d'Extrême-Orient*, published post-humously by J. Dauviller and L. Hambis (Paris, 1973), pp. 47–48, nn. 1 and 2.

[49] Yule, *Cathay*, III, 32.

[50] These were two priests (Francis and Raymond of Provence), two lay brothers (Lawrence of Alessandria and Peter of Provence), 'and Master John of India, a black man, belonging to the third order of St Francis, who had been converted by our friars'. Yule, *Cathay*, III, 32.

This was not the end of the mission outpost at Almalyq. In the next year Ali Sultan was deposed by Kazan (1339–46), who, one year later, gave warm welcome to a papal embassy led by John of Marignolli, and permitted its members to preach freely at Almalyq.[51] Marignolli reported 'there we made a church, bought a site, made fonts, sang masses and baptized many'.[52] When his party departed for Cathay, they probably left some of their number to man the new installation at Almalyq. Unfortunately, nothing further can be reported concerning the mission in Chaghatai. There is no record of successor bishops for the see of Almalyq, and no firm evidence that Franciscans continued to staff a mission there.[53]

This brief summary of mission history and of the mission in Central Asia in the fourteenth century demonstrates the perils associated with undertaking missionary conversions. What impelled the mendicants, at such great personal risk, to enter lands totally foreign? Clearly, it was not the will of the various popes who, sometimes lukewarmly and often after the fact, blessed their undertakings. Rather, the friars who toiled and died in foreign lands were consumed by a deep passion to convert new peoples to Latin Christianity. Partly because of the support they received from the Mongol khans, the missionaries, and the popes who endorsed their efforts, entertained the hope that Mongol rulers might be converted, and through them the peoples over whom they exercised dominion. The missionaries' ultimate quest, however, was the conversion of those peoples, in fulfillment of apocalyptic prophecies, in the eleventh hour of human history. That same apocalyptic zeal also made them eager to embrace a martyr's death, and thereby convert earthly travail into eternal reward. From this melange of motivations, missionaries found the courage to enter liminal regions inhabited by strange and often frightening peoples to do the work of salvation. These sometimes-contradictory elements must be remembered in any assessment of the writings and deeds of medieval mission travellers, who surely had otherworldly motives for writing the descriptions of their voyages that have captured the interest of modern historians.

---

[51] The mission Marignolli helped lead was sent by Benedict XII after ambassadors of Togon Temür (1333–70) arrived at Avignon to request a bishop be sent to replace Montecorvino. *Fontes, VIII: Acta Benedicti XII (1334–42)*, ed. by A. Tautu (Rome, 1958), pp. 44–48. Marignolli's account of events in Almalyq, *Sinica Fran.*, pp. 527–28, is translated by Moule in his *Christians in China*, p. 254 ff.

[52] Moule, *Christians in China*, p. 255.

[53] Almalyq does occur on later lists of OFM convents in Asia, but several early establishments continued on the rolls, even if defunct. Richard, *Papauté*, p. 164.

Cum hora undecima:
The Incorporation of Asia
into the *orbis Christianus*

FELICITAS SCHMIEDER

'T his country was never reached by any Apostle or a pupil of an Apostle', that
is what the great missionary John of Montecorvino assured in a letter from
Beijing, China, in 1305.[1] Christ had ordered the apostles to go and teach all
nations,[2] to baptize all of the *orbis terrarum*—and John, following that order, demands
the incorporation of the Mongol lands (including China and much of Asia) into the up-
and-coming *orbis Christianus*. Thereby he formulates his perception that in Asia,
unlike, for instance, the Holy Land, no existing church has to be liberated and
reconstructed, but a new one has to be created. But at the same time, according to
Christian tradition, the apostles had indeed reached all nations. John, moreover, is
therefore—though implicitly, thus carefully—suggesting that the Mongols might not
be part of the well-known *orbis terrarum*. The *orbis terrarum* had been regarded as
complete and entirely described in the antique, biblical, and literary tradition until the

---

[1] Johannes von Monte Corvino, *Epistolae,* ed. Sinica Franciscana, I: *Itinera et relationes
Fratrum Minorum saeculi XIII et XIV,* ed. by P. Anastasius van den Wyngaert (Quaracchi, 1929),
book II, chapter 1, p. 347. The present text is a slightly changed version of the paper given at
Leeds 1997; for a broader context see Felicitas Schmieder, *Europa und die Fremden. Die
Mongolen im Urteil des Abendlandes vom 13. bis in das 15. Jahrhundert,* Beiträge zur Geschichte
und Quellenkunde des Mittelalters, 16 (Sigmaringen, 1994). For John and the late-medieval
mission in Asia in general, see Jean Richard, *La papauté et les missions d'orient au Moyen Age
(XIIIᵉ–XVᵉ siècles)* (Rome, 1977).

[2] Matthew 28. 19–20: 'Euntes ergo docete omnes gentes' (cf. Mark 16. 5, Luke 24. 47).

twelfth century. Now, in the beginning of the fourteenth century, the geographical horizon had widened for the Roman Christians who had to find out—among several other facts—that they themselves represented only a small fraction of the people of the world.

To make it worse, time was running out, since Christ's redemptive return to the world would not occur until the last heathen had been baptized or extinguished and the *orbis Christianus* thereby completed.[3] Eschatological necessity as the fundamental and final reason is the starting point in missionary summons commencing with *Cum hora undecima* (since it is the eleventh hour) by which the popes in the middle of the thirteenth century intended to promote wide-ranging missionary activities, enumerating long lists of heathen peoples about whom not much more than their names was yet known.[4]

The framework of mission, the legal grounds for such papal summons, was the popes' fully developed claim for true world domination. Following the general doctrine of canon law in the thirteenth century, the pope, Christ's vicar on earth, possesses jurisdiction and power over all humans, by law, even if not in reality (*de iure licet non de facto*). Consequently, he also claims the right and the duty to oversee the unbelievers' countries.[5] They may rule legally and also hold Christian subjects. But as soon as

---

[3] Matthew 24. 14: 'et predicabitur hoc evangelium regni in universo orbe in testimonium omnium gentibus et tunc veniet consummatio'.

[4] Those Bulls stressing the eschatological aspect were started by Pope Gregory IX. Interestingly, Pope Innocent IV did not include the Mongols in his Bull from the year 1245, when he first sent missionaries directly to the Mongols (*Bullarium Franciscanum*, ed. by Johannes Hyacinthus Sbaralea and cont. by Conrad Eubel, 7 vols (Rome, 1759–1904), I, no. 80, pp. 360–61), but only in 1253 (*Vetera monumenta historica Hungariam sacram illustrantia*, ed. by Augustin Theiner (Rome, 1859), I, no. 425, pp. 223–24). They then appeared in all *Cum-hora* Bulls of the thirteenth century, but disappeared permanently in 1307, the year when Pope Clement V started to organize a Mongol Catholic Church, cf. below (23.7; *Bullarium Franciscanum*, V, no. 84, pp. 35–37). For the Bulls, see James Muldoon, *Popes, Lawyers, and Infidels* (Philadelphia, 1979), pp. 36 ff.; esp. on their legal form, see Athanasius Matanic, 'Bulla missionaria "Cum hora undecima" eiusque juridicum "Directorium apparatus"', in *Archivum Franciscanum Historicum*, 50 (1957), 364–78.

[5] See Innocentius IV, *Apparatus in V libros decretalium* (Frankfurt, 1570), ad X.3.34.8, *verbo compensato*, 3–4; different and even opposite in many regards is his pupil Hostiensis, *Commentaria in libros decretalium* (Venice, 1581), *pro defensione* fol. 128vb, no. 27; cf. Schmieder, *Europa und die Fremden*, pp. 74–77. For some parallel and later developments on the field of the 'ius gentium', see Muldoon, *Popes, Lawyers, and Infidels*, and, for example, Felicitas Schmieder, 'Enemy, Obstacle, Ally? The Greek in Western Crusade Proposals (1274–1311)', in *The Man of Many Devices, Who Wandered Full Many Ways . . . Festschrift in Honor of János M. Bak*, ed. by Balázs Nagy and Marcell Sebök (Budapest, 1999), pp. 357–71; Paulus Vladimiri, *Opinio Hostiensis*, in *Paulus Vladimiri and his Doctrine Concerning International*

they suppress them or any Christian missionary activity in their countries, they lose their rights—and the pope has to intervene because of his duty to take care of all humans, especially all Christians. Like the general Christian duty to baptize all peoples, which had grown out of the same roots, this again made the whole *orbis terrarum* a virtual *orbis Christianus*.

Contemporary political interests supported the idea of mission: heavy military setbacks in the Holy Land had demonstrated the West's inability to easily defeat the Muslims, a people classified as too stubborn to be baptized. Allies were therefore needed against them. Those allies had to be Christians in order to conclude a reliable agreement, since mutual oaths could only then be trusted.[6]

Symptomatically for this political and legal, material and mental situation in thirteenth-century Latin Europe, the earliest indications of the movements of peoples in Asia (which reached European ears in the 1220s) were received positively, without fear. One reason for this uncommon expectation that a foreigner was no enemy but a friend was the presumed knowledge of the totality of the *orbis terrarum*: medieval Europeans expected potential intruders, good or bad, to belong to a limited pool of well-known peoples. They urgently needed help against the Muslims and, consequently, wished the approaching tribes to be good: Prester John, the legendary Christian king from India, was coming to attack the Muslims from behind in support of Roman Christianity and the Holy Land.

Then the Mongols, called Tartars by the Europeans, started to kill Christians. In 1241 they overran the eastern parts of Europe and at the same time threatened the remainder of the crusader states in the Holy Land. The image and chosen patterns of explanation were changed entirely, and fear became predominant: Gog and Magog, the peoples of the Antichrist, now were thought to have emerged from the four corners of Earth to bring the world to its end.[7]

Law and Politics, ed. by Stanislaus F. Belch, 2 vols (London, 1965), II, 845–84; cf. F. H. Russell, 'Paulus Vladimiri's Attack on the Just War: A Case Study in Legal Polemics', in *Authority and Power. Studies on Medieval Law and Government,* ed. by Brian Tierney and Peter Lineham (Cambridge, 1980), pp. 237–54; James Muldoon, 'Papal Responsibility for the Infidels: Another Look at Alexander's VI. *Inter Caetera*', *Catholic Historical Review,* 64 (1978), 168–84; Kenneth J. Pennington, 'Bartholome de Las Casas and the Tradition of Medieval Law', *Church History,* 39 (1970), 149–61.

[6] 'It is certain that unbelievers lacking the true faith (*fides*) cannot be tied by the bond of trust (*fides*). Neither do they admit any authority to our oaths of allegiance, nor is a Christian able to trust (*fides*) undoubtedly in heathen oaths': this principle was formulated in a letter by Pope Alexander IV and sent to King Béla IV of Hungary, who intended to marry a son or daughter to a Mongol prince's daughter or son (and so conclude a treaty). *Vetera monumenta historica Hungariam,* ed. by Theiner, I, no. 454, here p. 240.

[7] Apocalypse 20; for the historical context, see Gian Andri Bezzola, *Die Mongolen in abendländischer Sicht (1220–70). Ein Beitrag zur Frage der Völkerbegegnung* (Bern, 1974);

But no explanation was ultimately convincing, and hope was inextinguishable. In 1245, Pope Innocent IV, an important protagonist of the idea of papal world domination, took the initiative, fully aware of his universal position. He sent out explorers to learn more about the invaders. The envoys were no high ranking diplomats, but missionary monks of the new mendicant orders, who were, as the pope himself explained to the Tartar khan, the most likely to benefit the Tartars, which is to say, to convert them.[8]

Not only did the first missionaries fail, but the diplomatic embassies were even received as offers of submission by the Mongols, who had their own claim for world domination. This was entirely unacceptable to the Europeans, so diplomatic contacts were broken off for the moment. Even so, in spite of all set-backs, the following years saw missionary efforts responding to every hint of the Mongols' readiness to be converted. In 1253, they were included in the *Cum-hora* Bulls.[9]

But the Christian need for help against the enemies of the cross remained too urgent. While the Latin Christians in Eastern Europe, constantly victims of Mongol onslaughts, were and remained convinced that only a crusade against the Mongols would do any good, in the Near East things changed at the very moment that the Mongols themselves were looking for allies. In 1260, they were heavily defeated by the Mamluks. So, from 1262 onwards, the Persian Il-khans repeatedly turned to the Western

---

Schmieder, *Europa und die Fremden.* On Prester, see several works by John C. F. Beckingham, including *Between Islam and Christendom* (London, 1983), and many others.

[8] These ideas are especially stressed by the pope's letter to the Mongols carried by John of Plano Carpini OFM, who between 1245–47 reached Mongolia via Russia. See his report, the *Ystoria Mongalorum,* ed. by Paolo Daffinà et al., in *Storia dei Mongoli* (Spoleto, 1989), comm. and trans. in Johannes von Plano Carpini, *Kunde von den Mongolen, (1245–1247),* ed., trans., and comm. by Felicitas Schmieder (Sigmaringen, 1997); for a critical edition of this and all other papal letters to the Mongols, see Karl Ernst Lupprian, *Die Beziehungen der Päpste zu islamischen und mongolischen Herrschern im 13. Jahrhundert anhand ihres Briefwechsels* (Città del Vaticano, 1981), 1245, no. 21 (cf. no. 20 for Laurent of Portugal who did not certainly travel). The report by Simon de Saint-Quentin OP, companion of Ascelin OP to the Mongols via the Near East (1245–48) has only survived in extracts in the Dominican encyclopedist Vincent of Beauvais's *Speculum historiale* (Douai, 1624); see also Simon de St-Quentin, *Histoire des Tartares,* ed. by Jean Richard (Paris, 1965).

[9] For letters in response, see Lupprian, *Die Beziehungen der Päpste,* no. 32 ss. For the *Cum-hora* Bull of 1253, see n. 4. When (in the same year 1253) the Flemish Franciscan William of Rubruck responded to a rumour about a Mongol prince's baptism, he did not travel as envoy in spite of massive disadvantages; nevertheless, he had to accept and bring back an order of submission (Eric Voegelin, 'The Mongol Orders of Submission to European Powers, 1245–55', *Byzantion,* 15 (1940–41), 378–413). A very lively report can be found in *Itinerarium: The Mission of Friar William of Rubruck. His Journey to the Court of the Great Khan Möngke 1253–1255,* trans. and notes by Peter Jackson and David Morgan (London, 1990).

powers. Oriental Christians and Latin Christians well acquainted with the Orient preferred Mongol to Muslim rule for several reasons, and initiated massive propaganda for an alliance between Mongols and European crusaders. They tried to smooth away the main obstacle from the Western point of view, the above-mentioned need for a baptized ally. When joint actions were finally planned, the Europeans, for one reason or another, were persuaded to negotiate with a Christian khan.[10]

Also brought into play for this purpose were contemporary eschatological writings, texts dealing with the above-mentioned ultimate meaning of all missionary activity, with the coming of the Antichrist, the Final Judgement, and Christ's return to Earth. As these questions were crucial, eschatological prophecies were highly political, intending and actually achieving influence. Prophecies were a proper medium of propaganda; although rooted in real events, they also articulated and shaped a hoped-for future, and so reflected current fears and hopes.

Around 1260—the year which the great twelfth-century prophet Joachim of Fiore had identified as the crucial beginning of a new era—new Oriental prophecies were imported to the West. Supposedly written long before Christ's birth, the so-called Book Sidrac (*Fontaine des toutes siences*) thus seems to prophesy all history:[11] including the emergence of Islam and the crusades and the appearance of the wild Tartars, who will gain the entire East from the Saracens and kill their head, the Caliph (which indeed happened when Bagdad was conquered in 1258). From then on the narration turns to the hoped-for future: a final Latin crusade would destroy weakened Islam; the Christians would baptize all surviving peoples and would also defeat the Tartars, whose last survivors would eventually become friends with the Christians. All over the world, there would be peace under Latin rule until the final emergence of the Antichrist.

Faithful to real historical development, the Tartars are described as non-believing enemies with some apocalyptic overtones. Nevertheless, they fight the Muslims and so assist the Latins in liberating the Holy Land, which is exactly the constellation the Oriental Christians wished to be used by the West. By using prophecy they emphasised

---

[10] For papal letters up to 1300, see Lupprian, *Die Beziehungen der Päpste*; for those later, those from European princes, and lost letters, see Schmieder, *Europa und die Fremden*, pp. 328–35.

[11] The 'Sidrac' is unpublished; the best manuscript for the historical passages is Bibliothèque National, Paris, MS. BN franc. 1160, fol. 108 ff (s. XIV); unreliable transcriptions of some manuscripts of the Bibliothèque National are published in Ernest Renan and Gaston Paris, 'La Fontaine de Toutes Sciences du philosophe Sidrach', in *Histoire littéraire de France*, 31 (1893), pp. 285–318. On this (con)text, see Felicitas Schmieder, '*Nota sectam maometicam atterendam a tartaris et christianis*—The Mongols as Non-believing Apocalyptic Friends around the Year 1260?', *Journal of Millennial Studies*, 1.1 (1998) <http://www.mille.org/journal.html>; for the problem of the mainly Joachite (political) prophecy in the thirteenth century, see the literature quoted there, esp. Marjorie Reeves, *The Influence of Prophecy in the Later Middle Ages: A Study in Joachimism* (Oxford, 1969).

the eschatological aspect which had always been part of the ideology of the crusades. And they profited from the fact that in the special medium of prophecy the circumstances could easily be adapted to Christian conditions: the decisive victories and supreme power would be finally gained by Roman Christians. Other prophecies of the time were further adapted with more explicit prediction of the Tartars' eventual baptism —and of the final transformation of the *orbis terrarum* into a true *orbis Christianus*.

In the meantime the missionaries on the job were in fact labouring for this purpose and established a broad missionary network all over Asia. Around 1320, a total of thirty-four Franciscan and five Dominican monasteries were counted in Tartar empires —unfortunately we do not have information about their structure or the number of their inhabitants. The organization of Franciscan Asiatic vicarates goes back to the 1280s, when the Dominicans also organized their Asiatic missionary society.[12] The ecclesiastical organization followed immediately: in 1307 the above-mentioned Franciscan John of Montecorvino was consecrated first Catholic archbishop of Beijing, followed in 1318 by a Dominican at Sultaniyah/Persia, the second archbishopric founded on Mongol territory. Interestingly, in the same year, 1307, the Tartars disappear from the missionary Bulls beginning *Cum hora undecima*, from the catalogue of little-known, rather than unknown, heathen peoples to be baptized, but still lacking missionary organization. They were obviously now regarded as part of the *orbis Christianus*, at least from the organizational point of view. The missionaries' reports were full of successes, and this good news in particular was especially well received and often repeated in the West.[13]

In approximately 1364 the Carmelite monk John of Hildesheim wrote his legend of the Three Magi, which enjoyed broad circulation. According to his narrator, the Tartars have conquered the entire East so that nowadays there is no ruler mightier than

---

[12] *De locis Fratrum Minorum et Predicatorum in Tartaria,* ed. by Girolamo Golubovich, Biblioteca Bio-Bibliografica della Terra Santa e dell'Oriente Francescano, 5 (Quaracchi, 1906–27), II, 72 (dat. 1320–30). On Franciscan vicarates, see Bartholomew of Pisa, *De Conformitate Vitae Beati Francisci ad vitam domini Jesu* (1385–90), ed. Analecta Franciscana sive chronica aliaque varia documenti ad historiam fratrum minorum spectantia, ed. a patribus Collegii S. Bonaventurae, 4–5 (Quaracchi, 1906–12), IX, 2, pp. 556–57; cf. Golubovich, *De locis Fratrum Minorum et Predicatorum in Tartaria,* II, 260–74; the Dominican Societas Fratrum Peregrinantium Raymond Loenertz, 'Les missions dominicaines en Orient au XIVᵉ siècle et la Société des Frères Pérégrinants pour le Christ,' *Archivum Fratrum Praedicatorum,* 2 (1932), 1–83; 3 (1933), 1–55; 4 (1934), 1–47.

[13] For the events of 1307 (23.7), see Clement V, *Bullarium Franciscanum,* V, no. 84, pp. 35–37); on John, see n. 1; on the *Cum-hora* Bulls, see n. 4. Later, in Archivio Segreto Vaticano Reg. Vat. 62 (probably compiled at Rome after 1362, in order to put together texts regarding the oriental mission: Jules Gay, *Le pape Clément VI et les affaires d'Orient (1342–52)* (Paris, 1904), p. 8); the two *Cum-hora* Bulls (not mentioning the Mongols) by Clement V and John XXII (23.10.1321, *Bullarium Franciscanum,* 5, no. 443, pp. 211) appear under the common title 'to the Franciscans and Dominicans in the Tartars' realm'.

the Tartar emperor, the Great Khan of Cathay (Northern China). And this emperor fully supports Christianity.[14] 'And in a time which God will determine a very wise and mighty archbishop of Cologne will be chosen by God to conclude a marriage between the son and the daughter of the Emperor of the Romans and the Tartar Emperor [. . .] and by this contract and this friendship the Christians will recover the Holy Land. [. . .]' John does not, like Sidrac, explicitly connect this to the emergence of the Antichrist, but one hundred years later he still has the same goal: peace all over the world under Christian rule with the help of the Tartars. From both sides of the *orbis terrarum*, Christian or nearly-Christian rulers would emerge and embrace to unify into an *orbis Christianus*. Prester John would return, in new clothes, ironically, at the very moment when in fact Eastern Asia became practically unreachable again for Western missionaries, and at the very moment when Latin Christianity in that region, however strong it might have been, was once more to perish completely.

---

[14] *Historia trium regum,* written in 1364, probably for the two hundredth jubilee of the translation of the relics of the Three Magi to Cologne. See the Latin and English edition by C. Horstmann, Early English Text Society (London, 1886). A little earlier, a Mongol emperor as a ruler similar to the Last Emperor, can be found Johannes de Rupescissa, *Ostensor*, Vat. MS Ross. 753, fol. 50ʳ, text Schmieder, *Europa und die Fremden,* pp. 280–81, n. 431.

The Theology of Conversion

St Thomas Aquinas's
Theory of Conversion

PATRICK QUINN

The Context of Conversion

In his introduction to *Summa contra Gentiles*, book IV,[1] St Thomas depicts conversion as a turning towards God through a process of cognitive ascent upwards from creatures to divine reality. This particular text is quite a remarkable one since it calls into question Aquinas's own frequently reiterated claim to be a Christian Aristotelian. The text's remarkable character lies in its Neoplatonic approach to the question as to how human beings can come to know God. In it, Aquinas tells us that we rise to the knowledge of God in the context of an upward and downward movement:

> For since all the perfections of things come down from God the summit of all perfection, the human being begins from the lowest things and rising by degrees, advances to the knowledge of God: thus too, in corporeal movements, the way down is the same as the way up, and they differ only as regards their beginning and end.[2]

This noetic ascent to God is difficult, warns Aquinas, because of the weakness of the human mind which is constantly struggling for knowledge of what is essential and, in the end, will only succeed in providing us with a meagre knowledge of God by

---

[1] Hereafter *SCG, IV. The Summa Contra Gentiles of Saint Thomas Aquinas*, the Fourth Book, literally trans. by The English Dominican Fathers (London, 1929).

[2] *SCG*, IV.1.

natural means.[3] Divine revelation compensates for this by supplying the kind of knowledge about God that surpasses human understanding. This supernatural provision does, however, respect the movement of the human mind which gradually advances from what is imperfect to what is perfect. Aquinas explains what he means by this by stating that, initially, what is revealed is believed in terms of what is heard, though not understood. That is because, in this life, the mind is anchored to sensory data. However, when this connection is broken, as it is in death, then the mind intuitively sees what is revealed.

Aquinas then describes in *SCG,* IV.1 the three phases that comprehensively map this cognitive ascent to God. The first of these is when the human being, by the natural light of reason, noetically ascends to God through the knowledge of creatures. Secondly, there is the new supernatural phase of revelation when a more profound form of theological knowledge is heard and believed. Finally, there is the ultimate revelation 'when the human mind is raised to the perfect intuition of things revealed'.[4]

The movement away from the sensory world, where human reason must function discursively, to the ineffable realm of the divine where the human mind directly intuits the essence of God, is an identifiable Platonic theme, and it is in terms of this movement from the visible to the invisible that conversion as a turning towards God occurs, according to St Thomas. The culmination of this noetic search is understood by him as a form of knowing, not just that God is, but as an ultimate cognitive vision of what God is. This latter knowledge is only possible by supernatural, not natural, means since it involves an intuition of the divine essence not naturally accessible to the human mind, because of divine transcendence.

The noetic turning towards God that defines the nature of conversion is thus quite a complex phenomenon, a mysterious intermingling of both natural and supernatural forces difficult to distinguish in some ways from one another. This is indicated in the Thomistic concept of the human being as having a supernatural mode of existence from the outset since, as a Christian, Aquinas believes that we are all called to divine childhood. Yet he also strongly supports an Aristotelian-based theory of human nature. This dual interplay of what is natural and supernatural can be confusing when one tries to decipher precisely how the human mind's motivation to know God can involve both dimensions. Bernard Lonergan identifies a philosophical paradox here in the mind's natural desire to understand the supernatural.[5] It seems clear that the problems that arise as a result in Aquinas's attempts to deal with this issue present a challenge to the possibility of successfully applying a philosophical analysis, at least, to some theological issues.

---

[3] Patrick Quinn, *Aquinas, Platonism and the Knowledge of God* (Aldershot, 1996), pp. 25–35.

[4] *SCG,* IV.1.

[5] Bernard Lonergan, *Collection,* ed. by F. E. Crowe (Montreal, 1967), p. 87.

Conversion through Change

In religious terms, conversion is usually portrayed as a movement away from what comes to be increasingly seen as a profoundly undesirable, even personally destructive, state towards a more theologically enhancing way of life leading to eternal happiness. Plato's Cave narrative in *The Republic,* book VII philosophically portrays this dramatically as a turning away from the illusory world of shadows towards the ineffable brightness of being, where things are seen as they really are in the light of the Good. Plato's parable is explicitly constructed as a metaphorical description of conversion from darkness to light, from captivity to freedom, and from ignorance to knowledge. It depicts the human mind, together with the whole body, being

> turned around from the world of becoming together with the entire soul, like the scene-shifting *periactus* of the theater, until the soul is able to endure the contemplation of essence and the brightest region of being.[6]

Conversion occurs in the Cave narrative in the form of guidance that liberates the individual socially and involves a certain degree of compulsion, and ultimately requires the converted to give testimony to the new vision that is seen.

While many of these elements are implicit, whether consciously or not, in the Thomistic account of the cognitive ascent to God in *SCG,* IV.1, Aquinas also insists that conversion, as he understands it, is only possible in the changing environment which we presently inhabit and is intrinsic to our way of life before death. According to him, the very possibility of conversion is defined by change. In an interesting text on the Incarnation in *SCG,* IV.55, he argues that it was quite appropriate for God to have assumed a human nature because of the flexible form of decision-making that is permitted by the changing circumstances that characterize human life. The human mind can revise choices over time, thus making conversion and forgiveness possible right up until death. God's salvific purpose, which crucially involves forgiveness, was therefore better served by assuming human nature rather than, for example, an angelic nature since the latter essentially implies an irrevocable and inflexible form of decision-making.

In his *Compendium of Theology,* chapter 145, Aquinas repeats this view while discussing the claim that no sin is unforgivable before death. He argues as follows:

> Unyielding adherence to good or evil pertains to the end of life's course; immobility and cessation from activity are the terminus of the movement. On the other hand, the whole of our present life is a time of wayfaring, as is shown by man's changeableness in body and soul.[7]

---

[6] Plato, *Republic, 518c. The Collected Dialogues of Plato,* ed. by Edith Hamilton and Huntington Cairns (Princeton, 1964).

[7] St Thomas Aquinas, *Compendium of Theology,* trans. by Cyril Vollert (St. Louis, 1947), p. 155.

Our present human mode of change, to which our existing process of decision-making is related, marks the discursive rather than the intuitive nature of human thought and is thus essential to conversion, in St Thomas's view. It is a different matter altogether once death has occurred. Then there is no going back since the human will is now unchangeably fixed, as he explains in *SCG*, IV.91–95. Post-mortem disembodiment removes the soul from the world of change and confers immutability on human decision-making. In this respect, the Thomistic concept of the human soul is quite similar to that of angelic intelligence. Aquinas expands on this point in *SCG*, IV.95 by arguing that the human facility for reversing one's decisions in life before death exists because human beings often make mistakes whereas angelic intellects do not. Human error can, fortunately, be rectified as long as the soul is united to the body since our desires can be transitory or not strongly held. Our orientation towards our ultimate goal falls into this category. As long as we pursue it in our changing environment, then we can always change direction too. However, in death we are precluded from further change and our will remains fixed forever on what we ultimately sought:

> When [the soul] departs from the body, it will no longer be in a state of mobility towards the end, but of quiescence in the end. Consequently the will, as regards the desire for the ultimate end, will be immovable.[8]

Aquinas insists that such wilful immutability does not contradict freedom of choice. The essential nature of the latter is to adhere to what we want, irrespective of the conditions in which the will operates. Being free to choose does not intrinsically depend on whether we should be free to change our minds at some later stage. Conversion, however, does intrinsically depend on our ability to change and reverse our decisions and when this is no longer operative, the possibility of being converted also ceases. Even in the reunification of soul and body in the resurrected state, conversion is no longer an option, since the body is then under the total influence of the soul whose psychic direction is now immutable.

In the Thomistic account, conversion and the post-mortem state are wholly opposed. One might wonder whether this presents any difficulties for Aquinas's concept of purgatory. St Thomas deals indirectly with this issue in *SCG*, IV.91 where he defines the purgatorial state as one in which a soul is still defiled by sin by adhering 'inordinately to the things beneath it' and needs to be wholly purified or cleansed before it sees God. He distinguishes this process of purification from that of conversion by stating that souls in purgatory, despite their need for corrective sanctions, nevertheless, are ultimately fixated on God:

---

[8] *SCG*, IV.95.

> Now the souls that finally depart with something that needs to be cleansed, differ not from the souls of the blessed, in that they depart in charity, whereby we adhere to God as our end. Therefore they also have an unchangeable will.[9]

Aquinas incidentally admits that his concept of purgatory is based on an interpretation of Scripture, specifically I Corinthians 3. 15. *The Compendium of Theology,* chapter 181, also states that people who have not done full penance during their lives for the sins they have committed, but which they later regret, will undergo purgatorial punishment because the order of divine justice demands it. The implication also is that such punishment works in the case of such souls because they have the right disposition, whereas the damned do not.[10] Whatever one may think of the Thomistic account of purgatory, its function, like that of Plato's underworld myth at the end of *Phaedo* (107b–114e), is to argue for ultimate justice.[11]

The Disposition for Conversion

From a subjective point of view, one might wonder what kind of personal disposition is required for conversion and how this can be acquired. To some extent these issues are inaccessible to public investigation and analysis, given that they belong to the private psychological sphere of human life. Aquinas himself declares, as we have seen, that conversion cannot be understood as a purely natural process since its object, the beatific vision of God, transcends human rationality. If, however, conversion is a supernatural process and if the beatific vision is the object for all, then the candidates for this experience should, in justice, consist of all humankind. The very existence of non-Christians might then imply either a failure on God's part to put in place the necessary procedures for some people to acquire faith or, alternatively, denote an attitude of perversity on the part of non-Christians who refuse to convert. The latter possibility may have coloured the thinking of the medieval ecclesiastical Christian authorities and Christian communities which resulted in the kind of distrust and persecution of non-Christians which has been so extensively historically documented.

Aquinas insists that people have a natural desire to discover truth and are assisted in their efforts, not only by intelligence, but also by sensory experience and social communication since to be human is to be a social being. However, since the knowledge of truth ultimately implies seeing God as first truth, then the supernatural means to bring this about must be made available. In addition, the weakness of human reason, which leads to error and the adverse influence of emotional life and bodily weakness, also

---

[9] *SCG,* IV.94.

[10] *Compendium of Theology,* chap. 182, makes the latter point.

[11] There are other points of contact between Plato and Aquinas on this issue, for example, in the Platonic Socrates' description in *Phaedo,* 108b, of the soul that needs purification because it is still attached to bodily things.

argues for a special form of divine assistance in case human beings are turned away from their ultimate objective.

Aquinas's message here seems to be that supernatural assistance is essential in every way if human beings are to function appropriately in relation to what is of ultimate importance. Again, one might ask whether human reason plays any natural part at all in the conversion process or if it is simply subsumed under the supernatural dimension that is mapped on to it. In *SCG*, IV.148, we are told that such help respects the voluntary nature of human rationality and does not compel us to behave in any particular way. Such assistance is unmerited, claims St Thomas in *SCG*, IV.149, and he goes on to say that the soul 'works under God as the instrumental under the principal agent'. This means that human beings do not bring about in themselves the disposition to receive divine assistance. Aquinas gives a number of reasons in *SCG*, IV.150 why such divine help is described as grace, such as its being gratuitously given as a gift that surpasses human nature and leads human beings to God. Grace enables us to persevere in seeking good[12] and assists human beings to move back towards God if they have fallen away.[13]

Conversion and Intolerance

On the face of it, many of the features outlined above seem to be relatively non-controversial. However, there is another aspect of Aquinas's theory of conversion that is highly questionable. This concerns the conditions under which, according to Aquinas, it may be acceptable to compel certain categories of unbelievers to convert to Christianity. Such an issue was, of course, extremely topical at that time. In *Summa theologica*, II–II.10.8, which asks whether unbelievers should be compelled to believe, St Thomas distinguishes between unbelievers who have never received the faith, such as heathens and Jews, and, on the other hand, lapsed believers. The former two groups should not be compelled to convert, he claims, on the grounds that believing depends on free will. However, he cautions that Christians should actively defend their faith from such subversive influences by ensuring that such people do not hinder Christians 'by their blasphemies, or by their evil persuasions, or even by their open persecutions'.[14] These defensive measures, according to him, can be justifiably extended to Christians who wage war so as to prevent unbelievers from hindering the faith of Christ, as he puts it. In addition, he also states that lapsed unbelievers, such as heretics and apostates, should undergo bodily compulsion if necessary to enable them to reconvert. Keeping

---

[12] *SCG*, IV.155.

[13] *SCG*, IV.156.

[14] *Summa theologica* (hereafter *ST*), II–II.10.8. St Thomas Aquinas, *Summa Theologica*, literally trans. by The Fathers of the English Dominican Province (London, 1947–48).

the faith, according to Aquinas, is an obligation on all who believe, and this must be enforced on people for their own good.[15]

Apart from the unpleasant, discriminatory, and punitive aspects of such views, it seems only fair to add that neither are they philosophically coherent. If freedom of choice is crucial to conversion, then it seems contradictory to suggest that lapsed believers should be compelled to convert. In addition, the Christian adversarial tone of Aquinas's remarks is to be deplored from a contemporary theological standpoint. At best, his views on compulsory conversion teach us that theocratic politics can represent a considerable threat to individual freedom and may distort the intellectual nature of religious belief. Ultimately, even the convinced believer must recognise that any evaluation of the route to salvation lies beyond the human domain altogether and may not be usurped without serious implications for the dehumanization of others.

---

[15] *ST,* II–II.10.8 ad 2, 3. This view is also developed in various ways in *ST,* II–II.9, 10 in relation to maintaining limited forms of communication with unbelievers (article 9) and the problems of jurisdiction which Christians may confront under political rulers who are unbelievers (article 10).

Aquinas, the Intellect,
and Divine Enlightenment

Truth as Enlightenment

In his *Summa theologica,* I–II.109.1, Aquinas declares that to know truth involves 'a use or act of intellectual light'. He agrees with Aristotle that human beings naturally acquire truth through sensory experience and from imagination and memory but also insists that, at the highest level of truth, the mind is divinely enlightened in a way that transcends human nature. This does pose philosophical problems of coherence and integrity since Thomas claims to follow the Aristotelian view of how the human mind functions and of how knowledge is acquired.[1] In one of his earliest works, his Commentary on Boethius's *De Trinitate,* Aquinas discusses the nature of mental enlightenment. In question 1, article 1, he asks whether the human mind needs a 'new illumination of divine light' in order to know the truth. The background against which this particular discussion occurs is one in which Christian Platonists, like St Augustine, had suggested that some special form of divine enlightenment is always needed for the human mind to attain truth. This is mentioned in some of the objections at the start of article 1. The second objection, for example, restates with approval a claim of St Augustine's in *De magistro* that no one can naturally discover truth unless God illuminates the mind with a new light. The third objection is quite explicitly Platonic in tone, even though it begins with a reference to Aristotle's view in *De anima,* III, of the mind's perception of intelligible truth. The objection takes a similar approach to that of the Platonic Socrates in *Republic,* book VII, where the intellect is described as 'the eye of the soul' that can only see when it is illuminated by the invisible sun (the Good).

---

[1] Compare Patrick Quinn, *Aquinas, Platonism and the Knowledge of God* (Aldershot, 1996), pp. 48 f.

Aquinas substitutes God for this light source so that the objection then reads that God is the illuminating agent of the mind when it discovers and recognizes truth. These two objections, in conjunction with the other six, all argue that the human mind must be supernaturally enlightened in order to know truth.

As one might expect, given Aquinas's preference for Aristotle's philosophical views, he can argue as follows:

> Our mind possesses within itself the power of making things intelligible in act, namely the active intellect, and what is intelligible is proportionate to it; therefore it does not require another illumination in order to know truth.[2]

Just as one's eyesight, no matter how weak, can make things somehow visible, so too can our minds, irrespective of our mental stability, reach some understanding of truth.

Aquinas's view, which he claims to base on Aristotle's, is that the human mind is potentially and actually capable of making things intelligible and of receiving whatever intelligibility is so acquired. Technically, these mental abilities are respectively called the possible, active, and passive intellects.[3] The tendency to portray one or other of these at times as if they were substantially different intellects rather than intellectual powers led to some heated post-Aristotelian controversies among religious thinkers, especially those from a Neoplatonic-Islamic or Christian tradition.

The description of the active intellect or *intellectus agens* as the human power of actively striving for intelligibility by means of abstraction ensured that *intellectus agens* came to be metaphorically depicted as the illuminating source necessary for understanding to occur. Much of the post-Aristotelian medieval controversies on the intellect centred on whether there might be some kind of intellect common to all, an external mental influence operating on the human mind. Aquinas entered this debate with great vigour, opposing what he described as an erroneous doctrine of the intellect by thinkers who based their views on the works of Averroes. The issue, according to Aquinas in *De unitate intellectus*, is whether: 'The possible intellect [...] is evidently a kind of substance separate, by its very nature, from the body, yet in some way united to the body as its form; and further, that this possible intellect is one for all men'.[4]

---

[2] St Thomas Aquinas, *The Trinity and the Unicity of the Intellect*, trans. by Rose Emmanuela Brennan (St. Louis, 1948), p. 23.

[3] See *Summa theologica* (hereafter *ST*), I.79.2 ad 2, for a concise account of the passive and possible intellects. Cf. also *ST*, I.79.1–5; *Summa contra Gentiles* (hereafter *SCG*), II.59–62, 67. Translations are taken from St Thomas Aquinas, *Summa Theologica*, literally trans. by The Fathers of the English Dominican Province (London, 1947, 1948); and *The Summa Contra Gentiles of Saint Thomas Aquinas*, Books I–IV, literally trans. by The English Dominican Fathers (London, 1923–29). For a well written account of the debate on the active intellect in Islamic thought, see Oliver Leaman, *An Introduction to Medieval Islamic Philosophy* (Cambridge, 1985), pp. 87–107.

[4] Aquinas, *The Trinity and Unicity of the Intellect*, p. 209.

He forcefully rejects this view on a number of grounds. If true, it would mean no intellectual diversity, no individual human distinctiveness and no personal immortality. From a philosophic standpoint, he also thought that it represented a misreading of Aristotle. If it is true that there is one intellect for all, Aquinas contends we would all understand things in the same way, something not borne out by experience. Towards the end of *De unitate intellectus*, Thomas expresses himself strongly about the whole issue in uncharacteristically vehement and emotional language, showing the depths of his feelings on the topic:

> If any one, however, boastfully claiming a pseudo-science, wishes to say anything in contradiction to what we have written, let him not do his talking in out-of-the-way corners, or before mere boys who know not how to judge of difficult problems. But, if he dares, let him write an answer to what has been here written.[5]

It is interesting to note, however, that while Aquinas is so adamant about rejecting one possible intellect for all, he is not so adamant, at least in *De unitate intellectus*, about allowing that there may be one agent intellect for all. His reference to this occurs in the course of mentioning Plato's metaphor of the sun that enlightens all. Aquinas continues: 'But, whatever be said in regard to the active intellect, to say that there is one possible intellect for all cannot be true'.[6] This point becomes important when Aquinas identifies the divine enlightenment of the beatific vision in the divine mind as the directing intellect.

It is also noteworthy how aware Aquinas is, even at the very early stage of his writings, of the need to address the kinds of issues outlined above. In his Commentary on Boethius's Trinitarian text, St Thomas begins his account in question 1, article 1 by naming Avicenna as a key contributor whose views he rejects.[7] Aquinas states that his own position agrees with that of Aristotle and insists that we can naturally acquire knowledge of some first principles and deduce truth from them. No special form of intellectual enlightenment is needed for this though he emphasises that there are other truths which cannot be naturally obtained like the truths of faith and knowledge of future events. The latter occurs when the mind is 'divinely illuminated by a new light, superadded to what it naturally possesses'.[8] Aquinas adds that even when the mind is naturally enlightened, divine providence is always operating since God's creative activity made it possible for the mind to function intelligently in the way it does. This contrast between a natural, though divinely based, enlightenment and a special super-natural one, permeates much of the Thomistic discussion on the question of mental illumination.

---

[5] Aquinas, *The Trinity and the Unicity of the Intellect*, pp. 276–77.

[6] Aquinas, *The Trinity and the Unicity of the Intellect*, p. 256.

[7] Compare also *SCG*, II, chs 73, 74 and 76.

[8] Aquinas, *The Trinity and the Unicity of the Intellect*, p. 25.

Intellectus Agens *as* Lumen Intelligens

According to Aquinas, the natural source of mental illumination resides in the active intellect. In the course of a discussion on the intellectual powers in *ST,* I.79, he examines the existence and nature of *intellectus agens* in articles 3–5. Article 3 asks whether there is an *intellectus agens,* and Aquinas contrasts what he takes to be the major differences between Plato and Aristotle on this issue. Plato, he claims, has no need for an active intellect making things actually intelligible since he posits actually subsisting intelligible forms which are already in locus beyond the physical. These are recognized metaphysically by the mind and not abstracted from the physical environment, as Aristotle says. The extent to which our minds participate in these metaphysical forms constitutes in us, according to Plato, a corresponding level of knowledge.

Aristotle, however, claims that the forms of things do not exist outside the material conditions in which they are located. They remain unintelligible in the physical environment until the mind makes them understandable by abstracting them notionally from their physical context. This is the function of the active intellect, states Aquinas, who agrees with Aristotle's claim that just as vision requires light, so does understanding require intellectual illumination. There is a particularly interesting remark in *ST,* I.79.3 where Thomas declares that, although Plato rejects the concept of intellectual abstraction, there are definite implications in Plato's view for the theory that the active intellect provides intellectual light. This point is developed in *ST,* I.79.4 which asks whether the active intellect is something in the soul, the alternative being that it might be some kind of external mind that influences human thinking. Aquinas again cites Aristotle as his authority for asserting that the nature of the human mind is to strive for knowledge by argument and reasoning which involves movement from potentiality to act. Something must cause this, argues Aquinas. Even if we say that there is a substantial separate intelligence making things actually understandable, there must still be something in the human mind itself that makes these things intelligible to us. We know this from experience through our self-awareness of our own mental activity. This is why Aristotle in *De anima,* III compared the active intellect to light, claims Aquinas, and was what Plato had in mind when he used the sun metaphor. Aquinas concludes in *ST,* I.79.4:

> But the separate intellect, according to the teaching of our faith, is God Himself, Who is the soul's Creator, and only beatitude [. . .] wherefore the soul derives its intellectual light from Him.

Here Aquinas seems to identify the separate active intellect with God as the universal source of enlightenment. However, in the article that follows, which discusses whether there is one active intellect for all human beings, he rejects this view on the grounds that the multiplicity of human beings means a multiplicity of minds.[9] There is

---

[9] *ST,* I.79.5.

an interesting footnote to this in his reply to the third objection. This objection states that since all human beings agree on the primary intellectual concepts to which assent is given by the active intellect, the latter must be the same for all. Aquinas replies that, although as members of the same human species we all know in common the first intelligible principles, this does not mean that the power of knowing is identical in all of us. He adds:

> Yet [such knowledge] must be derived from one principle. And thus the possession by all men in common of the first principle proves the unity of the separate intellect, which Plato compares to the sun; but not the unity of the active intellect, which Aristotle compares to light.[10]

The point to be noted here is that, though Aquinas wants to say that the active intellect is the active power of abstraction, he also leans towards the view that it can be described as a separate substantial source of intelligence, to be identified as divine. There is the additional point that, in the beatific vision, all human minds presumably see God in a similar way, though Aquinas claims that this experience will be more perfect in some than others.[11]

The Human Mind and Supernatural Enlightenment

The human search for truth is finally achieved, according to Thomas, when the mind is supernaturally enlightened in order to see God. As the ultimate goal of all human endeavour, this will satisfy every human need and desire. This is a purely speculative mental activity in which knowledge of God's essence is perceived to be worth acquiring for its own sake.[12] The question is how can this ever be possible, something which is addressed in *ST*, I.12. Article 1 asks whether any created mind can see God's essence, and during the course of his reply, Aquinas identifies the dilemma central to the debate. This is that, though the divine essence as an intelligible object surpasses the ability of the human mind to grasp it, nevertheless there is a strong natural human desire to know what God is. Lonergan classically depicts this as a philosophical paradox.[13] Aquinas's position is that this natural human desire is satisfied by supernatural means. This occurs, according to *ST*, I.12.2, when the intelligible likeness of God's essence is divinely provided to the human mind. This intelligible likeness is the divine essence. In other words, God is seen through his own divine likeness, which is made possible by 'some similitude in the visual faculty, namely the light of glory

---

[10] *ST*, I.79.5 ad 3.

[11] *ST*, I.12.6 and *SCG*, III.58.

[12] *ST*, I–II.3.5.

[13] Bernard Lonergan SJ, *Collection*, ed. by F. E. Crowe (Montreal, 1967), p. 87.

strengthening the intellect to see God'.[14] What all this means is that God is the only agent responsible for enabling the beatified to see the divine essence by providing the intelligible species for the human mind to grasp and the disposition to permit the mind to do so. Aquinas describes the process of divine enlightenment in the beatific vision in this way in *ST*, I.12.5:

> Since the natural power of the created intellect does not avail to enable it to see the essence of God [. . .] it is necessary that the power of understanding should be aided by divine grace. Now this increase of the intellectual powers is called the illumination of the intellect, as we also call the intelligible object itself by the name of the light of illumination.

Thus, divine illumination refers both to the divinely created disposition to enable the mind to see God, and the intelligible object, namely God. The search for truth is then complete, according to *SCG*, III.51. In this divine takeover of the human mind, its activity and its intelligible object, God acts as an all-encompassing influence.

Conclusion

It is important to say that the human conditions which make this vision of God possible crucially involve a noetic state that is independent of sensory experience. I have argued elsewhere that the Thomistic account of the beatific experience implies a mode of existence and of thought from which the senses are either wholly absent (as with the disembodied soul) or so completely controlled (as in the state of rapture or bodily resurrection) that they cannot and do not continue to function.[15] This also means that Aquinas has to employ a Platonic epistemology and psychology to explain how the human mind operates during the beatific vision. It is therefore no coincidence that the Thomistic account of divine illumination reads so similarly in many ways to Platonism's theory of ultimate enlightenment.

Perhaps Aquinas himself, if challenged about the coherence of his account, might not be too put out. After all, he was well aware of the limitations of philosophical explanations and accepted that human beings need more than human reason alone to cope with the direction of their lives.[16] It was ultimately his belief that such knowledge was possible that inspired the Thomistic writings. From that point of view, it is fair to say that the inevitable limitations of his account simply demonstrate the difficulties that philosophical explanations must meet in the attempt to explain religious thought and belief.

---

[14] *ST*, I.12.2.

[15] Quinn, *Aquinas, Platonism and the Knowledge of God*, pp. 66–90.

[16] *ST*, I.1.1.

Conversio ad bonum commutabile:
Augustinian Language of
'Conversion' in Medieval Theology

DONALD MOWBRAY

T he phrase *conversio ad bonum commutabile* comes from Augustine, and was frequently cited by theologians when they talked about the different kinds of pain and punishment due for sin. The 'conversion' comprised a turning to worldly, changeable pleasures, and also implied an aversion to the unchangeable, divine good. 'Conversion' of this sort was closely related to the way in which the human will could determine a person's salvation or damnation and how re-ordering of the soul by a 'conversion' might lessen its own suffering. It is the intention of this paper to trace ideas about the conversion of the will according to a group of thirteenth-century masters of theology at the University of Paris. The theme of conversion will be addressed in three contexts: first, the definition of punishments for unbaptized infants dying with original sin will be considered in relation to any personal conversion of the will on their part; second, the theories advanced by these masters of theology about how the soul could turn back towards God through bodily affliction and fasting will be analysed. The final section will attempt to draw on both of the two previous areas by suggesting that the practice of certain good works through bodily affliction could diminish suffering of

This paper was originally delivered at the International Medieval Congress, IV at the University of Leeds in July 1997 as part of the session entitled 'Conversion or Punishment: Experience and Theory in Otherworldly Visions and Medieval Theology'. I owe special thanks to my co-organizer Dr Michelle L. Roper for making this session such a success. Dr Carloyn Muessig chaired the session with her usual skill and keen interest in the subject. She also provided many interesting comments and advice on the present paper.

the damned in the fires of hell. Moreover, the evidence considered here suggests that masters of theology and the authors of medieval visions of the otherworld addressed analogous issues and came to similar conclusions about them.

Augustinian Ideas about 'Conversion'

Augustine's account of his own conversion is very well known. Of course, he had made his first conversion to Manichaeism, impressed at the time by the Manichaean solution to evil and human freedom, according to which a God who is good opposes a principle of evil which is equally powerful.[1] In his conversion to Christianity, Augustine's decision was clearly influenced by the polarity between the mutable and the immutable, the changing and the unchanging. The episode is recalled in his *Confessions*:

> [Nebridius] [. . .] used to ask what the imaginary powers of darkness, which the Manichees always describe as a force in conflict with you [God], would have done if you had refused to join battle with them. If they answered that this force could have done you some harm, they would, in effect, be saying that you were subject to hurt and corruption. If on the other hand they said that the powers of darkness could not harm you, there would be no purpose in a battle. [. . .] Therefore, whatever you are—that is, whatever the substance by which you are what you are—if they admitted that you were incorruptible, all their theories were proved to be false and repugnant. If they said you were corruptible, it would be an obvious falsehood. [. . .] I ought to have disgorged these men like vomit from my over-laden system [. . .].[2]

The concept of the incorruptible and unchangeable was an important concern for Augustine when he discussed the nature of the will and its relation to God. In *De libero arbitrio*, Augustine described the will as an intermediate good. When this good adheres to the immutable good, which is common to all, then man will lead a happy life. The will commits sin by turning away from immutable and common goods, and turning or converting to its own private good, which is something either external to, or lower than, itself. It converts to its own private good when it desires to be its own master; it converts to external goods when it concerns itself with the affairs of others or what does not concern it; and it converts to goods lower than itself when it loves bodily pleasures.[3] He concluded:

---

[1] A. J. Krailsheimer, *Conversion* (London, 1980), p. 17; P. Brown, *Augustine of Hippo* (London, 1969), pp. 47–53. For a detailed account of the origins of the Manichaean religion, see G. Bonner, *St Augustine of Hippo: Life and Controversies* (Norwich, 1986), pp. 157–92.

[2] St Augustine, *Confessions*, trans. by R. S. Pine-Coffin (Harmondsworth, 1961), VII, 2, p. 135.

[3] *De libero arbitrio*, 2, 196–200, Corpus scriptorum ecclesiasticorum Latinorum (henceforth CSEL), 74 (Vienna, 1956), pp. 86–87: 'Voluntas ergo, quae medium bonum est, cum inheret incommutabili bono eique communi, non proprio, sicuti est illa de qua multum locuti sumus et nihil digne diximus veritas, tenet homo vitam beatam. [. . .] Voluntas autem aversa ab incom-

> Evil is an aversion to the immutable good, and a conversion to changeable goods. This aversion and conversion result in the just punishment of unhappiness, because they are not compelled, but committed voluntarily.[4]

The conversion and aversion described by Augustine determined the nature of human beings and explained why they should be punished in specific ways. Thirteenth-century theologians owed much to Augustine as an authority when they debated theological issues. How did this language impinge upon their ideas about the human will, sin, and suffering?

Defining the 'Unwilled': Children in Limbo

One major concern in theological discussions of the afterlife was the fate of infants who died unbaptized, and whether they would be punished by infernal fire.[5] In a series of questions in his *Disputed Questions on Evil*, written in Rome between 1266 and 1267, the Dominican theologian Thomas Aquinas went into some detail about the kind of punishments due to unbaptized children.[6] In the second article of *quaestio* five, Aquinas asked whether original sin is due *poena sensus*, that is, some kind of pain of the senses.[7] He stated the common perception of this issue: children dying only with original sin are not due *poena sensus*, but rather *poena damni*: privation of the vision of God (*carentia visionis dei*). This is defensible for three reasons, argued Aquinas. First, actual sin is fault (*vitium*) of the person, whereas original sin is the fault of nature. Grace and the divine vision are above human nature and thus the privation of both of these is not due only to someone who has committed actual sin, but also to someone who has original sin.[8]

---

mutabili et communi bono et conversa ad proprium bonum aut ad exterius aut ad inferius, peccat. Ad proprium convertitur, cum suae potestatis vult esse, ad exterius, cum aliorum propria vel quaecumque ad se non pertinent cognoscere studet, ad inferius cum voluptatem corporis diligit'.

[4] *De libero arbitrio*, 2, p. 87: 'Malum sit aversio eius ab incommutabili bono et conversio ad mutabilia bona; quae tamen aversio atque conversio quoniam non cogitur, sed est voluntaria, digna et iusta eam miseriae poena subsequitur'.

[5] For a detailed discussion of the importance that definitions of pain and suffering held for the intellectual development of the concept of the *limbus puerorum*, see D. Mowbray, 'A Community of Sufferers and the Authority of Masters: The Development of the Idea of Limbo by Masters of Theology at the University of Paris (c. 1230–c. 1300)', in *Authority and Community in the Middle Ages*, ed. by D. Mowbray, R. Purdie, and I. P. Wei (Stroud, 1999), pp. 43–68.

[6] *Quaestiones disputatae de malo*, Issu Leonis XIII. P. M. Edita (Paris, 1982), q. 5, aa. 1–3, pp. 129–36.

[7] *De malo*, q. 5, a. 2, pp. 133–35: 'Utrum peccato originali debeatur pena sensus'.

[8] *De malo*, q. 5, a. 2, p. 134: 'Dicendum, quod sicut communiter dicitur, peccato originali

The second reason is that *poena* (pain or punishment) is proportionate to *culpa* (guilt, or fault). Aquinas explained the differences between mortal and original sin with reference to the theory of the 'conversion to changeable goods'. Mortal sin involved a deliberate rejection of the divine, which is unchanging, and a conversion to worldly goods, which are changeable. In terms of the pain received for this sin, privation of the vision of God corresponded to the rejection of the divine, whilst the *poena sensus* corresponded to the 'conversion'. In original sin there is no conversion because the children have been unable to use their free will. There is only a rejection, or something which comes very close to it: the abandoning of the soul by original justice.[9]

The third reason is that *poena sensus* is not due someone who has a disposition (*habilis*) to commit a certain act. Aquinas gave the example that someone who is disposed to steal is not punished for this reason, but for the act of stealing. However, disposition to privation without any act deserves some sort of loss: just as someone who is unlearned (*non habet scientiam litterarum*) is unworthy of being promoted to the dignity of the episcopacy. In original sin, there is *concupiscentia*, or desire: in children, there is a revealed propensity to have this disposition; in adults it is demonstrated by the act of desire. Thus, a child who dies with original sin, is not deserving of *poena sensus*, but only *poena damni*. The latter punishment was merited because the child was not fit to be led to the divine vision on account of the privation of original justice.[10]

---

non debetur pena sensus set solum pena dampni, scilicet carentia visionis diuine. Et hoc uidetur rationabile propter tria: primo quidem quia persona quelibet est alicuius nature suppositum; et ideo ad ea que sunt nature per se immediate ordinatur, ad ea uero que sunt supra naturam ordinatur mediante natura. Quod igitur detrimentum aliquod patiatur aliqua persona in his que sunt supra naturam, potest contingere uel ex uitio nature uel etiam ex uitio persone; quod autem detrimentum patiatur in his que sunt nature, hoc non uidetur posse contingere nisi propter uitium proprium persone. Ut autem ex premissis patet, peccatum originale est uitium nature, peccatum autem actuale est uitium persone. Gratia autem et uisio diuina sunt supra naturam humanum, et ideo priuatio gratie et carentia uisionis diuine debetur alicui persone non solum propter actuale peccatum, set etiam propter originale'.

   [9] *De malo*, q. 5, a. 2, p. 134: 'Secundo quia pena proportionatur culpe; et ideo peccato actuali mortali, in quo inuenitur aversio ab incommutabili bono et conversio ad bonum commutabile, debetur pena dampni, scilicet carentia visionis divine respondens aversioni, et pena sensus respondens conversioni. Set in peccato originali non est conversio, set sola aversio, vel aliquid aversioni respondens, scilicet destitutio anime a iustitia originali'.

   [10] *De malo*, q. 5, a. 2, p. 134: 'Tertio quia pena sensus numquam debetur habituali dispositioni: non enim aliquis punitur ex hoc quod est habilis ad furandum, set ex hoc quod actu furatur; set habituali priuationi absque omni actu debetur aliquod dampnum: puta, qui non habet scientiam litterarum ex hoc ipso indignus est promotione ad episcopalem dignitatem. In peccato autem originali inuenitur quidem concupiscentia per modum habitualis dispositionis que paruulum facit habilem ad concupiscendum, ut Augustinus dicit adultum autem actu concupis-centem. Et ideo paruulo defuncto cum originali non debetur pena sensus set solum pena dampni,

The Augustinian canon, Giles of Rome addressed the same issue in his *Commentary on the Sentences of Peter Lombard* sometime in the mid-1270s.[11] He compared original sin to actual sin in a general sense. Generally, actual sin corresponds to the aversion to an immutable good and the conversion to a mutable good. In the punishments meted out for this, the aversion corresponds to the *poena damni*, which is the loss of the vision of God, and the conversion deserves *poena sensus*, pain of the senses. Giles gave his reasons for this: firstly, the aversion from the divine light deserves the privation of the vision of that light; secondly, the sinner himself converts to the changeable, and thus it is correct for this conversion to the changeable and created good to be punished by the pain of material fire.[12]

In original sin, Giles continued, there is a turning away from the unchangeable good because there is a lack of original justice which orders us towards this good, but there is no conversion to a changeable good. Such sin merits the *poena damni*, but not the *poena sensus* because there is not personal guilt *per se*. There is, however, natural guilt *per se*. If there is any actual guilt, it is in as far as nature infects the person. This is not through the application of evil, but rather through the subtraction of some good in original justice.[13]

The punishment of mortal sin required a pain which corresponded to its conversion to changeable pleasures. The soul's concern with the changeable and the worldly meant that it deserved a punishment commensurate with such a sin: material hell-fire. The rejection of the divine, unchanging good demanded the deprivation from its vision. Both kinds of punishment faced the damned in hell, and what kind of punishment was to afflict them more was also a subject for debate among theologians.[14] However, un-

---

quia scilicet non est ydoneus perduci ad uisionem diuinam per priuationem originalis iustitie'.

[11] *Egidio Romano Archiepiscopus Biturciensis Ordinis Sancti Augustini in secundum sententiarum* (Venice, 1482), *In II sententiarum*, d[istinctio], p. 33, q. 1: 'Utrum decedentes in originali tantum doleant de eo quod carent visione divina', no foliation.

[12] *In II sententiarum*, p. 33, q. 1: 'In omni peccato actuali generaliter loquendo est aversio ab incommutabili bono et conuersio ad commutabile. Auersioni ergo respondet pena damni. Conuersioni respondet pena sensus. Nam quia peccator se auertit a divino lumine dignus est quod careat visione diuini luminis. [. . .] Sed quia peccator se conuertit ad commutabile bonum et ad creaturam [. . .] dignus est quod [. . .] a materiali igne et pena sensibili puniatur'.

[13] *In II sententiarum*, p. 33, q. 1: 'Sed in peccato originali est ita auersio ab incommutabili bono quia est carentia originalis iustitie que nos subiciebat et ordinabat ad illud bonum quod non est ibi conuersio ad commutabile bonum, propter quod tale peccatum sic meretur penam damni, quod non meretur penam sensus, meretur enim penam damni ex eo quod est culpa. Sed non meretur penam sensus quia non est culpa actualis et personalis per se. Sed est culpa naturalis per se. Si autem est culpa personalis, hoc est inquantum natura natura inficit personam; sed ista infectio vt patet per habita non est per appositionem alicuius mali per se loquendo, sed solum per subtractionem alicuius boni in originalis iustitia'.

[14] In questions concerning whether the separated soul suffers more from the punishment of

baptized infants only received partial punishment for original sin. Aquinas and Giles both stressed the kind of punishments due to the movement of the will in sin. Aquinas explains that unbaptized children have had no opportunity to exercise their free will, and therefore would not have been able to make the conversion to changeable pleasures. This is one main reason why children in this case will not suffer from the pain of fire, for that requires the conversion of the will to the mutable good which arises in actual sin. Giles maintains that the pain of sense is merited for the act of changing to the sensible, and moving away from the spiritual. It is interesting to note that Augustine's own terminology is effectively being used against him.[15] Aquinas evoked Augustine as an authority to prove that the unbaptized would not be subject to hell-fire. Augustine himself, however, believed that these children would be damned and suffer the effects of material fire,[16] a claim which played a major part in his fight against the Pelagian heretics, especially Julian of Eclanum.[17]

---

hell-fire than the worm of conscience, certain masters argued that the soul which was corrupted by its conversion to changeable pleasures would be more accustomed to the punishment of material fire, than by the privation of the fruits of God, with which it was totally unaccustomed. See, for example, Matthew of Aquasparta, *Quaestiones disputatae de anima separata*, Bibliotheca Franciscana scholastica Medii Aevi, 18 (Karachi, 1959), q. 7: 'Quae poena erit gravior in inferno animabus separatis vel acerbior: vermis conscientiae vel ignis gehennae', pp. 120–34; Gauthier of Bruges, *Quaestiones disputatae*, Les Philosophes Belges, 10, ed. by E. Longpré (Louvain, 1928), q. 22: 'Quaeritur an damnati magis affligantur verme conscientiae quam igne gehennae', pp. 171–78.

[15] For a full development of this idea, see Mowbray, 'Community of Sufferers', pp. 49–57.

[16] Augustine discusses the fate of infants who have not been baptized in *De peccatorum meritis et remissione*, c. 16, 20: 'Infantes non baptizati lenissime quidem, sed tamen damnatur. Pena peccati Adae gratia corporis amissa. Potest proinde recte dici, parvulos sine baptismo de corpore exeuntes in damnatione omnium mitissima futuros': *Patrologia Latina* (henceforth *PL),* 44, col. 120. Augustine's assertion was in line with patristic authorities as well. See St Basil, *Homilia in sanctum baptisma*, xiii, *Patrologia Graeca* (henceforth *PG*), 31, col. 427; Gregory of Nyssa, *De baptismo, PG,* 46, col. 424b; and Gregory of Nazianus, *In sanctum baptisma*, XL, *PG,* 36, col. 390.

[17] Augustine gives evidence of the Pelagian position in *De anima et eius origine*, bk. 1, c. 9: 'Non baptizatis parvulis nemo promittat inter damnationem regnumque coelorum, quietis vel felicitatis cujuslibet atque ubilibet quasi medium locum. Hoc enim eis etiam haeresis Pelagiana promisit: quia nec damnationem metuit parvulis, quos nullum putat habere originale peccatum; nec sperat eis regnum coelorum, si non perveniunt ad Baptismatis sacramentum.' *PL*, 44, col. 481. See also 'Contra Julianum "Opus imperfectum"', III, 236, 34–56, ed. by M. Zelzer, CSEL, 85 (1974), pp. 349–50. For the Pelagian views surrounding the fate of the unbaptized, see E. A. Clark, *The Origenist Controversy: The Cultural Construction of an Early Christian Debate* (Princeton, 1992), pp. 194–240; Bonner, *St Augustine*, pp. 378–83; N. P. Williams, *The Idea of the Fall and Original Sin* (London, 1927), pp. 344–45.

Converting Back: Voluntary Affliction
of the Body and the Re-ordering of the Soul

The masters argued that the individual was born into a world of sin and had the opportunity, or misfortune, to convert to the changeable and reject the divine when he or she exercised free will. How did these same masters explain the process of returning to the immutable? In his *Commentary on the Sentences* produced sometime in the early 1250s, Bonaventure asked whether the passions of the soul were just *poenae*, pains or punishments, or whether they were sins as well.[18] Bonaventure explained that passions of the soul are not sins in as far as they are passions, but according to the disorder they provoke in the soul.[19] There are two sorts of passions: one kind comes from the exterior, the other from the interior of the soul. This second, interior kind is further subdivided into two: in one way, a passion can arise from natural corruption, in another from the free conversion of the will. Bonaventure distinguished two ways in which the will can convert to something. Firstly, it can convert to a simple good. This causes the will to detest everything which opposes this good, namely sin. Such a rise of passions is meritorious and just. However, sometimes the will converts to its own good. These passions are culpable and bad, and in this sense they are sins.[20]

Converting to a simple good was deemed virtuous. How therefore could the soul move towards this state of virtue? One way, it seems, was to subject the body to certain forms of rigorous discipline and affliction. In the mid-1250s, Bonaventure used this means of explanation when he asked whether fasting attains satisfaction for sin.[21] Fasting is a work of reparation (for sin), he argued, when it is painful and causes liberation from punishment. It is pleasing to God, for there is a re-ordering of the body

---

[18] *Commentarius in IV librum sententiarum* (Karachi, 1882–89), II, d. 36, a. 1, q. 2: 'Utrum passiones animae poenae tantum sint, an poenae simul et peccata', pp. 845–47.

[19] *IV Sent.*, p. 846: 'Licet autem huiusmodi passiones peccata sint, tamen peccata non sunt in quantum passiones [. . .] sed huiusmodi passiones peccata sunt ratione inordinationis voluntatis coniuntae vel antecedenter, vel consequenter'.

[20] *IV Sent.*, p. 846: 'Propter quod notandum est, quod quaedam est passio illata ab extrinseco. [. . .] Est et alia passio, quae ortum habet ab intrinseco. Et haec dupliciter potest oriri, quia quaedam oritur ex corruptione naturae, quaedam vero ex conversione voluntatis liberae [. . .] ex conversione voluntatis ad aliquod bonum amabile, sic, secundum quod voluntas habet converti dupliciter, passiones huiusmodi sunt in duplici genere. Voluntas enim aliquando convertitur ad bonum simpliciter, et tunc detestatur et odit quod adversatur illi bono, utpote peccatum; et hoc modo passiones inde consurgentes sunt iustae et meritoriae. Convertitur etiam voluntas aliquando ad bonum proprium et ad bonum ut nunc; et tunc passiones, quae inde consurgunt, culpabiles sunt et malae, sicut et voluntas, a qua oriuntur [. . .] Et sic patet, quod huiusmodi passiones animae peccata sunt, et in quantum oriuntur ex corruptione concupiscentiae, et in quantum ortum habent ex inordinato amore voluntatis deliberativae'.

[21] *IV Sent.*, d. 15, p. 2, a. 2, q. 2, pp. 372–73: 'Utrum ieiunio contingat satisfacere'.

and spirit, so that the body no longer stubbornly opposes the spirit. God is not pleased by the affliction of the flesh nor its mortification in itself, but in as far as the spirit is punished in the flesh. Bonaventure supported this argument by quoting Augustine who wrote that pain is not of the flesh, but of the soul in the flesh.[22]

Aquinas was also interested in the positive effects of fasting. In the *Summa theologiae*, he debated whether fasting was an act of virtue.[23] He stated that fasting has three main aims: first, to keep the concupiscence of the flesh in check; second, to allow the mind to rise freely and contemplate sublime things; and third, to make amends for sin. Here, Aquinas provided a quotation from Augustine which explained how fasting purged the mind and caused the senses to lift up, whilst the flesh was subordinated to the spirit.[24]

Like Bonaventure, Aquinas argued that fasting would give the mind freedom to raise itself to the contemplation of sublime things. He also stated that fasting would lead to reparation for sin. The relationship between soul and body was improved by the physical affliction of fasting.

On this subject, in about 1280, the Franciscan master of theology Matthew of Aquasparta debated whether maceration or affliction of the flesh was an act of virtue, a praiseworthy or meritorious act.[25] Matthew claimed that affliction or castigation of the flesh is virtuous and worthy of praise if it is done for the right purpose, with the right intention, and practised discretely and rationally; man must not mortify the flesh so that it is destroyed in the process.[26] The more the flesh is subjected to the spirit and sensuality to reason, maintained Matthew, the more the mind is subject to God. Through affliction, the flesh and sensuality are brought under reason, and the mind is thus

---

[22] *IV Sent.*, p. 373: 'Dicendum, quod ieiunium est opus satisfactorium [. . .] est, inquam, satisfactorium liberando a poena, cum sit poenale; et Deo est placitum, quia corporis et spiritus est reordinativum: ut corpus spiritui non repugnet contumaciter [. . .] dicendum, quod Deo non placit afflictio carnis sive eius maceratio secundum se, sed in quantum in ea punitur spiritus- quia "dolor non est carnis, sed animae in carne", ut dicit Augustinus'.

[23] *Summa theologiae*, Leonine edition (Rome, 1895–99), vols VIII–X (henceforth *ST*), 2a2ae, q. 147, a. 1, pp. 153–54: 'Utrum ieiunium sit actus virtutis'.

[24] *ST*, 2a2ae, q. 147, a. 1, p. 153: 'Assumitur enim ieiunium principaliter ad tria. Primo quidem, ad concupiscentias carnis comprimendas. [. . .] Secundo, assumitur ad hoc quod mens liberius elevetur ad sublimia contemplanda. [. . .] Tertio, ad satisfaciendum pro peccatis. [. . .] Et hoc est quod Augustinus dicit, in quodam sermone de *Orat. et Ieiun.*: "Ieiunium purgat mentem, sublevat sensum, carnem spiritui subiicit"'.

[25] *Quaestiones disputatae de anima separata, de anima beata, de ieiunio et de legibus*, Bibliotheca Franciscana scholastica Medii Aevi, 18 (Karachi, 1959), q. 1, pp. 365–86: 'Utrum maceratio sive afflictio carnis sit actus virtutis sive sit actus laudabilis vel meritorius'.

[26] *Quaestiones disputatae*, pp. 372–73: 'Ergo carnis mortificatio et afflictio sive castigatio est actus virtutis et laudabilis, si fiat eo fine, ea intentione qua debet, et eo modo, id est et discrete et rationabiliter, ut sic homo carnem mortificet quod non exterminet'.

subjected toward God.[27] Moreover, said Matthew, the desires of the flesh oppose those of the spirit: those of the flesh incline downwards and those of the spirit incline upwards. Therefore, the more the desires of the body are diminished, the more spiritual desires are elevated. The entire grounds for the virtue of this bodily affliction is the turning away from the flesh and its desires, and the conversion or elevation toward God through desire.[28]

What emerges from these questions on bodily affliction and fasting are the links between bodily control and the betterment of the soul. For the soul to convert back to its correct path, the love of the unchanging divine, the body must be hindered from its concern with the worldly and the changeable. Bodily affliction brings the body and soul back into the right order, and allows the soul to elevate upwards towards God. It is a spiritual conversion through corporeal affliction. The reasons behind this Franciscan concern with the positive effects of bodily affliction seems related to the positive portrayal of the body which David d'Avray has studied for Franciscan sermon literature.[29] In their assertion that the discipline of the body could convert the soul back to its right path, Bonaventure and Matthew of Aquasparta were not only alluding to the inseparable nature of body and soul, they may also have been reacting to the 'hard line' dualism of the Cathars, who perceived the flesh as intrinsically evil.[30]

Saving Souls through Painful Works: An Intersection between Theology and Visionary Literature?

But what chance was there for those who had permanently converted to changeable goods, that is, the damned in hell? If there could be a conversion to a simple good which would render the soul contrite and lead the sinner back to the unchangeable divine through meritorious works, could this be transferred to others in the afterlife? Didactic tales of suffering of the damned being mitigated through the works of those on earth

---

[27] *Quaestiones disputatae*, p. 374: 'Quanto autem magis subicitur caro spiritui et sensualitas rationi, tanto magis mens Deo subicitur. Sed caro [. . .] et sensualitas [. . .] per carnis macerationem et afflictionem rationi subduntur; igitur et mens per consequens ipsi Deo'.

[28] *Quaestiones disputatae*, p. 375: 'Desideria enim carnis et desideria spiritus contraria sunt: desideria carnis inclinant deorsum, desideria spiritus elevant sursum. Igitur quanto magis diminuuntur et remittuntur desideria carnis, tanto magis sublimantur desideria spiritus [. . .] Sed tota ratio virtutis est averti a carne et desideriis carnalibus et converti sive ferri sursum in Deum per desiderium'.

[29] D. L. d'Avray, 'Some Franciscan Ideas about the Body', *Archivum Franciscanum historicum*, 84 (1991), 343–63.

[30] D'Avray suggests that the reaction to the hard-line dualism of the Cathars was an important impetus behind some Franciscan sermons praising the virtue of marriage: 'Some Franciscan Ideas', p. 350.

abound in medieval visionary literature.[31] For example, in the ninth-century *Vision of Bernold* by Hincmar of Rheims, Bernold meets groups of bishops subjected to intense heat and intense cold. He asks his clergy to pray for their souls and the next time he encounters them, they have been washed, shaved, and well-clothed. In the same vision, Bernold discovers the emperor Charles the Bald being devoured by worms; more prayers on his behalf alleviate the emperor's suffering.[32] The historian of medieval popular culture, Aron Gurevich, identifies this link between prayer and the improvement of those suffering in hell as conforming to a certain type of belief which was in contradiction to the teaching of the Church:

> The idea that the prayers and intercessions of saints can alleviate the lot of sinful souls condemned to hell's torments was repeated in many stories of other-worldly visions, even if it did not express the official teaching of the church. A 'theology of feeling' contradicted the theology of doctrine.[33]

The masters of theology of the thirteenth century were clearly aware of accounts of hell in visionary literature. In their discussions about whether the separated soul could experience the punishment of corporeal fire, the masters used the archetype of later visionary sources, the *Dialogues* of Gregory the Great, as a basis for developing their own arguments.[34] Like the visionaries, the masters also seemed compelled to ask

---

[31] See, for example, P. Dinzelbacher, *Vision und Visionsliteratur im Mittelalter*, Monographien zur Geschichte des Mittelalters, 23 (Stuttgart, 1981); R. Cavendish, *Visions of Heaven and Hell* (London, 1977); *Visions of Heaven and Hell before Dante,* ed. by E. Gardiner (New York, 1989); C. J. Holdsworth, 'Visions and Visionaries in the Middle Ages', *History*, 48 (1963), 141–53.

[32] A. Gurevich, *Medieval Popular Culture: Problems of Belief and Perception*, trans. by J. M. Bak and P. A. Hollingsworth (Cambridge, 1988), p. 114; Dinzelbacher, *Vision*, p. 61. For the social and political significance of early visions, see M. L. Roper, 'Uniting the Community of the Living with the Dead: The Use of Other-World Visions in the Early Middle Ages', *Authority and Community*, pp. 19–41.

[33] Gurevich, *Medieval Popular Culture*, p. 114.

[34] Gregory the Great was a common authority used by theologians in their discussions about the afterlife: 'Quidam enim dixerunt quod anima separata patitur ignem hoc ipso quo videt; quod tangit Gregorius, in IV *Dialogorum*, dicens: Ignem eo ipso patitur anima quo videt. Sed cum videre sit perfectio videntis, omnis visio est delectabilis in quantum hujusmodi. Unde nihil in quantum est visum est afflictivum, sed in quantum apprehenditur ut nocivum': *St Thomas Aquinas Quaestiones de Anima: A Newly Established Edition of the Latin Text with an Introduction and Notes*, ed. by J. H. Robb, Pontifical Institute of Mediaeval Studies, Studies and Texts, 14 (Toronto, 1968), q. 21: 'Utrum anima separata possit pati poenam ab igne corporeo', p. 269. Albert the Great, Thomas Aquinas, and Bonaventure were also aware of the visionary tradition surrounding purgatory. See J. Le Goff, *La naissance du Purgatoire* (Paris, 1981), pp. 271, 345, 361, 371.

whether the pains of hell-fire could be mitigated by the charitable and painful works of others. In the fourth book of his *Commentary on the Sentences,* Albert the Great asked whether good works done outside of charity could diminish the fire of hell.[35] He concluded that such works will not diminish fire directly, but indirectly, just as fire is diminished when one stops wood being put on it. Where good forms part of the genus of good, it becomes accustomed to doing good and consequently withdraws from the habit and appetite of doing evil, thus causing sin to be diminished. Albert concluded with the argument that by diminishing the cause of fire, the fire itself is diminished.[36]

Aquinas asked a similar question in his own *Sentence Commentary,* that is, whether certain good works would have force in the mitigation of infernal fire.[37] He argued that infernal punishment can be understood in two ways. In the first sense, someone is liberated from the punishment which is merited. However, nothing is freed from punishment unless it is absolved from guilt, for the effect cannot be removed or diminish unless the cause is lessened or taken away. Such works, said Aquinas, can neither remove, nor lessen, the guilt and thus infernal punishment cannot be mitigated in this way.[38] There is a second way, however, and this concerns impeding the merit of the punishment due. In this sense, the works of charity can diminish infernal fire because firstly, man escapes the accusation of omitting to perform such works. Secondly, these works are, in some way, disposed to good, so that man will commit sin with less contempt, and through these works, he will be held back from committing many other sins.[39] Aquinas also replied to some critics who maintained that infernal punishment can be diminished by works, but not in terms of the subtraction of this

---

[35] *Super IV sententiarum,* in *Opera omnia,* ed. by P. Jammy, 20 vols (Paris, 1651), XVI, d. 15, a. 32: 'An bona opera facta extra charitatem diminuant incendium inferni', p. 292.

[36] *Super IV sententiarum,* p. 292: 'Dicendum, quod non diminuunt directe, sed indirecte: sicut dicitur diminuere ignem, qui prohibet ligna imponi: bona enim de genere bonorum assuefaciunt ad bonum, et per consequens elongat a mali consuetudine et appetitu, et ita diminuunt peccatum [. . .] et ita diminuendo causam incendii, diminuunt incendium'.

[37] *Commentum in libris IV sententiarum,* ed. by P. Mandonnet and M. Moos, 4 vols (Paris, 1929–47), IV, d. 15, q. 1, a. 3, q. 5: 'Utrum opera praedicta valeant ad poenae infernalis mitigationem', pp. 653–58.

[38] *Commentum in libris IV sententiarum,* p. 658: 'Dicendum quod diminuere poenam infernalem potest intelligi dupliciter. Uno modo ita quod quis liberetur a poena quam jam meruit. Et sic, cum nullus liberetur a poena nisi sit absolutus a culpa, quia effectus non diminuuntur neque tolluntur nisi diminuta vel ablata causa; per opera extra caritatem facta, quae neque culpam tollere neque diminuere possunt, poena inferni mitigari non potest'.

[39] *Commentum in libris IV sententiarum,* p. 658: 'Alio modo ita quod meritum poenae impediatur. Et sic hujusmodi opera diminuunt poenam inferni. Primo, quia homo reatum omissionis evadit, qui hujusmodi opera perficit. Secundo, quia hujusmodi opera aliquo modo ad bonum disponunt, ut homo ex minori contemptu etiam peccata faciat, ut etiam a multis peccatis per hujusmodi opera retrahatur'.

punishment as a substance, but rather by providing some sort of fortification to the human subject. This cannot be true, argued Aquinas, for fortification only exists when passibility (the ability to suffer) is taken away. Passibility exists according to the measure of guilt, and if guilt is not diminished, then the subject cannot be fortified.[40] Exactly to whom Aquinas was alluding here is unclear. However, both Albert and Aquinas maintained that there may be some diminution of eternal hell-fire, through the practice of works disposed to good. Though there is no demonstrable link between these questions and medieval visions, Gurevich's claim that one genre essentially contradicted the other does not stand up to scrutiny. The masters, it seems, were alive to this 'theology of feeling' as well.

The masters used the Augustinian language of 'conversion' to explain key areas of their theology. As a model of language, it could be applied to a variety of different theological contexts. It was also important because it meant that the masters could manipulate language for their own purposes and still remain faithful to a key patristic authority. In this way, for example, the theologians of the thirteenth century were able to exclude the possibility of unbaptized infants being burnt in eternal hell-fire, contrary to what Augustine himself had maintained. However, the movement away from or to God in the spiritual sense was not apparently beyond the reach of the sinner. Acts of bodily affliction and castigation were an important tool in the act of re-ordering soul to body, with the aim of converting to the divine good. This tells us much about the thirteenth century's preoccupation, not only with the body, but also how closely it was linked to the soul, and how each depended on the other. It was of utmost importance that the soul was extracted from the disordering influence of the body, so that it could pursue its true goal: the love of God. Works of this kind were also thought to have some beneficial effects on the intensity of fire in hell. The central idea behind the benefits of these works was that the soul became accustomed to the correct sort of good. When we ask what medieval theologians thought conversion to entail, it appears that it was the striving for the proper good, a simple good which was epitomized by the ordering of the soul and body towards God.

---

[40] *Commentum in libris IV sententiarum,* p. 658: 'Quidam autem dicunt quod diminuunt poenam inferni, non subtrahendo aliquid de ipsa quantum ad substantiam, sed fortificando subjectum, ut melius sustinere possit. Sed hoc non potest esse; quia fortificatio non est nisi ex ablatione passibilitatis. Passibilitas autem est secundum mensuram culpae. Et ideo si culpa non diminuitur, nec subjectum fortificari potest'.

Converting the Other and Converting the Self: Double Objectives in Franciscan Educational Writings

BERT ROEST

L ike many concepts that have both a historical and an analytical existence, conversion at first sight seems to have a straightforward signification. But subsequent reflection and additional reading quickly reveal tensions and confusion in the way the concept is used in the past and the present, and the ongoing need to define its meaning in the context of clearly delineated historical situations—especially after the work of Karl Morrison, who has raised important questions about the meaning of conversion as a metaphor and as a phenomenon.[1] This paper is just an initial attempt to analyse conversion in the thirteenth- and fourteenth-century Franciscan educational context, where this concept seemed to have had a series of related meanings, directed either outwardly (towards the conversion of the other), or inwardly (towards the conversion of the self). To clarify this I would like to present a short introduction to Franciscan conceptions of conversion and related phenomena, as they appear in several educational writings. To provide a background for these conceptions I also would like to include some reflections on older monastic ideas towards the same phenomenon, as well as a short foray into one of the pressing themes in the history of the Franciscan order, or rather the image-building around it (if in historiography these things can ever be separated).

First of all, I would like to take the reader back to the early years of the Franciscan movement, at a time when it consisted of a relatively small group of religious enthusiasts bound both by a very strongly felt commitment to what they conceived to

---

[1] Karl F. Morrison, *Understanding Conversion* (Charlottesville, 1992).

be a new and yet authorized life of Gospel perfection, and by the charismatic powers of its leader. According to sources like the *Dialogus sanctorum Fratrum Minorum*, the *vitae* devoted to Francis, and the writings of Leo *cum suis*, new members of this group underwent a very radical conversion, not only steered by the ideals and precepts formulated in the Bible and the Franciscan rule, but first and foremost by the charisma and the religious dynamics of the Franciscan community itself. The latter not only had a very appealing and compelling religious profile to new postulants, but also presented its members with an almost apocalyptic group consciousness.[2] Hence, the order in its early years could be described as a classic example of a so-called revitalization movement, in which conversion experiences were very important vehicles to account for God's special predilection.

When the order grew and started to take on new responsibilities, all kinds of changes occurred which fundamentally changed its character. Much has been written about this development, to stress the clericalization of the order, the decline of poverty standards, and the many internal conflicts (epitomized in the so-called *usus pauper* controversy). And, inevitably, scholars signal a loss of innocence, and a corruption of the initial idealism, which would have had repercussions both for the meaning of conversion to the Franciscan way of life and for the religious transformation of friars living their vocation in the order. Several medieval sources of course seem to be supportive for such a view. Look for instance at the Testament of Francis, the lamentations of Giles of Assisi, the polemic retrospective histories of Angelo Clareno, the *Speculum perfectionis*, as well as several of the most well-known rule commentaries.

Yet the order continued to attract growing numbers of postulants, who frequently described their own vocation and their subsequent immersion into the Franciscan life as a profound conversion with enormous personal consequences. With regard to the assumed decline of religious vigour we therefore might well ask ourselves whether we, as scholars, are not somewhat deceived by a romantic view of historical developments. The myth of pristine beginnings versus the slackening of the ideal is very deeply grounded in our modern poetic imagination, and I dare say that with regard to Franciscan studies this myth has grown very vigorous. Many important scholars since Renan, Sabatier, Gratien, and Little have emphasised the problems of institutionalization and decline, and either consciously or unconsciously have chosen to edit exactly those sources that could give fuel to such a representation of the history of the order.[3] This myth finds support in an underlying and not often acknowledged, deeply felt mistrust among modern humans of accepting the presence of idealism, sincere commitment, and charismatic situations within the boundaries of a well-regulated

---

[2] See, for instance, J. M. Phelps, 'A Study of Renewal Ideas in the Writings of Early Franciscans: 1210–1256' (unpublished doctoral dissertation, University of California, 1972).

[3] The latest representative of this approach is D. Nimmo's survey *Reform and Division in the Medieval Franciscan Order. From Saint Francis to the Foundation of the Capuchins (1226–1538)*, Bibliotheca Seraphico-Capuccina, 33 (Rome, 1987).

community. Every so often we intuitively connect idealism and an unconditional surrender to a new way of life with a state of revolutionary turmoil and unregulated religious enthusiasm, not hindered by institutional constraints. We seem to have difficulties in accepting the possibility of complete surrender to ideals within well-ordered institutions, which we suspect to be ossified and rigid.

Yet in a society where order and hierarchy have a very different status, going back to God himself, the situation might have been rather different. When we, if only for the sake of the argument, for the moment qualify the lamentation about declining standards in some of the now most famous contemporary sources, such as the *Historia septem tribulationum* of Angelo Clareno (which, after all, were highly ideological statements in polemical contexts, and not just reliable eye-witness reports of what was going on), we might find in the well-organized Franciscan communities of the later thirteenth and fourteenth centuries many mechanisms indicating extreme idealism, including very deep and sincere concerns for religious conversion.

There is nothing strange about such a vigorous idealism within narrow institutional constraints, especially not when we recall conversion ideals from earlier periods. According to Karl Morrison, twelfth-century authors claimed that true and lasting conversion was a long process of redemption, for which monasticism provided the great institutional form. Especially within this context, the process of religious conversion could hope to proceed through the monastic *imitatio Christi*.[4] The mentioning of Morrison's book immediately brings to mind my other problem, namely the question of conversion itself. Thus far I have been talking about conversion without clearly defining it, but in earlier paragraphs I used it in particular to denote the chosen entrance in a *religio* (such as the Franciscan order). This by no means exhausts the meaning of the word conversion. Throughout the Middle Ages it also meant the simple submission to the Church by accepting baptism and the creed. However, during the high Middle Ages this was regarded not so much as conversion properly speaking, but as no more than an initial affiliation. For high medieval authors the process of conversion was a turning of the heart towards Christ, and this took place within the discipline of the monastic life. Seen in this light, conversion denotes both the entrance into the order and the ongoing transformation of the person through constant prayer, the practices of liturgy, and disciplinary asceticism. Conversion in this view is a long formative pedagogical process full of pitfalls and reversals, rather than a moment of cataclysmic change. Although there are, of course, special moments of a supernatural dimension, when the infusion of divine grace induces the individual to radically alter his or her behaviour.

Franciscan authors inherited many of these twelfth-century conceptions as formulated by Cistercian and Victorine theologians. Yet more than many twelfth-century monastics, the Franciscans were concerned with mission, for which Francis and his friars had set many compelling examples, with the intention of converting the infidel

---

[4] Morrison, *Understanding Conversion*, pp. xvii, xix, 14

to the Christian faith and of converting the ordinary believers to a real life of evangelical perfection. These missionary objectives were central elements of the Franciscan way of life. Not surprisingly, they have found their way into the Franciscan rule itself. Conversion in the Franciscan context, therefore, could have a range of different meanings. It seems that the term itself most often was used either in the context of converting the infidel or for the actual entrance into the Franciscan order or one of its sub-branches. Converts in these contexts first and foremost were those made Christian, and those turned friar or lay penitent, hence people who had significantly changed their status as believers through an act of will facilitated by divine grace.

The ongoing process of reaching towards higher levels of religious life within a chosen *religio*, which was the central conversion topic of many high medieval authors, also could be called conversion by Franciscan authors. That is to say that in Franciscan writings the term conversion is also used to denote 1) the Franciscan way of life which *began* with the entrance in the order, and 2) the actual activity of the mind and soul *in the course of* this transition towards the divine. The first of these more specific meanings is found quite often in Franciscan hagiographic writings. Hence expressions such as 'in the sixth year of his conversion' (*sexto namque conversionis suae anno*), 'in the beginning of your conversion' (*in principio tuae conversionis*), or 'from the beginning of his conversion' (*a principio suae conversionis*).[5] Conversion in this sense is the way of life according to the precepts of evangelical perfection, in which friars continually aspire to reach higher levels of *christoformitas*. The actual turning of mind and soul to God in this way of life can also be called conversion, both in a technical epistemological sense (to account for the change in the cognitive and affective faculties of the soul by which a better knowledge and a greater love of Christ is acquired), and in an ontological sense (the way in which the creature is converted to his creator).[6]

The prolonged process and concomitant actions which make it possible for mind and soul to be converted during one's life as a friar are often referred to themselves in other terms; predominantly that of the itinerary (to stress the length and hardship of the process), or those of *imitatio, similitudo, conformitas,* and *christoformitas* (accentuating the mimetic aspects resulting from the process of sanctification, by which one's life was modelled on the precepts and examples of Christ and Francis).

Both the itinerary and the *imitatio/conformitas* metaphors were amply used. The first one, which finds its root in the classic *homo viator* topos, received its exemplary treatment in the famous *Itinerarium mentis in Deum* of Bonaventure, which was meant

---

[5] See, for instance, *Seraphici doctoris S. Bonaventurea legendae duae de vita S. Francisci seraphici*, editae a PP. Collegii S. Bonaventura (Ad Claras Aquas, 1923), pp. 97 and 146 (*Legenda maior*, IX, 5, and XIII, 10).

[6] The contrary movement of the soul away from God towards other (temporary) goods and delights also was called conversion, namely the *conversio ad bonum commutabile*. This movement was frequently discussed in commentaries on the third book of Lombard's *Sentences*, in the context of the passions of the soul.

to be a guide for friars to help them in their ongoing conversion. The work is Bonaventure's most systematic attempt to provide his fellow friars with the tools to engage in an ongoing conversion, from the very beginning until its prospective consummation in the afterlife. Taking as a point of departure Francis's stigmata miracle, which for most Friars Minor was the ultimate sign of full conversion to *christoformitas*, Bonaventure built a metaphorical structure of six *illuminationes*. These six *illuminationes* conformed to the six wings of the seraphic angel in Francis's own vision, and they represented the several grades or ways by which the soul of man could be prepared to arrive at peace.[7] The work makes it abundantly clear that man cannot lift himself to higher levels, unless he receives help from a superior virtue.[8] Spiritual transformation is dependent on grace. This grace is bestowed on those who ask for it from their heart—*humiliter et devote*—through fervent prayer.[9] Prayer, therefore, is the mother and origin of the upward movement of the soul.[10] The natural potencies of the soul have to be reformed towards grace by means of prayer; towards justice by means of holy conversation; towards illuminating knowledge by means of meditation; and towards perfecting wisdom in contemplation.[11]

We can compare this with the educational program designed by Gilbert of Tournai in his *De modo addiscendi*, written in the 1260s for a non-Franciscan aristocratic pupil. Gilbert argues that pupils should aim to reach the *status perfectionis*. This path of learning in this status consists foremost of *lectio, meditatio, oratio*, and *contemplatio*, which comprise the *doctrina claustralium et virorum perfectorum*. These four activities are taught by God himself (Christ, that is). Reading is described as the diligent inspection of the Scriptures and other inspired writings with due attention of the soul. Meditation is the studious activity of the mind, searching for the knowledge of hidden truth with the help of its own rational capacities. Prayer is the devout attention of the

---

[7] *Seraphi doctoris Sancti Bonaventurae tria opuscula, breviloquium, itinerarium mentis in Deum et de reductione artium ad theologiam*, edita studio et cura PP. Collegii a S. Bonaventura (Ad Claras Aquas, 1890), p. 331 (*Itinerarium mentis in Deum*, Prologus, 3): '[. . .] quasi quibusdam gradibus vel itineribus disponitur, ut transeat ad pacem [. . .]'.

[8] *Itinerarium mentis in Deum*, p. 334 (I, 1): '[. . .] supra nos levari non possumus nisi per virtutem superiorem nos elevantem'.

[9] *Itinerarium mentis in Deum*, pp. 334–35 (I, 1): '[. . .] nihil fit, nisi divinum auxilium comitetur. Divinum autem auxilium comitatur eos qui petunt ex corde humiliter et devote [. . .] per ferventem orationem'.

[10] *Itinerarium mentis in Deum*, p. 335 (I, 1): 'Oratio igitur est mater et origo sursum-actionis. Ideo Dionysius in libro de Mystica Theologia [. . .] primo praemittit orationem'.

[11] *Itinerarium mentis in Deum*, p. 339 (I, 8): 'Qui igitur vult in Deum ascendere necesse est, ut vitata culpa deformante naturam, naturales potentias supradictas [animae] exerceat ad gratiam reformantem, et hoc per orationem; ad iustitiam purificantem, et hoc in conversatione; ad scientiam illuminantem, et hoc in meditatione; ad sapientiam perficientem, et hoc in contemplatione'.

heart for God, in order to take away what is bad and to attain the good. Contemplation, finally, is the elevation of the suspended mind in God, tasting the joy of eternal light.[12]

In the religious life of friars these four activities are the main tools for an ongoing conversion process during the itinerary of their life, hopefully leading to pure wisdom, that is a pure *christoformitas* of the soul. Metaphors like *transformatio, imitatio, similitudo, conformitas,* and *christoformitas* were, for instance, used to describe the activity and the phenomenon of acquiring a qualitative likeness to Christ. This was attainable by each, and by Franciscan friars in particular. Metaphors like *transformatio, imitatio, similitudo, conformitas,* and *christoformitas* figure prominently in texts on the Franciscan life of Evangelical perfection, but they were most fully exploited in the context of describing Francis's own perfect imitation of and conformation to Christ. The most far-reaching attempts in this regard are the famous *Arbor vite crucifixe Jesu* of Ubertino of Casale, and the notorious *De conformitate Beati Francisci ad vitam Domini Jesu* of Bartholomew of Pisa. The latter work is of particular interest, in that it places Francis on an almost equal footing with Christ himself. The *conformitas* of Francis would not only have caused a qualitative similitude, but also a quantitative similitude with Christ. Therewith, the founder of the Franciscan order himself is not a real model for other friars any more, as he was in the *Arbor vite,* but an *alter Christus* beyond imitation.[13]

Yet Franciscan friars in their present stage of conversion could not afford to concentrate only on their own spiritual welfare. According to the missionary vocation explicit in the *religio* of their choice, they were bound to aspire to the conversion of the other as well. Going back towards the history of the order, we should be aware of the fact that complaints about the course the order had taken were not always directed against the lack of idealism in itself, but foremost against the heavy emphasis on pastoral work. There was concern that the conversion of the other could stand in the way of further conversion or sanctification of the self. Giles of Assisi had complained that Paris had destroyed Assisi, meaning that the simple Franciscan adherence to the Gospel precepts was jeopardized by the entrance of the friars into the university, which was necessary for an effective apostolate among heretics and the urban masses.[14] Several friars felt that the sacrifices needed to engage in an efficient conversion of the other were a threat to the Franciscan way of life itself. They felt that these sacrifices stood in the way of their own spiritual development as friars, and hence could lead to their own damnation. A very nice example of this concern can be found in the life story of Louis of Anjou, one of the sons of Charles of Serano (the later Charles II of Naples). After several years of being held hostage by the king of Aragon on account of a military

---

[12] Gilbert of Tournai, *De modo addiscendi,* ed. by E. Bonifacio, Testi e studi sul pensiero medioevale, 1 (Turin, 1953), pp. 265–90.

[13] See, in particular, Caroll Louise Erickson, 'Francis Conformed to Christ: Bartholomew of Pisa's "De conformitate" in Franciscan History' (unpublished doctoral dissertation, Columbia University, 1972), pp. 38, 77–103.

[14] *Dicta Beati Aegidii Assisiensis* (Ad Claras Aquas, 1905), p. 91.

conflict with the Kingdom of Naples over Sicily, he entered the Franciscan order to embark on a life of spiritual growth. Yet he was very soon made bishop of Toulouse, much to his own dismay. He even begged Pope Boniface VIII to release him from his burdensome pastoral duties, as they stood in the way of his attempts to take care of his own soul.[15]

The difference which set the Franciscan order apart from many earlier orders was exactly this combined and not always easily reconciled double objective: the ongoing conversion of the other and the ongoing conversion of the self. Although the balance was not always found, the conversion of the self and the conversion of the other were often seen to be concomitant activities that should reinforce one another. It is no accident that in Franciscan chronicles and saints' lives the saintly and homiletic qualities of famous friars are frequently hailed together, and presented as intrinsic elements of the life of the converted.[16] And thirteenth- and fourteenth-century Franciscan educational writings devoted to conversion and related topics essentially stress the same elements, whether they were directed towards the friars themselves or towards tertiaries and lay people who fell under the pastoral sway of the order.

This is in fact the result of a new view of the body of the faithful as a whole. High medieval sources stress that conversion is a matter of degrees, a process with beginners and veterans, and that true conversion beyond the initial level was limited to a few. Morrison, not accidentally, speaks about a strong aristocratic embedding of the monastic conversion ideal. Eventually it was seen to be the pursuit by a contemplative elite, more often than not within the murals of the cloister. Its monastic inspiration notwithstanding, the Franciscan ideal of conversion was somewhat more democratic, in that it eventually extended to all people, and in essence had the same message for all. This implies on the one hand that we are confronted with a large amount of rather elementary materials, which might seem rather shallow when compared to the refined poetic structures and literary masterpieces of twelfth-century authors on mimetic conversion. Yet the Franciscan conversion programme, on the other hand, aimed to raise all people above the initial levels, as many Franciscan sermons and Franciscan writings for lay penitents make clear.[17] In these writings we see a process of many stages unfold, to create a proper disposition of the soul, and to make genuine conversion possible. And the most important message of all was the acknowledgement of the need continuously to aspire to higher levels, and not to be satisfied by levels of virtue and insight reached, as the conversion process of the *homo viator* very easily could be undone by pride and self-conceit.

---

[15] J. Paul, 'Saint Louis d'Anjou, franciscain et évêque de Toulouse (1274–1297)', *Cahiers de Fanjeaux*, 7 (1972), 59–90.

[16] See, for instance, B. Roest, *Reading the Book of History. Intellectual Contexts and Educational Functions of Franciscan Historiography, 1226–1350* (Groningen, 1996), pp. 84–88.

[17] See, for instance, Peter Olivi's *Informatio ad virtutum opera*, in Pietro di Giovanni Olivi, *Scritti scelti*, ed. by J.-G. Bougerol, G. Mura, P. Siniscalco, Fonti Cristiane per il terzo millennio (Rome, 1989), pp. 145–50, 156–59.

Platonism and Plagiarism
at the End of the Middle Ages

'The existence of Islam was the most far-reaching problem in medieval Christendom. [. . .] [It] made the West profoundly uneasy'.[1] R. W. Southern

'For our cultural indebtedness to Islam, we Europeans have a blind spot. We sometimes belittle the extent and importance of Islamic influence in our heritage, and sometimes we overlook it altogether. [. . .] To try to cover or deny it is a mark of false pride'.[2] Montgomery Watt

'No historical student of the culture of Western Europe can ever reconstruct for himself the intellectual values of the later Middle Ages unless he possesses a vivid awareness of Islam looming in the background'.[3] Pierce Butler

Leo Strauss and his disciples have built distinguished careers arguing that great philosophers write esoterically in an effort to avoid persecution. The most powerful and influential thinkers, Straussians aver, conceal their genuine message inside an exoteric shell designed to mislead and manipulate the vast majority of readers away from the esoteric core. The teaching of the core is too difficult, threatening, or shocking for most and must therefore be hidden to prevent its author's

---

[1] R. W. Southern, *Western Views of Islam in the Middle Ages* (Cambridge, MA, 1962), pp. 3–4.

[2] Montgomery Watt, *Islamic Surveys: The Influence of Islam on Medieval Europe* (Edinburgh, 1972), p. 2.

[3] Pierce Butler, 'Fifteenth Century Arabic Authors in Latin Translation', in *MacDonald Presentation Volume: A Tribute to Duncan Black MacDonald* (Freeport, 1933), p. 63.

persecution. The esoteric author, however, encodes the exoteric shell with clues only the few most painstaking and dedicated interpreters can detect to discover the core.[4]

Strauss mentions that esoteric writing in Western Europe has its roots in 'the Jewish and Islamic philosophy of the Middle Ages'. He pinpoints Al-Farabi as its greatest proponent and lists Marsilius of Padua and Machiavelli as the tradition's 'most famous representatives in the West'.[5] Strauss says little more about the Middle Ages and turns his focus to early modern Europe. To be sure, after 1500 support for esoteric writing of one sort or the other turns up among Europe's most eminent thinkers. Marlowe has Dido say to Aeneas before she dies: 'Live false Aeneas! truest Dido dies'. Erasmus, More, Bodin, and Bacon, no strangers to persecution, all made use of dramatic instruments (utopia, dialogue, etc.) which make their real message elusive. Machiavelli, once tortured, advocated saying and doing anything to gain or maintain power. Descartes, who acknowledged his own fear of repeating Galileo's fate, wrote that 'to live well one must live unseen'. Spinoza's signet read *caute*, and the first of his three 'rules of living' enunciated in the *Treatise on the Improvement of the Understanding* was 'to speak in a manner intelligible to the multitude, and to comply with every general custom that does not hinder the attainment of our purpose'.[6] In Shakespeare 'all the world's a stage', and nothing can be taken at face value.

In this essay, I do not challenge Strauss or the Straussians. Rather, I aim further to probe the medieval origins of European esotericism that Strauss leaves largely un-investigated. In particular, I argue that a centuries-long encounter at the end of the Middle Ages with undeniably superior non-Christian neighbors, especially Muslims, fostered esotericism. But the argument goes far beyond the claim that Western medieval thinkers cloaked the truth they knew about Islamic civilization in order to avoid persecution in Christian Europe. I contend that their encounter with and treatment of Islamic culture led medieval intellectuals to cast doubt on, rather than merely disguise, their notion of universal truth. By the close of the Middle Ages they had little hope of even discovering a universal truth to hide. Put differently, nihilism (understood as the absence of a belief in universal truth) was around in Europe a long time before Nietzsche was, and the reason for this had much to do with the Latin Christian encounter with Islam.

Islamic Superiority

Over the course of roughly five centuries between 1000 and 1500 AD, Western Europeans experienced something akin to what Eastern Europeans have recognized over the past five decades, namely, their undeniable inferiority to their arch-rivals. By 1000,

---

[4] Leo Strauss, *Persecution and the Art of Writing* (Glencoe, 1952).

[5] Strauss, *Persecution and the Art of Writing*, pp. 8–15.

[6] Benedict de Spinoza, *Improvement of the Understanding, Ethics and Correspondence*, trans. by R. H. M. Lewis (New York, 1961), p. 5.

Europe's two greatest cities were Constantinople and Córdoba, neither controlled by Latin Christians. Latin Europe had no cities which could even remotely compare with the splendour, wealth, and vitality of these two metropolitan centres. R. W. Southern writes of the period: 'Viewing the matter from Constantinople in the tenth century, Europe must have appeared as an undeveloped hinterland'.[7] This was due to the fact that Western Europe lay outside a rich and expanding trading zone which spanned from the Mediterranean across the Indian Ocean to China. By the thirteenth century, argues Janet Abu-Lughod, this trading zone constituted a full-blown 'world system' characterized by 'economic integration and cultural efflorescence'.[8] Eurocentric views of history, Abu-Lughod complains, erroneously equate the state of Western Europe in the Dark Ages with the rest of the world. In reality, however, 'if the lights went out in Europe, they were certainly still shining brightly in the Middle East'.[9]

Not entirely dissimilar to the way in which the capitalist world economy has penetrated the second and third worlds, the medieval world economy eventually reached Western Europe. And Western Europe experienced this contact, like the countries of the second and third worlds, as an unmistakable inferior, as 'an upstart peripheral to an ongoing operation' to quote Lughod.[10] The new foreign products, institutions, ideas, and technologies the Latins encountered all surpassed their own counterparts in effectiveness, validity, and sophistication. Asian textiles, most notably silk, dazzled Europeans whose own fabrics were crude in comparison.[11] Islamic glass, pottery, and paper all surpassed European counterparts.[12] Córdoba's leathers were known as the finest in Europe.[13] Similarly, through trade with Asians, Europeans were introduced to dozens of new foods they had never tasted (oranges, bananas, rice, sugar).[14] Such products were made possible not only by different climates but also superior agricultural technologies. For instance, the rest of Europe had nothing to compare with the Arabs' La Campiña irrigated district of the eastern Guadalquivir Valley.[15] Throughout the Middle Ages, with the exception of Arab-controlled Spain, Western Europeans farmed with highly primitive methods. Indeed, as Denys Hay reports, retrogression took place as many of the technological advances achieved by the Romans fell into disuse or

---

[7] R. W. Southern, *The Making of the Middle Ages* (New Haven, 1961), p. 47.

[8] Janet Abu-Lughod, *Before European Hegemony* (New York, 1989), pp. 12 and 4.

[9] Abu-Lughod, *Before European Hegemony*, p. ix.

[10] Abu-Lughod, *Before European Hegemony*, p. 12.

[11] Michael Adas, *Machines as the Measure of Men* (Ithaca, 1989), p. 50.

[12] David Abulafia, 'The Role of Trade in Muslim-Christian Contact During the Middle Ages', in *The Arab Influence in Medieval Europe*, ed. by Dionisius Agius and Richard Hitchcock (Reading, 1994), p. 1.

[13] Robert Kern, *The Regions of Spain* (Westport, 1995), p. 21.

[14] Abulafia, 'The Role of Trade', p. 1.

[15] Kern, *The Regions of Spain*, p. 21.

disrepair.[16] The Arabs' accounting and business instruments and institutions were also superior to those of the Europeans and only became common in Europe through interaction with and emulation of Arab traders. Thus bills of exchange, letters of credit, checks, and private banks all have Arabic origins.[17] Other superior technologies possessed by Muslims in the Middle Ages range from the abacus to the conical valve to the astrolabe. Arabic medicines too surpassed those commonly used by Europeans. Francis Bacon advised his infirm king: 'Your Majesty's recovery must be by the medicines of the Galenists and Arabians and not of the Chemists or Paracelsians'.[18] No wonder that Alfonso X of Castile ordered the *Libros del Saber* written in 1277 for the expressed purpose of learning superior Arabic technology.[19]

Money often brings with it might. The vibrant Afro-Eurasian economy enabled the region's inhabitants to develop superior military strategies and technologies. Successful Arab attacks on European territories began as far back as the ninth century and then continued for centuries thereafter. Norman Daniel notes that the word European accounts of the battles most commonly associated with the Arabs was 'devastation'.[20] By the close of the tenth century, writes Southern, 'the communities which owed ecclesiastical obedience to Rome were hemmed in on every side by hostile powers'.[21] The encroaching Islamic threat drew the acute attention of the Western Europeans. In his speech to the Council of Clermont in 1095, for example, Urban II painted a detailed portrait of the many lands close and hostile to Christendom.[22]

Naturally, the Christians fought back, but with little success. By the end of the twelfth century, the Muslims had regained the territories lost to the Christians in the First Crusade. As Southern argues, Christians had to admit by that point that the advance of Islam could be halted neither by conversion nor conquest.[23]

As if the Muslims of the Mediterranean were not enough to handle, the Europeans had to concern themselves with the advancing Mongol threat in the thirteenth century. Kiev fell in 1240 and did not escape the 'Tartar Yoke' until 1480. The Mongols' reputation for ferocity exceeded even the Arabs'. Brilliant Mongol leaders, most notably

---

[16] Denys Hay, *Europe in the Fourteenth and Fifteenth Centuries* (London, 1989), p. 15.

[17] See J. H. Kramers, 'Geography and Commerce', in *The Legacy of Islam*, ed. by Thomas Arnold and Alfred Guillaume (Oxford, 1934).

[18] *The Works of Francis Bacon*, ed. by James Spedding, Robert Ellis, and Douglas Heath, 12 vols (London, 1857–74), XI, 312.

[19] Donald Hill, 'Arabic Fine Technology and its Influence on European Mechanical Engineering', in *The Arab Influence in Medieval Europe*, ed. by Agius and Hitchcock, pp. 29–37. Also see in the same volume Jim Allan, 'The Influence of the Metalwork of the Arab Mediterranean on that of Medieval Europe', pp. 44–62.

[20] Norman Daniel, *The Arabs and Mediaeval Europe* (London, 1979), p. 56.

[21] Southern, *The Making of the Middle Ages*, p. 25.

[22] Southern, *The Making of the Middle Ages*, p. 70.

[23] Southern, *The Making of the Middle Ages*, p. 73.

Jingiz Khan (1162–1227) and Timur (1336–1405), warred far and wide and built the largest land-based empire in history. Their superior military tactics, such as the draft and the decimal system, became legendary. According to Arthur Waldron, their campaigns 'have a character that is undeniably akin to the modern concept of total war'; the scale of their operations 'in terms of the number of troops engaged and the distances involved was not again equaled until the Napoleonic era'.[24] True, initially the Europeans greeted news of the Mongols with optimism. The Muslims finally had a military rival who could defeat them. Better yet, if the Mongols could be christianized, Islam would have its back to the wall. Yet, clear-headed Europeans entertained the opposite scenario with great trepidation. Upon hearing of the fall of Acre in 1291, for instance, Ramon Llull wrote: 'It is much to be feared lest the Tartars receive the Law of Mahomet, for if they do this, either by their own volition or because the Saracens induce them to do so, the whole of Christendom will be in great danger'.[25] Of course, Llull's worst nightmare became reality.

The most menacing Islamicized successor state to the Mongol Empire was that of the Ottoman Turks. By the end of the thirteenth century, the Ottomans had established themselves as the dominant Mediterranean power. They won critical battles with Christians at Nicopolis in 1396 and Varna in 1444; took Constantinople in 1453, Belgrade in 1456, Negropont in 1470, and Otronto in 1480; overran Hungary in 1542; and laid siege to Vienna in 1683. But no loss so shocked Europeans like the fall of their greatest treasure, Constantinople. It stood as the only city under Christian, if not Latin Christian control which rivaled the magnificent cities of non-European empires like Damascus or Samarkand. Cosimo de' Medici was said to have referred to the fall of the Byzantine capital as the worst tragedy in centuries. Even one-sided Christian accounts of the fall marveled at the Turks' military dexterity and technology.[26] Europeans never dreamed any one or thing could compromise the mammoth walls of Constantine's city. But Mehmet II brought with him the largest cannon yet known to man and breached the walls. The world over, the Ottomans were recognized as the most skilled warriors. K. N. Chaudhuri speaks of them as 'the acknowledged masters [. . .] of the art of gun-casting and the use of artillery', particularly the arquebus.[27] The Europeans realized they were no match for the Turks. Although a papal Bull called for a crusade to retake the city, no crusade materialized. Instead, all the Christian lands bordering the Ottoman Empire recognized the Sultan's suzerainty and paid the required tribute.[28] For their part the Turks displayed nothing but confidence. Mehmet II saw himself as the legitimate

---

[24] Arthur Waldron, 'Introduction' to *The Mongol Period*, by Bertold Spuler (Princeton, 1994), p. 12.

[25] Quoted in Southern, *Western Views of Islam*, p. 68.

[26] Robert Schwoebel, *The Shadow of the Crescent: The Renaissance Image of the Turk (1453–1517)* (New York, 1969), pp. 3–18, esp. p. 3.

[27] K. N. Chaudhuri, *Asia before Europe* (Cambridge, 1990), p. 102.

[28] Steven Runciman, *The Fall of Constantinople, 1453* (Cambridge, 1965), p. 166.

heir of the Roman Empire and the ruler of a universal world empire. Even as late as 1538, Suleyman the Magnificent could order inscribed in the citadel of Bender 'I am God's slave and the sultan of this world'.[29]

It is one thing to have richer, stronger neighbors or enemies, it is quite another to have finer ones. Early images of Islam in Europe were as unflattering as they were false. Muhammad comes forth as a magician given to epileptic fits as well as orgies; Muslims as barbaric, duped idolaters who believe in three gods in some accounts, up to forty in others.[30] But as Western European contact with Islamic culture deepened, particularly from the twelfth century on, a radically different picture of the arch-enemy emerged, at least among those scholars willing to study Islam. And in this new picture, it was the Christians who came out looking crude and barbaric.

Alfonso VI's conquest of Toledo in 1085 more than any other single event contributed to the new understanding of Islam. There the victors discovered in the mosque the extraordinary library compiled by al-Ma'mun. They came across hundreds of books and treatises of which they had neither knowledge nor understanding. Southern writes of the discovery: 'A comparison of the literary catalogues of the West with the lists of books available to Moslem scholars makes a painful impression on a Western mind, and the contrast came as a bombshell to the Latin scholars of the twelfth century, who first had their eyes opened to the difference'.[31] Thus began a centuries-long process, initiated by Peter the Venerable, to translate, comprehend, and absorb Arabic learning—to play catch-up, if you will, with the superior Islamic intellect. Southern explains that the Christian scholars of the time entertained no hopes of surpassing the Muslims. Just learning what they already knew amounted to a 'stupendous task, demanding the labors of many scholars through the whole of our period'.[32]

The new knowledge transferred in this 'one-way traffic in ideas'[33] from Islam to Christendom at the end of the Middle Ages was nothing short of staggering. It spanned every discipline from astronomy, to mathematics, medicine, philosophy, and poetry. It included many works of the ancient Greeks lost to the West after the break-up of the Roman Empire—works by such masters as Plato, Aristotle, and Euclid. But also transferred were the works of great Islamic and Jewish scientists and philosophers, such as al-Khwarizmi (author of *Algebra*), Ibn Sina (Avicenna), Maimonides, and Ibn Rushd (Averroes), to whom the ancient heritage had not been lost and who significantly expanded and deepened that heritage of scholarship.[34] Dorothee Metlitzki does not exaggerate when she refers to the conquest of Toledo as 'one of the most important

---

[29] Halil Inalcik, *The Ottoman Empire: The Classical Age 1300–1600* (London, 1973), p. 41.

[30] For details, see Southern, *Western Views of Islam*, pp. 14–33.

[31] Southern, *Western Views of Islam*, pp. 8–9.

[32] Southern, *The Making of the Middle Ages*, p. 188.

[33] Southern, *The Making of the Middle Ages*, p. 66.

[34] See Eugene Myers, 'Legacy of Arab Culture to the Western World', *The Muslim Digest*, 18.6 (December 1968), 61–65.

events not only in the political but in the intellectual history of medieval Europe. At one stroke the Christian world took possession of a civilization next to which the Latin West, to quote Daniel of Morley, seemed 'infantile', provincial and barbaric'.[35] Or as Will Durant has said of the twelfth century: 'Scholars descended upon Toledo, Cordova, and Seville, and a flood of new learning poured up over the Pyrenees to revolutionize the intellectual life of the adolescent North'.[36]

The Middle Ages, of course, knew not the secularism of today. Science and philosophy were not considered separate from theology. The transfer of new knowledge thus had serious theological implications. Many Christian beliefs failed to jibe with the lessons of advanced reason and logic, making the faith seem unreasonable. Christian scholars had to wrestle with these predicaments, Thomas Aquinas being the most famous of these Christian problem-solvers. Eugene Myers claims that Aquinas and his mentor Albertus Magnus made it 'the goal of their lives to reconcile Aristotelian and Moslem philosophy with Christian theology'.[37] Islam had already tackled many such quandaries with the implication that it was a more rational, more mature faith. It had expunged, for instance, the illogical concept of the Trinity. It had also devised a way to tolerate rather than persecute the peoples of the two other great monotheistic religions. Most disturbingly, Islam was winning converts and experiencing a 'vitality [which] had no equal in the medieval West'.[38] I have already mentioned the fear Westerners expressed over the Mongol conversions. But pagans were not the only ones converting. Large-scale, voluntary conversions of Christians, some civic leaders, to Islam had transpired in Andalusia.[39] And even those who did not abandon Christianity often assimilated to most other aspects of Arab culture. Listen to the laments of the committed Christian Alvaro of Córdoba:

> Oh, the pain and the sorrow! The Christians have even forgotten their own language, and in every thousand you will not find one who can write a letter in respectable Latin to a friend, while as soon as they have to write Arabic, there is no difficulty in finding a whole multitude who can express themselves with the greatest elegance in this language.[40]

---

[35] Dorothee Metlitzki, *The Matter of Araby in Medieval England* (New Haven, 1977), p. 11.

[36] Will Durant, *The Story of Civilization: The Age of Faith* (New York, 1950), IV, 909.

[37] Eugene Myers, *Arabic Thought and the Western World* (New York, 1964), p. 16.

[38] Southern, *Western Views of Islam*, p. 8.

[39] Charles Burnett, 'An Islamic Divinatory Technique in Medieval Spain', in *The Arab Influence in Medieval Europe*, ed. by Agius and Hitchcock, p. 106.

[40] Quoted in Marianne Barrucand and Achim Bednorz, *Moorish Architecture in Andalusia* (Cologne, 1992), p. 58.

Islam's greater appeal persisted right through to the end of the Middle Ages. As John Horace Parry has said of the fifteenth century, 'Islam, and not European Christendom, was the most obviously expanding community'.[41]

The Predominance and Power of Untruth

Superior Islamic achievements put European scholars in a precarious position. Were they to recognize these advances but thereby directly or indirectly laud the enemy? Worse, were they beknownst to themselves and the wider public to emulate their greatest foe, the anti-Christ itself? European thinkers responded to this sensitive situation not only by working tirelessly to catch and pass the infidels, as Southern documents so thoroughly, but also by often distorting, altering, or even disguising the truth as they knew it.[42] And over centuries of discovering and dealing with new truths emanating from the Muslim world, they gradually became more aware of and comfortable with the predominance and power of untruth. I deliberately choose the awkward term 'untruth'. 'Lies' or 'fictions' or even 'distortions' all carry with them a connotation of premeditation with which I am not entirely comfortable. I do not wish to suggest an orchestrated conspiracy. Rather, out of habit, happenstance, and sometimes desire, European intellectuals so increased the frequency of their contacts with untruths, conflicting truths, and new truths that they grew accustomed to them. The expectations they had before the encounter with Islam of discovering or possessing single, timeless truth wore thin as the contact intensified. By the end of the Middle Ages, it was neither rare nor radical to question the possibility and prudence of finding and preaching one superior truth. Nihilism had been born.

Keep in mind that the discovery of Islam's intellectual treasures was a self-discovery. Paradigm shifts usually occur alongside personnel shifts. The cleverer new guard ousts the stubborn old. Most medieval European scholars, by contrast, came face to face with the inaccuracy and immaturity of their own ideas without losing their jobs. For rare was the pope or prince who gathered Muslim and Jewish scholars to his side.[43] Thus arose the first and intimate experience with untruth. These medieval savants had to realize that they had long been esteemed throughout their society as the best and brightest when, in fact, they were not. Furthermore, as they scurried among themselves to absorb what their Islamic and Jewish counterparts already possessed, they continued to be regarded as learned authorities in Europe. They experienced in a most personal and, I think, unforgettable manner a sharp disassociation with truth and power.

Ample evidence of direct or indirect admissions of inferiority among the medieval elite exists. Alfonso the Wise, Peter the Venerable, and Frederick II represent just three

---

[41] John Horace Parry, *The Establishment of the European Hegemony, 1415–1715* (New York, 1961), p. 8.

[42] R. W. Southern, *Scholastic Humanism and the Unification of Europe* (Oxford, 1995).

[43] Though Alfonso the Wise did employ scholars from all three faiths.

well known cases of powerful men who ordered scholars around them to translate and study Arab works. One such scholar, Roger Bacon, put the matter plainly: 'Philosophy is the special province of the unbelievers: we have it all from them'.[44] Albertus Magnus, mentor of Thomas Aquinas, is known to have shared Bacon's view.[45] Adelard of Bath, one of the first exposed to the new ideas, scoffed at the imbecility rampant in his homeland: 'violence ruled among the nobles, drunkenness among the prelates, corruptibility among the judges, fickleness among the patrons, and hypocrisy among the citizens'. He looked forward to but one thing in this disagreeable place: *'Arabum studia'*.[46] Although Aquinas toiled to refute Arab philosophers, he must have reached moments of vexing frustration with European thought. For instance, in his attempt to refute Avicenna's claim that a created creature could not directly know God, Aquinas had to turn to Averroes—so irrelevant was Christian philosophy to the subject matter.[47]

To conceal their embarrassment no few European writers got sloppy with their sources. The most notorious case is that of Dante. Miguel Asin ignited a fierce controversy in the first quarter of this century when he argued that Dante's *Divine Comedy* was almost certainly inspired by abundant Islamic *miraj* literature. 'As this *Miraj*, was preceded by an *Isra*, or Nocturnal Journey, during which Mahomet visited some of the infernal regions, the Moslem tradition at once struck me as a prototype of Dante's conception'.[48] Asin's voluminous evidence has been put to tough, even mean-spirited scrutiny by Dante worshippers but has withstood the test. One recent assessment of the debate concluded: '*Divine Comedy* was a Christian counter-text to the *miraj*. He [Dante] would have been more interested in transcending his model rather than paying lip-service to it'.[49] Dante was not alone. We now know that Marco Polo never set foot in China; he lifted the stories and descriptions of the Far East from Persian and Arabic sources.[50] Aquinas too may have been similarly motivated. His treatment of light in *Lumen gloriae* bears such a resemblance to Ibn al-Arabi that it is hard to believe the great Christian scholar was not aware of it.[51] F. C. Copleston goes so far as to insist that 'the more we know about Aristotle and about Islamic and Jewish philosophy [...] the more we may be inclined to wonder what, if anything, is peculiar to Aquinas himself'.[52] Roger of Hereford took credit in 1176 for a treatise on astronomy which certainly had

---

[44] Quoted in Southern, *Western Views of Islam*, p. 59.

[45] Philip Kennedy, 'The Muslim Sources of Dante?', in *Arab Influence in Medieval Europe*, ed. by Agius and Hitchcock, p. 73.

[46] Metlitzki, *The Matter of Araby*, p. 13.

[47] See Southern, *Western Views of Islam*, p. 55.

[48] Kennedy, 'The Muslim Sources of Dante', p. 77.

[49] Kennedy, 'The Muslim Sources of Dante', p. 77.

[50] Frances Wood, *Did Marco Polo Go to China?* (Boulder, 1996).

[51] Wood, *Did Marco Polo Go to China?*, p. 69. In all fairness to Aquinas, he does, however, cite Averroes over five hundred times.

[52] F. C. Copleston, *A History of Medieval Philosophy* (New York, 1972), p. 181.

to be from an Arabic source.[53] Ramon Llull did not know or did not mention that Averroes was Muslim. But that did not stop him from writing a treatise on the philosopher—one in which Llull, according to Dominique Urvoy, 'is guilty of grave factual errors—even dishonesty'.[54]

Llull advocated appropriating Islamic literature for Christianity because of its superior mythical and allegorical element.[55] But as elements of Islamic literature found their way into popular European literature of the Middle Ages, the sources disappear altogether. 'We nowhere', Norman Daniel explains, 'find an explicit admission that there was an alien source for the new ideas of western Europe in the twelfth century in the lay world'.[56] Metlitzki gives the example of *Dame Sirith*.

> *Dame Sirith* shows how completely an oriental story was absorbed into the popular tradition of medieval England within a hundred years of its first appearance in the West. The characters [...] are given thoroughly English features and names. The setting is clearly marked on native soil and the voices are as distinctively English as Chaucer's.[57]

Though it is true that precise citation was 'unusual for the period', it is no less true that the practice came in handy when dealing with sensitive sources.[58]

One of the many growing experiences with untruth came with depictions and understandings of Islam itself. As mentioned above, Western portraits of Islam before the conquest of Toledo bore virtually no resemblance to the truth. To quote Southern, they were the result of 'the ignorance of confined space and the ignorance of a triumphant imagination'.[59] But a clearer, more correct understanding of Islam began to emerge at the beginning of the twelfth century. First, the recent convert (from Judaism) to Christianity, Petrus Alfonsi, who had actually lived among the Muslims of Spain, offered a not terribly inaccurate description of Islam and its beliefs. Not long thereafter, in 1143, a giant leap forward took place with Robert of Ketton's first Latin translation of the Koran at the request of Peter the Venerable. As contact and study multiplied, Western knowledge of Islamic beliefs improved.[60] By 1273, William of Tripoli could write an appraisal of the Muslims unthinkable in the eleventh century: 'though their beliefs are wrapped up in many lies and decorated with fictions, yet it now manifestly

---

[53] See Metlitzki, *The Matter of Araby*, pp. 39–40.

[54] Dominique Urvoy, *Ibn Rushd (Averroes)* (London, 1991), p. 131.

[55] Kennedy, 'The Muslim Sources of Dante', pp. 76–77.

[56] Daniel, *Arabs*, p. 107.

[57] Metlitzki, *The Matter of Araby*, pp. 98–99.

[58] Urvoy, *Ibn Rushd*, p. 129.

[59] Southern, *Western Views of Islam*, p. 14.

[60] For details, see Southern, *Western Views of Islam*, pp. 34–66.

appears that they are near to the Christian faith and not far from the path of salvation'.[61] Yet, this better understanding of Islam also represented another experience with the power of untruth. For these more learned students of Islam knew perfectly well that they, as well as those they instructed, had once swallowed the earlier fabrications hook, line, and sinker.

Furthermore, false representations of Islam hardly ceased soon or long after the conquest of Toledo or Robert's translation. The earlier views persisted among and were reproduced for the masses throughout the Middle Ages. Metlitzki, for example, maintains that medieval romances, such as *Beues of Hamtoun* or *The Sowdone of Babylone*, were 'essentially vehicles of fanatical propaganda in which the moral ideal of chivalry is subservient to the requirements of religion, politics and ideology. Pagans are wrong and Christians are right whatever they do. [...] It is the triumph of Christianity over Islam'.[62] Needless to say, neither portraits nor understandings of Islam took place in a political vacuum. When things went badly in battle, the portrait of the Muslims tended to worsen. Southern, for instance, documents just this for the period following the fall of Acre in 1291.[63] Naturally, medieval scholars had no better chance of wiping out propaganda than do modern scholars. But like us, they must have seen the propaganda for exactly what it was: untruth in action. Moreover, it seems unlikely, with respect to the critical issue of halting the advance of Islam, that as Latin scholars learned how easily the masses could be duped, they did not come to see it as expedient and prudent.

Even when communicating among themselves, Western intellectuals employed untruth and half-truth. In their understanding of the history of knowledge, for example, they (conveniently?) skipped over the pivotal role played by Muslim thinkers. Southern describes the view commonly held by scholastic humanists:

> In principle, they aimed at restoring to fallen mankind, so far as it was possible, that perfect system of knowledge which had been in the possession or within the reach of mankind at the moment of creation. It was generally agreed that this body of knowledge, after collapsing completely in the centuries from the Fall to the Flood, had thereafter been slowly restored by divinely-inspired prophets among the chosen people, and by the efforts of a succession of ancient scholars in the Greco-Roman world. The achievements of these great ancient restorers of the knowledge at the Fall had once more been corrupted, and partly lost, as a result of the waves of barbarian invasion which had overwhelmed Christendom in the fifth century and continued intermittently to threaten its existence until the eleventh. But, although the tradition of learning had been threatened by these disasters, the great texts of ancient learning had survived, and

---

[61] Southern, *Western Views of Islam*, p. 62.

[62] Metlitzki, *The Matter of Araby*, p. 160.

[63] Southern, *Western Views of Islam*, pp. 68–73.

it was the work of the new succession of scholars from 1050 onwards [. . .] to take up
once more the ancient task of restoring the knowledge that had been lost at the Fall.[64]

Islam's pivotal place in the actual story gets no mention. Implicitly, Muslim and Jewish
philosophers receive credit for acting as dutiful preservers and transmitters of ancient
knowledge, never, however, for being the sophisticated extenders and augmenters of
that heritage.[65] As mentioned above, no few medieval scholars were unaware of the
religious affiliations of great Muslim scholars like Avicenna and Averroes. Worse yet,
most medieval commentators simply failed to distinguish between Averroes and
Aristotle.[66] And thus only Aristotle received credit. It is perhaps telling that the 1210
prohibition by a provincial council at Paris of Aristotelean ideas (which were only
available through the commentaries of Avicenna and Averroes) mentioned only the
Greek's name. Rewriting history, in other words, became a common tool in the struggle
against Islam.[67]

The encounter with Islam also led European scholars to expect multiple and
competing truths. As already noted, the earliest Western accounts of Muslims treated
them as slaves to their appetites and/or their magician prophet. But as it became
undeniable that many Muslims were sophisticated thinkers, it became equally
undeniable that sophisticates do not always think alike. This must have come as a
surprise, even a shock, to Westerners who before the twelfth century were accustomed
to pervasive unity in Western thought. This broader awareness turns up in Roger
Bacon's address to the pope, *Opus maius*: 'there are few Christians; the whole breadth
of the world is occupied by unbelievers, and there is no one to show them the truth'.[68]
Bacon clearly did not convert to Islam; nor did he turn nihilist. Nonetheless, he was
keenly aware that other contenders to truth (even when themselves nothing more than
untruth) could and did move many.

The absorption of Islamic learning also caused fragmentation *within* Western
Christendom itself. Several different and competing schools of thought rose up around
the ideas of Aristotle, Avicenna, or Averroes.[69] The Averroists challenged the authority

---

[64] Southern, *Scholastic Humanism*, pp. 4–5.

[65] Myers writes: 'they [Arabs] did not simply transmit ancient knowledge; they created a new
one. In fact, it was the most creative movement of the middle ages to the fourteenth century.'
'Legacy of Arab Culture to the Western World', p. 64.

[66] See Vern Bullough, 'Medieval Scholasticism and Averroism', in *Averroes and the
Enlightenment*, ed. by Mourad Wahba and Mona Abousenna (Amherst, 1996), p. 45.

[67] Also see Américo Castro, *The Spaniards*, trans. by Willard King and Selma Margaretten
(Berkeley, 1971), pp. 27–47, for an account of how the Christian Spaniards rewrote history to
discredit or excise Muslims after they reconquered land back from them.

[68] Quoted in Southern, *Western Views of Islam*, p. 57.

[69] Bullough, 'Medieval Scholasticism', p. 46, for example, lists five distinguishable schools
in the thirteenth century trying to respond to the transmission of Aristotle.

of religion altogether, claiming philosophy represented a superior path to the truth. Thus Averroists like John of Jandun 'had no Christian belief behind their learning'.[70] Aquinas labored to defend the notion of a single, transcendental truth, but even he had to admit philosophy and religion offered different, though not incompatible versions of the truth. His attempt to protect Christianity from the seed of doubt planted by the great Muslim philosopher ultimately failed: 'there can be little doubt that Averroism played a large part in establishing a tradition in which it became possible to question the status of religion by comparison with reason'.[71]

After the contact with Islamic scholarship, difference of opinion proliferated in the West. Southern dates the 'breakdown of the unity of Western thought' to after 1312 and cites the condemnations of Marsilius of Padua, William of Ockham, Eckhart, the Spiritual Franciscans, and Dante's *Monarchia* as evidence.[72] The fourteenth and early fifteenth centuries would witness the collapse of papal authority whether in the great schism of 1378 or the protests of the likes of John Wycliffe and John Huss. Eventually patricians in Italy such as Cosimo de' Medici would found academies like the Platonic Academy of Florence which had no religious affiliation or obligation whatsoever.

Religious and philosophical conflict bred cynicism. The prospect, source, and holder of truth all sunk away into a murky sea of doubt. The once-believed necessary union between the possession of truth and the acquisition of worldly power waned. Might and marketing were the progenitors of power—untruth as opposed to truth. Listen to Petrarch in the middle of the fourteenth century.

> Turn where you will, there is no place without its tyrant; and where there is no tyrant, the people themselves supply the deficiency. When you escape the One, you fall into the hands of the Many. If you can show me a place ruled by a just and mild king, I will take myself there with all my baggage. [. . .] But it is useless to search for what cannot be found. Thanks to our age, which has levelled all things, the labour is unnecessary.[73]

A stronger statement of nihilism would be hard to find.

Platonism

Petrarch stands not far from Machiavelli. For it makes sense that if untruth reigns supreme, anyone wishing to rule should, indeed must, learn to employ it to his advantage. The kind of unprincipled pragmatism associated with Machiavelli has roots which stretch back to the conquest of Toledo when Western scholars first began to

---

[70] Fernand van Steenberghen, 'Averroism', in *Encyclopedia Britannica,* 24 vols (1971), II, 892–93.

[71] Oliver Leaman, 'Averroes and the West', in *Averroes*, ed. by Wahba and Abousenna, p. 65.

[72] Southern, *Western Views of Islam*, p. 73.

[73] Quoted in Southern, *Scholastic Humanism,* p. 54.

encounter untruth. It is tempting, then, to search for pre-Machiavelli Machiavellians, that is, for philosophers who advocated unprincipled pragmatism before the Florentine master.

Two groups stand out as potential candidates: the Averroists and the Neoplatonists. The former professed Averroes' theory of the 'two truths'. According to it, religion and philosophy represent different forms of knowledge, the former practical, the latter theoretical. Religion constitutes a simplified version of philosophical truth and performs the practical function of guiding the masses who cannot comprehend theoretical philosophy. Furthermore, Western Averroists maintained that the conclusions of religion contradicted those of philosophy and were therefore inaccurate. However, they permitted the philosopher to feign acceptance of religious conclusions in order to protect himself by not riling the masses.[74] Here then is the justification for the pragmatic use of untruth. But it falls well short of Machiavelli. For the toleration of untruth always represents a tool for the Averroists in their effort to attain a divinely inspired other-worldly truth. Machiavelli, in stark contrast, recognized no such divine, universal truth. Put differently, Averroists had not ascribed to relativism as Machiavelli would later.

Neoplatonists deserve attention because Plato, in *The Republic*, espoused censor-ship as a way to protect philosophy. Because the masses cannot understand the great philosophical conclusions of dialectics, the philosopher-king is justified in presenting them a simpler, more palatable version of the truth. He is likely justified in silencing, even eliminating, persons and ideas which threaten the project of pursuing wisdom. Plato's ideas did experience something of a renaissance in the West near the end of the Middle Ages as the influence of Neoplatonism spread. As Raymond Klibansky has sug-gested, Cosimo de' Medici's warm reception of Plethon in Florence in 1439 would have unlikely taken place had there not preceded it years of rising interest in Neoplatonism.[75] Others have insisted that some Aristoteleans were actually closet Neoplatonists.[76] Still, the Neoplatonists, however great or small their actual influence in the West, do not deserve the label 'proto-Machiavellian'. For like the Averroists, they never abandoned the idea of divine wisdom.

My use of the term 'Platonism' in the title of this essay does not designate an identifiable school of thought in the late Middle Ages. I employ the term rather as a way to draw a loose analogy that captures a growing mood or attitude toward universal truth which I detect at the end of the Middle Ages. In the heart of Plato's philosophy lies lodged a predicament in the relationship between philosophy and politics. Anyone who reads *The Republic* and is uncritically confident in the existence of the Forms, particularly the Good, and the philosopher's ability to comprehend them has no qualms about the absolute political power granted him in the form of the philosopher-king. But

---

[74] For a detailed description of the doctrine, see Oliver Leamann, 'Averroes and the West', pp. 57–65.

[75] Raymond Klibansky, *The Continuity of the Platonic Tradition* (London, 1981), p. 32.

[76] Asin, *Islam and the Divine Comedy*, p. 262, makes this argument regarding Dante.

on scrutiny the text reveals that the philosopher actually requires absolute political power in order to create the kind of social atmosphere which makes the intricate, life-long pursuit of the Forms possible. Put differently, in *The Republic* Plato does not grant absolute power to the philosopher because he already possesses knowledge of the Good; he grants him omnipotence so that he can seek such supreme knowledge. Plato and his devotees, of course, presume that the ends will justify the means, that the philosopher will discover the Good and allow it to direct him to use his absolute power to realize the just society. And this core presumption represents the critical predicament. For Plato cannot guarantee that the ends will justify the means. Indeed, if there is any wisdom in Lord Acton's famous remark about absolute power, there is good reason to expect that the ends will never justify the means.

I suggest that Western European scholars, as a result of their intensified contact with Islamic thought, experienced something akin to the Platonic predicament.[77] The European scholars who first discovered the intellectual treasures of the Muslims were indeed dismayed by their own immaturity. However, they remained confident that ultimate truth lay on their side because of the divine revelation. They presumed out of faith that they could and would eventually learn all the Muslims had and then surpass them.[78] To be sure, medieval scholars enjoyed nothing close to absolute power. However, confident in their presumption of ultimate superiority, they granted themselves considerable license to distort or hide the truth regarding the actual relationship between Islam and Christendom. Why concede their own inferiority if in the long-run it were but a temporary condition? But as the Middle Ages wore on, Western thinkers came face to face with the Platonic predicament. For, as supreme wisdom eluded them, they could not produce the ends to justify the means. Instead, mounting cynicism took root that there were no ends, just means. Moreover, they had become quite skilled in these means themselves. And if everywhere their enemies utilized them, as Petrarch noted, there could be little doubt over their own course of action.

Two brief examples will have to suffice to illustrate this change in mood between roughly the twelfth and fifteenth centuries. Between 1266 and 1268, Roger Bacon penned a treatise (*Opus maius*) to the pope advising him on how effectively to deal with the Muslims, though other religions received some attention as well. Two things stand out in the treatise in the context of the argument of this essay. First, Bacon implores the pope to promote the advance of philosophy in Christendom. He justifies his admonition by claiming only philosophy can win over the Saracens. Wars and miracles Bacon excludes as prudent strategies. But because the Saracens speak the language of philosophy, Christians must become well versed in that language in order to persuade the enemy of

---

[77] Whether or not they were aware of *The Republic* is irrelevant. I am employing 'Platonic predicament' only as an analogy to help characterize the experience the scholars had.

[78] Southern, in *Scholastic Humanism*, pp. 4–6, nicely captures this general mood of optimism in the twelfth century.

the wrongness of their ways. Bacon here exhibits an acute awareness of means. He essentially counsels the pope to market to the Muslims, to speak in their language rather than his own. Second, however, the means, philosophy, are totally justified by the ends. Indeed, there exists no conflict between philosophy and divine revelation: 'the power of philosophy agrees with the wisdom of God; it is the outline of the divine wisdom given by God to man, so that he may be raised up to the divine verities'.[79] It is for precisely this reason that the Saracens can be brought to Christianity through philosophy.

Contrast Bacon's optimism with the cynicism of Aeneas Silvius some two centuries later. In 1460 Silvius composed a letter to Mehmet II urging him to convert to Christianity. But the author makes his appeal with no reference to divine wisdom or eternal salvation. The reasons he supplies refer exclusively to the benefits of this world. After boasting, quite erroneously by 1460, of the great powers and treasures of Europe, Silvius writes:

> It is a small thing, however, that can make you the greatest and most powerful and most famous man of your time. You ask what it is. It is not difficult to find. Nor have you far to seek. It is to be found all over the world—a little water with which you may be baptized, and turn to the Christian sacraments and believe the gospel. Do this, and there is no prince in the world who will exceed you in glory, or equal you in power. We will call you emperor of the Greeks and of the East.[80]

Here Christianity is no longer an end in itself, merely a means.

Straussians revere Machiavelli as a thinker of virtually unparalleled genius.[81] While conventional textbooks on the history of Western thought credit him with inaugurating modern, secular thought.[82] This essay seeks not to cast doubt on Machiavelli's genius or originality. It does provide evidence, however, that Machiavelli was perhaps less a visionary who discerned future trends and more a keen observer of trends long in formation in Western Europe. And these trends began and grew in large part as a result of Christendom's encounter with Islam.

---

[79] Quoted in Southern, *Western Views of Islam*, pp. 59–60. Southern gives a full description of the *Opus maius* on pp. 56–60.

[80] Quoted in Southern, *Western Views of Islam*, p. 100. Southern offers a lengthy description of the letter on pp. 98–103.

[81] See Leo Strauss, *Thoughts on Machiavelli* (Glencoe, 1958).

[82] See George Sabine, *A History of Political Theory* (Hinsdale, 1973), pp. 311–31.

Conversion in Art

The 'Conversion' of King John and its Consequences for Worcester Cathedral

UTE ENGEL

P ersonal piety is difficult to judge, even in the case of King John Lackland
(1199–1216). Contemporary sources are critical about his moral and religious
integrity and tell us, for example, that he never received the holy sacrament
during his adult life, and how John pressed Bishop Hugh of Lincoln to finish his sermon
more quickly, because he wanted to get his dinner.[1] But we also hear that the king
visited Bishop Hugh on his deathbed, carried his corpse at his funeral, and donated a
golden chalice at the altar in front of which the bishop was going to be buried in Lincoln
cathedral. On other occasions, John visited shrines, gave alms, and made donations to
nunneries.[2]

---

[1] *Magna Vita S. Hugonis. The Life of St Hugh of Lincoln,* ed. by D. L. Douie and H. Farmer,
2 vols (London, 1962), II, 143 f.; see Josef Lehmann, *Johann ohne Land. Beiträge zu seiner
Charakteristik*, Historische Studien, 45 (Berlin 1904), pp. 15 f.; Sidney Painter, *The Reign of King
John* (Baltimore, 1949), p. 152; Karl-Friedrich Krieger, *Geschichte Englands von den Anfängen
bis zum 15. Jahrhundert* (München, 1990), p. 145; Ralph Turner, *King John* (London, 1994), pp.
1–19.

[2] *Magna Vita S. Hugonis*, pp. 188, 225; Ralph of Coggeshall, *Chronicon Anglicanum*, ed.
by J. Stevenson, Rolls Series, 66 (London, 1875), pp. 110 f.; Roger of Wendover, *Flores Histor-
iarum*, ed. by H. G. Hewett, 3 vols, Rolls Series, 84 (London 1886–89), II, 472; see Lehmann,
Johann ohne Land, pp. 16 f.; Painter, *King John*, pp. 152 f.; Austin L. Poole, *From Domesday
Book to Magna Carta, 1087–1216* (Oxford, 1951), pp. 428 f.; Elizabeth Hallam, 'Aspects of the
Monastic Patronage of the English and French Royal Houses, c. 1130–1270' (unpublished

And yet King John certainly suppressed the English Church ruthlessly, exploited its goods during the interdict, and was not very concerned about his personal excommunication from 1209 to 1213.[3] So it is not surprising that the worst verdicts about John Lackland stem from monastic chroniclers (some of whom, incidentally, wrote only after the king's death),[4] and which culminate in the famous words of Matthew Paris: 'Foul as it is, Hell itself is defiled by the foulness of John'.[5] This contradictory record of King John in thirteenth-century documents probably mirrors the truth.[6] Concerning his piety we might carefully conclude that John was not particularly religious in medieval terms, and in marked contrast to his son, Henry III. But there are two things which suggest a different image of King John: the foundation of the Cistercian abbey of Beaulieu, which was even noted by Matthew Paris, and John's veneration of St Wulfstan of Worcester.[7]

The king founded a Cistercian monastery at Faringdon in 1203, which was transferred to Beaulieu the following year.[8] This deed on the one hand seems to be a kind of

---

doctoral thesis, University of London, 1976), pp. 143, 147–49; W. L. Warren, *King John* (London, 1978), pp. 171 f.

[3] Painter, *King John*, p. 201; Warren, *King John*, pp. 166–69; Krieger, *Geschichte Englands*, p. 145; see *Magna Vita S. Hugonis*, p. 141.

[4] James Clarke Holt, *King John*, Historical Association Pamphlet, G 53 (London, 1963), pp. 4, 16, 19, 22 f.; Warren, *King John*, pp. 7–16, 171; M. T. Clanchy, *England and its Rulers, 1066–1272. Foreign Lordship and National Identity* (London, 1983), pp. 191 f.

[5] Trans. by Clanchy, *England and its Rulers*, p. 192; Matthew Paris, *Chronica majora*, ed. by H. R. Luard, 7 vols, Rolls Series, 57 (London, 1872–83), II, 669: 'Anglia sicut adhuc sordet foetore Johannis, / Sordida foedatur foedante Johanne gehenna'. See also Warren, *King John*, p. 16. Compare the judgement of Gerald of Wales, *De principis instructione*, in *Opera*, ed. by J. F. Dimock, 8 vols, Rolls Series, 21 (London, 1861–91), VIII, 328: 'catulum tyrannicum, crudentissimis a tyrannis parentaliter exortum ipsumque tyrannorum omnium tyrann[ic]issimum' (a tyrannous whelp who issued from the most bloody tyrant and was the most tyrannous of them all; trans. by Holt, *King John*, p. 63).

[6] Hallam, *Monastic Patronage*, pp. 143–46; Warren, *King John*, pp. 257–59; Clanchy, *England and its Rulers*, p. 195; James Clarke Holt, *Magna Carta and Medieval Government* (London, 1995), p. 190.

[7] Matthew Paris, *Chronica majora*, II, 668: 'Sperandum est autem et certissime confidendum, quod quaedam bona opera, quae fecit in hac vita, allegabunt pro eo ante tribunal Jesu Christi; construxit enim abbatiam Cisterciensis ordinis de Bello loco [. . .]'; see John Tate Appleby, *Johann 'Ohneland', König von England* (Stuttgart, 1958), p. 233.

[8] Harold Brakspear and W. H. St John Hope, 'The Cistercian Abbey of Beaulieu', *Archaeological Journal*, 63 (1906), 129–32; Frederick Hockey, *Beaulieu, King John's Abbey. A History of Beaulieu Abbey Hampshire, 1204–1538* (Old Woking, 1976), pp. 14–22; Virginia Jansen, 'Architectural Remains of King John's Abbey, Beaulieu', in *Studies in Cistercian Art and Architecture*, ed. by Meredith Parsons Lillich, 2 vols (Kalamanzoo, 1984), II, 76, 102 n. 3; Christopher Holdsworth, 'Royal Cistercians. Beaulieu, her Daughters, and Rewley', in *Thirteenth-Century*

compensation following John's conflict with the Cistercians in 1200.[9] On the other hand, the king presumably intended this abbey originally to be his burial place.[10] In this way he continued a pattern well established by his family and other royals: the foundation of a monastery serving especially as the mausoleum of the patron and his inner family circle.[11] John endowed Beaulieu generously in comparison to other Cistercian houses in England,[12] but by the time he died in Newark in 1216 he changed his intentions concerning his last resting place, probably led by the second topic mentioned above: John's veneration of St Wulfstan.

This veneration could have originated from about the same time as the foundation of Beaulieu. Wulfstan, the last Anglo-Saxon bishop of Worcester and of England in general, who died in 1095, twenty-nine years after the Norman Conquest, was canonized in 1203. From 1204 onwards, King John visited Worcester nearly every year,[13] prayed at the saint's tomb, and granted the cathedral priory manorial rights and money for the repair of its cloister buildings.[14] Emma Mason and Peter Draper have shown that the reasons for the king's sudden turn towards the new saint were to a great deal political. John was able to employ one of the most famous legends of St Wulfstan in his own struggle with Innocent III about lay investiture. According to this legend, Archbishop Lanfranc of Canterbury pressed Wulfstan to resign his bishopric. But Wulfstan resisted, answering that he would return his office only to the one who invested him with it, and this was Edward the Confessor. As the scene took place in

---

England, ed. by P. R. Coss and S. D. Lloyd, Proceedings of the Newcastle-upon-Tyne Conference, 4 (Woodbridge, 1992), p. 139.

[9] Lehmann, *Johann ohne Land*, p. 209; Hallam, *Monastic Patronage*, p. 151; Hockey, *Beaulieu*, pp. 11–13; Jansen, 'Architectural Remains of King John's Abbey', pp. 76 f.; Holdsworth, 'Royal Cistercians', p. 140; see also *Magna Vita S. Hugonis*, p. 232.

[10] Elizabeth Hallam, 'Royal Burial and the Cult of Kingship in France and England, 1066–1330', *Journal of Medieval History*, 8 (1982), 377 n. 5; Holdsworth, 'Royal Cistercians', p. 140. The foundation charter of Beaulieu does not mention King John's wish to be buried there, but several sources record John's intention to found a Cistercian monastery as his burial place: see *The Beaulieu Cartulary*, ed. by S. F. Hockey, Southampton Record Series, 17 (Southampton, 1974), pp. 3–5; Hockey, *Beaulieu*, pp. 13 f., 212–15; *Annales de Margam, Annales Monastici*, ed. by H. R. Luard, 4 vols, Rolls Series, 36 (London, 1864–69), I, 25; Coggeshall, *Chronicon*, p. 109.

[11] Hallam, *Monastic Patronage*, p. 289; Hallam, 'Royal Burial', pp. 367–70; Holdsworth, 'Royal Cistercians', pp. 142–44.

[12] Brakspear and Hope, 'The Cistercian Abbey of Beaulieu', pp. 132–35; Hockey, *Beaulieu*, p. 22; Holdsworth, 'Royal Cistercians', p. 145.

[13] Except for the years 1210, 1211, and 1213, see Emma Mason, 'St. Wulfstan's Staff. A Legend and its Uses', *Medium Aevum*, 53 (1984), 158.

[14] Peter Draper, 'King John and St. Wulfstan', *Journal of Medieval History*, 10 (1984), 45 f.; Mason, 'St. Wulfstan's Staff', p. 158.

Westminster Abbey, Wulfstan pushed his bishop's staff into the Confessor's tomb, and no one besides himself was able to remove it. Consequently, Wulfstan retained his see. This story, of course, was very apt to be interpreted as supporting the power of royal investiture against the claims of the Church, and King John is reported to have used it in this way.[15]

But the king's veneration of St Wulfstan must have been more deeply rooted. On his deathbed he recommended his soul especially to this saint and stated in his testament that he wished to be buried at Wulfstan's cathedral at Worcester.[16] His will was fulfilled, and his last remains were positioned in the place of honour in Worcester cathedral: in front of the high altar and 'inter sanctos Oswaldum et Wulstanum', as the medieval records state.[17] This refers to the shrines of Wulfstan and Oswald, the latter the other saintly Anglo-Saxon bishop of Worcester, which we can assume lay on the north and south side of the choir of the cathedral.[18] Furthermore, when King John's tomb was opened in 1797 his head was covered with a monk's cap.[19] Was this a sign of humility —of conversion—during his last earthly minutes? Or was John accepted as a *confrater* by the monks of Worcester?

In any case, the Cistercians of Beaulieu were not happy to lose the royal bones which had been promised to them. After they had moved into their choir in 1227, they urged their new patron, the young King Henry III, to write to the pope in 1228, asking him to allow the translation of his father's remains from Worcester to Beaulieu, their rightful resting place.[20] The petition failed. At Worcester, in the meantime, the monks and their bishop had commenced their own sumptuous rebuilding of the cathedral choir

---

[15] Draper, 'King John and Wulfstan', pp. 46 f.; Mason, 'St. Wulfstan's Staff', pp. 158–70.

[16] *Testamenta Vetusta, Being Illustrations from Wills [. . .] from the Reign of Henry II to the Accession of Queen Elizabeth,* ed. by N. H. Nicolas, 2 vols (London, 1826), I, 5; Draper, 'King John and Wulfstan', pp. 41–43; Mason, 'St. Wulfstan's Staff', p. 157; Ute Engel, 'Die Kathedrale von Worcester' (doctoral thesis, University of Mainz, 1993), p. 422 (publication forthcoming).

[17] *Annales Prioratus de Wigornia, Annales Monastici,* ed. by H. R. Luard, 4 vols, Rolls Series, 36 (London, 1864–69), IV, 407; other sources are cited in Engel, 'Die Kathedrale von Worcester', p. 426 n. 21. In 1216 King John was buried in the Romanesque predecessor of the present cathedral of Worcester. It was replaced by a Gothic building from 1224 onwards (see below).

[18] This position of the shrines can be reconstructed for the Norman and the Gothic cathedral buildings; see Engel, 'Die Kathedrale von Worcester', pp. 413–21.

[19] Valentine Green, *An Account of the Discovery of the Body of King John in the Cathedral Church of Worcester, July 17th, 1797* (London, 1797); see also Engel, 'Die Kathedrale von Worcester', p. 429 f.

[20] 'De corpore Johannis quondam Regis Angliae ad domum Belli-loci [. . .]', *Foedera [. . .],* ed. by A. Clarke and F. Holbrooke, vol. 1, part 1 (London, 1816), p. 192; Brakspear and Hope, 'The Cistercian Abbey of Beaulieu', pp. 136, 138; Engel, 'Die Kathedrale von Worcester', pp. 362 f.

in 1224, and in 1232 King John was placed in a new tomb (Figure 1).[21] The slab of this still exists as the earliest figured tomb of an English king on English soil.[22] The putting-up of this lavishly equipped tomb with its Purbeck marble and, originally, manifold gems obviously brought the rivalry between the cathedral and the Cistercians to an end, and King John was to rest at Worcester for ever.

Interestingly, this decision seems to have been accepted by John's son, Henry III, at once. The day after the translation of King John into his new 'sarcophagus', Henry III started his long series of donations to Worcester—to the cathedral fabric, the priory, and the bishops—which was to last for over thirty years.[23] From 1232 to 1253 he continuously donated wood for the rebuilding of the eastern arm of Worcester cathedral —179 oaks in all;[24] he put the proctors, who collected money for the fabric, under his special protection;[25] he initiated a papal indulgence for the new work in 1252[26] and gave several liturgical vestments to the cathedral.[27] He also turned out to be a benefactor of the bishop and priory in general: he allowed them to hold several markets at Worcester and on their manors, and he transferred many privileges of land use to them.[28]

---

[21] *Annales Monasterii de Theokesberia, Annales Monastici*, ed. by H. R. Luard, 4 vols, Rolls Series, 36 (London 1864–69), I, 84. In 1232 the Early English choir of Worcester was not yet finished (see below), so King John's new tomb presumably was still put up in the old Romanesque building and transferred to its present position in the Early English choir when this was finished about the middle of the 1250s, Engel, 'Die Kathedrale von Worcester', pp. 244–58.

[22] Jane Martindale, 'The Sword on the Stone. Some Resonances of a Medieval Symbol of Power (The Tomb of King John in Worcester Cathedral)', in *Anglo-Norman Studies*, ed. by M. Chibnall, Proceedings of the Battle Conference, 15 (Woodbridge, 1992), pp. 199–243. The Purbeck marble slab of King John's tomb today rests on a late medieval base, which was constructed around the original stone coffin in 1529; see Engel, 'Die Kathedrale von Worcester', p. 429.

[23] See Engel, 'Die Kathedrale von Worcester', pp. 359–65.

[24] 1232: 100 oaks, 1238: 50 oaks, 1242: 15 oaks, 1253: 10 oaks, 1256: 4 oaks; see *Calendar of the Close Rolls [. . .]*, 59 vols (London, 1892–1956), 1231–34, pp. 64, 92; 1237–42, pp. 51, 396; 1251–53, p. 376; 1254–56, p. 371. In 1267 Henry III donated a further 24 oaks 'ad maeremium' to the bishop of Worcester, but these presumably were no longer needed for the Early English choir; ibid., 1264–68, p. 290. See Engel, 'Die Kathedrale von Worcester', p. 216.

[25] 1252, 1258, and 1268, *Calendar of the Patent Rolls [. . .]*, 67 vols (London 1891–1948), 1247–58, pp. 165, 633; ibid., 1266–72, p. 263.

[26] *Calendar of Entries in the Papal Registers Relating to Great Britain and Ireland: Papal Letters, 1198–1404*, ed. by W. H. Bliss, 4 vols (London, 1893–1902), I, 282.

[27] A chasuble in 1244, *Cal. Close Rolls*, 1242–47, p. 270; and a cope in 1253, *Calendar of the Liberate Rolls [. . .]*, 6 vols (London, 1971–64), IV, 113.

[28] Engel, 'Die Kathedrale von Worcester', pp. 314–16. For donations to the priory see *Ann. Wigornia*, pp. 407, 443; *Rotuli Litterarum Clausarum*, 1204–44, ed. by T. D. Hardy, 2 vols (London, 1833–44), I, 356; *Calendar of the Charter Rolls [. . .]*, 6 vols (London, 1895–1920),

Additionally, he put the church of Worcester under his special protection[29] and visited the place nearly every year.[30] Henry III's last gift to the cathedral community dates from 1268.[31]

None of the king's predecessors had supported the church of Worcester with such intense patronage.[32] Henry III himself expressed the reason for this commitment in all his relevant documents: the concern for his father, buried in Worcester cathedral.[33] The fate of King John's soul in after-life genuinely seems to have worried his son, and Henry obviously hoped that his gifts promoted the effectiveness of the monks of Worcester in their task of praying his father into heaven—to use a phrase of Christopher Holdsworth.[34] Henry III even gave the church of Bromsgrove, with its revenues, to the cathedral in order to finance the celebration of the anniversary of his father and himself after his death.[35] The monks of Worcester carried out this duty until the Reformation, putting candles around King John's tomb, decorating it with a wreath, and distributing alms for the sake of the king's soul.[36]

I, 220, 443; III, 207; *Cal. Close Rolls*, 1234–37, p. 293; 1251–53, p. 148; *Cal. Patent Rolls*, 1247–58, pp. 5 f.; *The Cartulary of Worcester Cathedral Priory (Register I)*, ed. by R. R. Darlington, Pipe Rolls Society, n.s., 38 (London, 1968), no. 321, p. 169; no. 461, p. 239; no. 458, p. 237; no. 468, p. 244. *Original Charters Relating to the City of Worcester [. . .]*, ed. by J. H. Bloom, Worcester Historical Society (Oxford, 1909), no. 1600, p. 152; Worcester Chapter Library, B 1600.a. For donations to the bishop, see *Ann. Wigornia*, pp. 410, 431; *Ann. Theokesberia*, p. 64; *Rot. Litt. Claus.*, I, p. 359; *Cal. Charter Rolls*, I, pp. 102, 248, 332, 443; *Cal. Close Rolls*, 1253–54, p. 143; *Cal. Patent Rolls*, 1232–47, p. 235; 1247–58, p. 306, 345; *Cartulary of Worcester Cathedral Priory*, no. 327, pp. 172 f.

[29] 1236 and 1256, *Registrum sive liber irrotularius et consuetudinarius prioratus Beatae Mariae Wigorniensis*, ed. by W. H. Hale, Camden Society, 91 (London, 1865), p. 26ᵇ; *Cal. Patent Rolls*, 1247–58, p. 530; *Cartulary of Worcester Cathedral Priory*, no. 459, p. 238.

[30] *Itinerary of Henry III, 1215–72*, Typescript, Public Record Office (London, 1923).

[31] *Liber Pensionum Prioratus Wigorniensis [. . .]*, ed. by C. Price, Worcester Historical Society (London, 1925), no. 130, p. 41; see also *Cal. Patent Rolls*, 1266–72, p. 263.

[32] See *Cartulary of Worcester Cathedral Priory*, p. xxiv.

[33] See, for example, *Cal. Close Rolls*, 1253–54, p. 143: '[. . .] pro nobis et heredibus nostris pro anima domini J. regis patris nostri [. . .]'; or *Cartulary of Worcester Cathedral Priory*, no. 459, p. 238: 'Sciatis quod suscepimus in protectionem et defensionem nostram specialem priorem et monachos ecclesie sancte Marie Wygorn in qua corpus J[ohannis] regis patris nostri ecclesiastice traditum est sepulture [. . .]'; Engel, 'Die Kathedrale von Worcester', p. 316.

[34] Holdsworth, 'Royal Cistercians', p. 149: 'No Becket or Swithun would distract the attention of their Cistercians from what, to their royal founders, would be their job in hand, praying them into heaven'.

[35] *Cal. Charter Rolls*, I, p. 154; *Cal. Close Rolls*, 1234–37, p. 341; *Ann. Wigornia*, p. 432; *Cartulary of Worcester Cathedral Priory*, no. 330, p. 176; *Liber Pensionum*, no. 72, p. 20.

[36] See *Early Compotus Rolls of the Priory of Worcester*, ed. by C. Gordon and J. M. Wilson,

The fact that Henry's and many other donations to the rebuilding of the east arm of Worcester only began in 1232 and lasted well into the 1250s suggests that by 1232 this great Early English part of the cathedral cannot have been near completion, as has formerly been assumed.[37] Indeed it can be shown that the eastern parts of Worcester were erected in four stages, which were complicated by the necessity to incorporate the crypt of the old Romanesque building underneath the new choir (Figure 2, I–IV).[38] The first part was the retrochoir, which was certainly ready to be roofed when Henry III gave wood for rafters in 1232. Presumably the eastern transepts, the next stage, were also under way at this time, and were finished when the next gift of timber occurred in 1238. The third phase only comprised the first bay of the choir from the east. After this there is a clear building break which Robert Willis was the first to observe (Figure 1, left).[39] The disruption was probably caused by structural problems in the crypt. The Annals of Tewkesbury record that in 1243 a crypt at Worcester collapsed.[40] In fact the excavation of the east end of the cathedral's crypt has shown that its ambulatory broke down under the load of the new choir piers at one stage and was infilled hastily afterwards.[41] During the last building phase the choir of Worcester was finally completed until about the middle of the 1250s, when news of building ceases.

So the monks, bishops, and builders of Worcester cathedral rewarded the interest of their patron Henry III with a splendid architectural setting for his father's tomb. The Early English choir of Worcester incorporates elements of the three main architectural *modi* which were developed in the north, west, and south of England around 1200.[42] The plan and general outline of the eastern arm as an aisled rectangle with projecting east bay and the one-bay eastern transepts with their huge lancet windows are modelled on

---

Worcester Historical Society (Oxford, 1908), C 292, p. 60; C 482, p. 41; Worcester Chapter Library, C 426; *Cartulary of Worcester Cathedral Priory*, no. 332, p. 177; *Liber Pensionum*, no. 76, p. 21; *Registrum*, pp. 88[b], 108[a], 109[a]; *De missis celebratis quotidie in ecclesiam cathedralis Beate Marie Wigorniensis*, Worcester Chapter Library, A 12, fol. 133[r], transcribed by James M. Wilson, Worcester Chapter Library, Add. MSS 145, pp. 38–40.

[37] See, for example, Barrie Singleton, 'The Remodelling of the East End of Worcester Cathedral in the Earlier Part of the Thirteenth Century', *Medieval Art and Architecture at Worcester Cathedral*, British Archaeological Conference Transactions, 1 (Leeds, 1978), p. 108; cf. Engel, 'Die Kathedrale von Worcester', pp. 251–56.

[38] Engel, 'Die Kathedrale von Worcester', pp. 299–302.

[39] Robert Willis, 'The Architectural History of the Cathedral and Monastery at Worcester', *Archaeological Journal*, 29 (1863), pp. 102 f. (reprinted in *Architectural History of Some English Cathedrals*, 2 vols (Chicheley, 1973), II.

[40] *Ann. Theokesberia*, p. 133.

[41] Christopher Guy, 'Excavations at Worcester Cathedral', *Transactions of the Worcester Archaeological Society*, 3rd ser., 14 (1994), pp. 17–20; Engel, 'Die Kathedrale von Worcester', pp. 278–85.

[42] Engel, 'Die Kathedrale von Worcester', pp. 314–40.

northern English and Scottish examples (Figures 3, 4). The architecture of the interior
with its complex pier forms and lavish use of *en délit* shafts and Purbeck marble follow
the southern English tradition developed from Canterbury to Salisbury and Lincoln
(Figure 1). West Country vocabulary, on the contrary, is restricted to the exterior and
the subordinate aisle bays. In this way Worcester can be interpreted as a kind of
synthesis of the modern, today called Gothic, architecture, which prevailed in John's
and Henry's English realm in the 1220s.

Additionally the east arm of Worcester is lavishly decorated—in fact on an unprecedented scale—with figure sculpture: in the spandrels of the dado-arcading, the
triforium, and on the roof bosses. The subjects can be more or less closely connected
with King John. The Early English sculpture of Worcester cathedral has been much
neglected because of the assumption that it is almost entirely a product of Victorian
restoration. But careful observation can show that only the heads and protruding parts
of the figures are restored; the bodies and lower relief elements, however, are original
and also preserve a lot of medieval paint.[43]

In the dado-arcading of the retrochoir and the eastern transepts we find a curious
mixture of beasts, men fighting monsters, and, in between, biblical events, partly
referring to St Mary, one of the patron saints of the cathedral. The most consistent
programme is developed in the southeast transept, where a Last Judgement is enfolded
in single scenes like a twentieth-century comic strip. Probably not by accident, in one
of these the large figure of a king is the first to be led into heaven by an angel (Figure
5). The series finishes on the west wall with a bishop standing beside a tomb, which
may be interpreted as an illustration of the legend of St Wulfstan's staff recounted
earlier (Figure 6). The head of the bishop was replaced in the nineteenth century, but
his figure is original, as well as the tomb chest, and a projecting piece on the tomb can
possibly be reconstructed as the staff, which the bishop held in his raised right hand.

In the Early English choir, King John's tomb is positioned in the first bay from the
east, where it has always been, as can be concluded from the medieval sources (Figures
1, 3, no. 11).[44] The main altar stood in the eastern crossing, and east of it a broad screen
extended between the crossing piers, the outline of which is apparent from the late
medieval Prince Arthur's Chantry on the south side (Plate 3, K). On this platform the
two shrines of St Wulfstan and St Oswald could have been placed, towering behind the
high altar and at the same time be accessible to pilgrims from the retrochoir in the east,
as with similar arrangements in York and Beverley.[45] So King John was laid down at

---

[43] Engel, 'Die Kathedrale von Worcester', pp. 106, 302–4. For the iconography of the sculpture of Worcester see ibid., pp. 433–45.

[44] For example John Rous, *Historia Regum Angliae*, ed. by T. Hearne (Oxford, 1745), p.
198; see Engel, 'Die Kathedrale von Worcester', pp. 427–29.

[45] Engel, 'Die Kathedrale von Worcester', pp. 378–82, 411–21. Figure 3 shows the thick
wall east of the high altar (L), which presumably incorporated the original altar screen and was
destroyed in 1812. Concerning the position of the shrines in York or Beverley, see Nicola

the feet of his patron saint. But he did not only look up to Sts Wulfstan and Oswald. The imagery also included Christ himself on the roof boss of the eastern crossing, further depictions of the two bishops on the bosses of the retrochoir, as well as St Mary, and, one should note, a holy king. Moreover John is flanked by his name saints on the vaults of the eastern transepts: St John the Baptist to the north and St John the Evangelist to the south (Figure 7).[46]

The spandrel figures in the triforium of the choir should also be added to this iconographical programme concentrating on the monarch: there King John is accompanied by angels to his right on the south side (Figure 8). Their heads and musical instruments are replacements of the nineteenth century, but their original wings and bodies are clearly discernible. In their medieval state they also must have been shown praying or making music, and were thus the direct forerunners of the Angel Choir of Lincoln.

On the north of the choir a series of enthroned figures is depicted, which the Victorians interpreted as kings and queens by adding new heads. This interpretation is correct in all probability: David with his harp can be recognized clearly in the eastern bay (Figure 9); and the pairs of females and males towards the west could be Salomon and Bathsheba or Salomon and the Queen of Sheba. So these figures seem to represent a series of Old Testament kings and queens, a veritable kings' gallery. But two figures in the second bay from the east offer a different interpretation or a second layer of meaning: one of them has crossed legs and a sword, and both of them hold shields (Figures 10, 11). On one shield a bear or a *lion rampant* is represented, on the other one three lions *passant guardant*. These lions have been the arms of the kings of England since the late twelfth century.[47] So we might be dealing with a succession of English kings here, perhaps including some of the numerous Anglo-Saxon ones. There are several reasons in favour of this hypothesis:[48] the memory of England's Anglo-Saxon rulers was revived in the twelfth and thirteenth centuries and aroused the special interest of Henry III.[49] England was the first country where, in the second half of the twelfth century, living monarchs were represented within a series of holy predecessors.[50] In

---

Coldstream, 'English Decorated Shrine Bases', *Journal of the British Archaeological Association*, 129 (1976), pp. 21 f.

[46] Engel, 'Die Kathedrale von Worcester', pp. 396, 430 f, 439.

[47] *British Heraldry from its Origins to c. 1800*, ed. by R. Marks and A. Payne (London, 1978), p. 103.

[48] Engel, 'Die Kathedrale von Worcester', pp. 442–45.

[49] Coldstream, 'English Decorated Shrine Bases', p. 32; Paul Binski, *Westminster Abbey and the Plantagenets. Kingship and the Representation of Power, 1200–1400* (London, 1995), pp. 52–54, 82.

[50] Ursula Nilgen, 'Amtsgenealogie and Amtsheiligkeit. Königs- und Bischofsreihen in der Kunstpropaganda des Hochmittelalters', *Studien zur mittelalterlichen Kunst, 800–1250*, Festschrift für Florentine Mütherich (München, 1985), pp. 217–34.

Worcester itself, which had been a stronghold of Anglo-Saxon tradition since the time of St Wulfstan, four Anglo-Saxon kings and two princesses were especially venerated.[51] And in the late medieval glass paintings in the north aisle of the choir, nine Anglo-Saxon royals were shown as patrons of the church of Worcester. Interestingly, the series is completed by King John, Henry III, and St Wulfstan, in the first bay from the east, which is the bay where King John's tomb was put up.[52]

We can conclude that King John was distinguished at Worcester cathedral as the offspring of a genealogy of holy kings, lead by King David directly above John's tomb, the ideal monarch of the Middle Ages, who provided the link with Christ himself—depicted on the boss of the eastern crossing. They all—supplemented by John's name saints in the eastern transepts—would support the king's spiritual welfare, and the eternal song of the angels to his left would echo the prayers of the monks of Worcester in their stalls. So the 'conversion' of King John proved itself highly effective, whether for the king's soul, we cannot judge, but certainly for Worcester cathedral. The task to establish the burial place of a king spurred the bishops and monks of Worcester to develop a highly sophisticated programme in which architectural and pictorial means interlocked and by which they must have wished to convince their generous patron, Henry III, that his father's soul was well cared for at the place of his choice.

---

[51] Engel, 'Die Kathedrale von Worcester', pp. 37, 443.

[52] Thomas Habington, *A Survey of Worcestershire*, ed. by J. Amphlett, Worcester Historical Society, 2 vols (Worcester, 1895–99), II, 457 f.; Engel, 'Die Kathedrale von Worcester', pp. 428, 444.

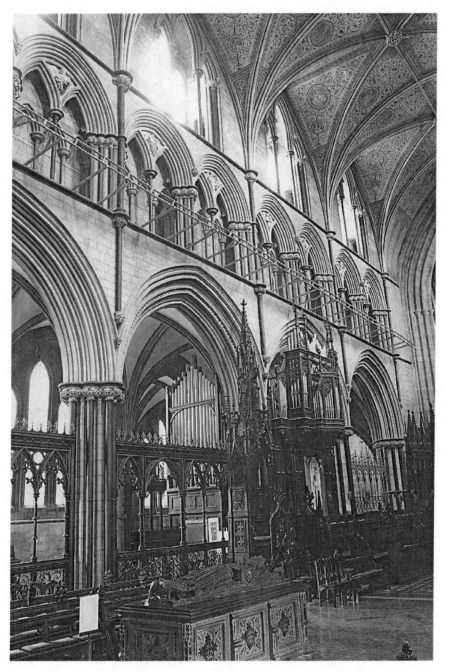

Figure 1. Worcester, cathedral, choir to southwest
with the tomb of King John. Photo: Engel.

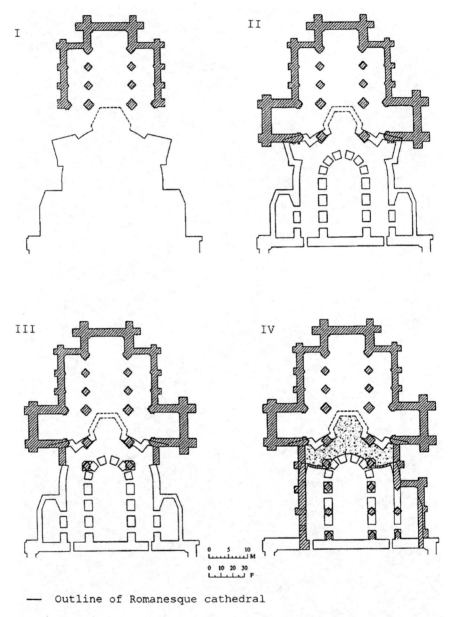

I

II

III

IV

—   Outline of Romanesque cathedral

⬜   Romanesque crypt

▨   Early English choir

Figure 2. Worcester, cathedral, building phases of the east arm, 1224–1250s.
Drawing: Engel.

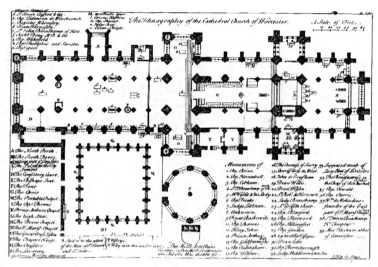

Figure 3. Worcester, cathedral, plan.
Reprinted from Browne Willis, *A Survey of the Cathedrals of York [. . .], Worcester, Gloucester, and Bristol* (London, 1727), I, 623.

Figure 4. Worcester, cathedral, east arm from north. Photo: Engel.

Figure 5. Worcester, cathedral, southeast transept,
dado-arcading on south wall with spandrel figures. Photo: Engel.

Figure 6. Worcester, cathedral, southeast transept,
dado-arcading on west wall with spandrel figure. Photo: Engel.

Figure 7. Worcester, cathedral, southeast transept,
vault boss in outer bay. Photo: Engel.

Figure 8. Worcester, cathedral, choir, south side, triforium,
bay 3 from east, spandrel figure. Photo: Engel.

Figure 9. Worcester, cathedral, choir, north side, triforium,
bay 1 from east. Photo: Engel.

Figure 10. Worcester, cathedral, choir, north side, triforium,
bay 2 from east, spandrel figure. Photo: Engel.

Figure 11. Worcester, cathedral, choir, north side, triforium,
bay 2 from east, spandrel figure. Photo: Engel.

Conversion As Depicted on the Fourteenth-Century Tring Tiles

T he efforts of the medieval Christian Church to achieve conversion of the Jews
assumed many forms in Christian art. One such representation of Christian
concerns is presented on a series of red clay English tiles called the Tring Tiles,
dated to the first quarter of the fourteenth century.[1] These tile images portray scenes
from the apocryphal Infancy of Christ Gospels, which were in existence before the
second century. The gospels describe miracles purportedly performed by the child Jesus
from birth to eight years of age.[2] In these stories, Jesus kills other boys and two of his
teachers. In addition, he revives the dead persons and performs miraculous acts of
trickery, healing, and charity. Though the infancy stories were excluded from the
canonical Bible, they survived in multiple languages within oral culture and in written
texts, most notably the Gospel of Thomas and the Protoevangelium of James from the
second century, and the compilation of these two texts, the eighth- or ninth-century
Gospels of Pseudo-Matthew. These infancy stories enjoyed renewed popularity in the
thirteenth and fourteenth centuries, with new manuscript production and the only known

---

[1] This topic is drawn from my master's thesis, 'The Apocryphal Infancy of Christ as
Depicted on the Fourteenth-Century Tring Tiles' (University of Arizona, 1995).

[2] The major sources for the Apocryphal Infancy of Christ Gospels are C. Tischendorf,
Evangelia Apocrypha, 2nd edn (Leipzig, 1876); M. R. James, *The Apocryphal New Testament*
(1924; repr. Oxford, 1955), pp. 38–90; Oscar Cullmann, 'Infancy Gospels', in *New Testament
Apocrypha*, by Edgar Hennecke, ed. by Wilhelm Schneemelcher (Philadelphia, 1963), pp.
414–69; and J. K. Elliott, *The Apocryphal New Testament* (Oxford, 1993), pp. ix–xxv, 46–122.

depiction outside manuscripts, the Tring Tiles. The most comprehensive, illuminated collection of the stories known is the early fourteenth-century, Anglo-Norman Bodleian MS Selden Supra 38, which has a close recensional relationship to the Tring Tiles.[3] Since the tiles contain no inscriptions, the stories as told in this manuscript and the old texts provide a better understanding of the tile images. Like the medieval cleric or friar who may have used a manuscript like Selden Supra 38 to aid and direct viewers' comprehension of the tile images, I will utilize the text and illustrations of that manuscript to decipher the path to conversion of the Jewish figures as set forth in the Tring Tile images.

The Tring Tile series is the only extant example of the infancy stories which might have been designed for public viewing. It has been suggested that the eight tiles, one shard, and a related drawing now held at the British Museum and the two tiles and two shards at the Victoria and Albert Museum are the remains of a longer series which might have been mounted as a frieze on the walls of Tring Parish Church in Hertfordshire.[4] Their siting in Tring Parish Church is based upon the circumstantial discovery of most of the tiles and shards in Tring in the mid-nineteenth century. Determination of their original location is made more difficult by the rarity of their technique, as they are the only extant example of major fourteenth-century English tile work produced by *sgraffito*, the incising of designs in white slip. The tiles vary in size, but measure approximately 325 mm long by 162 mm high and are 34 mm thick.[5] The placement of these tiles on the wall of an English parish church, in a manner similar to wall paintings, would have satisfied the desires of the parishioners to know more about the childhood of Jesus. The apocryphal stories could have also been used to impress

---

[3] Maureen Boulton, *Les Enfaunces de Jesu Christ* (London, 1985), pp. 4, 28. Also in 'The "Evangile de l'Enfance": Text and Illustration on Oxford, Bodleian Library, MS Selden Supra 38', *Scriptorium*, 37 (1983), 54–55, 62–65, where Boulton compares the close similarity of an old French manuscript to Selden Supra 38, along with four other related manuscripts. For other discussions on the relationship between the Tring Tiles and Selden Supra 38, see M. R. James, 'Rare Medieval Tiles and their Story', *Burlington Magazine*, 42 (1923), 32–37; Otto Pacht and J. J. G. Alexander, *Illustrated MSS in the Bodleian Library, Oxford* (Oxford, 1973), III, 53; L. F. Sandler, *Gothic Manuscripts 1285–1385. A Survey of Manuscripts Illuminated in the British Isles*, 5 vols (London, 1986), II, 62–63, no. 54; J. J. G. Alexander and Paul Binsky, *Age of Chivalry* (London, 1987), pp. 277–78, 283–84.

[4] The Tring Tiles are discussed by Elizabeth S. Eames, *Catalogue of Mediaeval Lead Glazed Tiles in the Department of Mediaeval and Later Antiquities of the British Museum* (London, 1980), I, 14, 39–40, 56–61. Eames also suggests that the tiles might have been mounted as a frieze on the walls of the chancel in *St Peter and St Paul, Tring. A Short Guide to the Parish Church* (Tring, n.d.), p. 6.

[5] Eames, *Catalogue of Mediaeval Lead Glazed Tiles*, and records at the Victoria and Albert Museum.

upon the mostly illiterate audience a variety of mainstream Christian messages, including the essential concept of conversion.

This paper will discuss two intertwined concepts of conversion which are exhibited in the Tring Tile infancy images. Of primary interest is the spiritual conversion of Jews to Christianity. This theme of conversion is facilitated by a second technique of conversion: the textual additions and alterations made within the apocryphal tradition to the straightforward stories in the ancient texts. These changes produced a magnified re-telling in late-medieval manuscripts. The Tring Tile apocryphal images, infused with medieval symbolism, demonstrate the historic tendency to expand the details of Jesus's actions, rather than to purge the stories of the more objectionable material. These alterations incorporate the religious, social, and cultural attitudes of the period.

The spiritual conversion of the Jews, historically blind to Jesus's divine status, develops within the narrative progression of the infancy episodes. The tile stories begin with scenes of harsh confrontation but evolve to present a solution for these conflicts in the final tile images, as Jesus's miracles not only exhibit his divine nature, but act as catalysts to alter the attitude of the Jewish characters towards him.

The dating of the Tring Tiles to the first quarter of the fourteenth century places them just a few decades after the Jews were expelled from England in 1290. In the time following this event, the banished Jews were described in a clichéd, stereotypical manner in manuscripts, sermons, pamphlets, and in oral culture. The memory of Jewish presence persisted with the proliferation of images of the Host depicted as the Christ Child, which when bleeding recalled the accusations of Jewish ritual murder. The conflation of these factors retained the spectre of the Jews in the minds of Christians and defined their perceived purity of their faith.[6] Ruth Mellinkoff, in *The Outcasts*, describes the visual details used in Christian art to identify and stereotype Jews, such as large eyes and noses, foolish expressions, and pointed hats.[7] The facial features of the Tring Tile figures echo such Christian prejudicial characterization, over and above the expressiveness of the English linear style in which they are drawn. The villagers' features are even more exaggerated than those of their corresponding figures in Selden Supra 38, the manuscript which contains the most extensive expansion of anti-Semitic sentiment among existing apocryphal infancy manuscripts.[8] For example, in the Gospels of Thomas and Pseudo-Matthew, the word 'Jew' appears only a few times. Yet, in the expanded Selden Supra 38 text, the word occurs over two dozen times, always in confrontational scenes, in which Jesus uses debasing terms to rebuke the boys or scold

---

[6] Denise L. Despres, 'Cultic Anti-Judaism and Chaucer's Litel Clergeon', *Modern Philology*, 4 (1994), 415–20.

[7] Ruth Mellinkoff, *The Outcasts: Signs of Otherness in Northern European Art of the Late Middle Ages* (Berkeley, 1994), I, 127–29.

[8] Kathryn A. Smith, 'Canonizing the Apocryphal: London, British Library MS Egerton 2781 and its Visual, Devotional and Social Contexts' (unpublished doctoral dissertation, Institute of Fine Arts, New York University, January, 1996), pp. 245–46.

and lecture the teachers and villagers. Such alterations extend to the final verses of the text where the author of the manuscript asks Jesus, the 'all-powerful, to curse the treacherous Jews'.[9]

From the beginning, the apocryphal stories show the villagers' hostility and anger towards the child Jesus and their insensibility to his divine status, which inhibits any possibility of their conversion. An atmosphere of confrontation is established in the scenes of the first two tiles, where Jesus kills two boys who accost him. In the first story Jesus at age five builds three pools of water on the Jordan River bank (Figure 1). When a boy breaks the pools down with a stick, Jesus strikes him dead by withering him, a condition associated with Judaic non-belief. This tile episode is presented in a time-compressed scene of Christian iconographic layering. Jesus, his cherubic face surrounded by curls emphasizing his childishness, wears the gracefully draped, floor-length kirtle of adults in the Gothic period. The absence of a halo must be an oversight by the tile artist, as the texts and other tile images present Jesus as divine. Jesus is shown using a large compass to build only three pools, reduced from the seven in the texts, possibly to fit the limited tile space. Only the Tring Tiles and Selden Supra 38 include the compass in the depiction of this story. Maureen Boulton, in her study of Selden Supra 38, attributes the depiction of the compass in this scene to a literal fourteenth-century French, as opposed to Anglo-Norman, interpretation of the verb *compassar* by the artist or iconographer of the model for the Tring Tiles and Selden Supra 38.[10] The appearance of the compass here also recalls this instrument of creation as held by God the Architect in the frontispieces of medieval manuscripts such as the Queen Mary Psalter and the Holkham Bible Picture Book.[11] The compass is not a child's toy, but here identifies Christ as the creating Word of God, separating the firmament from chaos. Gesturing with his left hand, Jesus kills the boy who breaks down a water pool with a stick. Simultaneously, the boy is depicted as dead, in an upside-down position.

In the first scene of the second tile, Jesus kills another boy who jumps on his back with the intention of harming him (Figure 3). The boy appears in a crumpled, upside-down position behind Jesus. The seated man is a Hebrew teacher, Zacharias, who is not involved in this story but is introduced in Selden Supra after the killing of the boys when Joseph, fearful of the parents' threats against Jesus, takes his son to school. The teacher is depicted as a large, hieratic figure reflecting his respected position as a Hebrew master who attempts to teach Jesus the Judaic law. However, his mask-like facial features indicate his ineffectiveness with the all-knowing child, and point out his foolish lack of wisdom in not recognizing Jesus's divinity. In the eyes of the Christian

---

[9] MS Selden Supra 38, lines 1989–98, as ed. by Boulton, *Les Enfaunces de Jesu Christ*, pp. 87–88.

[10] Boulton, 'The "Evangile de l'Enfance"', p. 61.

[11] Queen Mary Psalter, British Library, Royal 2.B.VII, fol. 1ᵛ; Holkham Bible Picture Book, British Library, Additional MS 47682, fol. 2ʳ.

donor or iconographer of the Tring Tiles, he would have represented one of the major characters in need of conversion.

The right panels of these first two tiles show Jesus reviving the dead boys, begrudgingly, to please his mother. He does this with a touch of his foot, and then, with a hand gesture to the second boy's back (Figures 2, 4). In the right panel of the first tile, Mary acts as intercessor, aggressively admonishing Jesus to revive the dead boy. She wears an elegant Gothic gown, as well as the crown of the Queen of Heaven and Ecclesia, a pertinent role for her here. This complex image contrasts with her depiction in Selden Supra 38, where she appears seated, holding her book, with a simple shawl covering her head.

The women in the right panel of the second tile show parents, complaining to Joseph. While they appear to be smiling, possibly in response to Jesus's revival of the dead boy, the apocryphal parents typically exhibit defiant anger at the children's deaths, as seen in a tile from the Victoria and Albert collection (Figure 5). Their foolish expressions are more exaggerated than on their counterparts in Selden Supra 38, even though that text describes the parents in maligning, anti-Semitic terms.

The gospel texts state that the first boy was withered and the second one killed, but they do not refer to an upside-down position, as seen only in the Tring Tiles and Selden Supra 38.[12] While it is possible that the Tring Tile artist placed the boys vertically because of limited tile space, compression is not an issue in Selden Supra 38. It seems more probable that the boys were depicted in that position because, as Jews, they represented a people who were enemies of Christ. In Christian iconography the upside-down position has been used to denote death or punishment for sin and the resulting fall into hell of three types of evil beings: the rebel angels, heathen idols, and sinful humans. These figures are traditionally depicted falling head-first with arms extended, as they begin their metamorphosis into demonic beings.[13] The boys' similarity to these evil beings suggests a fourteenth-century characterization of these boys not just as pranksters, but as sinful humans.

This interpretation is reinforced in the Selden Supra manuscript by the sequence of images which places the boys and heathen Egyptian idols in proximity to each other. Beginning this sequence, the idols appear in the story of the Holy Family's flight into Egypt. When Jesus, accompanied by his parents, approaches an Egyptian temple, the evil heathen idols fall from their pedestals, breaking into pieces. In this scene the manuscript artist has utilized a comic style to depict one demonic idol falling, as the

---

[12] For example, the Oxford, Bodleian Library, MS Douce 237 includes this story, but the dead boy is portrayed in an horizontal position.

[13] Examples of these three types of falling beings include the fall of the rebel angels (the origin of evil) as they are expelled with Lucifer from heaven, in Oxford, Bodleian Library, MS Junius 11 (Caedmon); their successors, the heathen idols, in the relief sculpture from the north portal at Moissac; and sinful human beings doomed to hell, as Simon Magus, depicted in an eleventh- century sacramentary, Udine, Blblioteca Capitolare, 76.v.t., fol. 48ᵛ.

other flies from the window of the temple, depicted as a medieval church (Figure 6). The next image in the sequence shows the Egyptian king, Frondise, and two of his people on their knees in adoration of this miraculous child who has overpowered their gods (Figure 7). This image is immediately followed by the depiction of Jesus killing the first boy, the duplicate of the first image in the Tring Tile series (Figure 8). This narrative progression in the manuscript from the idols to the boys establishes the possibility of an association between the wicked idols and the malevolent boys. This relationship is strengthened in the Selden Supra text by the repetitive use of the verb *trebucher*, meaning 'to fall head over heels'. It is used to describe first the fall of the idols and then the death of the second bad boy depicted in the Tring Tiles.[14] In addition, it describes the falling death of a third boy who attacks Jesus in Selden Supra, but who is not present in the extant Tring Tile images. The upside-down position of the dead boys suggests that in the model manuscript for the Tring Tiles and Selden Supra 38 these verbal and visual associations may have influenced the artist or iconographer to transfer the upside-down position of the falling idols to the boys. Fourteenth-century anti-Semitic attitudes would have also invested the boys with the wickedness of the idols.

Hostility towards the boys as non-believers appears first in the apocryphal Gospels of Thomas and Pseudo-Matthew where Jesus angrily calls the first boy an 'insolent, godless ignoramus' and withers him. In the expanded Selden Supra 38 text, Jesus's language takes on an even more strident anti-Semitic tone. He complains to Mary about that 'bad boy, the traitor, who is a treacherous son of Satan', and states 'that is why he had to die', reinforcing the anti-Semitic connection with the devilish idols. With this emphasis upon their Jewishness, the mischievous boys become representatives of a people who rejected the true faith and were blamed for Jesus's death.

From these initial stories, the Tring Tile narrative proceeds in exaggerated terms to exhibit Jesus's miraculous capacity to provide grain for the poor and heal the crippled, but also his power to punish those who defy and attempt to trick him. The villagers express amazement and awe at his miracles, but without statements of conversion. Jesus's reputation as a killer of children has caused one father to lock his son in a tower, to keep him from playing with this holy child (Figure 9). Described in Selden Supra as a wicked Jewish father, his damaged face on the Tring Tile still shows the stereotypical large nose and bulging eyes. Jesus 'saves' the child by pulling him through a small slit in the tower wall.

The foolishness of villagers who believe that they can outwit Jesus is seen on the faces of three men who have hidden their children in an oven to protect them from Jesus (Figure 10). When they lie and tell him that pigs are in the oven, Jesus changes the children into pigs. This literal response to the parents' words is an appropriate punishment for a people whom Christians accused of rejecting Jesus because of their tendency

---

[14] The verb *trebucher* appears in line 358 in the idols story, then in lines 494 and 508 with the two episodes of the dead boys.

for literalness.[15] The episode also exhibits the Christian metaphor of blindness, as these fathers, as well as the one who locked his son in the tower, were guilty of hiding their children to prevent them from seeing Jesus and his miracles.

A defining episode with adults occurs when a group of agitated villagers, exhibiting a shift in concern for Jesus, threaten Joseph for allowing his son to play with wild lions (Figure 11). When the lions are tame with Jesus, the holy child berates the villagers, calling them treacherous and deceitful. He states that the lions are wiser than the villagers, since the lions recognize him as their master, and the humans do not. This incident exemplifies the importance to Christians of the Jews' recognition of Jesus's divinity. Here, as in each confrontational episode, Jesus's benevolent miracles shift the villagers' response from anger to amazement.

However, alteration in attitudes equivalent to conversion occurs only in Jesus's contact with the Jewish masters. The theological conflict between Jesus and Judaism is the central concept behind the message of conversion presented in the fourteenth-century Tring Tile and Selden Supra 38 versions of the apocryphal stories. Three times Joseph takes Jesus to the Hebrew teachers to control his unruly behaviour and to mollify the villagers' anger. When the respected Jewish masters attempt to teach him the alphabet and the law, Jesus berates and lectures them, declaring his total knowledge and divine wisdom. In each instance the masters are confounded by their helplessness with Jesus. Two of the teachers slap him for his insolence. The Tring Tile image includes a duplicate figure of Jesus as he berates one of the teachers for the assault (Figure 12). In the second slapping episode, depicted in Selden Supra but not contained in the extant Tring Tiles, Jesus kills the teacher.

But the defining scene of conversion must be viewed in a Selden Supra image, as it is not present in the extant Tring Tiles. At this point the manuscript must again be used to decipher what appears to be the theme of the Tring Tile narrative. In a story recalling his canonical visit to the temple in Jerusalem at the age of twelve, Jesus makes a final trip to the teachers (Figure 13).[16] Upon entering, Jesus picks up a book and begins to read of the Holy Spirit. The Jewish masters, who had previously not recognized him as a holy child, now speak in terms that Christians want to hear. In amazement and in fear, they state that they recognize the wise, knowing child who has demonstrated his power by word and deed. Like the Egyptian king, Frondise, they fall at this feet, asking for mercy, and relate that they now know 'in truth, that he is God Almighty, the God of power. This he has demonstrated in childhood'. Such recognition and admission on the part of the Hebrew masters would have been seen by the medieval Christian church as a hopeful sign for the conversion of Jews to Christianity. This episode also demonstrates the rewards of Jesus's struggles with the non-believers. As an addition to the old texts, this story lends credibility to the infancy gospels, bringing them more in line with the accepted Christian canon.

---

[15] Smith, 'Canonizing the Apocryphal', p. 271.

[16] Jesus's teaching of the doctors in the temple at Jerusalem appears in Luke 2. 41–52.

The legitimizing of the apocryphal infancy stories is seen in yet another narrative not contained in the old texts, but added to several later medieval texts, including Selden Supra 38 as well as to the Tring Tiles. It depicts a wedding feast drawn from the canonical wedding feast at Cana (John 2. 1–12). The final Tring Tile scene depicts the marriage of Architeclin where, as at Cana, Jesus changes water to wine (Figure 14). The importance of this episode in the Tring Tile series is indicated by its being the only scene covering an entire tile and encased in a double border. Although there are six jugs in the canonical gospel, and seven in Selden Supra 38, the Tring Tile scene contains only three jugs, a holy number which also balances the three pools in the first tile image. In addition, this tile story of resolution and goodwill stands in symmetry with the first scene where Jesus holds the compass of creation and with the swiftness of Old Testament judgement strikes down those who defy him and alter his creation. Jesus, in this final miraculous tile scene, having consistently exhibited his supernatural status to the Tring Tile villagers and, more critically, gained recognition and conversion of the Hebrew Masters, defines the path to conversion and eternal life for all those who recognize and believe in him.

Thus, as these apocryphal tile images provided viewers with stories of Jesus's childhood which exhibited his supernatural powers from an early age, they didactically presented an argument which made clear the dangers of non-belief and the rewards of faith. The alterations made to the old apocryphal texts, as they appear in the Tring Tile images and in the Selden Supra 38 manuscript, served to intensify the extent of hostility towards Jewish non-belief in fourteenth century England. By emphasizing the threats to Jesus, and therefore Christianity, the magnified stories provided justification for his shocking acts of killing, actions which were then balanced by miracles of revival and charity. And finally, these Tring Tile images provided Christian viewers with reassurance of Christ's victory over the non-believing Jews and the inevitability of their Christian conversion, an event critical to the coming of the last days.

Figure 1. Tring Tile. Jesus builds
pools and kills boy who destroys
them. Reproduced by courtesy of the
Trustees of the British Museum.

Figure 2. Tring Tile. Mary tells Jesus
to revive boy, who walks away.
Reproduced by courtesy of the
Trustees of the British Museum.

Figure 3. Tring Tile. Zacharias; boy
jumps on Jesus and is struck dead.
Reproduced by courtesy of the
Trustees of the British Museum.

Figure 4. Tring Tile. Joseph talks
with parents, Jesus revives dead boy.
Reproduced by courtesy of the
Trustees of the British Museum.

Figure 5. Tring Tile. Angry parents with Joseph.
Reproduced by permission of the Victoria and Albert Picture Library.

Figure 6. MS Selden Supra 38, fol. 8ʳ. Holy family and Egyptian idols.
Reproduced by permission of the Bodleian Library, University of Oxford.

Figure 7. MS Selden Supra 38, fol. 8ᵛ. Egyptian King Frondise kneeling before Jesus. Reproduced by permission of the Bodleian Library, University of Oxford.

Figure 8. MS Selden Supra 38, fol. 9ʳ. Jesus builds pools and kills boy who destroys them. Reproduced by permission of the Bodleian Library, University of Oxford.

Figure 9. Tring Tile. Father locks son in tower; Jesus pulls son through slit.
Reproduced by courtesy of the Trustees of the British Museum.

Figure 10. Tring Tile. Father puts sons in oven; Jesus changes them into pigs.
Reproduced by courtesy of the Trustees of the British Museum.

Figure 11. Tring Tile. Jesus scolds villagers for not recognizing him, as did the lions.
Reproduced by courtesy of the Trustees of the British Museum.

Figure 12. Tring Tile. Teacher slaps Jesus; Jesus scolds teacher.
Reproduced by courtesy of the Trustees of the British Museum.

Figure 13. MS Selden Supra 38, fol. 30ʳ. Teachers kneel before Jesus in recognition of his divine powers and are converted. Reproduced by permission of the Bodleian Library, University of Oxford.

Figure 14. Tring Tile. Marriage of Architeclin. Jesus changes water to wine. Reproduced by courtesy of the Trustees of the British Museum.